# The Authenticity of the Book of

# Genesis

**by**
**Bill Cooper**

**a study in three parts**



Published by the Creation Science Movement, est. 1932

ISBN: 978-0-950-20-90-8-1

**For**

# David and Joan

~ * ~

## About the Author

Bill Cooper is a Vice President of the Creation Science Movement in England. He is also a member of the Master Faculty of the Institute for Creation Research School of Biblical Apologetics. He is the author of *After the Flood* (1995); *Paley's Watchmaker* (1997); *William Tyndale's 1526 New Testament* (old-spelling ed., British Library. 2000); and *The Wycliffe New Testament of 1388* (British Library. 2002). He has also authored numerous technical articles on Creationism, Palaeoanthropology, Bible Apologetics, the Reformation and the History of the English Bible. Graduating with Honours at Kingston University (England), he went on to obtain both his PhD and ThD from Emmanuel College of Christian Studies (Springdale, Arkansas) under the good auspices of the College Dean, Dr Gene Jeffries, and the expert supervision of faculty member Dr James J Scofield Johnson. He lives in England, is married to Eileen (for nigh 40 years now), has two daughters, numerous foster children, and three fine grandsons.

~ * ~

## Acknowledgements

My thanks must go firstly to Dr James J Scofield Johnson, my teacher and mentor in so many subjects; to Dr Gene Jeffries, Dean of Emmanuel College of Christian Studies, Springdale, Arkansas, for his untiring encouragement, and without whom, under the Lord, so much would not have been possible; to Dr Johnny Sanders of Downsville, Louisiana, for his untiring encouragement; to Dr David and Joan Rosevear who seem always to have been there, and to whom this book is gratefully dedicated; and as always to my very dear wife, Eileen. What would I do without her?

~ * ~

# Part One

# The Antiquity of Genesis

## Contents

# Introduction

This entire book begins and ends with the oft-proven assumption that the Bible is all that it claims to be, the Word of God. It is a definition that embraces and supports the historical accuracy of the Bible in all its parts, prophetical, geographical, linguistic, and doctrinal. The Bible is, in short, inerrant in its original autographs. God does not lie. But this is not a fashionable view. It is, unsurprisingly, a view which invites hoots of derision in most academic circles today. But then, it always has.

For men to choose not to believe the Bible on an individual level is one thing. But the world has seen, in the past few hundred years especially, a concerted drive on an institutional level to rubbish the Scriptures altogether. It is nothing new, of course. It's just the scale of the enterprise which takes the breath away. And it's not just international. It's global.

In fact, such is the scale of the effort that one wonders if this really is just about the literary criticism of a book. Most other written works of man have been subjected to the discipline of literary criticism, from historical epics down to the crossings-out and scribblings of the Lakeland poets. But how many colleges, universities, seminaries and schools around the world are dedicated solely to the literary criticism of just one book? Very few, I'll warrant. But for the denigrating of the Bible, very many. Hundreds, in fact.

As we proceed, we shall see a strange yet consistent phenomenon when it comes to Biblical criticism (the destructive kind, at least). The phenomenon is consistent down the ages and across the world, and involves a countless multitude of hammers being worn down to nothing ,or shattered to pieces as they strike against this particular anvil, and all to none effect. Indeed, so consistent, predictable and inevitable is the phenomenon, that one wonders why they bother. But bother they do, and they must be answered.

This book is an attempt to supply such an answer. The book of the Bible that most of its critics have focused upon down the centuries is the Book of Genesis. Not only have its historical statements been challenged on every level, but in particular its age has been challenged. It is currently said, as it has been for the past two hundred years, that it was written out at a time so remote from the past that it claims to deal with, that it cannot possibly be an accurate account. Indeed, it is said nowadays to be a borrowed and edited account, filched from the myths of Babylonia. Such claims demand to be tested, and tested they shall be. After all, with no Book of Genesis, there is no Creation. And with no Creation, there is no Fall of Man. And with no Fall of Man, there is no Gospel. So the matter is of immense import. Whether the Book of Genesis can stand up to its critics... well, we shall see.

To show something of the sheer authenticity of the Book of Genesis, this book is divided into three parts. Part One deals with the antiquity of Genesis, showing how each of its component parts is considerably older than any of the sources proposed for it by the modernist school. Part Two deals with the pre-Christian Flood traditions that are found around the world, which together present a formidable body of evidence for the truth of Genesis when it speaks of the Flood of Noah. Finally, Part Three draws the reader's attention to a certain clay tablet which makes a nonsense of the modernist claim that the Flood account found in Genesis was modelled on or derived from the Epic of Gilgamesh. We call it here the Genesis Flood Tablet.

*Bill Cooper.*

## Chapter One: The Critics

The initial challenges to the historical accuracy of the Bible, and to the Book of Genesis in particular, were laid down in the very first centuries of the Christian era. By far the most radical of its critics was Marcion (fl. AD 140). Marcion was a wealthy ship-owner, and the son of the bishop of Sinope in Pontus. He bears the dubious distinction of having been excommunicated by his own father for gross immorality, and this seems to have fired within him the determination to demolish the Bible, and with it, the Christian faith.[1] He was to seek the accomplishment of his design from within the Church by posing as a Christian scholar whilst at the same time destroying at least faith in the Scriptures as the inspired Word of God. He made his way to Rome in ca. AD 140 and attached himself to the Christian church there, making his application to join them all the sweeter by donating the enormous sum of 200,000 sesterces to the church coffers.[2] This should have set many alarm bells ringing, but to the everlasting regret of that church it didn't, and Marcion was welcomed into the fold as a scholar and as a well-to-do benefactor.

It is distressing to consider what happened next. Marcion, having arrived on the scene in a blaze of glory, disappeared for a while, whether on board one of his own ships or elsewhere is not known, but when he returned it was to announce the completion of a radical edition of the Bible, and a paring away of anything in the Scriptures which did not conform to Marcion's own strange and devilish views. As Gontard tells us:

> "The seafarer became a Bible critic. Conceiving numerous doubts about the purity of the text, he examined the Gospel to discover the portion that Paul had spoken of as being genuine. What did it treat of? Which was really the original? What had been added? Had there been arbitrary textual additions and substantial errors? After his comparative examinations Marcion rejected Matthew's Gospel with its accommodations of the Old Testament. In Mark's Gospel he disapproved of the scanty relation of Jesus' words. Nor would he accept John's Gospel, finding the statement, 'Salvation is of the Jews,' unauthorized and of no avail for the rest of the

world. Luke's was the only Gospel which, in his view, retained its authenticity, though even here he considered he was forced to 'operate' in order to free it of falsifications and interpolations made by alien hands."[3]

It is wonderful to think that the modernist school, which has carried on the work of Marcion so faithfully, using exactly the same methodology as he, should boast of being so modern when its ideas and methods are in fact so ancient. But no matter. Marcion went on to announce to the church that the Father of Jesus was not the God of the Old Testament (whom he said was 'evil'), and that the Old Testament indeed had nothing to say to the true believer - all very wearisome stuff.

The demonstrably foolish notion around which Marcion had built his 'edition' of the Bible, was that the Gospel of Jesus was purely a gospel of love. So far so good. But it was a gospel of love to the utter repudiation and exclusion of the Law of God. In his *Antitheses*, which mercifully seems not to have survived, he explained to his readers that this was why he rejected the Old Testament in its entirety. He claimed that the Creator that was spoken of from Genesis onwards, being a God of law, could have nothing in common with that God who called Himself the Father of our Lord Jesus Christ and was a God of love. Marcion's 'studies' - if such they might be called - convinced him that the God of the Old Testament was "fickle, capricious, ignorant, despotic and cruel," and was not at all the loving Father whom Jesus had come to reveal to the world, and whose one purpose was to overthrow the law-loving (but paradoxically "wicked") Creator. Or so he claimed.

Such notions cannot be read or considered without distress to the Christian heart, but they lead us on to the subject of Marcion's "editing" the Bible down to what he claimed to be a more trustworthy document. For him to arrive anywhere near to his strange ideas, it is clear that most of the Bible would have to be thrown out of the window, and it is interesting to see how he actually accomplished his grand design.

He began by stating that his strange ideas were fully appreciated only by Paul, and that the twelve apostles and evangelists, as well as numerous other disciples, were completely blind to the truth of what Marcion was saying through having lived under Jewish influences. He seems never to have considered that all the apostles and evangelists were dead by his time, and therefore could not approve of his views even if they'd wanted to; nor that Paul had lived not only under Jewish influences, but was himself a Pharisee of the Pharisees, a veritable fount of Jewish influence who knew more about the Law than most other men then living - Marcion included, it seems.

Briefly though, his paring away the Biblical text until he had something that might lend a little credibility to his ramblings, meant that he was left with only ten of Paul's epistles (edited of course), and a yet more heavily edited version of Luke's Gospel. And that's it. That is all he was left with once he applied his own foolish notions to the Word of God. It is truly amazing. He got over the loss, of course, by embracing the Docetic heresy,[4] announcing that Jesus had not been born, but had suddenly materialized in the synagogue at Capernaum where He began His ministry, His later suffering and death being the work of the ("evil") Creator-God whom Jesus' real ("good") Father was in the process of destroying.

It is thus seen that Marcion's intention toward Scripture was solely to cut it down and to get rid of most of the Bible, or at least those parts of it - like the *entire* Old Testament! - which did not agree with his own ideas. Thus he hoped to destroy the Bible in men's eyes, and their saving faith in Christ along with it.

Alas for the critics who were waiting in the wings, Marcion had moved too quickly. His attack on the Scriptures was simply too abrupt and violent to persuade the believer to doubt them and, finally, to turn from them. He had panicked the flock. But it was a lesson to be learned. The critic, if he was to be successful, had in future to move more slowly. He had to be subtle in his approach, more circumspect, masquerade as a scholar concerned only for the Truth, and cover the deceit with a cloak of honest inquiry. Some of them became very skilled at it. And so the work went on.[5]

It went on quietly enough, leaving little record behind of its activities. But amongst the more public attempts to denigrate the Word, we may think of Irenaeus (late 2nd cent.) who rejected the authenticity of Paul's letter to the Hebrews, though he acknowledged the Gospels, all of Paul's other letters, *some* of the other pastoral epistles and Revelation.[6] After him, and writing in AD 230, Origen counts the four Gospels, the Acts of the Apostles, Paul's thirteen epistles, 1 Peter, 1 John and Revelation as canonical, whilst disputing the canonicity of Hebrews, 2 Peter, 2 and 3 John, James and Jude.[7] We say nothing of the apocryphal books that he accepted as inspired. Others lent their own wisdom to the dispute, and such was the disagreement amongst certain of the "church fathers" regarding which books were canonical and which not, that it is a mystery how we finished up with the canon that we have.

Origen (185-232) got himself into difficulties with many because of his excessive allegorising even of those books of Scripture that he did accept, as did some of his later admirers. But nigh a thousand years had to pass before, in the 12th century, Hugo of St Victor's came out with the notion that Solomon was not the author of the Song of Songs, and that Daniel 11 could only be properly understood by reference to I and II Maccabees.

The reluctance of critics to make their voices heard, in public at any rate, was due no doubt to the death penalty being in place - in Protestant countries as well as Catholic - for any who bore about them the whiff of heresy, which was seen in those days as political as well as religious subversion. The Italian philosopher, Giordano Bruno, whose views on the Creation and on the Bible were bizarre in the extreme, was burned alive in 1600 for expressing those views. But others, more humble than he, and even far more discreet, suffered a similar very public and exemplary fate. Little wonder then that those who found the Bible hard to accept and who wished to persuade others of their views, did not raise their heads above the parapet until after the Reformation was long past, and society had become more humanistic, and thus more tolerant, in its sympathies.

Waiting in the wings for just such a moment, was Huig de Groot (1583-1645), a diplomat of the Netherlands. Under his literary name, Grotius, he launched a systematic attack against the Scriptures. To escape too much censure by the authorities (though he was finally imprisoned), he cleverly avoided identifying himself directly with the views that he was expressing. It was a matter of, "It is believed...", or

"Christians have exercised their wits...", and so on, as if he were a detached and indifferent commentator on views that were not of his making or opinion.[8]

Thomas Hobbes (1588-1679) added his own twopennyworth to the effort, his political researches bringing the legal works of Grotius to his attention. Something of an odd-ball of his time, Hobbes was first and foremost a political theorist. He thought that this gave him the intellectual authority to pronounce upon the Scriptures, and this he did with pleasure. He decried Moses' authorship of the Pentateuch, saying that it was manifestly written long after Moses' time. From Joshua 4:9 onwards, the Book of Joshua and that of Judges were written after the Babylonian Exile of the 6th century BC. The Books of Samuel, Kings, Chronicles, Ezra and Nehemiah were written later still. Jonah, of course, was a complete nonsense.[9]

In short, it was his political theorizing that had got him into such a muddle. It was all a question of authority (or so he pretended). He claimed not to find Scripture authoritative, because he couldn't say who had authorised Scripture. Was it the church? No, because the church is not a person. Therefore, it must rest upon the king. But Hobbes was the last man to find any king trustworthy, so therefore Scriptural authority did not exist. If only he had remembered what the Bible claims for itself. It is the word of neither church nor king. It is the Word of God, plain and simple, and God was his problem, not churches or kings.

The more modern 'putsch' against the Bible, however, has been going on since the mid-18th century, when the arch-Rationalist philosopher David Hume announced to the world in so many words that nothing can be trusted by the human intellect except the intellect of David Hume – and with it, of course, his godless views on miracles – thus making himself, drinker and gambler that he was, the only sure point of reference in the universe. It is sad when a man of his many obvious talents comes to such a pass. But it is even sadder when others, sometimes numbered in their millions, are led astray by him. David Hume's one regret was that he had been unable to destroy Christianity. He had done his level best to disparage it and the Scriptures that proclaim it. But to no avail. He dies, while the Christian faith - with its Bible - lives on. It was all very tedious for him.

But David Hume was merely one of a company. Others of his day in England and Scotland, carried the same banner, pursued the same mission: Anthony Collins (1724); Thomas Sherlock (1726); Robert Lowth (1753); William Blake (1790); the opium addict Samuel Taylor Coleridge (1825); Thomas Arnold (1829); Benjamin Jowett (1860); and Matthew Arnold (1873) – to name but the better known. There were others, of course. John Drury, Dean of King's College, Cambridge, delights in each one of them, describing in his 'Introductory Essay' the men and their work as "brilliant."[10]

Well, brilliant or not, they were as yet disorganised. Scraps or jottings from the occasional stoned poet or irascible political theorist were not going to replace the Bible in the affections of the people. Millions still loved to read it, quote from it, live by it, and to worship the God whose Word it is, and this simply would not do. It needed a concerted and organised effort of education and publishing by high-ranking scholars, and as if in answer to that need, there arose in 19th-century Germany a school of thought. It was not a school of science or the arts, but one dedicated solely to the overthrow of the Bible.

It had grown out of the so-called Rationalist Movement of the 18th century, sometimes laughingly called the Enlightenment, and the ambitious goal that it set itself, the destruction of the Bible, was to consume vast sums of money over many years, (a consumption that is still going on today). It was to occupy - and still occupies - the lives of thousands of scholars. All over the world, there are hundreds of colleges and universities dedicated to its cause. Publishing houses and worldwide electronic media exist solely to promote its aims and spread its doctrine. Not even medical research can boast the like of its funds and amenities, nor, indeed, its governmental support on the global stage. Never in all history has any human enterprise attracted so much over such a long period of time in the way of financial investment, talent and sheer devotion, and it flourishes today just as vigorously as ever it did in the past - and with the added help of modern technology too. And all this just to ridicule the Bible.

It is very strange. After all, it's not as if the Bible were the only 'religious book' out there. There are dozens of others. The Koran of Islam, the Hindu Vedas, the scriptures of Buddhism, Taoism and so on, just to mention the most prominent among them. Yet, apart from being mentioned in passing - if only to convey the impression that the scholar concerned has read a lot - these are all largely ignored. I am not aware of a single college or university anywhere in the world that is dedicated solely to the destruction of any one of them, and howls of protest would very soon close such an institution if it ever tried to get started. Yet, when it comes to the Bible, no human endeavour is considered too large or expensive to achieve its demise. Astonishing.

Yet, what is even more astonishing is this. For all the incalculable costs and sacrifices that have been made over the last two centuries and beyond, this school of thought is further from its goal today than it ever has been. The Bible stands today as it has always stood, the dearest treasure on earth to millions – millions who are not in the least concerned about what the critics might have said over the years. But exactly why do the critics bother? If God truly does not exist, then it should matter not a fig to them that someone somewhere happens to believe that He does. If the Bible is truly the meaningless nonsense that they proclaim it to be, then what should it matter if some people happen to love reading it? Is it really a problem of such gargantuan proportions that it requires the investment of trillions of dollars, pounds and euros over centuries of hard academic toil to solve it? No one seems in the least bit bothered that the Koran is read and believed in most countries. And the knowledge that the Hindu Vedas are, at this very moment, being printed, read and discussed in India doesn't even raise an eyebrow. Yet if someone opens the Bible to read it? Ah, now that's another matter altogether.

We are all familiar with the fact that on every good ship there are notices telling you where the lifeboats are, where the life-jackets are kept, and where to go in order to claim your seat in the life raft should the ship begin to founder. The owners of the ship have obviously gone to a great deal of time, trouble and expense to put up those notices. And it's a good thing, too! But, imagine you are on a ship which has no lifeboats on board, nor any equipment which might help you stay afloat. Does it make any sense, when the ship begins to sink, for some passenger or other to spend what little time he has left printing out and sticking up posters saying that there are no lifeboats, just in case someone on board might be spending their time hoping that there might be? Of course it doesn't. He'd surely be better occupied either swimming for it, or trying to pump the water out of the ship to keep it afloat just a little longer. Anything else would be madness and a waste of whatever precious time he has left.

Richard Dawkins, the famously vociferous atheist, recently put his weight behind a campaign in England to put up posters on public buses saying: "There's probably no God. Now stop worrying and enjoy your life." – which is all well and good, except that the one person in that campaign who was worried to bits by the mere possibility of there being a God, seems to have been Dawkins himself! He has spent his whole life and thousands of his own money proclaiming his hope that God does not exist. Why?

In any other circumstance, it might be said that just the thought that God *could* exist terrifies him – indeed, that it terrifies him so much that he can't stop shouting about it, even to the open embarrassment of his colleagues. That isn't science. It isn't academe. It isn't even philosophy. It's despair, pure and simple, and it has nothing to add to the fund of human happiness. What comfort it can be for the passengers on our sinking ship to read that there probably is no lifeboat, and that they must stop worrying and enjoy the few minutes they have left before they drown, is surely none at all, and making the public feel the urgency of that discomfort must be the greatest service that Richard Dawkins could possibly have rendered the Gospel. Our heartfelt thanks to you, Richard.

Such pointless and counter-productive activity, of course, isn't new. But it raises the question of what is so terrible about the knowledge that salvation is free to all and that man can live forever in the Kingdom of God, that a man of such talent should spend his life and his very soul seeking to persuade people away from it? What is so wrong with the notion that God is Truth, that His Word is true, and that He is faithful to all His promises – the very *best* of Fathers? And why is it such an urgent necessity in the eyes of so many to expunge that knowledge and notion at whatever the cost?

The fact of the matter is that the immeasurable amount of time, money and energy that has gone into the disparagement of the Bible over the past two thousand years and more, is simply a measure of its inestimable value. No other book in the history of the world has attracted such venom and hate. In times past, whole armies were employed in its confiscation, destruction and burning – often along with its owners. As for times future, we may only guess what will be done. But whatever kind of war will continue to be waged against the Bible (and it is all the same war), we can be assured that it will be pursued with rigour and with all the ferocity and determination that men can muster. The Bible will survive it, of course. It always does. God's Word is eternal, even as He Himself is eternal. Man, on the other hand, for all his endeavours, is somewhat less, and it is the end-game of the war that will always defeat him.

But to return to our school in 19th-century Germany. Its setup and purpose had to do with the systematic documentary criticism of the Bible, its members being pleased to call themselves the 'Higher' Critics. Now, criticism, in the literary sense of the word, is like a hammer. It is a tool which can be usefully and constructively employed, or it can be used destructively. In itself, it is an indifferent thing, whose use is determined solely by the one who wields it. Unhappily, and for reasons known only to themselves, the 'Higher Critics' of Germany sought (and still seek) to use it in a wholly destructive sense, destructive of the Bible and the Christian faith.

Eichhorn (1752-1827) seems to have been the first of the German school, himself having been inspired by Jean Astruc, the French physician (1684-1766). Astruc saw his first book published when he was only 19 years of age. It was on the processes of decay and decomposition which human bodies undergo after death. Today we would fear for the mental health of any teenager who liked to spend his time observing dead bodies decaying at close quarters. But perhaps it was just a phase that he was going through, because he eventually seems to have grown out of it, turning his attention instead to writing the work that really made him famous, *De Morbis Veneriis libri sex* (1753), an edifying multi-volume treatise on syphilis and other sexual plagues of 18th-century France. But the work that endeared him most to Eichhorn and colleagues, was his *Conjectures on the Reminiscences Which Moses Appears to Have Used in Composing the Book of Genesis*.

Eichhorn was delighted with both book and author, eulogizing Astruc because he "...did that which no professional critic dared to attempt: dissected the whole of Genesis into separate fragments."[11] In short, Astruc had assigned the sources used by Moses in compiling the Book of Genesis to several different authors. Quite why this should excite the 'higher' critics of Germany so much is hard to explain. It never seems to have bothered the lower ones. Indeed, even conservative Bible scholars down the centuries have long recognised that the Book of Genesis is composed of successive documents. We ourselves shall see this aspect of Genesis at close quarters as we proceed in contesting the modernist view. But the entire purpose of the 'higher' critical hypothesis was to denigrate Scripture from being the Word of God into the words of mere men. That is the difference between a conservative Bible scholar and what we today call a modernist. In Germany of the 19th century, however:

> "...a new spirit and mode of enquiry were at work in the educated world. It was the spirit of inductive science, cautious, tentative, and sceptical. It was a spirit which would no longer accept a belief because it was traditional, which demanded reasons, and insisted upon working back from the known to the unknown. Nothing was sacred to it; everything had to be brought before the bar of human reason. Man became, as he had never become before, the measure of all things; but it was as educated man, as a member of the scientifically-trained society of Europe."[12]

If only the 'scientifically-trained society of Europe' had been up to the task. It simply had not occurred to anyone that the Book of Genesis had not been written in, or for, a Europe of *any* description, let alone that of the 19th century. Its contents and purposes are, and always have been, foreign to any man-made society. Why, even the Jewish sages came to grief when they thought that they could stretch it to meet their own manly criteria of interpretation and 'logic'. So, when the critics of Germany, high and low, began their dissection of the Bible, they began their work with a complete inability to understand the Bible's nature and its very purposes. It is not a task that the wise and prudent should ever undertake. The Bible was written for babes and little children, and one can only understand it by approaching it with the heart and mind of a little child. That is why the Bible says of itself that its Gospel is nonsense and foolishness, but tellingly, only to those who perish (1 Cor. 1:18). For the redeemed child of God, it is joy and life everlasting!

## Footnotes to Chapter One

1. Most of Marcion's biographical details are taken from the *Oxf. Dict. Of the Christian Church*, p. 870; and from Gontard, pp. 70-6 (see Bibliography).

2. Gontard. p. 72.

3. Ibid.

4. Docetism would have been truly laughable had it not been for the damage it caused within the church. It ascribed a phantom-like quality to Jesus, whose sufferings were more apparent than real, and who was said to have changed places either with Judas Iscariot or Simon of Cyrene just as the crucifixion occurred, thus escaping death. What the soldiers who were charged with carrying out the crucifixion and the on-looking members of the Sanhedrin who had demanded it, thought of this sudden swapping of victims, we are nowhere told.

5. It is interesting to see that Marcion, and his many followers after him, attacked only the *canonical* books of the Bible, the same books that we know today. Not once did any of them try to 'edit' or eradicate an apocryphal book. This means that, contrary to what the critics tell us, the canon of the entire Bible, both New Testament and Old, was established and in place by *before* AD 140 at the latest, some 250 years or more before the Council of Hippo, where, it is alleged by the critics, the canon was formally decided upon. Amazing.

6. *New Bible Dict*. vol 1. p. 242-3.

7. According to Eusebius, *Hist. Eccl.* Vi. 25., cit. Bruce, *Books and Parchments*, p.112.

8. *Interpreter's Dictionary of the Bible*, vol. 1, p. 409.

9. Ibid, pp. 409-410.

10. Drury, pp. 1-20.

11. cit. *Interpreter's Dictionary of the Bible*, vol. 1, p. 411.

12. Sayce, *The Higher Criticism*, p. 11.

## Chapter Two: The Critics and the Book of Genesis

By way of introduction, we need to be clear in our minds about what this chapter, and all that follows, is not. It is not an argument from the fossil record, or biology, DNA, or any other such discipline for the truth of the Book of Genesis. That Truth is assumed throughout. There are already multitudinous books and volumes available in which all the evidence for Genesis from the physical sciences, particularly concerning its account of the Creation, may be found. This is rather an exploration of all those hallmarks that tell us that the Book of Genesis is more ancient than *all* the sources that the critics propose for it. After all, if the Book of Genesis is indeed a late compilation, edited from several pagan sources, as its critics claim, then evidence from the physical sciences, abundant though that is, would count for very little. Genesis would hardly be worth the parchment it is written on, and we would be reduced to the consideration of a silly and worthless philosophy.

It would be asking too much of the reader to take in the impossibly ponderous and tangled web of hypotheses upon hypotheses upon endless and vain hypotheses that is the fare of 'Higher Criticism'. It is like aiming for rubber goalposts set on castors, there being for every difficulty yet another imaginary 'editor' for them to fall back on. Even the critics are dizzied by it all. We may briefly note here, though, that, having painted themselves into the corner of 'forever learning, yet never coming to a knowledge of the Truth', there's nowhere else for the critics to go. They have to stick to their theories whatever the archaeological and palaeographical evidence, not to mention plain common sense, might say against them.

Their fault lies in this. 'Higher Criticism' is conducted with the view that we may discern ancient history only through philology – the 'straining out the gnat' of the meaning, senses and provenance of ancient words and syllables, and yes, even single letters. And they build all their theories on this, assuring us the whole time that these theories have proved 'scientifically' that the Bible is false, even though they acknowledge that their understanding of the ancient languages – yes, even of Hebrew - is decidedly and demonstrably imperfect. But it is the consideration of single letters that leads us on to the first point in our investigation into the antiquity of the Book of Genesis. I am referring now to a version of the Hebrew Bible (just the first five books in this case) known as the Samaritan Pentateuch.

## The Samaritan Pentateuch

What interests us here is not the textual corruption and compounded errors of its text, though even that has something to tell us. It is the fact that the Samaritan Pentateuch exists at all, because according to all the tenets of modernism and the 'Higher Critics', it shouldn't – certainly not in the form that it possesses. Let us see why.

Simply put, the written Hebrew alephbet is known to us in two forms: the K'tav Ivri, or Hebrew Script, which is the ancient form pre-dating the Babylonian Captivity of the 6$^{th}$ century BC; and the K'tav Ashuri, or 'Assyrian' [square] Script which has been used (with developmental variations) since the return of the Jews to Jerusalem under Cyrus of Persia. It is in the Assyrian Script that modern Hebrew is written and read. The significance of which lies in the fact that the Samaritan Pentateuch (or Torah), in its earliest copies, is written in a cursive form of the K'tav Ivri, the form of Hebrew which pre-dates the Captivity.[1]

By far the most ancient copy of the Samaritan Pentateuch, again written out in the cursive form of the ancient Hebrew Script, is the one known as the Nablus (or Abisha) Roll, so named from the town in Israel where it is zealously guarded by the Samaritan community. This community, which has been at theological odds with the Jews now for thousands of years, is claimed to be the 'oldest religious community in the world.'[2] Interestingly, Nablus is the Biblical Shechem (or Sychar) where our Lord encountered the Samaritan woman, a direct ancestor of the present-day Samaritans, who had come to draw water from Jacob's Well (John 4:5-42). But how much further back than that do the Samaritans go?

Well, their continued use of the earliest form of Hebrew writing should tell us something, namely that they were established in Israel long before the Babylonian Captivity which began in earnest in 587

BC. In fact, the Hebrew Old Testament first makes mention of them back in 2 Kings 17:29, where, thanks to the efforts of a solitary Jewish priest, who no doubt had a copy of the Torah or Pentateuch with him, the Samaritans took on board something at least of the knowledge of God, even though they continued to serve graven images as well. Their previous history, of course, had something to do with that.

The Samaritans were transplanted into the land of Israel after the Assyrian Conquest of that land in 722 BC. The first settlers came from the Mesopotamian cities of Cutha (the Jews still refer to the Samaritans as *Cuthim*), Babylon, Hamath and so on, followed later by settlers from other cities. But the Samaritans have always claimed for themselves that they are in fact Israelites who were first deported to those cities in 722 BC along with the rest of the Israelite population, but were then sent back by the Assyrians 55 years later (667 BC) to re-settle the area.[3]

Even leaving aside their claims of Israelite descent, the date that they give for their re-settlement in Israel is oddly precise, suggesting that it is based on a chronicled historical event. But that, at least, allows us to place the Samaritans, Israelite or not, in the land of Israel in the early 7th century BC, some 200 years *before* the return of the Jews from Babylon under Ezra and Nehemiah - which is important to note, as it allows us to answer several questions.

We know from the Bible itself that the returning Jews were no friends of the Samaritans, whose offer of help in rebuilding the Temple of Jerusalem was firmly rebuffed by the Jews, and who then slandered the Jews to the king of Persia (Ezra 4:2-3). Still smarting long after the rebuff, the Samaritans always referred to Nehemiah's colleague as that "accursed Ezra", and the enmity between the Jews and the Samaritans has sadly lasted down to this day, after some two and a half thousand years.[4] But all this is important to our purpose, because it answers the Bible's critics when they say that the Samaritan Pentateuch was merely copied from the 'scriptures' that Ezra and Nehemiah wrote out between themselves to enforce their priestly claims over their fellow Jews - in other words, that the Hebrew Bible (the entire Old Testament in fact, not just the Torah or Pentateuch) is itself a patent fraud and invention perpetrated by the post-Exilic Jews, the Samaritan version of it being no more than a poor and very corrupt copy. But is that contention at all feasible?

Given the enmity that has always existed between the Jews and the Samaritans, an enmity that must have been far more fierce in its early days than it is today, and the opinion of the Samaritans concerning Ezra that he was 'accursed', is it reasonable to suppose that they would have copied out the Jewish Scriptures which they would have known were forgeries of his – or even that they would have been granted access to them? Why would they not have denounced the Jewish Bible for what it was? And why, if they really had wanted to copy it all out, would they not have used the form of Hebrew – the K'tav Ashuri – in which that forgery had been made and which everyone could read? Why use an archaic form of the alephbet which by the date of the Return was entirely obsolete and which few could have made any sense of? Is it feasible? Not at all. Not that we would ever learn that from the 'Higher Critics' of course.

The Samaritan Pentateuch, moreover, contains a great number of corruptions and variant readings from the Hebrew Bible, such a number in fact (more than two thousand!) that requires the passing and vicissitudes of some centuries to accumulate.[5] Apart from deliberate substitutions, such as Mount Gerizim for Mount Zion, such corruptions cannot and do not happen overnight. But there is one glaringly obvious fact here that needs to be appreciated but which the modernists continue to ignore, and that is the fact which tells us that, whatever the age of a given copy, it can only ever have been made from an original that is older than itself. It is a self-evident fact which seems to have escaped the notice of our 'Higher Critics'. The Samaritan Pentateuch's script alone, never mind its corruptions and innovations, belies the notion that it was ever copied from a post-Exilic forgery. Rather, copied as it was *before* the Babylonian Captivity of the Jews, a fact that is demonstrated by the earlier form of Hebrew that it uses (the K'tav Ivri), the Samaritan Pentateuch can only have been copied from, or based upon, a Torah scroll which was manifestly older than itself, and indeed older than the Captivity when the K'tav Ivri had fallen into disuse. That alone places the Hebrew Pentateuch, which the Samaritan Pentateuch is based upon, and the Book of Genesis which opens the Pentateuch, firmly into pre-Exilic, that is into pre-6th-century BC Israel, a time in which the Pentateuch did not even exist according to the 'Higher Critics'.

One source of merriment in all this is a colossal howler made by the critics Graf and Wellhausen, authors of much of the nonsense which passed – and still passes - for scholarship in modernist circles. Karl Graf came up with the brilliant notion that the Law, or Torah (the Pentateuch in other words), was invented by the prophets of Israel (who didn't exist, by the way; or who, if they did exist, did so after the return of the Jews from Babylon when, even so, their books were written by others and not by the prophets themselves – quite so). In other words, the books of the prophets came first, and the Torah came after. Because that made Genesis, which opens the Torah, a lot younger than even he had dared to hope, Wellhausen seized upon the notion immediately, and, without further thought, adopted it, this giving rise to the famous - or infamous - Graf-Wellhausen Hypothesis.

If only he *had* given it thought. What Graf and Wellhausen had failed to consider is the fact that the Law, or Torah, is specifically mentioned by many of the prophets when they berate the people for not obeying it. The Torah is, in fact, appealed to *by name* by Isaiah twelve times; by Jeremiah twelve times (including once in Lamentations); by Ezekiel six times; by Daniel four times; and by Hosea three times. Amos, Micah, Habakkuk, Zephaniah, Haggai, and Zechariah, all mention it once; and finally, Malachi mentions the Torah no less than five times. How on earth these prophets could possibly have appealed to a Torah which did not yet exist because they themselves had not yet invented it, is not explained by our critics. Obviously, the Torah *had* to be there first and in place amongst the Jews in order for the prophets to refer to it and for their hearers and readers to know what it was that they were talking about. But it does make us wonder. Did these two actually *read* the Bible before they came up with these brilliant ideas in order to convince us of how untrue it all is?

We know that the Torah is specifically intended in these instances, because the word Torah is used for it. There were other words that the prophets used for law or laws in general – *dath*, for example, or *choq*, or *mishpat* – but the word Torah is specific, and there is absolutely no doubt as to what it is referring to. The silliest argument against this fact comes, of course, from certain members of the modernist profession, who say that because Torah is not written with a capital T in these instances, the term must be general rather than specific.[6] (It is hard not to laugh.) Perhaps someone should inform these gentlemen that, unlike Greek and English, or even German for that matter, Hebrew doesn't have capital letters. One might have hoped that this fact would not have been unknown to scholars who pretend to be authorities on the Hebrew Bible - authorities enough at any rate to be able to tell us how false it all is. But with some of them not knowing even the rudiments of the Hebrew alephbet, we may be excused for receiving their wisdom with some reserve.

But the fact that Isaiah specifically mentions the Torah by name, surely places the existence of the Torah firmly in the time of Hezekiah, king of Judah (ca 715-687 BC) under whom Isaiah ministered. (Interestingly, the Siloam Inscription, carved into the rock in Hezekiah's day, uses the same early Hebrew characters -K'tav Ivri - that the Samaritan Pentateuch is written in). But the Torah is traceable under its specific name even further back, to the reign of David in fact, and he was reigning by 1000 BC. Indeed, the Book of Psalms, most of which comes directly from David's pen, mentions the Torah no less than 35 times! Even the Book of Job, acknowledged by most scholars, modernist and otherwise, as being much older still, mentions the Torah once by name: "Receive, I pray thee, the Torah from His mouth...." (Job 22:22). And, of course, the Torah is mentioned no less than nine times in the Book of Joshua.

But, Graf and Wellhausen's hilarious hypotheses notwithstanding, by considering the characteristics of the Samaritan Pentateuch, we have been able to see that the Hebrew Book of Genesis, which is the first book of the Pentateuch, is patently far more ancient than is taught these days. It pre-dates the Babylonian Captivity of the early 6th century BC by what is necessarily a very long time indeed – half a millennium and more. But there are additional evidences, both internal and external, which enable us to carry the date of the Book of Genesis back much further. We shall consider that evidence now.

## Footnotes to Chapter Two

1. MS Cotton Claudius B VIII in the British Library is a splendid example of the Samaritan Pentateuch written out in K'tav Ivri.

2. Phelan, *The Inspiration of the Pentateuch*, p. 74.

3. *Interpreter's Dictionary of the Bible*, vol. 4, p. 191.

4. Ibid.

5. Easton, p. 598.

6. "...it is very awkward for them that the name Torah is found in the prophetic writings of that period. The Critics take refuge in the argument that the word here is not Torah with a capital T, but the common noun meaning 'teaching', and the word is used in a general sense." Phelan, p. 84.

~ * ~

## Chapter Three: The 'Mystery' of the Toledoth

Having seen that the existence of the Torah is traced back historically to at least the time of Joshua, we come now to the time of the Torah itself, the time when the Book of Genesis in particular was compiled by Moses, whose name has been historically linked to the Torah (or Pentateuch – the Five Books of Moses) ever since. But there is something distinctly odd to the modern western eye about the literary structure of the Book of Genesis which may yet have a lot to tell us about its age and antiquity. I refer to that strange literary device that is found in several places throughout Genesis, and which scholars call the Toledoth.

The word '*toledoth'* is a plural (it is never used in Genesis in the singular form, *toled*) which has several shades of meaning when translated into English. The English language, unfortunately, has no single word or term which exactly corresponds with it. Depending on the context, it can mean in English a genealogy, a history, an order of events, a simple story and so on. That is why sometimes what is clearly not the best shade of meaning is given in translation, as in Genesis 2:4, which the English Bible renders: "These are the generations (*toledoth*) of the heavens and of the earth when they were created..."[1] A better translation might have been, "These are the *origins* (or even the *bringing forth*) of the heavens and of the earth when they were created..." – shades of meaning which the word toledoth would allow. The English word 'generations' belongs more properly to tables of genealogical descent, which is not what Genesis is talking about in this instance. The heavens and the earth do not have ancestors, children or descendants, but they do have their *origins* (and therefore their *bringing forth*) in the creative act of God.

The next occasion on which we encounter a toledoth is in Genesis 5:1, "This is the book of the generations (*toledoth*) of Adam." – and it is here that the 'mystery' of the toledoth begins to make itself felt.[2] Some scholars, conservative as well as liberal, see the toledoth as titles which *begin* a section of Genesis. Others see them, with equal legitimacy, as colophons which mark the *close* of a section.[3] Jewish scholars have always seen them as colophons, referring back to the section which has gone before, on the following grounds. Concerning the first toledoth which appears in Genesis 2:4, Jewish commentators add together the numerical values of each Hebrew letter of the singular noun, *toled*, this giving a product (known as the *gematria*) of 434, which happens also to be the exact number of Hebrew words that make up the first account of the Creation (Genesis 1:1 – 2:3).[4]

I personally don't doubt the significance of that. But if we read through the Book of Genesis as a continuous whole, then we can see that, because of the multiple shades of meaning that the word toledoth possesses, the toledoth actually marks both the end of the preceding section, *and* the opening of the new. It is like the stitches that hold together two pieces of the same garment. The stitches form an integral part of *both* pieces, not just one. Instead of marking a division, in other words, the stitches bring together and unify the two pieces, making a whole out of parts - which is exactly what the toledoth accomplish in the Book of Genesis. In more senses than one, it seems, "...the Scripture cannot be broken." (John 10:35).

We can see how this works in Genesis 5:1, which the English Bible translates as, "These are the *generations* (toledoth) of Adam." Again, it would seem that what is given here is not the best shade of meaning for the word toledoth. The word 'generations' is simply too narrow for the baggage it has to carry. What follows Genesis 5:1 is indeed a table of genealogical descent that begins with Adam, but the toledoth which marks the beginning of that table, also marks the end of the long *history* of Adam which goes before, and which appears from Genesis 2:7 running all the way to Genesis 4:26, the close of the fourth chapter. But in English, unlike the Hebrew, we have no single word which combines the senses of both generations *and* history. So perhaps in this instance, the word 'histories' would have been the better translation, as it is a much wider term than the more specific 'generations', and hence can carry more baggage. 'Histories' would adequately describe both what comes before the toledoth of 5:1 as well as what comes after.

The fact that Genesis uses only *toledoth* (the plural), and not *toled* (the singular) is a telling point. If the toledoth of Genesis 5:1 refers solely to the genealogy or history of Adam which follows, or solely to the history of Adam which precedes it, then surely the singular form (*toled*) would have been used. But because it refers to the sections which come before *and* after, then naturally the plural is required. Thus the toledoth has more than one function. But what does that dual function tell us about the age and antiquity of Genesis?

We begin by taking on board the fact that Genesis consists of several successive documents that were written under inspiration at successive times. This in no way subscribes to the entirely spurious and misguided Documentary Hypothesis of the 'Higher Critics' though. Most of the documents of Genesis are clearly marked out for us by the appearance and function of the toledoth, and if we must look for a source for these various documents, then we can look no further than God. He is their source and Author, and each document in Genesis is as much the Word of God as is the next. Even as God is, each document is inerrant and infallibly true.

It would seem that when Moses brought together, or was given, these successive documents to make a single book of them, either he himself provided under inspiration the toledoth which 'stitch' these documents together, or the toledoth already existed in the documents themselves. The latter would seem the most likely option, because when the toledoth supplies a colophon to one document and an identifying preface or title to the next, it is merely fulfilling the same functions as the titles and colophons that appear at the beginning and end of clay (or stone) tablets. It is a most ancient method of record-keeping which largely fell into redundancy once writing was committed to parchment scrolls and papyrus, this allowing the unbroken continuation of long texts. Any clay tablet which formed part of a series would contain a preface or title at the beginning and a colophon at the end, so that the reader would know which tablet followed in the series or preceded the one that he was reading. Tablets, whether of clay or stone, were always a cumbersome medium for writing, just a small series or collection taking up an inordinate amount of space. Their collective weight was also a problem, although they did have one quality – durability. They were both waterproof and fireproof, and impervious to insects and vermin. Many are in as good a condition today as when they were written on and baked in the sun four and a half thousand years ago. Amazing.

It would seem, though, that from the very beginning, the Torah itself has been written on leather or parchment scrolls. Leather, parchment and papyrus scrolls were not unknown to Moses from his time in Egypt, so their use would have seemed perfectly natural. Moreover, it was possible to write the entire Pentateuch onto a single scroll when many hundreds of cumbersome clay tablets would have been required to meet the same task. The advantages of the scroll were immediate and obvious. But the use of clay tablets for the writing of Scripture, it would seem, did not altogether die out with the writing of the Torah on parchment.

Of all the books of the Pentateuch, it is significant that Genesis contains eleven of the Bible's toledoth. Nowhere else in Scripture do we find such a concentration.[5] Indeed, we do not see another until Numbers 3:1 – "These also are the generations (*toledoth*) of Aaron and Moses..." - which is also dated - "...in the day that the Lord spake with Moses in Mount Sinai." - in accordance with the already age-old conventions of the clay tablet. Then we do not meet another in the Bible until the Book of Ruth (4:18) – "Now these are the generations (*toledoth*) of Pharez..." – which marks the short genealogy which follows as well as all that has gone before, indicating surely that the Book of Ruth was originally written on clay tablets. Then we come to the last, being that which is given in 1 Chronicles 1:29 – "These are their generations (*toledoth*)...."

So for the Book of Genesis to contain so many toledoth, we may assume that a whole collection of clay tablets contained the already-inspired records and histories of Genesis that came into Moses' care and keeping. In itself, that suggests an antiquity for the Book of Genesis which far surpasses any of those modernist notions which would have us believe that this most ancient of Books is but a late compilation and the work of 6th or 5th-century BC forgers. But this is not the only evidence that we have for the antiquity of the Book of Genesis. There is more. Much more.

## Footnotes to Chapter Three

1. The English rendering 'generations' first appeared in Genesis 2:4 of the Wycliffe Bible of 1388, being itself a translation of the Latin Vulgate's *generationes*. It was then simply perpetuated through all the English versions up to (and even beyond) the King James Bible.

2. The other nine toledoth in Genesis are to be found in 6:9, 10:1, 11:10, 11:27, 25:12, 25:19, 36:1, 36:9, and 37:2. We need not worry ourselves too much about the headaches which these toledoth give the 'Higher Critics'. The very presence of toledoth in the Book of Genesis makes a complete muddle of all that they hold dear, cutting right through the baseless notions of J, E, P and D. This, of course, is very distressing for them and we mustn't laugh.

3. Phelan (pp. 211-250) gives an excellent account of the different schools of thought on these questions.

4. Ibid, pp. 224-225.

5. The word *toledoth* does actually appear in several other places in the Old Testament: twice more in Genesis, for example; twice in Exodus; eleven more times in Numbers; and eight more times in 1 Chronicles. But, though it is always translated as 'generations' in those places, it doesn't mark an ending or beginning (title or colophon) of a copied document. So none of these instances is *a* 'toledoth' in the same sense that we've been considering.

~ * ~

## Chapter Four: Genesis and the 'Babylonian' Epics

Perhaps the longest, the loudest, the most persistent, and at the same time, the most *inaccurate* allegation that has been laid against the Book of Genesis, especially in its opening chapters, is the 'Higher Critics' assertion that it is but a monotheistic rehash of the Babylonian epic(s) of creation. For well over a hundred years now, since the *Enuma Elish* tablets of Babylonia were first discovered and translated, that has been the mantra of those who pretend to know. In short, it is alleged that the Creation account of Genesis is but a late and edited version of the much older Babylonian story.[1] But does that allegation have any basis in fact? We shall see.

It is one thing to say that any given item is older or younger than another, but quite another thing to demonstrate and so prove it, and prove it forensically. It is therefore highly significant that during the past 137 years or so, after an enormous and concerted effort requiring the worldwide consumption of who knows what level of funding and man-hours, the critics have failed dismally to provide any such proof. How is that possible? Repeating an empty mantra for more than a century, however loudly, is no fit substitute for furnishing good old fashioned proof – proof that is of the honest, objective and forensic kind. We shall therefore consider here the evidence concerning both Genesis and the Babylonian epics, and see what that tells us about which came first. It promises to be a most enlightening exercise.

### The Enuma Elish

The *Enuma Elish*, otherwise known as the Babylonian *Epic of Creation*, burst onto the academic scene in the 1870s. Its discoverer and first translator was the Assyriologist, George Smith.[2] It caused a great deal of excitement amongst both Bible-believers (of which George Smith was one) and the critics, and the table below (based on George Smith's table) shows why:

Tablet 1 of the *Enuma Elish* 'agrees' with Gen 1:1-2 (the Prologue of the Creation);

Tablet 2 'agrees' with Gen 1:3-5 (the 1st day of Creation);

Tablet 3 'agrees' with Gen 1:6-8 (the 2nd day of Creation);
Tablet 4 'agrees' (probably, due to its fragmentary condition) with Gen 1:9-13 (the 3rd day of Creation);
Tablet 5 'agrees' with Gen 1:14-19 (the 4th day of Creation);
Tablet 6 'agrees' (probably, due to its fragmentary condition) with Gen 1:20-23 (the 5th day of Creation);
Tablet 7 (only probably, due to its fragmentary condition) with Gen 1:24-25.[3]

The word 'agrees' is perhaps a little unfortunate. The *Enuma Elish* certainly doesn't 'agree' with Genesis in anything like a theological sense. Nor does it 'agree' in any sense with Genesis over the days of creation, the orders of created beings, and so on. Rather, the Babylonian epic only agrees with Genesis loosely about the chronological order of the Creation, but even that is achieved only by straining things a bit. One has to admit that it starts nobly enough:

> "When on high the heavens proclaimed not, (and) earth beneath recorded not a name, then the abyss of waters was in the beginning their generator...."[4]

But from this point on, and in *every* sense of the term, all hell breaks loose. Suddenly the 'creation' is peopled with hideous monsters and demons: long-toothed serpents; raging vampires; "...the dragon, the great serpent...the great reptile, the deadly beast...the scorpion-man, the devouring reptiles, the fish-man, and the zodiacal ram, lifting up the weapons that spare not, fearless of battle."[5]

These are all whipped up into a colossal frenzy of war by Tiamat, the goddess of chaos, and what follows is but a hellish parody of anything that Genesis speaks of. Even the chronological order of the Creation itself is but a superficial thing. How anyone, Bible-scholar or not, can read the opening chapters of the Book of Genesis, and then suggest that it owes its authorship to such malevolent nonsense as this, I do not know.

The joy amongst the Higher Critics, however, was not to last. They could see the difficulty immediately of convincing their readers that

Genesis was born out of Babylon. The literary difficulties alone were insurmountable - but only if they published the text for their readers to see for themselves. Even today, try finding a modernist commentary on the Bible that includes the text of the Babylonian creation epic, so that the student or reader can compare it for themselves with the opening chapters of the Book of Genesis. I warrant you will find none. The commentator, using the most convincing academic jargon he can muster, will simply tell his readers that it is so, and that for the origins of the Genesis account of the Creation, we need look no further than the *Enuma Elish* and other Babylonian epics like it. And that is the mantra that has been repeated without proof for more than 130 years. Doubtless, it will continue for years to come, so we have taken the liberty of reproducing the text of the *Enuma Elish* in Appendix One of this book. That way, people can see for themselves how like, or unlike, Genesis it really is.

As for Genesis being the younger of the two accounts, A H Sayce, Professor of Assyriology at Oxford, largely took over George Smith's work of translation after Smith died in 1876. He was particularly interested in the *Enuma Elish*, translating it afresh and bringing all his expertise to bear on the text. He had little time for the 'Higher Critics', denouncing their subjective guesswork and often childish puns, and after examining the *Enuma Elish* in great depth - and, tellingly, publishing its text - he has this to say of it:

> "Since the death of George Smith other fragments of the Epic have been discovered, and we now know more exactly what it was like. It was an attempt to throw together in poetic form the cosmological doctrines of the chief Assyrian or Babylonian schools and combine them into a connected story. But the attempt breathes so thoroughly the air of a later philosophy which has reduced the deities of earlier belief to mere abstractions and forces of nature, that I much doubt whether it can be assigned to an earlier date than the seventh century BC."[6]

Now this is interesting, very interesting indeed. We have seen already how the Book of Genesis is traceable all the way back to Moses (and even beyond in its clay tablet form, particularly the early chapters).

In other words, it is immensely older than the 7th century (700-600) BC in which the *Enuma Elish* was composed. But what happened about a hundred years earlier than the writing of the *Enuma Elish*, to account for the 'air of a later philosophy' which had such a telling and mollifying effect upon the more demonic excesses of earlier Babylonian beliefs?

We must recall here the taking captive of the Ten Tribes of Israel by Assyria in the year 722 BC, perhaps a hundred years or more before the *Enuma Elish* was composed. Now, it has to be said that the Israelites of the Northern Kingdom were not exactly Biblical fundamentalists when it came to theology. The very reason why God expelled them from the land was their idolatry and their refusal to repent of that. Nevertheless, the knowledge of God was never entirely lost amongst them (it never is), and the sudden flooding of the land of Assyria (and with it Babylonia), with those who were once the Chosen People of God, must have had a considerable cultural impact on the native populations. Amongst the Israelites were some, if not many, who remembered the teachings of the Book of Genesis on the Creation. These would often have been told and listened to by the native population over that one hundred year span, and would certainly have had an impact upon those who, 55 years after the Assyrian Conquest, were sent back to settle a now empty Samaria, even claiming for themselves (rightly or wrongly) that they were Israelites.[7]

Which means that we have a situation here that is most strange. It would seem from this that, rather than the Babylonian mythology affecting the Book of Genesis, as the critics have claimed for so long, it is the other way about. It is the Book of Genesis, or the somewhat dimmed memories of it amongst the displaced Israelites, which affected the Babylonian myth. That is why the *Enuma Elish* borrowed something of the structure of Genesis with regard to the order of creation, certainly enough for us to recognise one or two details, however vague. But who would have thought it? Things are opposite concerning the history of the Bible to what the critics and modernists have been telling us all these years.

But what of the *earlier* Babylonian myths concerning the Creation, those that go way back to the earliest years after the Flood? Could they not have given birth, as the modernists claim, to the Book of Genesis, or at least to its account of the Creation? Consider, they say, that the Jews of the 6th century BC spent seventy years in captivity amongst the Babylonians, plenty of time for them to be influenced sufficiently to concoct the Genesis lie.

But the suggestion is made too glibly. Just how easy would it have been for the common Jew to read up on the mythology of Babylonia, or even to understand what he might have been told about it? Well, let us hear from one who knows. He is quoted here at length, and what he says bears repeated reading:

> "It was difficult enough for the foreigner to learn the language of the Babylonians sufficiently well to be able to write it. But it was far more difficult to learn the cuneiform system of writing in which it was expressed. The cuneiform syllabary contains nearly five hundred different characters, each of which has at least two different phonetic values. In addition, each character may be used ideographically to denote an object or an idea. But this is not all. The cuneiform script was invented by the primitive population of Chaldaea who spoke, not a Semitic, but an agglutinative language, and in passing to the Semitic Babylonians not only did the pre-Semitic words denoted by the single characters become phonetic values, but words denoted by two or more characters became compound ideographs, the characters in combination representing a Semitic word the syllables of which had no relation whatever to the phonetic values of the separate characters which composed it. It thus became necessary for the learner not only to commit to memory the actual syllabary, but also the hundreds of compound ideographs which existed by the side of it. When we further remember that the cuneiform characters are not pictorial, and that their shape therefore, unlike the Egyptian hieroglyphs, offers nothing to assist the memory, we shall begin to understand what a labour it must have been to learn them….."[8]

In other words, it would have taken an exceedingly clever man to have mastered enough of the Babylonian tongue to make any sense at all of their mythology, a mythology made all the more difficult by the many archaisms it contained. Next to such a task as that, learning Hebrew is a walk in the park, and the captive Jews of Babylon would have been hard enough put to it just to make their way through the working day.

But does that mean that there were no Jews who were clever enough to master not just the Babylonian language but its writing as well? Certainly there were. We can even name some of them. Daniel, Hananiah, Mishael, and Azariah were some (Daniel 1:6). Ezra and Nehemiah also, of course. These, and there must have been others whose names we are not told, mastered both the language and the horrendously difficult cuneiform writing system of Babylon. They had to. They were important and exceedingly able administrators, Daniel the chief of all. But there is one thing about these men which the modernists and critics forget to mention. They were all of them godly men in the *Biblical* sense of that term – faithful to God and faithful to His Word.

How drawn to the idolatry and mythology of Babylon were they? They were drawn not at all. Indeed, Daniel's three colleagues consented to be thrown into the burning fiery furnace rather than bow the knee to an idol. Daniel himself faced death by lion rather than cease praying to the God of Israel. So how likely is it that they would even have countenanced, let alone engineered, the infiltration of Babylonian mythology into the Scriptures – the very Word of God Himself – and Scriptures, by the way, which were already ancient by the time of the Exile, the Book of Genesis not the least of them? They would have given their very lives first.

King Darius himself bore testimony to Daniel's faithfulness to God: "Thy God, *whom thou servest continually*, He will deliver thee." (Daniel 6:16); and even the great king of Babylon himself, Nebuchadnezzar, was moved to worship the God of Israel by the testimony and godliness of both Daniel and his colleagues. These tributes were paid to these Jews not because they compromised with, but because they heartily withstood the attempted encroachments and demands of paganism. So again we must ask the question. How likely is it that such men as these would have written the Babylonian blasphemy into the Scriptures? The question answers itself, I think.

## Creation Account from Sumer

But again the reader is referred to Appendix One, where the *Enuma Elish* is not hidden away from readers' eyes as in modernist Bible commentaries, but rather laid out for open inspection. Please, take the time to read through it carefully. If anyone can show from it how the Book of Genesis can possibly derive from such an 'epic' as this, then I for one will be interested to hear of it. We have seen, of course, that the Book of Genesis dates back to extremely remote times, which the *Enuma Elish* patently does not. But there is a creation account that is much older than the *Enuma Elish*. It dates from the time of the ancient Sumerians, and is well worth considering to see if *it* can possibly stand as the source for Genesis. As it is only a short document, it appears below out of Sayce (punctuation mine):

> "The glorious temple, the temple of the gods, in the holy place (of Eridu) had not yet been made. No reed had been brought forth. No tree had been created. No brick had been made. No roof had been formed. No house had been built. No city had been constructed. No city had been made, no dwelling-place prepared. Nippur had not been built. E-kur (the temple of Nippur) had not been constructed. Erech had not been built. E-Ana (the temple of Erech) had not been constructed. The deep had not been created. Eridu had not been constructed. The glorious temple, the temple of the gods, its seat had not been made. All lands were sea. When, within the sea, there arose a movement, on that day Eridu was built. E-Sagila was constructed; E-Sagila where the god Lugal-du-azaga dwells within the deep. Babylon was built. E-Sagila was completed. The gods and the spirits of the earth were created all together. The holy city (Eridu), the seat of the joy of their hearts, they proclaimed supreme. Merodach bound together a reed-bed on the waters. Dust he made, and he poured it out on the reed-bed, that the gods might dwell in a seat of the joy of their hearts. He formed mankind. The goddess, Aruru, created the seed of mankind along with him. He made the beasts of the field and the living creatures of the desert. He made the Tigris

> and Euphrates, and set them in their place. He declared their names to be good. The ussu-plant, the dittu-plant of the marshland, the reed and the forest he created. He created the verdure of the plain, the lands, the marshes and the greensward also, oxen and calves, the wild ox and its young, the sheep and the lamb, meadows and forests also. The he-goat and the gazelle brought forth (?) to him. Then Merodach heaped up an embankment at the edge of the sea. As it had not before been made, he caused it to exist. [Bricks] he made in their place...Roofs he constructed. [Houses he built]. Cities he constructed. [Cities he made]. Dwelling-places he prepared. [Nippur he built]. E-kur he constructed. [Erech he built]. E-Ana he constructed."[9]

It is difficult to see even a superficial likeness here to any part of the Genesis account. There is a reminiscence of Genesis 1:2, where the Creation begins properly when, '…the Spirit of God moves upon the face of the waters' - "When, within the sea, there arose a movement, on that day Eridu was built" – but that is far more likely to be a reminiscence on the part of the Sumerians concerning a faint knowledge of Genesis 1:2 rather than the other way about. Otherwise, with its bricks, roofs and houses, it reads more like a report on some building project or other. Certainly there is nothing within the Sumerian creation myth to which we may point and say that such-and-such could have been the inspiration for the Hebrew account, or even any part of it. Absolutely nothing. As Pinches points out to us:

> "For the rest, the fact that there is no direct statement of the creation of the heavens and the earth; no systematic division of the things created into groups and classes; no reference to the Days of Creation; no appearance of the Deity as the first and only cause of the existence of things, must be held as a sufficient series of prime reasons why the Babylonian and the Hebrew versions of the Creation-story must have had different origins."[10]

It is significant that this is the very earliest creation myth from Mesopotamia, certainly pre-dating the bringing together by Moses of the even earlier documents of Genesis. Yet, not surprisingly, the Book of Genesis is as far removed from the Sumerian myth as the east is from the west. If anything in the history of the world were to be the critics' source for Genesis, this surely must be it. But alas for the Wellhausens of this world, there is not even the *faintest* resemblance between the two. Not that we would learn that much from the Wellhausens, of course. Quite where this leaves the contention of the critics and modernists, though, I shall leave the reader to judge.

## Footnotes to Chapter Four

1. The term 'Babylonian' is used here in its loosest sense, embracing also the creation legends and theogonies of Assyria, Sumer, Akkad and Babylonia.

2. For Smith's discussion of the epic, see *The Chaldean Account of Genesis*, pp. 61-112.

3. Ibid, p. 72.

4. Sayce, *The Higher Criticism...*, p. 63. In Babylonian, the opening words read: *enuma elish la nabu-u shamamu....*

5. Ibid, pp. 63-64.

6. Ibid, p. 62.

7. We mustn't forget either the impact that Jonah's arrival in Assyria had had upon the population some 30 years or so *before* the Northern Kingdom of Israel fell. He identified himself to the Phoenician sailors as, "...an Hebrew, and I fear the Lord, the God of Heaven, which hath made the sea and the dry land." (Jonah 1:9). He would doubtless have introduced himself in these terms to the Assyrians when he began his preaching there, awakening an interest within them in the Creation.

8. Ibid, pp. 50-51.

9. *Early Israel and the Surrounding Nations*, pp. 139-140.

10. Pinches, *The Old Testament…*, p. 63. In one Creation tablet at the British Museum (S2013), there is a vague reminiscence of Genesis 1:6-8, in which reference is made to the dividing of Tiamat into the "Upper Tiamat" and the "Lower Tiamat" – the waters above the firmament and the waters beneath the firmament, in other words. But even that is a poor resemblance of what the Book of Genesis tells us.

~ * ~

## Chapter Five: Sun, Moon and Stars

There is one very important hallmark which answers the question of the antiquity of the Genesis account of the Creation. I have dealt with this briefly elsewhere, but the subject deserves a fuller treatment. It involves Day Four of the Creation, when God created the sun, the moon and the stars (Genesis 1:14-19). Critics and modernists have expressed much amusement over the years concerning the alleged naivety and simplicity of the account, alleging that it is misplaced, and so on. But whilst they are busy giggling amongst themselves, they miss – or ignore – the magnitude and importance of what they are criticizing. They certainly ignore it in their commentaries, anyway.

If what the critics have been saying these past 150 years were in any way true regarding the Genesis account of the Creation, then the phenomenon which we are about to notice would simply not have occurred. They have been saying, of course, that Genesis is younger than the Babylonian creation myths from which it is copied, but whilst repeating the mantra *ad nauseam*, they have noticeably failed to show any such thing. On the contrary, they have willfully ignored the academic requirement to *prove* a proposition. So let us begin with the following statement from the Book of Genesis:

> "And God made two great lights; the greater light to rule the day, and the lesser light to rule the night. He made the stars also." (Genesis 1:16)

What is important here, and it is hard to overstate the importance of it, is how the Book of Genesis refers to what is clearly the creation of the sun and the moon. It calls them simply the 'greater light' (*maor gadol* in Hebrew), and the 'lesser light' (*maor qaton*). Notice that it doesn't name them. Genesis only states what they are – lights – and describes the kind of lights they are, greater and lesser. The greater light, we are told, is to rule the day, while the lesser of the two is to rule the night, so there is absolutely no mistaking what is meant here. And, all importantly, it is *God* who created them.[1] But, if Genesis deals with the creation of the sun and moon like this, how do the earliest *pagan* creation-myths deal with them – the ones that Genesis is supposed to be copied from? The answer makes interesting reading.

Happily, we can save ourselves some trouble by ignoring the later myths of Babylonia, because they will, quite naturally, name the sun and the moon (*Shamash* and *Sin* in their language). That is because the sun and moon had been given names by man long before. What we need to go to are the very earliest myths, the creation-myths of Sumer which long pre-date those of Babylonia and Assyria. And on that note, one world-authority on Sumerian texts and mythology (though no friend of Genesis he), has the following to say:

> "For the origin and nature of the luminous bodies – moon, sun, planets, and stars – practically no direct explanation is given. But the fact that, as far back as our written sources go, the Sumerians considered the moon-god, known by the two names Sin and Nanna, to be the son of the air-god Enlil….And since the sun-god Utu and the Venus-goddess Iananna are always referred to in the texts as children of the moon-god, the probability is that these two luminous bodies were conceived as having been created from the moon after the latter had been fashioned from the atmosphere. This is also true of the remaining planets and stars…."[2]

Clearly, and quite contrary to all that we have been told over the years, there is no component in the Sumerian myth that could possibly have given rise to the account that we have in Genesis. Moreover, apart from its obvious astronomical and other inaccuracies, the Sumerian myth gives proper names for the sun and moon: *Utu* for the sun, and *Sin* or *Nanna* for the moon. Now this requires the most careful consideration. As an analogy to help us understand the matter thoroughly, imagine that you come across two slips of paper, one to say that a baby boy was born in your house this morning at seven o'clock, and the other which says that Baby Stephen was born in your house this morning at seven o'clock. Which of the two notes were written first? Clearly, the note which names the baby was written after the note which does not name him. That is simply because when the first note was written, the baby didn't yet have a name. But by the time the second note was written, he had.

Likewise, Genesis does not name either the sun or the moon because, when this portion of Genesis was written, neither the sun nor the moon had as yet been given names. The names came long after. Utu and Nanna were names of gods dreamed up by the Sumerians after the Flood. The Creation account of Genesis, however, bears all the hallmarks of having been written before the Flood, indeed, within the very earliest years after the Creation. So, the question that the critics need to answer is, how can Genesis possibly be based upon myths, the very earliest of which were written long after the opening chapters of Genesis? – some 2,000 years after if chronology is anything to go by?

Later, Genesis does use the common names for the sun and the moon: *shemesh* in Genesis 15:12 for the sun (its Babylonian name); and *yareah* in Genesis 37:9 for the moon (its Canaanite name). The first is in the time of Abraham, who lived some hundreds of years after the Flood, and the second occurs in the time of Joseph when he was yet a young man. Now surely, if Genesis is happy enough to accommodate pagan names for the greater and lesser lights in chapters 15 & 37, then it would have been happy enough to have used those same names in its first chapter, but only if those names had existed back then. Clearly, they didn't. The first chapter of Genesis, at least, was written long before the myths which, critics would have us believe, gave birth to the Book of Genesis. Given that no child can be older than its parents, then that surely leaves the critics up a gum-tree.

The worship of the sun and the moon as gods is probably the oldest and most widely practiced form of idolatry. Even the Jews fell into the ritual of offering honey-cakes to the moon, and were roundly condemned for it. But idolatry seems, if the silence of Genesis is anything to go by, to have been a *post*-Flood phenomenon. The Book of Genesis does specifically state that the old world was destroyed by the Flood for three predominant sins of mankind: namely consorting with angels; for an inordinate love of violence; and for the fact that, "every imagination of the thoughts of his [man's] heart was only evil continually." (Genesis 6:5). Idolatry, or the worshipping of false gods and graven images, is not mentioned. Only after the Flood does idolatry raise its ugly head and corrupt mankind. Hence, if the earliest chapters of Genesis were written before the Flood, and we shall be considering good evidence that they were, and if idolatry did not become a universal sin until after the Flood, then that gives an antiquity for the earliest chapters of Genesis that even some conservative scholars have failed to realize.

## Footnotes to Chapter Five

1. Not so as far as the Sumerians are concerned: "In a tablet, which gives a list of the Sumerian gods, the goddess Nammu, written with the pictograph for primeval 'sea,' is described as 'the mother, who gave birth to heaven and earth.' Heaven and earth were therefore conceived by the Sumerians as the created product of the primeval sea." Kramer, p. 77-78.

2. Ibid, p. 79.

~ * ~

## Chapter Six: Pre-Flood Geography and the Present Tense

As we read through the earlier chapters of the Book of Genesis, our attention is drawn to certain geographic details and place-names that are written into the text (chapter 2:8-14). These details discuss and name places and geographic features of the world as it stood before the Flood of Noah. But what startles us is the fact that these details and descriptions are all written, not in the past tense as in a history book, but in the present tense as if by someone who knows them as present features and places. He addresses his details to the reader as if the reader himself is there with him, living out his daily life in the early pre-Flood world. Now that is unexpected to say the least.

It is all the more startling when we consider the fact that the pre-Flood world was destroyed beyond all recognition by the Flood.[1] The valleys, the hills, the rivers, and other contours of the earth's land-masses, were simply obliterated, and when the Flood-waters finally receded, there was nothing left of the Old World that anyone could point to and name.

Names were given to places after the Flood, of course, which recalled and paid nostalgic homage to the pre-Flood geography of the world, but it is easy to see, as we shall see in a moment, that these names did not always fit the new landscape. We can see as much in the name that the earliest people after the Flood gave to the plain that we know as Babylonia. The Babylonians themselves called it *edinu*, which in turn was known in the Assyrian tongue as *bit-idinu*, both names being an attempt to perpetuate the pre-Flood name of Eden. But there was one enormous and very obvious geographic difference between the old Eden and the new. Let us first consider the geography of Eden as it is given in the Book of Genesis, where the writer describes for us the rivers which once watered that country:

> "The name of the first (river) is Pison; that is it which compasseth the whole land of Havilah, where there is gold. And the gold of that land is good. There is bdellium and the onyx stone. And the name of the second river is Gihon. The same is it that compasseth the whole land of Ethiopia. And the name of the third river is Hiddekel. That is it which goeth

> toward the east of Assyria. And the fourth river is Euphrates."
> (Genesis 2:11-14)

Thus much for the old Eden, but what of the new? The old Eden was watered by *four* rivers, whereas Mesopotamia (wherein lay the Babylonian *edinu*) is so named from the fact that it has only two. The names given to these two rivers by the earliest settlers of Mesopotamia are names that we have already encountered in the pre-Flood description of Eden, namely the Tigris and the Euphrates. The name Tigris is derived through Greek from the Old Persian (*Tigra*), which was derived from the Akkadian/Sumerian *id Idikla*, which in turn was merely a transposition of the original and most ancient Biblical name of Hiddekel.[2]

Delitzsch, the German Assyriologist of the 19th century, proposed that the lack of the other two rivers, the Pison and Gihon, could be made up for by adding the *Pallukatu* and *Arahtu* canals of Babylonia.[3] But man-made canals are not rivers, and even Delitzsch must have seen the inadequacy of the proposition. The Babylonians certainly did, for they never even dreamed of claiming as much. Moreover, there are no etymological links between *Pallukatu*, *Arahtu*, and the Pison and Gihon of Genesis.

Clearly, much had changed because of the Flood. When we consider the desolation and emptiness of the world which the earliest families of Noah and his descendants had to settle into, and which most other Flood accounts bear witness to, then it is not to be wondered at that they should try to perpetuate the names of the old pre-Flood world, a world that they had heard so much about from those who had known it, and who had come safely through the Flood in the Ark. Having named one of the major rivers of the country that they were now settling, the Tigris, (the Hiddekel of Genesis), it was only natural that they should also name the land adjacent to it, Assyria, after the pre-Flood land of that name which had also once stood by a river Tigris.

This was to do no more than what settlers have done down the ages. North America, particularly, with its New England, Boston, London, Cambridge, and so on, testifies to the practice perfectly. Now we cannot say that the American Boston is the same city as the one in England just because they share the same name. Clearly, one was named after the other, and they are two distinct and separate cities. Likewise, we cannot say with the critics that the pre-Flood Assyria is the same as the post-Flood land of that name. The one is merely named after the other. Besides, there was one significant difference between the pre- and the post-Flood lands named Assyria. In the Assyria that existed before the Flood, the Tigris lay on the east side of the land. But in the post-Flood land of Assyria, the new Tigris lay on the west.[4]

There are, of course, other place names appearing in Genesis 2:11-14 which we encounter again in the post-Flood world, though most interestingly they do not belong to any part of Mesopotamia. Indeed, they are separated from Mesopotamia by considerable distances. Havilah, for example, is a name that was given to three countries in the years after the Flood, two of which lay within what is today Saudi Arabia. The first (peopled by descendants of Ham whose progenitor was actually named Havilah – Genesis 10:7) lay along the east coast adjacent to the Persian Gulf, whilst the second (a Semitic settlement) lay along the west coast of Saudi Arabia overlooking the Red Sea. (Yakut, an Arabian cosmographer, informs us that the dialect of these people, *Hawil*, was spoken by the 'descendants of Midian, the son of Abraham').[5] The third was another Semitic settlement, and this lay on the east African coast just west of the narrow strait (the Bab-el-Mandeb) which separates Saudi Arabia from Djibouti, just above the Horn of Africa.

Ethiopia and Cush (there were two lands given the name of Cush) are also countries which were named in remembrance of pre-Flood lands. But, as Dr Henry Morris points out to us, none of them are 'compassed' by great rivers, and their locations alone preclude them from being identified with the pre-Flood Ethiopia and Cush.[6]

Noting such discrepancies as these, we can say that, clearly, the writer of Genesis 2:11-14 knew absolutely nothing of the geography of the post-Flood world. How could he? He was writing in pre-Flood times of the pre-Flood world that he saw and knew, hence his use of the present tense when describing that world, as well as the glaring disagreements between the pre-Flood and the post-Flood geographies.

Perhaps the most obvious objection against what we have said concerning post-Flood Assyria, is that the country was plainly named after its eponymous founder, Asshur, a man later deified by his descendants. That may in fact be the case, yet the post-Flood Asshur was doubtless named after the pre-Flood patriarch who gave his name to the old Assyria. We see the same thing happening with Havilah and with Cush. In fact, there are two lands named Cush in the post-Flood era; one named after the pre-Flood land of Cush, and the other being named after its own eponymous post-Flood founder (Genesis 10:6). This Cush, the eldest son of Ham, named one of his own sons, Havilah, doubtless in honor of, and to perpetuate the name of, his pre-Flood predecessor. His other sons all came in time to give their names to the nations they founded. In other words, there is nothing in all this to cast the slightest doubt or concern over the antiquity of this part of the Book of Genesis. It all fits like a glove, which is more than we can say for the 'Documentary Hypothesis' of the critics.

## Footnotes to Chapter Six

1. Required reading in this field is Whitcomb and Morris', *The Genesis Flood*, especially chapter 5, pp. 116-200 (see Bibliography).

2. *Interpreters Dictionary of the Bible*, vol. 4, p. 642 (which transliterates the name as *Idigna*). Interestingly, Daniel (10:4) calls the river by its ancient name Hiddekel. Had the Book of Daniel truly been written in the 5th century BC or even later, under the Persians as modernists and critics continue to claim, then the writer would surely have used the Persian form of the river's name, *Tigra*, (whence the modern Tigris). Otherwise, his post-Exilic readers would not have known which river he was talking about. But the fact that Daniel uses its most ancient and pre-Persian name, Hiddekel, is one of the many hallmarks which tell us that the Book of Daniel was finished *before* the return in 536 BC of the Jews to Jerusalem under Nehemiah and Ezra, of whom Daniel seems to know nothing, even though all three had served under the same Persian kings, Darius and Cyrus. Daniel was most likely dead by the time Ezra and Nehemiah entered the scene.

3. Pinches, *The Old Testament*..., p. 70.

4. A point brought out very well by Henry Morris: *The Genesis Record*, p. 89.

5. Cooper, *After the Flood*, p. 177.

6. Morris: *The Genesis Record*, p. 89.

~ * ~

## Chapter Seven: The Temptation and Fall of Man

We are all of us familiar with the account in the Book of Genesis (chapter 3) regarding the Temptation and the Fall of Man. Even those who have never read a Bible in their lives are familiar with it. In the ancient world, folk were more familiar with it still, remembering for a very long time what had happened - and what had been lost - on that infamous and tragic day. Genesis 3 tells us what happened in full. But how did the pagans recall the Temptation and Fall of Man? And, more to the point, is there any pagan account of it that can be said to be older than that contained in the Book of Genesis? That is *the* vital point to establish.

A somewhat dimmed and distorted memory of the Temptation and Fall is definitely preserved in the following lines, taken from what was initially thought to be the third tablet of the Babylonian creation epic, the *Enuma Elish*:

> "In sin, one with another in compact joins.
> The command was established in the garden of the god.
> The Asnan-tree they ate, they broke in two,
> Its stalk they destroyed,
> The sweet juice which injures the body.
> Great is their sin. Themselves they exalted.
> To Merodach their Redeemer he (the god Sar) appointed their fate."[1]

There are several points to be recognized in this fragment. The compact between Adam and Eve (though unnamed) to eat of the forbidden fruit; the command not to eat it being established in a divinely-appointed garden; the 'Asnan' tree seeming to be the Tree of the Knowledge of Good and Evil; the effect of its juice in injuring the body, bringing death to the body, in other words; of the greatness of their sin in eating the fruit; and their act of self-exaltation in wanting to be like God, knowing good and evil. Whoever wrote the lines was clearly not gleaning his facts from the Book of Genesis, and it is also clear that Genesis was not gleaned from this fragment either, or any other like it. Rather, we have here two independent accounts of the same event, one, Genesis, reporting the scene with perfect accuracy, and the other relying on a dim and very distant collective memory. But which is the older of the two? We shall see.

Fox Talbot, the early 19th-century pioneer of modern negative/positive photography, and one of the earliest decipherers of the cuneiform inscriptions from Nineveh, once made the antiquity of the Book of Genesis his especial study. In his 'pre-cuneiform' days, he searched the ancient Greek and Latin poets and historians for recognizable references to the events of the early chapters of Genesis (missing several, it has to be said), and he argues most persuasively for the early Greek fable of Pandora's Box being a very dimmed memory of the Fall of Man.[2] I'm sure he's right:

> "[Pandora] is the story of the woman, *the wife of the first-created man*, upon whom the gods had showered every blessing which it is possible to imagine; but had laid upon her one injunction, had hid from her one secret which she was never to attempt to discover. But alas! her curiosity tempts her to violate this fatal command! Immediately all happiness flies away from earth; and in its place sorrow, misery, and all manner of evils invade the abode, and embitter the existence of mankind. Can it be said that the author of this fable had never heard of the temptation of Eve?"[3]

He then goes on to make the following observation:

> "Now, then, I argue thus:- Since this tale is related by Hesiod, one of the most ancient of profane authors, the Biblical history of our first parents must be more ancient than *him*."[4] (All italics are Fox Talbot's).

It is generally considered that Hesiod flourished during the late eighth century BC, but as he was clearly drawing on a yet more ancient myth, Fox Talbot reasoned with impeccable logic that the third chapter of the Book of Genesis upon which the Greek myth is based, must be older still. Until the later discovery of certain cuneiform inscriptions that touch upon the matter (some of which were translated by Fox Talbot himself), that was as far back as he was able to go in 1839.[5] It was an important and well-argued achievement, and was certainly a forceful answer to the Bible critics of his time. But more has surfaced since then.

Again, we may save ourselves the trouble of ploughing through all the later myths from Babylonia. Our remit, after all, is to see if there are any remembrances of the Temptation and Fall of Man that are *older* than the third chapter of Genesis, which means that our considerations must now be focused on the ancient land of Sumer.

Sumerian mythology is interesting. It is the earliest that was developed by man, and is remarkable for several reasons. It contains a very real and detailed memory of the events described in the earlier chapters of Genesis, and at the same time a surprising level of the corruption which that remembered detail underwent. The corruption is the more surprising element simply because it happened so early, in the very earliest years after the Flood when Noah and his descendants were alive, teaching, and able to keep the record straight. But not able enough, it seems.

There's something strangely unexplained about the way paganism was conceived so quickly, developed its mythologies and priestly systems so soon, and took a very firm hold indeed upon the vast majority of mankind. It is recognized by many that all of the world's various pagan religious systems are essentially the same, with only the names of the gods being changed from culture to culture.

The suddenness of the rise of paganism, and the immediacy of its highly complex organization in Sumer, belie the notion that religion is something that has 'evolved' down the ages. The entire disciplines of modernism and Bible criticism are founded very firmly indeed upon that assumption, yet it has no basis whatever in fact. Paganism exploded onto the world stage with such frightening suddenness that there seems to have been no time for any to challenge its irrationalities and false teachings. Its grip was immediate and permanent.

But paganism is, for all that, a post-Flood phenomenon. If the sixth chapter of Genesis is anything to go by, and I'm sure it is, then the sins for which God destroyed the old world did not include the worship of false gods and graven images. We may be sure that had such been the case, then it certainly would have been mentioned in Genesis, if only as a warning to mankind not to repeat the experiment. But the real point is this. If the Sumerian mythology concerning the Creation and the Fall of Man is but a dimmed and distant memory of the events recorded in Genesis 3, then it must surely stand to reason that the Genesis 3 account is the earlier of the two. It is impossible, even for Bible critics, to remember things that do not yet exist, and if Genesis 3 had not yet been written in the time of Sumer, then how could the Sumerians possibly have distorted the memory of it among themselves? But the matter is surely settled by the following two most interesting pieces of archaeology.

## The Temptation Seal

The first is illustrated below (Fig. 1) and is an impression from a cylinder seal. The seal itself dates back to ca 2200 BC, which places it among the earliest cylinder seals known.

Fig. 1

It resides today in the British Museum, where it is simply known as ME 89326. The seal had been discovered in 1846, and had belonged to the J R Stewart collection before the British Museum acquired it. We shall consider its details in a moment, but we can take note here of the strange embarrassment that comes over the British Museum these days when forced to acknowledge the seal:

> "This cylinder seal was related to the temptation of Eve in the Garden of Eden (Gen. 3:1-13) by George Smith of the British Museum (1840-76).... Such an interpretation has been given many times since. In fact the seal belongs to a well-known genre of the Akkadian and post-Akkadian periods in Mesopotamia (twenty-third and twenty-second centuries BC), and shows a seated male figure, identified by his headdress as a deity, facing a female worshipper. Both figures are fully clothed. The date-palm between them and the snake may have had fertility significance and there is no reason to connect the scene with the Adam and Eve story. "[6]

Well that's a relief. But what is wrong with the Museum's somewhat dismissive description of the seal? Many things. Firstly, female worshippers were *never* depicted as sitting in the presence of their 'god'. On every other depiction of worshippers - male *or* female - they are invariably shown standing, sometimes with their arms or hands formally raised in adoration, or being led toward or introduced to the 'god' by a priest or another deity. They are, moreover, depicted as being noticeably smaller than the 'god' or even king before whom they stand.

The fruit-bearing tree is interesting inasmuch as it bears seven branches, like the later Menorah, and two fruits, they being the fruits of the knowledge of good and evil. It also shows that the female figure was not alone in eating that fruit.

But a more interesting figure on the seal is surely the serpent which stands behind the female figure, watching from over her shoulder with great attention as she reaches out, with the man, to pluck the fruit. It is hard to imagine that the events depicted in Genesis 3:1-6 could ever have been portrayed more concisely, or more accurately, than this.

And what are we to make of the next seal that is shown in Figure 2? This again shows two figures, clearly male and female, but naked now and cowering in terror. Again, behind them stands a serpent, the three of them all looking intently toward the same point to the right of the seal. It is, in short, a perfect depiction of Genesis 3:10-19. No Babylonian or other account that has come to us depicts man's fall as

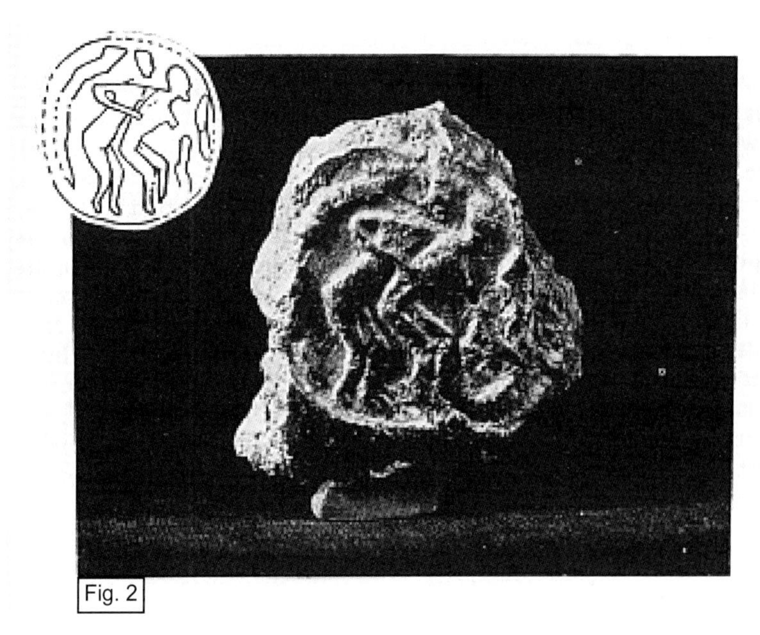

Fig. 2

Genesis does and as these two seals illustrate, so clearly the events depicted in Genesis covering the Fall were known in close detail in Babylonia in the very earliest years after the Flood, at the latest by 2200 BC, *before* the pagan Babylonian myth-makers had corrupted the memory of them.[7]

## Footnotes to Chapter Seven

1. Sayce, *Higher Criticism…*, p. 102. Though the fragment's provenance was once hoped to be the third tablet of *Enuma Elish*, nothing like it appears in any of the restored tablets of the epic, and certainly not in Sayce's own translation of that tablet (*Early Israel and the Surrounding Nations*, pp. 134-135). For the suggestion that it might have been from the epic, he cites, *The Babylonian and Oriental Record*, vol 4, p. 2 (1890), attributing the opinion to Theophilus Pinches. It is not known whether the fragment was the subject of any further investigation or attribution.

2. Fox Talbot, *The Antiquity of the Book of Genesis…..*, 1839, pp. 47-56. Actually, Hesiod tells us that Pandora's 'box' was

a *pithos* (πιθος), a large earthenware jar. The mistranslation is due to Erasmus of Rotterdam (1466-1536) who rendered the poem into Latin during the early 16th century, giving the Latin word for box, *pyxis*, for the Greek πιθος. And so it remains a box to this day.

3. Ibid, pp. 11-12.

4. Ibid, p. 12.

5. A more thorough search would have rewarded Fox Talbot with much more interesting material. Lucian's account of Deucalion (the Greek 'Noah') from his *De Dea Syria* (*On the Syrian Goddess*), and Cicero's *De Natura Deorum* (*On the Nature of the Gods*), for example. But richer pickings yet were to be had in Fox Talbot's day from Faber's 3-volume *The Origin of Idolatry* (1816), which brought everything together on the subject - see Bibliography.

6. Mitchell, *The Bible in the British Museum*, p. 24.

7. Even the fragment that we considered at the beginning of this chapter, gives a somewhat garbled account of the Fall, close though it is to that given in Genesis. A photograph of a modern impression taken from the Temptation seal may be seen at http://www.britishmuseum.org/explore/highlights/highlight_objects/me/a/adam_and_eve_cylinder_seal.aspx - while the seal depicted in fig. 2 may be seen at the following website: http://www.bible-archaeology.info/adam.htm

~ * ~

## Chapter Eight: Genesis 5 and the Sumerian King List

One of the more fascinating items to have surfaced from archaeology since the 19th century, is surely the Sumerian King List. This survives in several cuneiform documents, and is interesting to us inasmuch as it speaks, in its earliest portion, of kings who had reigned before the Flood. We had already known of such a list that had been supplied by the Babylonian priest, Berosus (Akkad. *Bel-re-usu*). He had translated it into Greek for his *Babyloniaca*, a work he composed in ca 280 BC for Antiochus I (324-261 BC), one of Alexander the Great's successors. Modernists had, of course, treated the work as spurious until the cuneiform inscriptions came to light which vindicated Berosus' claim that he had translated such a list. But now it is the cuneiform inscriptions which are suspect, especially as they appear to shed *some* light of corroboration upon a much-maligned section of the Book of Genesis known as Chapter 5, *The Book of the Generations of Adam* - or, at least, upon one particular aspect of it.

Now it has to be said that the Sumerian King List does *not* appear to be a Sumerian account of the ten pre-Flood patriarchs of whom Genesis 5 speaks. There are, after all, only eight kings mentioned in the list whose names, moreover, bear no resemblance at all to any of those in Genesis 5. Moreover, Genesis does not describe its patriarchs as kings. But the List's interest lies in its use of the Flood as a chronological dividing line, and in the longevity that is ascribes to the kings who lived before the Flood.

Genesis 5 also ascribes what is thought of by some today as unnaturally long life-spans for the pre-Flood patriarchs, the general longevity of mankind progressively tailing off after the Flood to its more 'natural' modern value of three score years and ten (70 years). This tailing off is also displayed in the Sumerian King List concerning the kings that reigned after the Flood. But the stick with which modernists beat the Sumerian King List today (and through it, Genesis 5) consists of the reigns of these monarchs running impossibly into tens of thousands of years for each of them. Such time-spans are impossibly long even by the standards of Genesis 5. But even this problem has a simple solution, and one that is not unknown to the modernists - though they invariably forget to mention it.

The Sumerian list of the pre-Flood kings and their reigns, in standard translation, may be summarized as follows:

A-lulima(k) reigned 28,800 years.
Alalgar reigned 36,000 years.
En-men-lu-Anna(k) reigned 43,200 years.
En-men-gal-Anna(k) reigned 28,800 years.
Dumu-zi(d) the Shepherd reigned 36,000 years.
En-sipa(d)-zi(d)-Anna(k) reigned 28,800 years.
En-men-dur-Anna(k) reigned 21,000 years.
Ubar-Tutu(k) reigned 18,600 years.

The list goes on to explain that there were thus eight kings who ruled over five cities, their successive reigns totaling 241,200 years. And then, "The Flood swept thereover."[1]

After the Flood, the List records a dramatic decrease in life-span, the first king after the Flood, Ga…ur of Kish, reigning a mere 1200 years; a successor of his, Aka, reigning only 625 years; and a later king of E-Anna(k), Mes-kiag-gasher, who fell off the throne after a piffling 324 years. All of which follows the pattern that we recognize from the Book of Genesis – very long life-spans before the Flood, which progressively tail off in the aftermath. But what are we to make of the astronomical figures for each of the reigns in the Sumerian King List?

Astronomical is actually the right word to use. The unit of measurement that is used in the List is known as a *saros* (pl. *sari*), an astronomical unit which equals 3,600 (or 60 x 60). So Dumuzi the Shepherd is said in the List to have reigned for 10 sari, or 36,000 years, and so on. The *saros* had its fractions, of course, which, like the *saros*, were also based on the number 60, and these also were used in combination to express the lengths of some of the other reigns. But there is something very strange going on here, because on analysis these figures actually begin to mean something. Let us see how.

To begin with, the List has come down to us in two forms, that of the cuneiform and that of the Greek translation of Berosus. Strangely, the two do not agree in the figures that they give us, yet even this might tell us something. The cuneiform, for example, gives us a total of

241,200 years (or 67 *sari*) for the pre-Flood era, whereas Berosus gives us *ten* kings who ruled for 432,000 years (or 120 *sari*), nearly double the cuneiform figure. So what significance does Berosus' figure hold for us?

To begin with, and so that we don't get lost in all this, we must bear firmly in mind the historical number of years that Genesis gives us for the pre-Flood era. That number is 1,656 years. Yet Berosus gives us 432,000 years for that period, and here's where it gets interesting. We know that the Sumerians employed what is known as a 'sexagesimal' system of mathematics – one that is based on the number 60 in other words. Well, 60 months equal 5 years, and if we divide 432,000 by 5, we are left with the product of 86,400, which happens also to be the number of *weeks* in the 1,656 years which Genesis gives us! Curious, isn't it? Yet not so curious when we consider that the calendar used by the Sumerians (and hence by Berosus) was the lunar calendar. They simply didn't measure things by the solar year as we do, and it becomes clear from this that Berosus wasn't giving us a period of time measured in years (a word he does not use), but one that is measured in lunar months, and the seven-day units (or quarters) of those months. So it seems that the common assumption that these figures pertain to years is entirely mistaken, and is yet another example of the modernists applying their own familiar values to those of the ancient past in order to ridicule it.

So much for the Greek version, but what of the cuneiform Sumerian King List's figure of 241,200 for the pre-Flood era? – or at least for the combined lifespans of its kings? Lopez has worked on this, basing his calculations on the translation of T Jacobsen (1939), and what Lopez proposes is this: that the scribe (being a Sumerian who used the sexagesimal system), was translating a document concerning the pre-Flood kings that was written out under the decimal system, both systems, as we know, using the same cuneiform signs as each other. Hence, under the decimal system the pre-Flood era is very much reduced from the figure of 241,200 (or 67 *sari*). Moreover, by applying this to the eight Genesis 5 Patriarchs who lived between Adam and Noah (excluding their times from the calculation), and by rounding the figures involved, a pretty close approximation is achieved between the figures given in Genesis 5 and the Sumerian King List.[2]

But even this is not all. Further to Lopez, we can say that the above values for the *saros* rely wholly on the assumption that it was the astronomical *saros* which was intended in these figures. As we have seen, that *saros* equaled 3,600 in value. The value was so large because astronomical calculations involve immensely large measurements. But there was another, smaller, *saros* used by the Babylonians which goes unmentioned in these figures, and that smaller *saros* had a value of only 18.5. It was used, of course, in smaller more everyday calculations.[3] Thus, if we use the smaller *saros*, then the 432,000 years of Berosus is reduced immediately to a period of only 2,220 years (if solar years were ever intended). Likewise, the 241,200 'years' of the cuneiform Sumerian King List, is reduced immediately to a mere 1,239.5 'years' – again assuming that the solar year was meant. Considering that the Sumerian King List counts only eight kings against Genesis 5's ten patriarchs, to whom Genesis 5 ascribes a period of 1,656 years, then the King List's 1,239.5 years suddenly seems to be not far off the mark.

To read Genesis 5 is clearly to read the older, and hence the original, of these accounts. That much is made immediately plain by a simple comparison between them. Genesis 5 is concise and precise in all that it tells us. It is also amazingly consistent with itself and with the rest of the Book of Genesis. There is so much that is unknown both to Berosus and the Sumerian King List, and what they do know is confused and imprecise, one counting ten kings, one counting eight, and both giving wildly different totals for their reigns – even though those totals are not without significance for our investigation. So once again, and in distinct contradiction to all that the modernists say, Genesis shows itself to be the older and by far the purer account. Moreover, the longevity of its patriarchs – a point of much scoffing in the modernist camp – is seen to be corroborated to a surprising degree by two independent and very ancient sources.

## Footnotes to Chapter Eight

1. Lopez, R E. 'The Antediluvian Patriarchs and the Sumerian King List.' *Creation Ex Nihilo Technical Journal*. December 1998. 12 (3). pp. 347-357. Jacobsen's translation cited by

Lopez is found in, Jacobsen, T. *The Sumerian King List*. 1939. University of Chicago. See: http://www.answersingenesis.org/tj/v12/i3/sumerian.asp

2. Ibid.

3. The information concerning the two Babylonian *sari* comes from Suidas, a Greek lexicographer who flourished in the late 10th century CE. He was frequently quoted by Eustathius in the 13th century, so this information would not have been unknown to our latter-day exponents of Babylonian science and history. (Suidas, cit. Jones, F A. *The Dates of Genesis*. 1912. Kingsgate Press. p. 114). It's just strange that the value of the smaller *saros* seems never to have made its way into public knowledge.

~ * ~

## Chapter Nine: The Antiquity of the Genesis Calendar

> "In the six hundredth year of Noah's life, *in the second month, the seventeenth day of the month*, the same day were all the fountains of the great deep broken up, and the windows of heaven were opened....And the waters returned from off the earth continually, *and after the end of the one hundred and fifty days* the waters were abated. And the ark rested *in the seventh month, on the seventeenth day of the month*, upon the mountains of Ararat." (Genesis 7:11 & 8:3-4. Italics mine)

Military strategists and those involved in the planning of covert warfare, will often speak of hiding things in plain sight. It is a time-honoured and trusty way of deceiving the enemy whilst protecting one's own troops and equipment (if they have any). Likewise, there is something in the Book of Genesis which seems to be hidden in plain sight. Few ever notice it, even though they may read Genesis repeatedly for many years. It is the calendar that Genesis uses. It has no match in the present day, and indeed has not had its equal since the days of the Flood, its unique characteristic being that all its months were of 30 days duration. From the 17th day of the 2nd month to the 17th day of the 7th month, were 150 days – no more, no less. That's 5 months of 30 days duration each. In that regard, this calendar is certainly unique, and it is one of the great indicators of the sheer antiquity of the Book of Genesis.

Virtually every calendar in the ancient world was governed by the moon. Indeed, the Jews and the Arabs (and others) still use the lunar calendar, measuring the beginning of each month (the word is itself derived from 'moon') by the appearance of the new or crescent moon. The problem with the lunar calendar these days, though, is that the month no longer lasts for 30 days. It lasts only for 29.5 days (roughly), and that has been the state of play since the very earliest years after the Flood. What happened to alter the length of the moon's orbit around the earth is another subject altogether, and has been dealt with elsewhere.[1] Suffice it to say that the Flood of Noah had astronomical effects as well as terrestrial. Our remit here is to consider just how the use of a 30-day month marks out the calendar of the Book of Genesis to be more ancient than all other known calendars.

We must begin by sparing a thought for the Sumerian and Babylonian astronomers who first noticed the new and somewhat erratic behaviour of the lunar month. With careful measurement, of which they were more than capable, they saw that the new lunar month was not even fixed. One month could be 29.26 days in length, whilst another would require up to 29.8 days to pass. To make any calendrical projection, therefore, they had to assume that each future lunar month would average out at 29.530588 days (which, in real money, is somewhat equal to 29 days, 12 hours, and 44 minutes – but *only* somewhat).

Twelve such months would therefore be equal to 354.367056 days, which has to be subtracted from the average length of the solar year, which is 365.2422 days, leaving it necessary to intercalate (or artificially insert) 10.875144 days to bring the lunar calendar somewhere into line with the solar.[2] Quite! The Sumerian and Babylonian astronomers loved to play with such figures, of course, a baffling pastime that has been inherited and is still enjoyed by their modern counterparts. But for the poor farmer who has to count upon his fingers, or the mariner who has to guess when the next high-tide is due so that he doesn't ground his boat upon the rocks, it is no fun at all.

Originally, of course, such erratic time-keeping was not intended. The Book of Genesis tells us that when God created the sun, the moon and the stars, He built into them the quality and attributes of being used to measure time – "Let them be for signs and for seasons, and for days and years." (Genesis 1:14). The Flood changed all that, of course, by bringing chaos to not just the lunar calendar. The solar calendar itself is fraught with problems, and the Flood's effects upon the earth have affected even the timekeeping of the stars. The earth's day, measured by the sun's zenith, lasts for exactly 24 hours (an artificial measurement devised by man merely for its convenience). But the stars behind the sun, the so-called fixed stars by which are measured sidereal time, are seen to go around the earth not once in 24 hours like the sun, but once every 23 hours, 56 minutes and four seconds (roughly)! That's a difference between the stars' and the sun's orbits of nearly four minutes a day, or roughly one whole day every year! Clearly, things had gone horribly wrong with the calendar.

But to appreciate the antiquity of the Genesis calendar, we need to consider the lunar calendar as it was devised by the Babylonians. To begin with, they gave names to the lunar months, which is something that Genesis doesn't do, its account of the Flood having been written out at so remote a time that the months had not yet been named. From day one, however, (no pun intended), the Babylonians named their months as follows:

> **Nisan**, which corresponds roughly with our March-April; **Iyyar** (April-May); **Sivan** (May-June); **Tammuz** (June-July); **Ab** (July-August); **Elul** (August-September); **Tisri** (September-October); **Marcheswan** (October-November); **Chisleu** (November-December); **Tebet** (December-January); **Sebat** (January-February); and **Adar** (February-March).[3]

The first lunar month of the year, Nisan, was reckoned to have a duration of 30 days, whilst the second, Iyyar, was reckoned as 29 days. The third was 30 days, the fourth 29, and so on. This is how they solved the problem of the true lunar month lasting an awkward 29.5 days. As calendar reforms go, it was ingeniously simple, and it has worked well enough for more than four thousand years. But the significance of all this is seen in the following.

The Jews returned to Jerusalem under Ezra and Nehemiah toward the close of the 6th century BC.[4] At some time after 515 BC, or so it is alleged by the critics, the Book of Genesis with the rest of the Torah was 'composed.' Now if that were true, how comes it that the Book of Genesis does not reckon its calendar dates according to the Babylonian calendar, which was the only calendar that the returning Jews were familiar with? The Jews who came out of Babylon were third or fourth generation from those who had been exiled there back in 587 BC. They used the Babylonian calendar then, and they use it still to this day, naming the months after the Babylonian fashion, and not numbering them as the Book of Genesis does. Moreover, if we take the 17th day of the 2nd month in the post-Flood Jewish/Babylonian calendar, and count forward by five months to the 17th day of the 7th month, we will count in that period not 150 days as does Genesis, but 147 days (29+30+29+30+29 = 147). And yet that is not what appears in Genesis

– nothing like it, in fact. There the months are numbered, not named, and each consists of an invariable duration of 30 days.

To work out from all this the pre-Flood values of the calendar, is hardly rocket-science. With the year consisting of 12 lunar months of 30 days apiece, the solar year consisting of 360 days, and the stellar or sidereal year being of like value, time-keeping and calendar projections were simplicity itself. The entire universe ticked away the hours, the days, the years, the signs and the seasons, with perfect consistency, precision and reliability. But not so after the Flood, which raises the following questions.

Of the Genesis and Babylonian calendars, which is the older? And can we possibly say that the older Genesis calendar was copied from the younger Babylonian? Hardly. That would reverse any historical sequence of events; it would reverse time; and it would reverse every notion that we have of logic and plain common sense. Yet that is no more than what the critics have been doing all these years – making their claims on the strength of a philology whose mechanics were little understood, and which was applied to languages which were even less understood. Little wonder that nothing but nonsense has flowed from it – and continues to flow to this day.

## Footnotes to Chapter Nine

1. Morris, J. 'In the Early Earth, Were All the Months Exactly Thirty Days Long?' *Acts & Facts*. 2005. 34 (12): "[T]he great Flood of Noah's day forever altered Earth's systems....With the fountains of the great deep relocating a huge volume of liquid, moving continents, possible asteroid bombardment, etc., shifting the location of much mass, the length of the day, the length of the year, and the tilt of the axis could have all changed." – see also Cooper, B. 2009. The Calendar and the Antiquity of Genesis. *Acts & Facts.* 38 (6): 19; or on-line at /www.icr.org/article/calendar-antiquity-genesis

2. Website http://www.ghazali.net/calander/Linar_v_Solar/body_linar_v_solar .html - the typographical errors in this address (linar for lunar x 2) are original to the website.

3. The modern Jewish calendar still uses these ancient Babylonian names for its months, as it has since the days of Ezra and Nehemiah and their return from the Babylonian Captivity, with just a slight variation in spelling: Nissan; Iyar; Sivan; Tammuz; Av; Elul; Tishri; Cheshvan; Kislev; Tevet; Shevat; and finally, Adar. For a fuller treatment, see: http://www.jewfaq.org/calendar.htm

4. The Return from exile took place over time between 538 BC, the date of Cyrus' edict, and 515 BC when the Temple in Jerusalem was restored.

~ * ~

## Chapter Ten: The Tower of Babel

> "And the whole earth was of one language and of one speech. And it came to pass, as they journeyed from the east, that they found a plain in the land of Shinar, and they dwelt there. And they said one to another, 'Go to, let us make brick and burn them thoroughly.' And they had brick for stone, and slime had they for mortar. And they said, 'Go to, let us build us a city and a tower whose top may reach unto heaven, and let us make us a name lest we be scattered abroad upon the face of the whole earth.'" (Genesis 11:1-4)

The building of the Tower of Babel, and the Confusion of Tongues which followed it, are among the best attested events of the ancient world. Like the Great Flood, most cultures around the world – even those separated by thousands of miles and many centuries of time – have some account or other of the Tower. Intriguingly, these accounts are all pre-Christian, and yet are not a million miles removed from that which Genesis gives us (11:1-9). But our task here is to see which is the eldest among them, and then to ask which of those accounts – if any - is older than the one which we have from the Book of Genesis.

We have known for centuries that the Greeks and Romans knew all about the Tower. Alexander Polyhistor (105-35 BC) tells us what he knew about it in his *Chaldean History*:

> "The Sibyl says that when all men formerly spoke the same language, some among them undertook to erect a large and lofty tower in order to climb into heaven. But God, (or the gods), sending forth a whirlwind, frustrated their design and gave to each tribe a particular language of its own, which is the reason that the name of that city is called Babylon."[1]

The 'Sibyl' referred to by Polyhistor is obviously not the pseudo-Sibylline Oracles which the Gnostics composed during the 2nd-5th centuries CE, for Polyhistor flourished some centuries before that. What he was alluding to were the original Sibylline Oracles which were already ancient by his time, and which have left us the following account of the Tower:

> "But when the judgments of Almighty God were ripe for execution; when the tower rose to the skies upon Assyrian's plain, and all mankind one language only knew, a dread commission from on high was given to the fell whirlwinds, which with dire alarms beat on the tower, and to its lowest base shook. It convulsed, and now all intercourse, by some occult [i.e. unseen] and overruling power, ceased among men. By utterance they strove, perplexed and anxious, to disclose their mind, but their lip failed them, and in lieu of words produced a painful babbling sound. The place was thence called Babel by the apostate crew, named from the event. Then, severed, far away they sped, uncertain, into realms unknown. Thus kingdoms rose, and the glad world was filled."[2]

It might, of course, be argued that the Romans got their account from the Greeks, who in turn had learned about the Tower from the Septuagint translation of the Old Testament from Hebrew into Greek. This translation is said to have been begun by ca 280 BC, so there's a kind of plausibility to the objection. However, Hestiaeus of Perinthus, a writer who studied under Plato (428-348 BC), and who thus lived some 200 years *before* the translators of the Septuagint, was not unfamiliar with the Confusion of Tongues at Babel, and tells us:

> "The priests who escaped took with them the implements of the worship of the Enyalion Jove, and came to Senaar [Shinar], in Babylonia. But they were again driven from thence by the introduction of a diversity of tongues, upon which they founded colonies in various parts, each settling in such situations as chance, or the direction of God, led them to occupy."[3]

Intriguing. Most intriguing. At this point in time, all we can say of Hestiaeus' source for this information is that it is lost to us. Doubtless, it was merely a part of that all-pervasive fund of knowledge concerning the Tower of Babel and its aftermath that was (and is) common to all nations and cultures. But, ancient though Hestiaeus' account is, it clearly has no part in the far greater antiquity of the Book of Genesis. The only challengers in that area are surely the Sumerians and

Babylonians. So, what do they have to say about the Tower, and, more importantly, when did they say it? Could their account possibly be so ancient that it pre-dates that of the Book of Genesis?

The Akkadians and Sumerians knew the locality of Babel under the name *bab-ilim*, meaning the Gate of (or to) the gods. The Babylonians later singularised the name to *bab-ilu*, the Gate of God. However, by Nebuchadnezzar's day, the Tower lay in ruins, and he leaves us this most interesting description of its history:

> "A former king built the Temple of the Seven Lights of the Earth, but he did not complete its head. Since a remote time, people had abandoned it.... Since that time, earthquakes and lightning had dispersed its sun-dried clay; the bricks of the casing had split, and the earth of the interior had been scattered in heaps."[4]

The 'former king' referred to here is doubtless Nimrod, whilst the 'Seven Lights of the Earth' refers to the seven planets that were known to the Babylonians, and which were created specifically to give light upon the earth and to measure the times and the seasons. Interestingly, Nebuchadnezzar does not say with other pagan sources that this Tower (which he names elsewhere specifically as *zikurat babili* – the Tower of Babel) was destroyed or ruined at the time its building ceased - and interestingly, nor does Genesis. Rather, he implies that its ruined conditioned was accomplished over a long period of time.

Nebuchadnezzar, however, lived and reigned in the 6th century BC, so we need a much older source than he if we are to approach anything like the time when the Genesis account of Babel was written. Happily, there is such a source, and it is seemingly very early. Its title is *Enmerkar and the Lord of Aratta*, and whilst it makes no mention of the Tower of Babel, it does hark back to the time when:

> "The whole universe, the people in unison (?), to Enlil in one tongue gave praise."[5]

The size of this 'whole universe' at the time when only one language was spoken is of immense interest. As given in this account, it consisted merely of the inhabitants of Shubur, Hamazi, Sumer, Uri, and Martu – all of them places contained within a small area in modern Iraq, otherwise known as Babylonia. In other words, no great migration or dispersal had yet occurred from this area. The absence in this account of any reference to the Tower of Babel itself tells us one thing that is very certain, and that is the fact that Genesis 11 was not – nor ever could have been - copied from it. Therefore, *Enmerkar and the Lord of Aratta* was not a source for this portion of Genesis.

Is there not, though, another account of comparable age which *does* mention the Tower of Babel? I can find only one. It was discovered by George Smith, the Assyriologist, in 1875, and it came at just the time when Smith was beginning to despair of ever finding a reference to the Tower among the cuneiform tablets. This general absence of mention is interesting in the light of what the modernist school has been claiming all these years. If their suppositions had been true, accounts of the Tower of Babel should at least have been plentiful enough to have inspired the later Hebrew forgers of Genesis. Yet, amongst the mountains of cuneiform tablets and inscriptions that have come down to us, there is, it seems, just this one single case which Smith tells us of:

> "Early this year [1875] I was astonished to find, on having one of the Assyrian fragments cleaned, that it contained a mutilated account of part of the story of the tower. It is evident from the wording of the fragment that it was preceded by at least one tablet, describing the sin of the people in building the tower. The fragment preserved belongs to a tablet containing four to six columns of writing, of which fragments of four remain."[6]

Smith then gives a literal translation of the inscription into English. In its literal state, it is stilted and difficult to read, so I have taken the liberty here of rearranging Smith's translation into a more natural English:

> "[Line 1]....them(?) the father....
> [2]....of him, his heart was evil....
> [3]....was wicked against the father of all the gods,

[4]....of him, his heart was evil (*sic*),
[5]....brought Babylon to subjection,
[6] small and great he confounded their speech.
[7]....brought Babylon to subjection (*sic*),
[8] small and great he confounded their speech (*sic*).
[9] all the day their strong tower they founded.
[10 & 11] in the night, he entirely made an end to their strong place.
[12] thus he poured out word also in his anger.
[13] he set his face to scatter abroad.
[14] he gave this command. Their counsel was confused."[7]

Unfortunately, Smith does not tell us the number of the tablet, and it is now seemingly untraceable. We do know, however, that it hailed from Nineveh, and belonged to the library of Ashurbanipal, meaning that it was a 7th-century BC copy of an older tablet. But just how old the original was, we cannot say. There is sufficient internal evidence, though, to suggest that even the original was of fairly late composition. God having been debased by the title 'father of all the gods', is one indicator. Such debasement only takes place over time. More telling, however, is the depiction of Nimrod as a king whose 'heart was evil' and who brought Babylon 'to subjection'. No contemporary – or even near-contemporary – writer would ever have dared to pen such words. So it seems that even the very best contender that Assyriology has unearthed so far, (unless there are others about which we have not yet been told), cannot hold a candle to the account of Genesis for sheer antiquity and originality.

There are many instances throughout Mesopotamian history when serious attempts were made to repair the damage done at Babel. As far back as Sargon of Akkad (ca 2300 BC according to conventional dating), it was written of him that "he appointed that all places should form a single kingdom."[8] Empire-building was thereafter the sole consuming passion of every Mesopotamian ruler. There was, moreover, the concerted effort to make Babylonian the *lingua franca* of the diplomatic world, which did succeed for a while, though the people themselves preferred to stick to the languages that they knew. But as far as a Babylonian or even Sumerian source for the Genesis account of the Tower of Babel is concerned, there is not a solitary trace in all the 2000 years or more of cuneiform literature, be it Sumerian, Akkadian, Babylonian or Assyrian. Strange, then, that modernists should persist in telling us that there was.

## Footnotes to Chapter Ten

1. Hodges (ed). *Cory's Ancient Fragments*. 1876. p. 75 (see Bibliography)
2. Ibid, pp. 75-6. I have modernised some of the punctuation in this passage.
3. Ibid, p. 74.
4. http://www.answers.com/topic/tower-of-babel#Sumerian_parallel
5. Kramer, *From the Tablets of Sumer*, p. 259.
6. Smith, *Chaldean Account of Genesis*, p. 160.
7. Ibid.
8. Sayce, *The Higher Criticism*, p. 156.

~ * ~

## Chapter Eleven: The Table of Nations

Speaking of antiquity and originality, the Table of Nations (Genesis 10 and 11) stands pre-eminent among all the documents of the ancient – or even the modern – world. Modernists, typically enough, assign its writing to the 5th century BC or thereabouts (the 'Persian' period), and pass off its composition as being merely a copy (if it wasn't pure fiction) of an earlier (pagan) document or documents. Well, we shall see in this chapter just how well this assertion stands up to the evidence.

The Table of Nations occupies chapters 10 and 11 of the Book of Genesis, and is such a complete and autonomous document that it may be studied in isolation. What is instantly noticeable about the Table is its comprehensiveness, its complexity, and its conciseness. It is, in short, a masterpiece of informative historical writing. But above even these qualities, it possesses an accuracy that is breathtaking. I spent more than 25 years digging into the Table of Nations, looking for a fault, an error, a false statement, or an historical inaccuracy. I found not one.[1] Whether the Table speaks of the early nations historically, geographically, linguistically, or ethnologically, it does so with 100% accuracy. Nothing remotely like it exists from the ancient world. It has no predecessor, and it has no imitator. It is, in every sense and in every way, unique.

As for its antiquity, we may generally note that even though it is very much an autonomous document, it is nevertheless an integral part of the Book of Genesis, and was clearly already in existence when Moses, under God, came to compile the Book of Genesis and the rest of the Torah at some time around 1300 BC.

More specifically, concerning the modernist claim that the Table of Nations was copied from an earlier source at some time during the 'Persian' period – in other words, around the 5th century BC or even later – we note the following phenomenon: the name of Persia is entirely absent from the Table! Now the Jews of the Persian period owed to Persia their national salvation and restoration. From Persia's Ahasuerus, (whose wife, Queen Esther, was herself a Jewess), came the edict that the Jews could destroy those who had sought their destruction, an event celebrated to this day by the feast of Purim. From Persia's King Cyrus came the decree (in 536 BC) that the Jews could return to Jerusalem from their Exile and Captivity. And from Persia's King Darius came the decree (in 515 BC) that the Temple, which had been destroyed and looted by the Babylonians, could be restored in Jerusalem. In other words, under God, the Jews owed Persia *everything*, and it is unthinkable that Persia's name would be omitted from the Table of Nations had that Table been compiled during the Persian period.

Persia herself first comes to the notice of recorded history in 836 BC, when she is mentioned in the inscriptions of the Assyrian king, Shalmanezer III. Intriguingly, the nation was descended from the Medes, and the Medes (Madai) certainly are mentioned in the Table of Nations (Gen. 10:2). What effort would it have been then for the scribe to add just three small consonants (*prs*) next to the name of Madai, to thus include Persia in the Table? It would have been no effort at all, and these three small letters would doubtless have been written into the Table had the name of Persia been known when the Table was compiled. But they are simply not there. They are absent from the Table for the simple reason that neither the name nor even the people of Persia had yet been heard of. That fact alone places the date for the Table of Nations - at the very latest! - to well before 836 BC, well over 400 years before its writing according to the modernist school. But there's more.

There are other examples of nations and peoples being known to dateable history that are not mentioned in the Table of Nations, for the simple reason that they did not yet exist; just as there are those who are mentioned the once in the Table of Nations, but whose names had sunk into oblivion by the 1st millennium BC or even earlier. Both point with equal force to the antiquity of Genesis 10 and 11.

The Zamzummim, who display both aspects of this phenomenon, are an interesting case in point. They make no appearance in the Table of Nations, even though they had once inhabited and were a major political component of early Canaan. Yet by Abraham's day they had virtually disappeared from the world stage. This is an important indicator for the antiquity of the Table of Nations. That Table must originally have been compiled before the time of Abraham, and before the Zamzummim had become a recognised people who had died out by the 19th century BC (when Abraham lived). Harking back to them, Moses, writing under God in ca 1300 BC, tells us what a great nation the Zamzummim had once been:

> "...and the Ammonites call them Zamzummims, a people great and many, and tall as the Anakims. But the Lord destroyed them before them, and they [the Ammonites] succeeded them and dwelt in their stead." (Deut. 2:20-21).

Remarkable. Equally remarkable, though, is the following fact. The Zamzummim were looked upon with some disdain by the early Ammonites. That disdain is reflected in the name which the Ammonites gave them, Zamzummim. It depicts someone who is so barbarous in his speech that it sounds as though he's trying to speak with his mouth full of food.[3] This leads us to the following question, a question which is addressed to those of the modernist school who have so far commented so disparagingly on this portion of the Bible:

> Were the post-Exilic forgers of the Jewish Bible, then, so expert in the ancient Ammonite tongue that they were able to invent this authentic though unkind nickname for a people who otherwise had no significant role in Jewish history?

We may hardly think so. Such forgers, removed from their subject by some 1500 years, could not have known that the speech of the Zamzummim had sounded barbarous to the Ammonite ear. Nor could they have been so learned in the ancient Ammonite tongue that they could make puns out of it and construct such an authentic and derogatory nickname for this people. For be assured, the name that Deuteronomy gives us is entirely authentic. Moreover, given the fact that the Zamzummim had not even a minor role to play in the history of the Jews, why should these forgers have gone to all this bother to tell us about them in the first place?

But let us also consider the Ammonites, the very same people who had held the Zamzummim in such contempt. Once again, the Table of Nations is silent concerning this people, and yet they were truly major players in the Middle East from ca 1300-580 BC.[4] It would have been impossible to ignore them had the Table of Nations been written at *any* time within their period. It is true that the Book of Genesis mentions the origins of the Ammonites elsewhere, Genesis 19:38 to be precise, yet – and this is a most telling point – the compiler of the Table of Nations should have had no knowledge of what the composer of the 'Abrahamic Saga' was going to write if what the modernists have always suggested was in any way based on fact. It is all rather extraordinary.

The Jebusites are a good example of a people who were great and famous at the time the Table of Nations was originally compiled. The eponymous name of Jebus is found in Genesis 10:16. Yet after the conquest of Canaan under Joshua, when the then city of Jebus (Jerusalem) was isolated by the Israelites, and more specifically, after the capture of Jerusalem by King David in ca 1000 BC, nothing further is heard of them. They simply sink into historical oblivion.[5] Surely, no 5th-century BC forger could have known anything of *their* existence either.

Not wishing to labour the point, the Perizzites belong to the opposite class, namely to those early peoples which are not mentioned in the Table of Nations, yet which are attested historically, and who died out by the beginning of the first millennium BC. They, again, were a major component of the Canaanite population, yet, whenever it was that they arose as a nation, it was clearly after the Table had been compiled, for it knows nothing of them. They had died out as a population by Solomon's day.[6]

Such examples could be multiplied, but they would all tell the same story. In short, the modernist assertion that the Table of Nations is a late post-Exilic composition is not just plainly wrong. It is sheer nonsense. Lacking any credible evidence, it actually flies in the face of a whole host of historical facts – well known historical facts! - that speak against the idea. And yet the same tired old phrases are trotted out in publication after publication alleging its late composition without any reference to the evidence which speaks of the antiquity and originality of Genesis 10 and 11. That is a truly shameful state of affairs. But it is again what passes for Bible scholarship these days – in modernist circles, at least.

Sadly, there are many who call themselves conservative Bible scholars who must take their share of the blame in all this. It is commonly said that all it takes for evil to triumph is for good men to do nothing. For that reason modernism has 'triumphed' on the world stage. Those who should have stood their ground and defended the Word when the attacks began, simply kept silent. Worse, many went over to the other side, fearing that the ridicule which modernism heaps upon all its opponents would damage their precious careers. Hence, many colleges and universities which began their lives as Biblically conservative institutions, have abandoned the very Bible-believing Christian constitutions upon which those places of learning were founded. Abandoning the Truth, what else can they write but nonsense?

## Footnotes to Chapter Eleven

1. Cooper, Bill. *After the Flood.* 1995. New Wine Press.
2. *Interpreter's Dictionary of the Bible*, vol. 4, p. 934.
3. Ibid.
4. Ibid, vol. 1, pp. 108-114.
5. Ibid, vol. 2, pp. 807-808.
6. Ibid, vol. 3, p. 735.

~ * ~

# Chapter Twelve: Abraham

Chapters 12 and 13 of the Book of Genesis tell us about the call of God to Abraham (then called Abram) to leave his city of Ur and settle in the land of Canaan, which God promises to him and to his heirs for a perpetual inheritance. With this episode we see the beginning of God's plan of Redemption unfolding in the history of the world. No longer just a promise (Genesis 3:15), it now takes on a very physical aspect, finally to be realised in the crucifixion and resurrection of Jesus Christ, and culminating in His future return to take the redeemed to Himself and then to judge the world. And it all began here with Abraham, the Friend of God and child of faith.

Without Abraham, the unfolding of the Gospel would make no sense, so it hardly comes as a surprise to see the modern reluctance to acknowledge that Abraham even existed as a man, let alone did all the things which the Bible attributes to him. Abraham, it is currently said, is merely the fictional 'hero' of the 'Abrahamic Saga', a pious myth, no less, which was incorporated into the text of Genesis by equally pious 'editors' (post-Exilic, of course), the motive being to give the Jews a sense of their own past and dignity. The main flaw in this nonsense is its refusal to acknowledge the findings of field archaeology and various items of ancient and extra-Biblical documentary evidence which speak overwhelmingly of the fact that, yes, Abraham did exist as a flesh and blood man, and yes, that he belongs very firmly to the historical times in which the Bible sets him.

We first meet the name of Abram outside the Bible in a contract. Interestingly, this contract was made out in about the year 1950 BC under the reign of Abil-Sin, who, importantly for our purpose, was the 4th king of the 1st dynasty of Babylon. Of added pertinence is the fact that this king was the predecessor but one of the famous Hammurabi whom we shall meet again in the next chapter. Between these two kings lies a period of just 38 years, and given that Abraham was in his 70s by the time of Hammurabi, the dates accord well with each other - very well indeed. In Abil-Sin's day, Abram was of a sufficient age to be signing contracts.

The name of Abram is rendered Abi-ramu in the contract, and I for one do not hesitate in the conclusion that Abi-ramu and the Biblical Abram are one and the same person. The date is exactly right, as is the locality, and the prospect of there being two men of that unusual name living and operating at the same time as each other in the same small area under the same king is unlikely in the extreme. Moreover, both men would have to have been men of substance to enter into a contract in the first place.

But given the fact that this contract exists, and that it has the name Abi-ramu written upon it, it is surprising to come across the following assurance from the modernist camp:

> "Although cuneiform parallels have occasionally been cited, neither 'Abram' nor 'Abraham' has yet been discovered in Akkadian texts."[3]

This is entirely specious. It depends how one interprets the term 'Akkadian'. The writer (R Lansing Hicks, erstwhile Professor at Berkeley Divinity School, New Haven) might have gone on to say that the name has nevertheless appeared in early Babylonian texts, but he doesn't. He simply says – with perfect truth in his view – that it is absent from Akkadian texts. Throwing such dust in students' eyes is nothing new for modernism, of course, but it is an entirely reprehensible practice.

The same writer goes on to say that the name of Abraham is philologically unsound, which, given that it is the name given to Abraham by God Himself, is indicative of the low view entertained by Hicks and his school both of God and His Word, as if God – if He exists at all - is incapable of good grammar. Little wonder, then, that Hicks entertains a similar contempt for his students and the public – sufficient at any rate for him to forget to mention the fact that the finer nuances of Biblical Hebrew are today imperfectly understood, not the least by himself.

Fortunately, not all modernist scholars are quite of this brand. A H Sayce, himself a modernist of sorts, yet one who is not afraid to bring Biblical evidence before his readers, is happy to tell us openly that:

> "The name of Abram – Abu-ramu 'the exalted father' – is found in early Babylonian contracts"[4]

There are indeed other contracts from the same time taken out under the auspices of Ammizadugga which bear the name Abram, one of them bearing the date 20th Ulul in the 11th year of Ammizadugga, which is conventionally dated to 1965 BC. These contracts bear witness to this Abram hiring an ox (through his agent, Kishti-Nabium), leasing some land, making rent payments, and so on – all of which fits exactly the picture of Abraham that Genesis presents us with – not of some civil servant or pampered princeling, but an agriculturalist and cattle owner, who, by the time that God called him, was wealthy enough to up-stakes and move himself and his entire people out of the country.[5]

Abraham's departure from Ur (Gen. 12:1-4) was a long-remembered event in Babylonia. The Babylonian historian, Berosus, writing at the beginning of the 3rd century BC, recalls for us:

> "...moreover...there lived, the thirteenth in descent, a man named Abraham, a man of noble race and superior to all others in wisdom. Of him they relate that he was the inventor of astrology and the Chaldean magic, and that on account of his piety, he was esteemed of God. It is further said that under the directions of God, he removed and lived in Phoenicia, and there taught the Phoenicians the motions of the sun and moon and all other things, for which reason he was held in great reverence by their king."[6]

The king was Abimelech of Gerar, whom Genesis tells us of.[7] Ignoring the magical and astrological nonsense, the interesting detail here is that Abraham is said by Berosus to have gone to Phoenicia. Now, the land called Phoenicia in Berosus' day, was called Canaan in Abraham's time, and any 'pious' forger working from Genesis, would surely have said Canaan, and not Phoenicia. All of which indicates that Berosus was working out of authentic Babylonian records and not the Book of Genesis.

The mention of magic and astrology, though, tells us even more about the authenticity of what Berosus has passed down to us. It is such a departure from the truth, that no 'pious' forger would have coloured his narrative like this. He would simply have rehashed Genesis, and, moreover, would not have made the mistake of saying that Abraham was thirteenth in descent (from Noah), when Genesis says that he was really only tenth.[8]

But even that is not all. The following fragment concerning Abraham and his journey from Chaldea to Canaan, is from Book IV of the 144 volume *Universal History*, by Nicolaus of Damascus (born 64 BC). It is very interesting indeed, not only for the fine internal detail of its subject, but for the explanation that it gives of an otherwise unexplained circumstance:

> "Abram was king of Damascus, and came hither as a stranger, with an army, from that part of the country which is situated above Babylon of the Chaldeans. But after a short time he again emigrated from this region with his people, and transferred his dwelling to the land which was at that time called Canaaea, but is now called Judaea; together with all the multitude which had increased with him, of whose history I shall give an account in another book. The name of Abram is well known even to this day in Damascus, and a village is pointed out which is still called the House of Abraham."[9]

Of particular interest is the use of the name Abram instead of Abraham in the earlier portions of the passage. Abram's name was only changed by God to that of Abraham long *after* he had settled in Canaan (Genesis 17:5), and was in his 99$^{th}$ year, which means that Nicolaus was clearly working from local (Syrian) records when he wrote this toward the end of the 1$^{st}$ century BC. (The word translated 'army' in this account, would equally well be rendered 'host', or multitude).

A forger would not have used the birth name of Abram. He would not have said that Abram was ever king of Damascus either. Genesis, which he would have followed, makes no such mention. In fact, Genesis 12:4-5 tells us that Abraham simply journeyed from Haran, in northwest Mesopotamia, down into Canaan, without mentioning any stop being made at Damascus which lay in between. But it is a most interesting detail, and here we come to the otherwise unexplained circumstance that Abraham's household steward should have been Eliezer of Damascus (Genesis 15:2), who, under the laws at that time, was deemed to be Abraham's heir should he, Abraham, not have a son of his own. Damascus, it seems, had good reason to record Abraham's passing that way.

But there is one other item of evidence for the antiquity of these chapters of Genesis which should have given the critics pause for thought, and it is this. Abraham, we know, came from ancestors who were renowned in the ancient world. Several major cities bore their names: Haran, Nahor, Terah, and so on. In the 19th century BC they were flourishing centres of trade and pagan worship (mostly to do with the moon). Yet, by the 6th century BC, they had long been desolate and ruined heaps (except Haran) covered over by the sand. Their names appear in Assyrian inscriptions of the time as *Til-Nakhiri* (the Mound of Nahor), and *Til-Turakhi* (the Mound of Terah).[10] Indeed, the city of Terah was abandoned to the encroaching sands at such an early date, that its mound was known to the Akkadians, who had themselves sunk into oblivion by the 18th century BC. They called it, *Til sa tuhari.*[11] The Jews of the Exile would not even have been aware of the existence of the mounds or the names by which the Assyrians and especially the earlier Akkadians had known them. Nor would they have had either reason or motive to adopt these names as ancestors for their fictional Abraham, the cities being so thoroughly associated with paganism. Nor, like the early explorers of the 19th century CE, would they have had reason to think that underneath these mounds lay once-great cities. The first man to realise that under these tells lay ruined cities, was the archaeologist Flinders Petrie, and he didn't discover that fact until AD 1890.[12] Yet, whenever Genesis speaks of these cities, they are still thriving centres of civilisation, vibrant with life and people. That alone should tell us something of its antiquity.

## Footnotes to Chapter Twelve

1. Pinches, *The Old Testament...*, p. 148

2. Sayce, *Early Israel.....*, p. 107-8.

3. *Interpreter's Dictionary of the Bible*, vol. 1, p. 15.

4. Sayce, *The Higher Criticism...*, p. 159.

5. http://www.docstoc.com/docs/21374098/ABRAHAM-AND-ARCHAEOLOGY

6. Charles Horne. *Sacred Books and Early Literature of the East*, p. 26. The work of Berosus' cited by Horne is his *Babyloniaca*, which he wrote out before the Old Testament was translated into Greek. He therefore could not have filched his information from the Septuagint as is suspected by some.

7. ibid. Abimelech of Gerar appears in Genesis 20:2-18; 21:22-32; and 26:1-26.

8. Shem-Arphaxad-Shelah-Eber-Peleg-Reu-Serug-Nahor-Terah-Abraham (Genesis 11:10-26).

9. Cory, p. 78.

10. Unger. *Archaeology and the Old Testament*, p. 112-3. See also: *Interpreters Dictionary of the Bible*, vol. 3, p. 497.

11. *Interpreters Dictionary of the Bible*, vol. 4, p. 574.

12. http://www.age-of-the-sage.org/archaeology/flinders_petrie.html

## Chapter Thirteen: The Kings of Genesis 14

> "And it came to pass, in the days of Amraphel king of Shinar, Arioch king of Ellasar, Chedorlaomer king of Elam, and Tidal king of nations, that these made war...." (Genesis 14:1-2a)

Thus says Genesis. But what say the modernists?:

> "It may be said at once that *none* of the names of kings mentioned in this chapter can be identified with *any* certainty as corresponding with the names of *any* kings known to us from contemporary records." (Italics mine). *Peake's Commentary*, p. 188.

The confidence with which these words are written is stunning, and the unwary reader could quite easily be forgiven for thinking that they must be true. After all, written by a leading academic of his day, they appear in one of the most widely-read Bible commentaries available, a commentary which is used in colleges and seminaries around the world. And yet, they are, in every sense and in every way, false. They do not even begin to reflect the truth of the matter. Worse still, the assumptions on which they were written, were widely known to be false at least fifty years *before* these words were first published.

The statement, however, merely perpetuates – and perpetuates unthinkingly – an earlier rash statement by the archetypal higher critic, Theodor Noldeke. As far back as 1869, Noldeke published an article called, 'The unhistorical character of the fourteenth chapter of Genesis'[1] In that article:

> "He declared that 'criticism' had for ever disproved its [Genesis 14's] claim to be historical. The political situation presupposed by it was incredible and impossible; at so distant a date Babylonian armies could not have marched to Canaan, much less could Canaan have been a subject province of Babylonia. The whole story, in fact, was a fiction based upon the Assyrian conquest of Palestine in later days. The names of the princes commemorated in it were etymological inventions; eminent Semitic philologists had already

> explained those of Chedorlaomer and his allies from Sanskrit, and those of the Canaanitish princes were derived from the events in which they were supposed to have borne a part."[2]

Astonishing. One would think that even by Noldeke's day, philologists of the modernist school would have learned their lesson. How many times in the past have they had to swallow their words concerning the reliability of the Bible or the discoveries of archaeology pertaining to the Bible? Initially, of course, Noldeke did at least have the excuse that 1869 was a little too early for him to have known about the discoveries of archaeology concerning the kings and political scene set out so concisely in Genesis 14. In fact, these details were not to come to light until the 1880s. Noldeke, however, lived on until 1930, yet in the forty or more years in which he was aware of those discoveries, it is not known that he ever once corrected his statements concerning Genesis 14, an omission which must stand to his lasting shame.

But let us now consider the kings of Genesis 14 and what archaeology has to tell us about them. Perhaps the most contested notion in the controversy, is the name of Amraphel, and the suggested possibility that he might in some way be identified with Hammurabi, the great king of Babylon and famous law-giver. But lest we are confused, *Peake's Commentary* once again explains it all to us, sharing with us the author's own wry amusement as he guides us into a true knowledge of affairs:

> "The name **Amraphel** used to be confidently equated with Hammurabi of the first Amorite dynasty of Babylon, famous for his [Law] Code: but the identification is no longer accepted, and we also now know that there were at least three other kings of that name ruling city-states during this period."[3]

Alas for Genesis, then. It seems to have got that bit wrong. Or has it? If only our author's knowledge had matched his confidence in the matter, we might have been able to believe him and accept that Genesis is in error here. But before we see what the evidence really says, let us briefly examine the methodology used here, and consider the sleight of hand that is offered to the uninformed reader.

Firstly, our author states that the identification of Amraphel with Hammurabi is no longer accepted, but avoids telling us who no longer accepts it. If it was some important and recognised authority in the field, then a name would be but a simple thing to supply. Indeed, if it was someone who really knew what he was talking about, then there could be no arguing with our author's statement. But then he also neglects to mention the most important detail of all, namely *why* they do not accept it. If it's a matter of simple philology, then half a line explaining how Amraphel could not possibly transpose into Hammurabi would be useful. It would surely make all clear to us. But instead we are offered precisely nothing on the matter, and for good reason it would seem.

The author of the piece is one Samuel Hooke (1874-1968), who was Professor of Old Testament Studies at the University of London, and who wrote the 'Genesis' chapter for *Peake's Commentary*. So he would, or should, have been in a strong position to not just state his case, but to explain it as well, citing his authorities in the process. That is standard scholarly fare, after all. And surely, the question of whether the Book of Genesis is accurate or not is important enough to warrant such a little effort. But no, it seems not.

Fortunately, we have a better teacher in A H Sayce, Professor of Assyriology at Oxford, and a world-authority on the languages of Mesopotamia and their cuneiform writing. And he is better still for our purpose, because he is no fundamentalist when it comes to the Book of Genesis. As an accomplished archaeologist, he believes the 'Higher' Critics to fall woefully short in their discipline, and takes them to task at every opportunity. Yet he never accepted the Book of Genesis in its entirety as literally and historically reliable. For him, as for so many, the new doctrine of evolution was the answer to everything. However, when it comes to the question of identifying the Amraphel of Genesis with the Hammurabi of Babylon, he is on very sure ground indeed, and makes no hesitation in bringing the following facts to our attention – facts that demand repeated reading:

> "Khammu-rabi, like others of his dynasty, claimed divine honours, and was addressed by his subjects as a god. In Babylonian *ilu* is 'god,' the Hebrew *el*, and *Ammu-rapi ilu*

would be 'Khammu-rabi the god.' Now *Ammu-rapi ilu* is letter for letter the Amraphel of Genesis."[4]

The name Hammurabi, as it is commonly spelt in English, is admittedly some way from the cuneiform letters of his name when they are transcribed thus: *Ammu-rapi-ilu*. As Professor Sayce confesses, he himself initially found the points of identity between Amraphel and Hammurabi difficult to recognise. That is because Amraphel is an English transposition of the Hebrew, when Hammurabi is an inadequate and incomplete transposition into English from the Babylonian cuneiform. But directly match the Hebrew with the cuneiform, and we have a different outcome altogether. The two names are, in every sense, identical, or 'letter for letter,' as Professor Sayce tells us. For all that modernists say to the contrary, the Amraphel of Genesis 14 *is* the Hammurabi of Babylon.

As for Professor Hooke's clinching statement that besides there were not one, nor even two, but at least *three* kings (suggesting yet more) all named Hammurabi ruling city-states at this time, he would have done better to inform his readers that Babylon was, in the days of Hammurabi, an empire, a fact which cannot have been unknown to him. It was a political entity which had expanded to embrace under its governance other city-states. Even so, it was never an enormous territory, and the chances of three or more kings all named Hammurabi living and ruling in the same small space at the same time is unlikely in the extreme. Archaeology certainly knows nothing of them. But consider, there are currently 49 countries in the British Commonwealth, yet there are not 49 Queen Elizabeth IIs to constitutionally rule over them. There is only one Queen Elizabeth II, and she heads the Commonwealth. Likewise, Hammurabi ruled at least three city-states together, with their documents and records all noting his name, as is only to be expected. But it was the name of only one Hammurabi, and not three.

Besides, even if there really had been three Hammurabis all living next door to each other, there would have been only one who ruled Shinar (or Babylon), and Genesis states very clearly that this Amraphel was king of Shinar. And of Shinar there was only ever one king whose name matches 'letter for letter' that of Amraphel. In his own records, he is known as *Ammu-rapi ilu*. Modern archaeologists know him as Hammurabi.

It is hard not to sigh. The introduction of three Hammurabis is, of course, the age-old modernist trick of throwing dust in the reader's eyes. It sends confusing signals which tell the unwary, on the authority of a leading academic no less, that even if the names Amraphel and Hammurabi did turn out to be one and same, then as there were at least three of them, the case of identification is hopeless anyway, and it would be fruitless to look into the matter further. It is, I'm afraid, what passes for Bible scholarship these days – in the modernist school, at any rate.

Amraphel, of course, is not the only king whom Genesis 14 mentions by name. There are seven others altogether, along with the territories that they ruled over. (The eighth king remains unnamed for some reason, though his city is spoken of). All these, naturally, are included in the sweeping dismissal that modernism affords this chapter, and it is profitable to spend a little time considering what the archaeological record says of them.

The remaining kings are given as: Arioch of Ellasar; Chedorlaomer of Elam; and Tidal, king of Nations. These are on the side of Amraphel of Shinar, and have descended into Canaan on a punitive expedition. The expedition was in answer to a concerted rebellion by the following kings, who after twelve years of submission, had thrown off the Mesopotamian yoke. And they are: Bera, king of Sodom; Birsha, king of Gomorrah; Shinab, king of Admah; and Shemeber, king of Zeboiim. Unnamed is the king of Bela, a city of the Plain that was later known as Zoar.[5]

Genesis 14:5-7 describes in great detail the sequence of battles and events as the expeditionary force moved south towards the Plain of Jordan, each place-name and people described being known from elsewhere in both the Bible and the archaeological record. What is more, they belong firmly to the time of which Genesis 14 speaks.

Regarding the Canaanite kings who met the expeditionary force in full battle at the Vale of Siddim, they were routed and slain, the kings of Sodom and Gomorrah perishing in the local slime (or bitumen) pits, whilst the others who survived the battle fled to the mountains (Genesis 14:10). Due to the later destruction of the cities of the Plain, no direct monument appears yet to have survived concerning these kings, but the archaeological record does hold some interesting facts concerning their names.

Shinab, king of Admah, has a name that appears in the Akkadian tablets from Ur as *Sin-ab-i*, meaning 'Sin [the moon god] is my father'.[6] Whether the inscription refers to this particular king, we cannot now know. But it does at least tell us that the name is no scribal invention of the 6th century BC. It is authentic, it is known outside the Bible, and it belongs to the time of which Genesis speaks.

Shemeber's name (that of the king of Zeboiim) is also known to us, this time from the Mari tablets of the period, where it is rendered *Su-mu-ebuh*.[7] So again, even if it is not the king of Zeboiim whom the Mari texts name (and it could be), we at least know by its appearance in those tablets that it is again authentic, and belongs firmly to the times in which Genesis 14 is set.

This is unexpected fare indeed when we consider what the modernists have always claimed about this chapter of Genesis. But the records are more obliging still when it comes to the names and cities of the Mesopotamian kings of Genesis 14 – very obliging, in fact.

The king whose name appears as Arioch in the Book of Genesis, didn't just have a name that belonged to the times. He actually left us an inscription – several inscriptions, in fact. One of them mentions the 'holy tree of Eridu', evidently revered by those of his day as the Tree of Life (Genesis 3:24), this tree's motif being commonly displayed on seals and amulets of the period. Arioch, or *Eri-Aku* as his name appears in his native tongue, tells us in this inscription of a temple which he had built to the honour of Nin-girsu, his god:

> "To the god Nin-girsu, his king, Eri-Aku, the shepherd of the possessions of Nipur, the executor of the oracle of the holy tree of Eridu, the shepherd of Ur and the temple of E-Udda-im-tigga, *king of Larsa*, king of Sumer and Accad; on the day

> when Anu, Bel and Ea, the great gods, gave into my hands the ancient city of Erech, I built to the god Nin-girsu, my king, the temple Dugga-summu the abode of his pleasure, for the preservation of my life."[8] (Italics mine.)

Eri-aku tells us in this inscription the main city over which he rules, namely Larsa. Genesis transposes the name into Hebrew as Ellasar. This, in turn, is simply the Hebrew form of the Babylonian *al-sarri*, which means simply 'the city of the king'.[9] But the story doesn't end there. On an inscribed brick from his reign, Eri-Aku tells us the name of his father.[10] It is an Elamite name, that of Khudur-Mabug. The first element of the name means simply 'servant', and the second element is the name of an Elamite god. So Eri-Aku's father announced in his name that he was the Servant of Mabug.

Interestingly, we meet the same first element in the name of another king, Khudur-Lagamar, whom Genesis 14 knows as Chedorlaomer, a perfect transposition into Hebrew (again 'letter for letter') from the Elamite. This name in turn announces Chedorlaomer as the Servant of Lagamar, the Elamite moon-god. We see then that Genesis calls Chedorlaomer the king of Elam with perfect precision. Moreover, Genesis correctly uses the ancient Elamite word for servant, a long-obsolete word which would have been entirely unknown to a 6th or 5th-century BC Jewish forger. Likewise, no Jew of the post-Exilic period would have known what was, 1500 years previously, the name of the Elamite moon-god, Lagamar. All of which is highly convincing evidence of the antiquity, integrity and authenticity of Genesis 14.

But the reason why the name of Chedorlaomer is transcribed here as Kudurlagmal instead of Khudur-Lagamar, as we noticed earlier, is that Khudur-Lagamar is the Elamite spelling of his name, where the tablets we are considering are Babylonian. It is interesting that the writer of Genesis 14 has used the Elamite spelling in his transcription of the name into Hebrew, (given that Chedorlaomer was king of Elam, as both Genesis and the tablets testify), and has not used the Babylonian. Professor Sayce always believed, along with many others since his day, that Genesis 14 was based on a Babylonian document.

But even the name Tidal, whom Genesis (14:1) calls 'king of nations', is not unknown to us from outside the Bible. Tudhalias I, a Hittite king of the time, is one candidate whose name has often been mooted for Tidal, but a better by far is *Tud-chula*.

In 1895, the magnificently named Theophilus Goldridge Pinches discovered in the collections of the British Museum, three clay tablets.[11] The tablets were found in a mutilated and broken condition, but the fragments contain the names of all four of the Genesis 14 kings, namely Amraphel, Chedorlaomer, Arioch and Tidal. Amraphel's name appears as Hammurabi; Chedorlaomer's appears as Kudurlachgumal; Arioch's as Eri-akua; and Tidal's as Tudchula. The tablets are later copies of earlier originals, but interestingly, all four kings are recorded as contemporaneous and interacting politically with one another. All this and more appears in Appendix Two of this book. But, more briefly, here is what appears on the first two tablets concerning Chedorlaomer and Arioch:

> "The gods....in their faithful counsel to Kudurlachgumal, king of the land of Elam, said (?) 'Descend', and the thing that unto them was good [they performed and] he exercised sovereignty in Babylon, the city of the king of the gods, Merodach....Dur-mach-i-lani, the son of Eri-akua, who [had carried off?] the spoil, sat on the throne of dominion."

and:

> "Who is Kudurlachgu[mal], the maker of the evils? He has gathered also the Umman-man[da]....he has laid in ruins...."[12]

Tudchula's (or Tidal's) name appears on the third tablet of the series. But there is an added detail to this name which no 6th-century BC 'editor' would have been aware of. The Babylonian syllabaries tell us that during the 2nd millennium BC, the final element (- 'a') in names like Tud-chula, was silent, a fact that neither J, E, P or D, or any other inventor of false scriptures could possibly have known, for such silent final vowels had long fallen into disuse by the time of the Jewish Exile of the 6th century BC. But the writer of Genesis knew it, which is why he correctly omitted that final vowel from his transposition of Tudchula's name into Hebrew as Tidal.[13]

In another inscription altogether, we see an interesting but entirely conventional form of dating which demonstrates the fact that Hammurabi (or Amraphel) had immediate dealings with Eri-aku (or Arioch):

> "On the 23rd day of Shebat, in the year when Khammurabi, through the might of Anu and Bel, established his possessions, [and] his hand overthrew (?) the *ad*(?)-*da* of Jamutbal, and King Eriaku."[14]

I do not suppose for one moment that we have exhausted this subject. Indeed, in Appendix Two we give the text of yet a *fourth* cuneiform inscription, a letter from Hammurabi of Babylon (the Amraphel of Genesis) to Sin-iddina, king of Larsa, concerning Chedorlaomer (see also Postscript below). Doubtless there are others awaiting rediscovery. Yet what comes immediately to hand is an awful lot of names and historical detail from outside the Bible concerning kings who, according to the critics, did not even exist; or, if they did exist, cannot now be identified. We see here that archaeology has proved them yet again to be wrong, utterly wrong. The offence that has been committed here is that this evidence has been known about and published within scholarly circles for more than a century, and the modernists and critics have undoubtedly been aware of it. Yet they continue in their chosen course to deceive the public into believing that this evidence does not exist, and that the Word of God is a lie. Shame on them. Shame on them all.

But we are not quite finished with Genesis 14. As if all the above were not enough, the geographic and ethnographic details supplied in the chapter also confirm its antiquity. As Professor Sayce observes:

> "We may now accept with confidence the geographical details which the narrative of Chedorlaomer's campaign brings before us. We have in them a picture of Southern Canaan *older than the oldest* which the monuments of Egypt have bequeathed to us. The earlier populations are still in the land.

> The kinsfolk of the Israelites – the Ammonites, the Moabites, and the Edomites – have not as yet supplanted them. The Zamzummim still occupy the future land of Ammon, the Emim are where the twin capitals of Moab afterwards arose, and the Horites are undisputed masters of Mount Seir."[15] (Italics mine)

Sayce goes on to observe that even the Rephaim, their name to be found in the ancient Jordanian city of Anau-repa, are still present in the land, the time of their destruction awaiting the later arrival of the Israelites under Joshua. Only a contemporary, who was intimately familiar with the populations and geography of Canaan long before the Israelite conquest of that land, could possibly have written about them as they appear in Genesis 14.

But before we leave the 14th chapter of Genesis, there is one very important hallmark of its antiquity which we should not ignore. It is a word which appears in the 14th verse of that chapter, and it is *chanik*. It is a Hebrew noun which means 'armed retainer', in other words a 'trained fighting-man'.[16] Used in this sense only here in the Bible, it is also met with in Egyptian texts of the 19th century BC, and is last encountered in a 15th-century inscription from Taanach in Israel.[17] Intriguingly, the word did not disappear from Hebrew after the time of Abraham (19th century BC), but it had changed its meaning quite drastically by the time of Moses, who compiled the Book of Genesis some 500 years after Abraham. Its derivative, *chanak*, which is given in Deuteronomy 20:5 (written by Moses), has the meaning of 'dedicate', and it has actually come down to us in this sense as the Jewish feast of *Hannukah*.[18] But in Genesis 14:14, it holds its ancient meaning of 'trained fighting-man', a meaning which it had lost in the 500 years leading up to the time of Moses. Certainly, no post-Exilic (6th-century BC) 'editor' could have known of the word's ancient 19th-century BC meaning, and so he would not – indeed *could* not - have used it in the context in which it has come down to us in the Book of Genesis.

## Postscript Concerning Chedorlaomer

The appearance of Chedorlaomer's name in a letter from Hammurabi caused considerable disquiet in the modernist camp. At a stroke, it undid almost everything that 'Higher Criticism' was trying to achieve, and some ingenuity had to be employed in order to get over the awkward fact. This was achieved by portraying the identification as an understandable mistranslation brought about by a blemish on the clay tablet:

> "In 1896, amid great excitement, a letter of Hammurapi was published which was said to contain the name of Chedorlaomer in a line interpreted to read: 'the day of (the defeat of) Ku-dur-nu-uh-ga-mar.' Closer examination showed that four of the cuneiform signs in that line had been misread, partly because of a later scratch on the tablet, and that the line in fact ran: 'the troops under the command of I-nu-uh-sa-mar'…."[19]

The reader is referred to Appendix Two of this book, where (toward the end) the full cuneiform text of the letter is given. Now it has to be remembered that cuneiform signs were not scratched or incised into the clay, but were impressed into it with a stylus. There is therefore a world of difference between a sign impressed into wet clay, and a later scratch on its dry surface. It is impossible to see, therefore, how a later single scratch can be of such a nature that it is mistaken for not just an impressed sign, but for four impressed signs. At the least, it would need to be of the same shape and size as the other cuneiform signs on the tablets, and would also need to be of such a nature that it altered – intelligibly! – not just one sign, but four, and altered, also intelligibly, not just the name of an individual, but a whole line of accompanying text. Should it be suggested, as it is clearly implied in the objection, that the scratch rendered the signs beneath it illegible enough to give rise to the mistranslation, then how comes it that the obliterated signs can now be interpreted in a way which no longer challenges the modernist cause? It is wonderful to think that the modernist school should now be asking us to believe in a miracle.

However, the proffered retranslation might just have been a little more plausible if it had made any sense. But it doesn't make any sense at all. The original translation by Theophilus Pinches reads:

> "Hammurabi sends thus to Sin-iddina. I shall hand over to thee the goddesses [idols] of Emutbalu (on account of) thy heroism on *the day of Chedorlaomer*. When they demand them back from thee, overthrow thou their people with the people who are with thee, and let them restore the goddesses to their shrines." (My italics)

The retranslation, which leaves the rest of the passage unchallenged, would read:

> "Hammurabi sends thus to Sin-iddina. I shall hand over to thee the goddesses [idols] of Emutbalu (on account of) thy heroism on *the troops under the command of I-nu-uh-sa-mar*. When they demand them back from thee, overthrow thou their people with the people who are with thee, and let them restore the goddesses to their shrines."

Once again, the modernist approach has churned out nothing but gobbledygook. Their argument in this case might have had some substance if the retranslation had made better sense than the alleged mistranslation. But under the most specious of objections, they have replaced a perfectly good translation with a perfectly bad one – and all in the name of a scholarship which would have us believe that Chedorlaomer did not exist, and that the Book of Genesis is therefore in error by mentioning him as someone who did. Amazing. What they have forgotten, of course, is the damning fact that this is not the only clay tablet to bear Chedorlaomer's name. Their explanation of those other occurrences is yet to be given, but I fear that we shall have a long wait – a very long wait indeed.

## Footnotes to Chapter Thirteen

1. It was first printed in *Untersuchungen sur Kritik des alten Testaments*, Abhandlung III, pp. 156-172. 1869. Kiel. And, *Jahrbucher fur wissenschaftliche Theologie*. 1870. pp. 213 et seq.

2. Sayce. *Monument Facts and Higher Critical Fancies*, pp. 54-55.

3. *Peake's Commentary on the Bible*, p. 188.

4. *Monument Facts*, p. 60.

5. Genesis 14: 1-2.

6. *Interpreter's Dictionary of the Bible*, vol. 4, p. 332.

7. Ibid, vol. 4, p. 323.

8. Sayce, *The Higher Criticism...*, pp. 102-3.

9. Ibid, p. 165. Larsa, or Ellasar, is today called Senkereh (Sin-qara).

10. The name Eri-Aku is rendered *Arriwuk* in the Mari tablets, and *Ar-ri-uk-ki* in the Hurrian tablets of Nuzi. *Interpreter's Dictionary of the Bible*, vol. 1, p. 219.

11. Pinches published his findings in the *Transactions of the Victoria Institute*, vol. 29, (1897). pp. 56-65.

12. Hogarth, pp. 42-43.

13. The tablet on which his name appears is catalogued in the Brit. Museum as Sp. iii. 2. See Appendix Two.

14. Hogarth, p. 42. Shebat was the eleventh month in the Babylonian calendar. When George Smith first translated this text in 1874, not realising that the cuneiform characters had a phonetic value beyond their pictographic value, he presented the name Eri-aku as reading Rim-agu.

15. Sayce, *The Higher Critics...*, p. 168.

16. Wigram. *Englishman's Concordance....*, p. 446; and *Young's Analytical*, p. 997.

17. McDowell. *The New Evidence....*, p. 445, citing Sarna, Nahum. *Understanding Genesis*, 1966, p. 111.

18. My thanks to Dr James J Scofield Johnson for pointing this out to me.

19. Bermant & Weitzman, *Ebla: A Revelation in Archaeology*, p. 188.

## Chapter Fourteen: The Melchizedek of History

> "And Melchizedek, king of Salem, brought forth bread and wine; and he was the priest of the Most High God." (Genesis 14:18)

Thus is Melchizedek first introduced to the reader in the Book of Genesis. But hitherto, Melchizedek has been a mysterious figure, for conservative Bible scholars as much as for liberal. Just who, or what, was he? For the liberal, he is a myth, a fanciful made-up character who is merely there as a literary prop for the rest of the Genesis 14 fable. For the conservative, he is rightly held, first and foremost, as a type and shadow of the Lord Jesus Christ, sharing the same titles as He, the 'King of Righteousness' (which Melchizedek means in Hebrew), and the 'Prince of Peace' (King of Salem). Like our Lord, he was Priest also of the Most High God (*El Elyon*) as well as king. But whether he was also *historically* a flesh-and-blood king of Salem, even conservative scholars can't agree, some saying he was, and some saying he wasn't. How, then, can we solve the riddle?

Like all historical riddles, we turn to the written record, (if there is one), and happily we have such a record - not just inside the Bible, but from outside the Bible - which compels the view that Melchizedek was indeed a flesh-and-blood historical priest and king of Jerusalem. Not that he himself has left us such a record - not one that we have been told about, at any rate. But one of his successors certainly has. And it makes very interesting reading.

As we look at what this historical record says of the priesthood and kingship of Salem, we must bear in mind that the historical record takes nothing away from what Scripture says of Melchizedek when it speaks of his being a type and shadow of Christ. On the contrary, it illuminates it. But so closely is Melchizedek's priestly and kingly office spoken of in relation to the Lord Jesus Christ in Paul's letter to the Hebrews, that many have come to assume that Melchizedek and Jesus are one and the same. This is because Melchizedek is spoken of as having neither father nor mother, nor even beginning or end of his life. But Scripture is very clear on this.

Firstly, Hebrews 5:6-7 speaks very plainly of '...Melchizedek, who, in the days of his flesh...' This says nothing less than that the days of his flesh are in the past. In other words, his earthly life is over. It is his priesthood that is eternal, and not his body.

Secondly, it says both in the Psalms (110:4) and Hebrews (5:6) of Jesus that He is a Priest forever 'after the order of Melchizedek'. If they were one and the same person, then surely Scripture would simply say to Jesus, 'Thou art Melchizedek,' instead of saying that He is of the order of Melchizedek. That is important to understand clearly. But that being said, what does the extra-Biblical record have to tell us?

The record that interests us here is a series of letters to the Egyptian pharaoh, Amenophis IV, preserved amongst the Tell el Amarna tablets. The letters, discovered in 1887, are from the hand of another priest-king of Salem who came some time after Melchizedek, a man named Ebed-tob. The letters are preserved on cuneiform tablets amongst much diplomatic and other correspondence, and they have a very interesting story to tell.[1]

Generally, the letters are a complaint from Ebed-tob to the pharaoh of incursions made by a confederacy of tribes near to Jerusalem, appealing for immediate help from the Egyptian king who has already sent his Commissioner to Ebed-tob to see events for himself.[2] Interestingly, this confederacy is called the *Khabiri*, a word from which the town of Hebron in Israel gets its name, and which still means 'confederacy'. Thus, the repercussions of these events and incursions are seen and felt today after nearly four thousand years. Though Hebron was known to Abraham as a place and was certainly a confederacy in his day, the modern town of Hebron, as a political entity, was actually born of the events that Ebed-tob complains about.

Ebed-tob, however, provides us in these letters with some fascinating insights regarding his priestly and kingly office. Bearing in mind the words of Hebrews 7:3 when it speaks of Melchizedek as being 'without father, without mother.' Ebed-tob, a successor to Melchizedek in his office of priest-king of Salem, reminds the pharaoh how he came to hold such office:

"Behold, neither my father nor my mother have exalted me in this place...."[3]

He repeats and expands upon this reminder later in the correspondence:

"Behold, this country of the city of Jerusalem, neither my father nor my mother has given to me; the arm of the Mighty King gave it to me, even to me."[4]

This is of immense interest and significance, because it helps us to understand historically the very nature of Melchizedek's combined office of priest and king of Salem. It was, in short, a non-hereditary office. The historical priest-king of Salem was put into office either by lot or by election. It was not an office that was handed down from father to son.

This has a vital bearing on the purity and sanctity of the priesthood at Salem of which Melchizedek was a member. The priestly lines of both Aaron and Levi were hereditary, and the sometimes unfortunate effect of that was that often young men inherited the office who were entirely unsuited to it. The priest Eli and his sons, Hophni and Phineas, are a first-class example of what can happen under such automatic elevation to the priesthood (1 Samuel 2:12-17). Ananias and Caiaphas are other, later, examples.

But the important point is that here such tragedies were averted by a non-hereditary priesthood. It is likely, given the choices of lot or election, that the priest-kings of Salem were chosen by lot rather than by election, and we may think that likely for this reason. When John, in the first chapter of his Gospel, speaks of believers being given power to become the very sons of God, he says that such are born '...not of blood, nor of the will of the flesh [inheritance], nor of the will of man [human election], but of God [who often made His choices known through the casting of lots – the *Urim* and *Thummim*].' (John 1:12-13).

Hereditary titles hold obvious dangers, and the voting majority, it has been observed, do not always bring in the best governments. Casting the lot, however, places the matter entirely in the hands and the will of

God. Thus, it seems, was Melchizedek and all his predecessors and successors chosen for office.

That there was something especially peculiar about the man Melchizedek and his calling with regard to this priestly office, is seen when we compare his name with that of Ebed-tob. Melchizedek means King of Righteousness, where Ebed-tob means simply Good Servant. Both names, of course, foreshadow the Lord Jesus Christ in His role as Messiah, because though He was King of all, He made Himself Servant of all, and He most certainly was the *Good* Servant. So it would appear that both the priesthood and the kingship of Salem were a living and decidedly historical foreshadowing of Him Who was to come, the promised Seed of the woman (Genesis 3:15).

It is at this point, however, that we need to clear up a serious misunderstanding. It is something which has given modernists and critics a field day, and has even confused such eminent archaeologically-conservative scholars as A H Sayce, and it is this. Because Melchizedek was king and priest of a Canaanite city (Jerusalem), it is assumed that he must have worshipped and served a Canaanite deity. Indeed, he would have worshipped and served the entire host of Canaanite deities. This is said in order to debase the Genesis record, and is said in defiance of that record when Genesis itself emphasises the fact that Melchizedek was no pagan idolater, but was priest to the Most High God (Genesis 14:18).

Now, as elsewhere in the ancient world, the Most High God was indeed known of in Canaan, for they included Him as head of their pantheon under His Biblical title, *El Elyon*. But their acknowledging Him and His Supremacy in this way, cannot reduce Him to the level of the many false gods that they worshipped. Would Abraham have even thought of paying tithes to a *pagan* priest? That is hardly likely. And where was Melchizedek when Abraham was commanded by God to sacrifice his son Isaac (Genesis 22:1-14)?

On this occasion, Abraham was led by God to the mount called Moriah, which lies as it has always lain, within the boundaries of Jerusalem, then a Canaanite city. The sacrifice of a son was entirely a pagan practice with which the Canaanites were all too familiar. So, had

Melchizedek indeed been the sole pagan priest of the Canaanite 'gods' at Jerusalem, would it not logically have followed that he would officiate at such a sacrifice? For not only was it to be a pagan sacrifice, but it was to be conducted at the holiest place within Melchizedek's own city of Jerusalem. It is unthinkable that Melchizedek would not have officiated as the city's priest at such a ritual if he was himself the city's only pagan priest. And yet he is notable throughout this episode (Genesis 22), not by his officiating, but by his absence.

Which in turn raises a question concerning the city of Jerusalem in pre-Davidic days. From its very beginning, the city bore a strange and unusual name. Even in Assyrian records, it was always *uru-salim* – the City of Peace – which the Egyptians likewise knew, even from before the days of Abraham, as *Urushalim*.[5] Within the city was Mount Moriah, a place of especial sanctity, which the Egyptians referred to (again before the days of Abraham) as *Har-el*, the Mount of God.[6] It was the place where, in later times, the Temple of Solomon was to be built, and throughout the first half of the 2nd millennium BC at least, the city was served by a long line of single priests who also officiated as its king. Melchizedek was one of them, of course, and his successor, Ebed-tob, another.

Whatever else it was, it would seem that Jerusalem was never a pagan sanctuary, at least not before the days of Israel's apostate kings. Ebed-tob, in sentiments that Melchizedek would certainly have echoed had he written of himself, states emphatically to Amenophis IV that he is not the pharaoh's vassal, but holds his kingship as a gift from the 'Mighty King'.[7] This is perpetuated in the Biblical term when it calls the city of Jerusalem, the City of the Great King (Psalm 48:2). Which is all very simple and plain enough. So why was AH Sayce so confused by it all, confused enough to state erroneously that Ebed-tob, and by implication Melchizedek, worshipped, of all things, the Canaanite sun-god? – a misinformed opinion from the conservative quarter which the modernists and critics have been only too happy to perpetuate.

The root of his confusion was the fact that, conservatively inclined though he was as an archaeologist and philologist, he never would fully accept the idea that Genesis could be true in any literal sense. Decrying the 'higher critics' at every turn, he nevertheless spoke their language, talking fluently of the 'Elohistic Narrative', and so on, ascribing the Book of Genesis to entirely fictional sources. He would claim that Genesis is probably based around historical events that were the inspiration for the Genesis 'stories', and in that sense was an historical account. But it was a sorry fudge, and a sorry fudge, I'm afraid, can never lead to the furtherance of knowledge and understanding.

That fudge led him on to his woefully mistaken conclusion concerning Melchizedek being a pagan priest, and resulted in him enforcing that error by simply misreading the honorific formula preceding Ebed-tob's second letter to Amenophis IV. That letter begins:

> "To the king, my lord, my Sun-god, thus speaks Ebed-tob thy servant...."[8]

From this, Sayce concludes that Ebed-tob worshipped the sun. But we should get this very clear. To whom was Ebed-tob writing? To the pharaoh of Egypt, a man held by the Egyptians to be the very personification of the sun – Ra, Horus and Osiris, the threefold and chief deity of Egypt. But through whom was he writing? Did he write the letter himself? Kings do not generally write their own multilingual diplomatic correspondence. Clearly, a secretary wrote it for him. And was that secretary a Canaanite? No, he was an Egyptian, opening a correspondence to the pharaoh with a formulaic greeting – a greeting which appears again in the correspondence *concerning* Ebed-tob, but this time from the pagan, Suwardatum (see footnote 1) who was complaining about him. An Egyptian scribe dare not open such a letter to the pharaoh with anything less than this greeting. But how do we know it was an Egyptian scribe who wrote the letter? Simple. He renders Ebed-tob's name into his native Egyptian as Ebed-khiba ('khiba' meaning 'good', as does 'tob'), and the letter closes with another formulaic sentence:

> "To the Secretary of the king my lord, Ebed-tob, thy servant.... Make a clear report of these my words to the king my lord, that thy faithful servant is he."[9]

The formulaic greeting of 'my Sun-god' thus consisted of words which were not Ebed-tob's own. They were written by an Egyptian scribe in accordance with strict scribal and diplomatic rules. Notably, out of the six that he sent, this (the second of the series) is the only letter from Ebed-tob to the pharaoh which contains that greeting. All others omit it, doubtless because of objections from Ebed-tob himself, who was quick to remind the pharaoh more than once in his letters that, though he was indeed his friend and ally, he was not the pharaoh's vassal, but held his kingship of Jerusalem from the Mighty King, whom he certainly did worship.

Had Sayce taken the Scriptures seriously in this matter, he would have seen the ridiculousness of those Scriptures saying of the Lord Jesus Christ, 'Thou art a priest forever after the order of a pagan priest of Canaan' – which is not what the Scriptures say at all. But then, modernism has made fools of mightier scholars than he.

Returning to the question of the historical Melchizedek and the long succession of priest-kings at Jerusalem to which he belonged, it is interesting to note the period in which Ebed-tob, one of Melchizedek's successors, lived. If conventional dating is correct on this issue, the Tell el Amarna correspondence dates from the 14th century (1400-1300) BC.[10] Given that Melchizedek lived in the latter half of the 19th century BC, then that means the priesthood and kingship of Jerusalem had lasted 500 years at the very least. How long it had been established before the time of Melchizedek, it is impossible to say, even as it is impossible to say exactly when it ended. Paul, writing of Melchizedek in his letter to the Hebrews, doubtless said more than he knew when, under inspiration, he described Melchizedek as having neither father nor mother, nor beginning nor end of his priesthood. The historical record bears him out perfectly.

As to the time when this priestly royal office ended at Jerusalem, we are afforded a possible glimpse in the Book of Joshua (10:1). There we hear of a king of Jerusalem named Adonizedek, his name meaning Lord of Righteousness. This name, as well as those of the two predecessors of his that we know about, is in accordance with all that we know concerning this royal line. Yet Scripture, intriguingly, calls him only king of Jerusalem. There is no hint of priesthood here.

Moreover, this king, Adonizedek, who was probably Ebed-tob's immediate successor, was slain at the Battle of Gibeon whilst resisting the Israelite possession of Canaan (see Joshua 10:15-26).

Did the priestly royal line of Jerusalem end then when the Tabernacle entered Canaan? It seems that it did. A newly established priesthood had arrived in Canaan in Adonizedek's day with the Tabernacle, and there was to be no other king over Israel save God Himself. So we can say with much certainty that the office held by Melchizedek back in the 19th century BC, lasted at least the 500 years from his own time down to that of Ebed-tob, and very likely 500 years before Melchizedek, from the earliest days after the Flood. It was, in short, a 1000-year living testimony to the promise that God made in Genesis 3:15. Even in the darkest periods of mankind's history, God does not leave Himself – or His eternal Word - without a witness.

To conclude, all this is a lot to say for a Melchizedek whom the modernists say did not exist. But he did exist. That much we may conclude from the archaeological and written records, let alone the Book of Genesis. Even the nature of the eternal priesthood to which he was called, is reflected with surprising detail in the same historical record that makes it clear that he once lived, and was, in every sense, all that Genesis and Hebrews say of him – 'priest of the Most High God and king of Salem...without father, without mother, without pedigree of descent, having neither beginning of days nor end of life....'[11] In short, it reflects not only the antiquity of this portion of Genesis, but its undoubted historicity too.

## Footnotes to Chapter Fourteen

1. The number of tablets found altogether was around 350, of which 200 were sent to Berlin, 82 to the British Museum, 50 to Cairo, and the rest were spirited away into private collections. Ebed-tob's correspondence is written on six tablets, with another concerning Ebod-tob from Suwardatum to the Pharaoh, and another from Labai. These eight tablets are among the 200 in the Berlin collection.

2. http://www.fullbooks.com/Early-Israel-and-the-Surrounding-Nations4.html - this website contains A H Sayce's valuable work, *Early Israel and the Surrounding Nations*, which reproduces the texts of the letters.

3. Letter I. http://www.fullbooks.com/Early-Israel-and-the-Surrounding-Nations4.html

4. Letter VI. http://www.fullbooks.com/Early-Israel-and-the-Surrounding-Nations4.html - elsewhere Sayce points out to us that the term, 'Mighty King', used by Ebed-tob, is quite distinct from the honorific title of king by which he addresses the pharaoh. The Mighty King is no earthly monarch. Sayce, *The Higher Criticism'*..., p. 175.

5. *Interpreter's Dictionary of the Bible*, vol. 2, p. 843.

6. Sayce, *The Higher Criticism'*..., p. 187.

7. http://www.fullbooks.com/Early-Israel-and-the-Surrounding-Nations4.html - this is stated in Letters I, II & VI of the correspondence.

8. Letter II. http://www.fullbooks.com/Early-Israel-and-the-Surrounding-Nations4.html

9. Ibid. See also Sayce, *The Higher Criticism'*..., p. 174 for Ebed-khiba.

10. *Interpreter's Dictionary of the Bible*, vol. 4, p. 529.

11. F F Bruce has something interesting to tell us regarding the lack of any mention of Melchizedek's parents: "The argument from silence plays an important part in rabbinical interpretation of Scripture where (for exegetical purposes) nothing must be regarded as having existed before the time of its first Biblical mention.... The argument is used extensively by Philo for allegorical purposes; thus Sarah is "without mother" ('αμητωρ,' the word here used of Melchizedek) because her mother is nowhere mentioned...." *The Epistle to the Hebrews*, p. 159.

# Chapter Fifteen: The Antiquity of the pre-Mosaic Laws and Customs

> "And Abraham ran unto the herd and fetched a calf, tender and good, and gave it unto a young man, and he hastened to dress it. And he took butter and milk, and the calf which he had dressed, and set it before them; and he stood by them under the tree, and they did eat." (Genesis 18:7-8)

Evidences for the antiquity of the Book of Genesis are not only to do with kings and royal battles. Sometimes, as here, they descend to the mundane, even to what people put on their tables to eat. This kind of evidence is incidental, and yet it is just as forceful as the other kind - sometimes even more so, simply because it *is* merely incidental. Moreover, this particular item of evidence is especially damning to the modernist cause, because if Genesis really had been written and edited by post-Exilic Jews, they would never - for *any* price - have written the two verses from Genesis which open this present chapter. Let me explain.

The Jews have always and ever extolled Abraham for his righteousness. That is as it should be. He was righteous. God Himself calls him so.[1] That regard for Abraham was as strong amongst the Babylonian Jews of 536 BC (the year they returned from the Exile) as amongst Jews of any age and dispensation, even from the days of Abraham until now. And yet here, in these two verses, Abraham appears to transgress one of the most important and assiduously observed Jewish dietary laws.

To transgress this one law is called sin by the rabbis of Israel,[2] and it is inconceivable that any observant Jew would have lain this sin to Abraham's charge if he was writing, or editing, a fictional account long after the time in which Abraham was said to have lived. It is doubly inconceivable when we consider that these so-called editors are called 'priestly' (P for short) by the modernist fraternity. Nothing was ever more important to the Jewish priesthood than the very strictest observance of the Law, and they would surely and certainly have edited out the details of the meal served by Abraham had those details already been in the text. And just as certain, of course, is the fact that had those details been absent, no priestly editor would ever have dared to insert them.

What interests us in all this is the following consideration. In the eyes of rabbinical law, Abraham would here have transgressed the thrice-given injunction of Exodus 23:19b, "Thou shalt not seethe a kid in his mother's milk." In other words, no calf or kid can be boiled or cooked in the milk of its own mother. The commandment is repeated in Exodus 34:26, and in Deuteronomy 14:21, and since the discovery in the 1930s of the Ras Shamra (or Ugaritic) tablets, we have been able to see why. One of the most important Canaanite sacrifices of the year was the boiling of a kid in its mother's milk, this being believed to persuade the fertility gods of Canaan to bless the crops.[3] Hence, the practice was particularly abominable in God's eyes (the kid was probably boiled alive), and He therefore *thrice* commanded His people not to imitate it.

Now this is Torah, and any commandment in the Torah which is given not once, not twice, but *three* times, receives very careful attention indeed from any Torah-observant Jew. However, under rabbinical interpretation, the observance of this *mitzvah* extended further than the command. Because it was impossible to tell if the milk in which the calf or kid was to be boiled had belonged to its own mother, or to the mother of some other kid or calf, to avoid transgressing the commandment, or *mitzvah*, the Jews very soon began to separate dairy products of all kinds from every kind of kosher meat. Even today, the kitchen of any observant household is divided into two, one half for the storage and cooking of dairy products and even the washing of their dishes, and the other for the storage and preparation of meat. It is why Jewish kitchen utensils and dishes are cleaned to the point of obsession, in case one of them has been in touch with both meat and dairy products.[4] Hence, the very idea of Abraham serving up the calf along with dairy products (butter and milk) in the same meal, and perhaps even in the same dish, would have been anathema to any Torah-observant Jew. Simply put, no Jew who lived after the time of Moses, would ever have charged Abraham with such a transgression of the Law.

Further to this is the following consideration. Not only would

Abraham have been remiss in later rabbinical eyes in serving up such a meal, but God and the two angels who ate the meal in front of Abraham would also have been guilty of grave sin. Now, which Jewish 'editor' – be he 'priestly' or no - would ever have dared to suggest such a blasphemy? None. None would ever have written such a thing. Which tells us this: Genesis 18:7-8 was not written by any Jew who lived after the time of Moses, let alone as late as the Exile. How could it possibly have been? Rather, it was written at a time long before Moses, before any such commandment had been given, and certainly before the advent and necessity of any Jewish sage to interpret the *mitzvot* of the Torah.

The rabbis got over the difficulty of these two verses, of course, by stating that God and the angels ate the dairy first and then, according to one school of thought, waited eighteen minutes before eating the meat.[5] Other schools suggest other lengths of time before it is safe to eat meat after dairy, but as Genesis makes no such statement (nor does Exodus, nor Deuteronomy), such reasoning is sheer sophistry. This order of things was chosen, because, according to rabbinical thought, if one ate the meat first, then anywhere between four to six hours would have to pass before one could eat the dairy products, and the thought of God and the angels waiting this long at Abraham's table was simply too much, even for the rabbis.

To conclude this item, nowhere in the Old Testament is the eating of meat with dairy products forbidden. Abraham committed no iniquity in serving up the meal, and God and the angels with Him committed no iniquity in eating it. The problem came with the arrival of the rabbinical and priestly interpretation of the Torah, and in this case, of Exodus 23:19b. But it does at least tell us with absolute certainty that no Jew of the Exile period would even have thought of writing these verses; by which token, the verses in question, Genesis 18:7-8, clearly pre-date the Mosaic Law, and hence the time of Moses.

With such matters in mind, Albright tells us:

> "It is now becoming increasingly clear that the traditions of the Patriarchal Age, preserved in the book of Genesis, reflect with remarkable accuracy the actual conditions of the Middle

Bronze Age, and especially of the period between 1800 and 1500 BC."[6]

Such refreshing words from the field of archaeology stand in stark contrast to those which we hear from the modernist philological school, which would have us believe that the story of Isaac, say, is merely a literary device invented solely for the purpose of connecting the Abraham and Jacob 'sagas'. On the contrary, Genesis, when it speaks of Isaac, speaks with the voice of history, and it speaks true. We can see the truth of it reflected most clearly in the laws and customs of the time.

We need to recall that in the time of the Patriarchs, Abraham, Isaac, Jacob and Joseph, there was as yet no God-given Law to guide them apart from their own innate sense of God's righteousness. When Joseph rebuffed Potiphar's wife, the commandment, 'Thou shalt not commit adultery,' had not yet been given. Nevertheless, Joseph was able to say with some vehemence, 'How then can I do this great wickedness and sin against God?' (Genesis 39:9).

Moreover, there was as yet no body of laws given by God which could govern the more secular lives of the Patriarchs, simply because they were still wanderers through other peoples' lands, and hence were not yet a nation. Thus, in their interactions between themselves and the societies around them, they necessarily relied upon and were governed by the secular laws of the nations through which they passed. And considering that such laws were devised by pagan societies whose religious practices could be so scandalous and cruel, these secular laws and customs were sometimes surprisingly wise and humane.

Much light has been shed on those laws in the past 100 years through the discovery of various codes of law and their commentaries. The city of Mari in Syria, buried since its destruction in 1746 BC, yielded some 20,000 clay tablets, many of which have to do with the law. The ancient city of Nuzi, which lies some 150 miles north of Baghdad, and which was destroyed in the early 13th century BC, also yielded some thousands of documents, many of which again have to do with the laws of those days, and they are most illuminating.

## The Setting Free of Hagar and Ishmael

When Abraham was approached by Sarah (Genesis 21:9-12) with the demand that he cast out Hagar and Ishmael, he hesitated in an agony of mind. He had good reason to do so. Sarah's demand meant that Ishmael, Abraham's first-born son through his slave Hagar, and whom Abraham loved dearly, would have no share in any inheritance from Abraham, simply because Ishmael (who had retained under law his slave status though he were Abraham's son) and his mother Hagar, would no longer be Abraham's slaves. That provision is made under a law of the Lipit-Ishtar Code which had already been in force for some two hundred years before Abraham's day. It's almost as if Lipit-Ishtar had anticipated the very event that Genesis tells us of, which, under God's good Providence, he may well have done:

> "If a man married his wife and she bore him children and those children are living, and a slave also bore children for her master but the father granted freedom to the slave and her children, the children of the slave shall not divide the estate with the children of their former master."[7]

As Genesis so rightly tells us in chapter 21, the question of Ishmael was all about inheritance. This is why Abraham did not simply disown Ishmael as his son. His love for him alone prevented such a denial. Had he done so, Ishmael would have continued to be a slave, *and* have lost his inheritance to boot. No. For Ishmael to be disqualified from the inheritance and yet remain Abraham's son, he first had to be set free, and this is what Abraham did, though not before God had given Abraham His own solemn assurance that He Himself would care for the lad and make him great, simply because he was – and continued to be -Abraham's son (Genesis 21:12).

The very fact that Abraham personally took the trouble to give Hagar and Ishmael provisions for their journey (Genesis 21:14), even personally hanging the bag that contained those provisions around Hagar's shoulders, shows that this was the setting free of a slave, and a beloved slave at that.[8] The fact that in the event, Hagar became lost in the wilderness of Beersheba was not Abraham's intention (nor even Sarah's, I dare say), though it was an event (as history has shown) which was firmly in the Providence of God.[9] Moreover, to show that Ishmael, who clearly relished his freedom, still loved and honored his father Abraham long after his release, the next time we meet him in the Book of Genesis is when he joins Isaac to perform, and perform honorably, Abraham's burial (Genesis 25:9). That is not the action of a slave who was cruelly abandoned to perish as certain modernist commentators assert. Nor is it a matter of dysfunctionality within Abraham's family as others like to think. It was a matter of a loving father freeing his slave-son from all further servitude by giving him his freedom, thereby lawfully transferring the inheritance to a son borne by his wife, and who now becomes his sole heir in accordance with the laws of that time – not to mention the command and the promise of God.

But the real point that we need to consider is this. These laws had been obsolete for many centuries by the time of the Jewish Exile when those returning Jews allegedly concocted the 'Abraham Saga'. The languages in which they had been written were entirely forgotten by that date, and the tablets on which they were written had been buried deep and out of sight for more than a thousand years by the 6th century BC, just as they would remain buried for the next two and a half thousand years. So how could such Jewish forgers possibly have known the legal conditions (even the very wording of the laws) of those days in which the hero of their 'saga' was supposed to have lived? In all truth, they could not possibly have known them, and therefore they could not possibly have invented such a fiction. The law which Abraham lived under and obeyed, was the law of his day, and only a contemporary writer could have known what that law required and allowed.

## Sister/Wife Contracts

We see a similar occurrence, of Genesis referring to the laws of Abraham's time, with that strange episode in which Abraham passes off his wife as his sister. A cursory reading, which, alas, is all that most people give this event, would suggest that Abraham has concocted a deceit, and that doesn't sit well with the righteousness of Abraham that the Bible speaks of elsewhere.

The fact that Sarah was, by birth, Abraham's half-sister (they shared the same father, Genesis 20:12), was only partly to do with the case in point. Isaac later had to present Rebekah as *his* sister (Genesis 26:7), and yet Rebekah was, by blood, no such thing. First cousin once removed she may have been (she was a granddaughter of Isaac's uncle, Nahor), but she was not his sister. No. This episode has to do, not with blood, but with the law, a fact that only recently was made plain to us by the discovery of the Nuzi tablets. These tablets have yielded a remarkable case in which a certain woman was made, by law, both the wife and the sister of a certain man. The first tablet in the case reads as follows:

> "Tablet of sistership of Akkulenni son of Akiya, whereby he sold his sister Beltakkadummi as sister to Hurazzi son of Ennaya."[10]

Then the second tablet concerning the very same individuals as the first, says this:

> "Tablet of marriage-contract of Akkulenni son of Akiya, contracted with Hurazzi son of Ennaya... Akkulenni shall give his sister Beltakkadummi as wife to Hurazzi."[11]

So, from a source outside the Bible, we can see a law from Abraham's time at work. Beltakkadummi was legally made both wife and sister to Hurazzi. At around this very time, exactly the same contracts would have been drawn up between Abram and Sarai, just as later they would have been between Isaac and Rebekah. Such legal transactions were a newly- established feature of the law which governed much of Mesopotamia where Abraham and his forebears came from. This is why the pharaoh was flummoxed by it, as Egypt knew no such provision; and so was Abimelech of Gerar, a Philistine king. Their puzzlement was doubtless due to the comparative novelty of the sister-wife law at that time, again attesting to the antiquity of these events. But it also explains why Abraham was sent away from both kings loaded with gifts. Abraham, no doubt, was able to demonstrate his lawful integrity by the presentation of the contracts under which Sarah had become first his sister and then his wife, even as Isaac would have been able to do at a later date. Kings who discover that they have been duped by a rascal, do not usually send him away the richer for his lies. He'd be lucky to escape with his life. But kings love law, and they honor lawful integrity when they see it, as in these cases they surely did. If Abraham, and later Isaac, hid behind anything for their safety's sake, it was not a lie. It was simply the provision and protection of the current law.

## Jacob and Laban

Amongst the legal tablets of Nuzi, there is one that is catalogued G51. It has been translated, of course, and reveals itself to be a contract of adoption between one Nashwi, the adopter, and one Wullu, the adoptee. The tablet bears three other names, those of Arshenni, the father of Nashwi; Nahuya, Nashwi's daughter; and Puhishenni, who was Wullu's father. Now the terms and conditions of the contract bear such a close resemblance to the state of affairs between Jacob and Laban which Genesis describes, that we present its full text below, with the Biblical names of Jacob, Laban, Bethuel, Isaac and Rachel substituted for those of the original parties. This exercise is perfectly legitimate as contracts of all ages tend to be more or less standard in the field that they deal with, and it will give us an excellent idea of just how close and faithful the Book of Genesis really is to the laws and customs of the Patriarchal Age. So, if Nuzi Tablet G51 had been drawn up between Jacob and Laban instead of between Nashwi and Wullu, it would have read as follows:

> "The adoption tablet of Laban, son of Bethuel. He adopted Jacob, son of Isaac. As long as Laban lives, Jacob shall give him food and clothing. When Laban dies, Jacob shall be the heir. Should Laban beget a son, the latter shall divide equally with Jacob, but only Laban's son shall take Laban's gods. But if there be no son of Laban's, then Jacob shall take Laban's gods. And Laban has given his daughter Rachel as wife to Jacob. And if Jacob takes another wife, he forfeits Laban's lands and buildings. Whoever breaks the contract, shall pay one mina of silver and one mina of gold."[12]

Interesting, isn't it? The contract explains so much that is mentioned by the Book of Genesis, revealing the true antiquity, as well as the historical authenticity and accuracy, of the story of Jacob. It also highlights the reason for and nature of Laban's deceit when he so craftily substituted Leah for Rachel at the wedding. The contract above, which would have been very close indeed, if not identical, in content to that between Jacob and Laban, states emphatically that if the adoptee marries any other woman than the contracted wife, then he loses all the lands, goods and chattels which he would have inherited by right of contract. Penalty clauses such as the fine of one mina (sixty shekels) each of silver and gold also explain why Jacob had to work for Laban an extra seven years before he could take Rachel. Quite simply, he would have had to work off any debt which such a penalty clause would have imposed upon him.

The contract also refers to the household gods, or *teraphim*, which belonged to the head of the household and which gave him in law his authority. Thus, when Jacob finally left Laban's household, the removal of the household gods robbed Laban of his lawful authority and transferred it to Jacob, and explains the desperate pursuit that followed. Before they fled Laban's household, however, Rachel and Leah asked Jacob a most interesting question:

> "Are we not counted of him strangers? For he hath sold us, and hath quite devoured also our money." (Genesis 31:15).

What interests us here is the word that they use for money. It refers to the 'bridal-price' that was set aside for them at their separate marriages to Jacob. The normal Hebrew word for this price (or dowry) is *mohar*, but they do not use that. They use instead the more legally-specialized word *keseph*, which is straight out of the Nuzi tablets.[13]

The fact that Jacob was married to two living sisters at the same time is yet another hallmark of this account's antiquity. By Moses' day, when God Himself was giving Israel the laws by which He wanted her to live, such unions were roundly condemned and forbidden (Leviticus 18:18), being described by God as a pollution for which nations had been uprooted and destroyed. It is inconceivable, therefore, that any 'priestly editor' would ever have charged Jacob – who gave his very name to Israel – with such iniquity.

It would labor the point to tell how much else in Genesis is found provided for under the ancient pre-Mosaic laws: oath-swearing by placing the hand under the thigh; marriage arrangements; adoption; concubinage; the status of slaves; the laws of inheritance; the laws of restitution; the city-gates as a place of justice; even the selling of the birthright; and so on.[14] Wherever and whenever they are mentioned in the Book of Genesis, they are all of them attested to be utterly faithful to the historical record, a record which was entirely lost to the Jews of the 6th century BC, and about which they would have known nothing. How, then, can it possibly be said that the Jews of that time concocted the Book of Genesis? One lucky guess might just be plausible, but a whole and very long series of highly complex lucky guesses? I don't think so.

## Footnotes to Chapter Fifteen

1. Genesis 15:6. Tellingly, Abraham was counted righteous before God, not because he fulfilled the Law by good works, for the Law had not yet been given, but because he *believed* God. And that is still the way in which God counts a man righteous: "Then said they unto Him, 'What shall we do that we might work the works of God?' Jesus answered and said unto them, 'This is the work of God, that ye *believe* on Him whom He hath sent.'" (John 6:28-29). Good works (righteousness) are the fruit of faith, and not the means of salvation.

2. http://www.seedofabraham.net/kosher.html - 'Kosher: Jewish vs Biblical' by Avram Jehoshua.

3. The Ras Shamra text which gives this information is called, *The Birth of the Gods*, and is listed as UT16 52:14. *Interpreters Dictionary of the Bible*, vol. 3, pp. 9 & 380.

4. This was the reason for the assiduousness of the Pharisees in cleaning the cup and the platter. Their error was that they had become so obsessed with avoiding the breaking of the rabbinical laws of mixing meat with dairy products, that they had forgotten about and neglected the real Law of God, which they

had misunderstood, following instead the traditions of their fathers. Matthew 23:25-6, and Luke 11:39.

5. http://www.seedofabraham.net/kosher.html - 'Kosher: Jewish vs Biblical' by Avram Jehoshua.

6. Unger. *Archaeology and the Old Testament*, p. 121, citing Albright.

7. http://www.justlawlinks.com/REFERENCE/codlistar.htm - see also Sarna, *Understanding Genesis*, p. 156.

8. A slave who was abandoned by an unkind master to his fate, would not have been given provisions of any kind, and certainly not by the master himself.

9. Just how Hagar managed to lose herself in the wilderness around Beersheba, we can only imagine (if we disregard the promise and the Providence of God). Then as now, Beersheba was no more than a day's walk away from the nearest town or village, or even caravanserai. Abraham did not cast her out in a place where shelter, water and sustenance were beyond any reach. That would have been tantamount to murder, and Abraham, even ignoring his own innate awareness of God's righteousness, would have answered to the law and to God for such a thing. Moreover, it would have violated his deep and genuine love for Ishmael. The bread and water that he gave Hagar and Ishmael for their journey would thus have been sufficient for at least a day's travelling on foot, certainly enough to see them to safety.

10. Sarna, *Understanding Genesis*, p. 103, citing *Annual of American Schools of Oriental Research*, vol. X (1930). p. 60.

11. Ibid.

12. Taken out of Vos, *Genesis and Archaeology*, p. 99.

13. Sarna, *Understanding Genesis*, p. 200.

14. "In one Nuzi tablet, there is a record of a man named Tupkitilla, who transferred his inheritance rights concerning a

grove to his brother, Kurpazah, in exchange for three sheep." MacDowell, p. 107. The parallel of Esau selling his birthright to Jacob for food is striking (Genesis 25:29-34). It was clearly a practice of some regularity for laws to be made necessary for its provision and governance. Sarna (*Understanding Genesis*) discusses several of these examples of law from the Nuzi tablets that are reflected in Genesis. So does Vos (*Genesis and Archaeology*).

~ * ~

# Chapter Sixteen: Joseph and Egypt

> "On the factual level it [the story of Joseph] may be compared to the stories in the first part of the book of Daniel. It is generally recognised that the historical setting of the stories of Daniel and his three companions at the court of Nebuchadrezzar and Darius is entirely imaginary. Similarly, the setting of the adventures of Joseph in Egypt at the court of an Egyptian monarch is not based on any knowledge of the contemporary Egyptian scene." *Peake's Commentary*, p. 200.

We could wish that those who aspire to comment adversely on the last fourteen chapters of the Book of Genesis would at least do us the honour of reading their history books. There could hardly be a less accurate statement than that which is contained in the above passage, that the story of Joseph "...is not based on any knowledge of the contemporary Egyptian scene." This arbitrary, not to say most *unscholarly* dismissal of the last fourteen chapters of the Book of Genesis as being nothing more than a work of imagination is disappointing enough when read in the newspapers or seen in a dumbed-down television documentary. But to be read in the pages of a Bible commentary which aspires to educate college and university students the world over on the Bible's *historical* narratives, well, words fail me.

With this statement, though, we come to one of the glaring weaknesses of the modernist argument for a late composition of the Book of Genesis. Briefly, most modernists will tell you that chapters 37-50 of Genesis – the 'Joseph Saga', or more correctly in the modernist view, the 'Joseph Romance'[1] - are a late composition ($6^{th}$ or $5^{th}$ centuries BC). This, as we have seen, is what they have said about the rest of the Book of Genesis. As previously, though, we shall come to see the inaccuracy – indeed, the irrationality! - of this opinion. We shall, of course, be killing two birds with the same proverbial stone, for by showing the authenticity of some of the fine detail of these chapters, we shall simultaneously be showing their antiquity, an antiquity which far outruns the dates proposed for these chapters by the modernist school.

We may begin by considering the antiquity of some of the words, names and phrases that appear in the Biblical story of Joseph. They are words, names and phrases that would have been entirely unknown to someone who was fresh out of Babylon and making it all up in his head. They are specific and technical terms which would have been unfamiliar to such a person who lived after the Exile (6th-5th centuries BC), yet known with accuracy and fluency by anyone who had lived in Egypt at around the time of Joseph (ca 18th century BC).

What, for example, should we make of the word *achu*? It is an old Egyptian word which appears in the Hebrew Bible in the 41st chapter of Genesis (verses 2 and 18), and so appears practically in the middle of the story of Joseph. It means a 'reed-meadow,' or (more generally), 'reed-grass'.[2] It occurs (as reed-grass or rushes) also in Job 8:11, and twice in a Ugaritic fragment of a clay tablet of ca 15th century BC.[3] Certainly not encountered in later times, how could a Babylonian Jew have known either the word or its meaning nearly 1500 years after the time of Joseph and nearly 1,000 years after the time of Moses? And why should he have used it? He would surely have used a current Hebrew word for meadow – *ma'areh*, for example - or even one that had been filched and adapted from the Babylonian, for reed-meadows are still a common feature around Babylon. At least then his readers would have understood what he was talking about.

But there's more. As one archaeologist tells us:

> "There are, moreover, a great many correct local and antiquarian details in the Egyptian narratives in Genesis and Exodus which, like the general fact of the sojourn of Jacob's twelve sons and their posterity in the land of the Nile, would be inexplicable as later inventions."[4]

Amongst these 'local and antiquarian details' are the names and titles by which certain public offices were known. These are always correct for the period, having fallen into disuse in later times. 'Chief of the Bakers,' is one such, as is 'Chief of the Butlers' (Genesis 40:2). When Potiphar appointed Joseph 'overseer over his house', the term used is a direct translation into Hebrew of the original Egyptian title, and is entirely authentic.[5]

Then there is the word contained in the Book of Genesis (chapters 39 and 40) for the prison in which Joseph was confined. Unknown elsewhere in the Bible, it is the Hebrew rendering of an Egyptian word for prison house, *bet ha-sohar*, signifying a circular or round prison, the kind that is found in fortresses of the period and which are well known to us from Egyptian texts.[6] How could any 6th-century BC forger, or inventor of false scriptures, have known about that? And why would he have used such a word when *beth has-surim* (house of the bound), *beth esur* (house of bondage), or even *beth kele* (house of restraint) were available to him, and which his readers would readily have understood? There were at least seven other Hebrew words for 'prison' which our forging editor could have used, and which, like the others, were current in the 6th century BC. Yet we are asked to believe that he opted instead for a long-obsolete (18th century BC) Egyptian word whose meaning would have been entirely unknown to his readers as well as to himself, and that, not only did he spell it correctly, but he used it in its correct context as well. I sigh. I really do sigh.

Also entirely authentic is the description which Genesis gives us of Joseph's inauguration as Pharaoh's Prime Minister:

> "And Pharaoh took off his signet ring from his hand, and put it upon Joseph's hand, and arrayed him in vestures of fine linen, and put a gold chain around his neck; and he made him ride in the second chariot which he had; and they cried before him, 'Bow the knee!'" (Genesis 41:42-3)

This inauguration ceremony is detailed exactly as Genesis tells it in several tomb-paintings and murals that date from the time of Joseph.[7] Moreover, the chariot, particularly the ceremonial chariot, was introduced into Egypt at this time,[8] as were horses which are mentioned for the first time in the Bible in Genesis 47:17.[9] The adulatory cry that was ordered for Joseph as his chariot passed by, is also of great interest to us. In the Hebrew of Genesis 41:43, it is *abrek!* – again, not a native Hebrew word, but an Egyptian, and one that is so archaic that many a scholar has torn a ligament in the attempt to translate it. The King James Bible renders it as, 'Bow the knee!' - which is probably as close as we shall ever get to its true meaning.

As for the alleged lack of evidence that the tribes of Israel were ever in Egypt in the first place, how comes it that so many Egyptian names appear in the genealogy of the tribe of Levi? Moses, Assir, Pashhur, Hophni, Phinehas, Merari, Putiel; they are all Egyptian names, not Hebrew.[10] And why should a Babylonian Jew have made them up? The mere presence of Egyptian names in Israel's priestly tribe of Levi reflects a most shameful episode in their past. In short, the early Levites had allowed themselves to become thoroughly embroiled in the worship of Egypt's false gods, more than any of the other tribes if the absence of Egyptian names in the other tribes' genealogies is anything to go by. That's why they were so quick (and able) to reinstitute the worship of the Golden Calf, which was none other than Hathor, the Egyptian divine cow with the sun-disc between her horns. They knew the complex rituals and mysteries both for the design and creation of the idol, and its worship[11] – and it required barely a twitch of provocation for them to plunge back into this familiar idolatry. Any Babylonian Jew (particularly P, the much-vaunted 'priestly editor' of Genesis and a Levite to boot) wishing to portray an heroic beginning for his people and their worship of just one God, would hardly have invented such a deplorable failing. But there's more.

If the children of Jacob were never slaves in Egypt in the first place, then how comes it that there lies in the Brooklyn Museum a papyrus, conventionally dated to around 1700 BC, which lists a number of Hebrew slaves, slaves who possessed such familiar names as Shiphrah and Menahem?[12] Shiphrah is of considerable interest to us, for that is the name of one of the Hebrew midwives mentioned in Exodus 1:15. Is it one and the same person? Who knows? However, not only the slaves' names, but their offices and duties are also listed – 'chief over the house' (the very same office, that of '*mer-per*', which Joseph held under Potiphar), 'house servant' and so on. Out of 95 slaves listed for this particular household, 37 no less are Hebrew.[13]

And what shall we say of the common assertion amongst

modernists that no Egyptian monument exists which bears the name of Joseph? Well, we can always point out the fact that about 80 miles south of Cairo, there lies the still-flourishing town of Medinet-el-Faiyum. It is a lush and fertile area, famed for its 'gardens, oranges, mandarines, peaches, olives, pomegranates and grapes'. It has been like this for well over 3,000 years, and owes its lush fertility to a 200 mile-long canal which still conveys to it the waters of the Nile in a constant year-round flow. It is an astonishing feat of engineering which to this day is known throughout Egypt as the '*Bahr Yusuf*' – the Joseph Canal. This has always been its name. Moreover, the people of Egypt are perfectly happy to tell you that it was built by the Joseph of the Bible who once was Pharaoh's 'Grand Vizier'.[14]

Now it is known by all that there exists little love for the Jews or their Scriptures amongst most Arabs, so it is astonishing that this canal still bears the name of Joseph. It would have been entirely natural if the invading Moslems of the early 7th century CE had renamed the canal either for Mohammed or some Islamic saint or hero. Yet here, from ancient Egypt, is a lasting monument to the Joseph of the Bible; not something that is six foot high, inert and which gathers dust in a museum somewhere, but one that is 200 miles long and is still in daily use, having provided the people of the area with life-giving water for nigh on 4,000 years. Now, that's what we may *call* a monument! Moreover, and to the chagrin of 'higher critics' everywhere, it does indeed bear the name of Joseph, just as it always has. No wonder they forget to mention it in their commentaries. But there's more.

On September 24th 2009, it was announced in Special Dispatch 2561 of the Middle East Media Research Institute that coins had come to light in the Museum of Egypt which bear the name and image of the Biblical Joseph. The dispatch, reported in the Al-Ahram daily newspaper, attributes the discovery to the research team led by Dr Sa'id Thabet, who were sifting through various hitherto unsorted items in the museum vaults. Dr Thabet has been engaged in a considerable research programme into the life and times of Joseph. Some of the coins were also found in the vaults of the Egyptian Antiquities Authority. Below is an extract of the report, which may be read in full on the internet:

> "The researcher identified coins from many different periods, including coins that bore special markings identifying them as being from the era of Joseph. Among these, there was one coin that had an inscription on it, and an image of a cow symbolizing Pharaoh's dream about the seven fat cows and seven lean cows, and the seven green stalks of grain and seven dry stalks of grain. It was found that the inscriptions of this early period were usually simple, since writing was still in its early stages, and consequently there was difficulty in deciphering the writing on these coins. But the research team [managed to] translate [the writing on the coin] by comparing it to the earliest known hieroglyphic texts…"

> "Joseph's name appears twice on this coin, written in hieroglyphs: once the original name, Joseph, and once his Egyptian name, *Saba Sabani*, which was given to him by Pharaoh when he became treasurer. There is also an image of Joseph, who was part of the Egyptian administration at the time."[15]

Coins (silver pieces) are, of course, mentioned in Genesis 23:14 when Abraham was settling with Ephron the price of the Cave of Machpelah; in 37:28 when Joseph was sold into slavery,[16] and later in Genesis 42:35, where 'bundles of money' are mentioned. We are firmly assured by Bible critics that no coinage existed at this time, but they also assured us until very recently – and with equal firmness - that writing was unknown in Moses' day and therefore he cannot have written the Book of Genesis. How wrong can one be?

Predictably, the world will have to wait some years – if not many years – for all the scholarly papers to be written up on the find, and we may expect to see the usual denials, expert opinions, and all the usual huff 'n' puff which always follows on the heels of any such discovery. But when the ink is finally dry and the pages have started to curl, the modernist school will once again have been proved wrong in their assumptions by plain archaeology.

## Footnotes to Chapter Sixteen

1. Such is the term used for Joseph by *Peake's Commentary* (p. 175): "Chs. 37-50 containing the story of Joseph. This is not saga, but what may be called romance with an historical basis."
2. http://www.bible-history.com/faussets/M/Meadow/
3. *Interpreters Dictionary of the Bible*, vol. 4, p. 23.
4. Unger. *Archaeology and the old Testament*, p. 132.
5. Ibid.
6. Sarna. *Understanding Genesis*, p. 217.
7. See Keller. *The Bible as History*, p. 103 for illustration.
8. Ibid, pp. 103-4.
9. McDowell. *New Evidence…*, p. 109.
10. Unger. *Archaeology and the Old Testament*, pp. 130-5.
11. It is yet another mark of the Pentateuch's age and authenticity when we are told that as Moses was coming down from the mountain with the Tables of the Law, '…he saw the calf and the dancing…' (Exodus 32:19), for, "Music and dance were part of the worship of Hathor like no other deity in Egypt. Hathor herself was the incarnation of dance...." http://www.touregypt.net/godsofegypt/hathor.htm - Again, we must ask our modernist scholars how a Babylonian Jew could possibly have known such a detail, and at such a remove in time.
12. The papyrus is Brooklyn Museum Papyrus No. 35 1446.
13. Sarna. *Understanding Genesis*, p. 214. See Wiseman. *Illustrations from Biblical Archaeology*, p. 39, for a photograph of the papyrus.
14. Keller. *The Bible as History*, p. 104.

15. Website http://www.memri.org/bin/articles.cgi?Page=archives&Area=sd&ID=SP256109

16. This is a most interesting sidelight. The going-rate for a slave in Joseph's time was 20 silver shekels, the price that the Ishmaelites paid for Joseph (Genesis. 37:28). Before then, it had been 10-15 silver shekels. After Joseph, however, the value of a slave rose to 30 shekels (Exodus 21:32); the point being, if this part of Genesis was written 1500 years or more *after* the events it speaks of, as modernists have been proclaiming since the 19th century, then how could the writer, be he J, E, P or D, have known what the price of a slave had been fifteen hundred years previously? I think we should be told.

## Chapter Seventeen: The Proven Antiquity of Genesis

What, then, shall we say to these things? One piece of evidence for the antiquity of the Book of Genesis would be intriguing. Two would begin to be persuasive. But the body of evidences that we have considered here (and we have not exhausted the subject by any means) is surely compelling to the highest degree. If the Book of Genesis were indeed as young as its critics have claimed, and if it really had been copied and edited from older sources, then there would be many items of hard archaeological evidence to that effect. Certainly, not one of the evidences that we have been considering would even exist. Yet when we look to the modernist school for just one item of hard evidence for their claims, we are met with silence - or merely the time-honored mantra of doubt and confusion.

Now it is no light thing to withhold evidence of any description, let alone when that evidence has to do with the Word of God. When we read the modernist claim that the kings of Genesis 14 are unknown to us from the historical record, and then see (as in Appendix Two of this book) that all four names of the Mesopotamian kings mentioned in that chapter are contained on a single clay tablet, and that they are also contained severally on other tablets of the time, then we have to ask what is really going on here. These tablets, though kept from the public eye, have been catalogued and translated, and have been lodged at the British Museum since the late 19th century. Their existence is well known to any enquiring scholar who cares to look into the subject. Yet the clear testimony that they bear to the truth of the Genesis 14 record is hidden away. But not only that. Their very existence goes unmentioned, and a deliberate and calculated lie is inserted in their place, the lie that the names of these kings are unknown to us from the historical record, and that the writer of the Book of Genesis either errs in his ignorance, or blatantly deceives those who read him.

The information that we have been considering is not just withheld from the public, of course. It is also withheld from all those students who are busy pursuing their degrees in modernist colleges and universities. Entirely unaware of the fact that they are learning and then propagating a lie, they go on to teach their own students and to write in their own publications the lie that they in turn have been taught. The education systems of the western world are geared to suppress independent thought, and open enquiry is discouraged at all levels. Let a student's dissertation once range beyond the lecture notes that he has been fed, and let his conclusions raise but the smallest question mark over what he has been taught, and he will be severely marked down for it - even failed altogether if the question mark is big enough to embarrass his tutors. The much-vaunted 'scientific method' in all this, is a sham.

This has always been the way of things, just as it always *will* be the way of things. No amount of evidence or persuasive argument will ever change that. The system is too big, too powerful, and is too firmly entrenched to offer the hope of ever being changed. Moreover, because the world itself rejects the Word of God out of hand, it welcomes a system which tells it how false that Word is, and will protect and nourish that system to the defiance of all logic and common sense. It therefore falls to conservative Bible scholars and teachers to do something which should have been done in the first place – enquire into the many evidences for the Truth of God's Word, and make sure that these evidences reach Bible believers and the general public everywhere.

As we have seen, the available evidence – of which there is a great deal – comes in several forms; archaeological, literary, philological, palaeolinguistic, ethnological, and so on. The great advantage for the conservative Bible scholar is that modernism has concentrated all these years almost wholly (and often inexpertly) upon the philological, making not only an appalling hash of things in the process, but ignoring the existence of the archaeological and other evidences to an astonishing and blatant degree – and to the great hurt and weakening of its own nefarious cause. The field is still to be won therefore, the critics' boasts of having already won that field in any 'scientific' sense being seen to be empty indeed. Modernism has won no such thing. It has spun a most deceitful web around the Bible and its integrity as an historical record - but that is all it has done. Pluck just once at the strings of this web with an enquiring mind, and it simply unravels and falls away. It cannot withstand, and never has withstood, the test. The Bible has withstood it, all of it, and, because it is the eternal Word of an eternal God - a God who cannot lie! - then we may safely rest assured that it always will.

# Appendix One: The Babylonian Epic of Creation (*Enuma Elish*)

translated from the cuneiform

by

Prof. A H Sayce

1894

[*Because critics persist in claiming that the Creation account of the Book of Genesis is derived from Babylonian mythology, the text of the* Enuma Elish – *the Babylonian* Epic of Creation – *is given below. Thus Bible students and readers can check for themselves how true that claim really is. The comments and parentheses interspersed in the text all belong to Professor Sayce. The punctuation and headings are mine.*]*

## Tablet I

When on high the heavens proclaimed not, (and) earth beneath recorded not a name, then the abyss of waters was in the beginning their generator. The chaos of the deep (Tiamat) was she who bore them all. Their waters were embosomed together, and the plant was ungathered, the herb (of the field) ungrown. When the gods had not appeared, any one (of them), by no name were they recorded. No destiny [had they fixed]. Then were the [great] gods created. Lakhmu and Lakhamu issued forth [the first], until they grew up [and waxed old] (when) the gods Sar and Kisar (the upper and lower firmaments) were created.

Long were the days [until] the gods Anu [Bel and Ea were created]. Sar [and Kisar created them]....

> 'Here the tablet is broken, and we have to pass on to what seems to be the seventeenth line of the third book in the series.'

## Tablet III

The gods have surrounded her (i.e. Tiamat), all of them. Together with those whom ye have created, (Merodach) marched beside her. When they had armed themselves (?) beside her, they approached Tiamat. (Merodach) the strong one, the glorious, who desists not night and day, the exciter to battle, was disturbed in heart. Then they marshalled their forces. They created *darkness* (?). the mother of Khubur, the creatress of them all, multiplied weapons not [known] before. She produced (?) huge snakes whose teeth were pointed. Unsparing was [their] edge. She filled their bodies with poison, like blood. She clothed with terror the raging vampires. She uplifted the lightning-flash. On high she launched [it]. She fills them with venom (?), so that with.... their bodies unbounded, though their breasts bent not. She stationed the dragon, the great serpent and the god Lakha[ma], the great reptile, the deadly beast and the scorpion-man, the devouring reptiles, the fish-man and the zodiacal ram, lifting up the weapons that spare not, fearless of battle. Strong is her law, not previously repeated. Thereupon the eleven monsters like him (i.e. Kingu) she sent forth. Among the gods her forces she [launched]. She exalted Kingu (her husband) in the midst. [Beside her, (he was) king. They marched in front before the army [of Tiamat].

> 'The lines that follow are so broken as to render a translation impossible. But we gather from what is left that the news of the preparations made by Tiamat was brought to the gods by Sar or An-sar, the primeval god of the Firmament. Then, it would seem, Sar sends forth one god after another among his family, beginning with Anu, the Sky-god, to oppose the forces of evil':

I sent forth Anu. He did not go forth. Ea feared and returned. I sent Merodach, the seer of the gods. He felt the courage to face Tiamat. He opened his mouth, and said.... I am [your] avenger. I will bind Tiamat!....

> 'Once more the mutilated state of the fragments makes further translation impossible, but we learn that eventually the gods made a feast, after having created the vine for the purpose, and retired to the highest heaven, leaving the issue of the

conflict in the hands of Merodach. The fourth tablet or book of the Epic is in an almost perfect condition, and runs as follows':

## Tablet IV

They (the gods) established for him (i.e. Merodach) the mercy-seat of the mighty. Before his fathers, he seated himself for sovereignty. 'Yea, thou (O Merodach) art glorious among the great gods. Thy fortune is unrivalled, thy festival that of Anu. O Merodach, thou art glorious among the great gods. Thy fortune is unrivalled, thy festival (that) of Anu. Since that day, unchanged is thy command. High and low entreat thy hand. May the word that goes forth from thy mouth, be established. Unopposed is thy festival. None among the gods has surpassed thy power, the sustainers of the...(and) the mercy-seat of the god of the canopy of heaven. May the place of their gathering (?), become thy home. O Merodach, thou art he who avenges us. We give thee the sovereignty, (we) the hosts of all the universe. Thou possessest it, and in the assembly shall thy word be exalted. Never may thy weapons be broken. May they reach thy foes. O lord, be gracious to the soul of him who putteth his trust in thee, and pour out the soul of the god who has hold of evil.' Then they laid upon their friend a robe. To Merodach, their firstborn, they spake, 'May thy destiny, O lord, be before the god of the canopy of heaven. A word and (the gods) have created. Command that they may fulfil it. Open thy mouth. Let the robe perish. Say to it, Return! and the robe will be there.' He spake with his mouth. The robe perished. He said to it, Return! and the robe appeared again. When the gods, his fathers, saw the word that came forth from his mouth, they rejoiced. They reverenced Merodach as king. They bestowed upon him the sceptre, the throne and reign. They gave him a weapon unsurpassed, consuming the hostile. 'Go,' (they said), 'and cut off the life of Tiamat. Let the winds carry her blood to secret places.' The gods, his fathers, determine the destiny of Bel (Merodach). The path of peace and obedience is the road they cause him to take. He made ready the bow. He prepared his weapon. He made the club swing. He fixed for it the thong (?), and the god lifted up the curved-sword. He bade his right hand hold (it). The bow and the quiver he hung at his side. He set the lightning before him. With the swift-glancing gleam he filled his body. He made also a net to enclose the Dragon of the Deep (Tiamat). He seized the four winds that they might not issue forth, any one of them: the south wind, the north wind, the east wind and the west wind. He brought to his side the net, the gift of his father, Anu. He created the evil wind, the hostile wind, the storm, the tempest, the four winds, the seven winds, the whirlwind, a wind unrivalled. And he caused the winds he had created to issue forth, the seven of them, confounding the dragon, Tiamat, as they swept after him. Then the lord (Bel) raised the deluge, his mighty weapon. He mounted the chariot, a thing not (seen) before – terrible! He stood firm, and hung the four reins at its side. [He held the weapon], unsparing, overflowing, rapid....

'The next few lines are much broken. Then we read':

On that day, they beheld him. The gods beheld him. The gods, his fathers, the gods beheld him. And the lord (Bel) approached. By the waist he catches Tiamat. She seeks the help (?) of Kingu, her husband. She looks, and seeks his counsel. But his plan was destroyed. His action was ruined, and the gods, his allies, who marched beside him, beheld how [Merodach] the first-born held the yoke upon them. He laid judgment on Tiamat, but she turned not her neck. With her hostile lips, she announced opposition. [Then] the gods [come to the help] of Bel. 'They approach thee. They gathered their [forces] together to where thou wast.' And Bel [launched] the deluge, his mighty weapon [against] Tiamat whom he requited, sending it with these words: '[War and] trouble on high thou hast excited. [Strengthen] thy heart and stir up the [battle]!'

'Then come five more mutilated lines, and after that the poem continues':

'...against my fathers thou hast directed thy hostility. May thy host be fettered. May they bind thy weapons. Stand up, and I and thou will fight together!' When Tiamat heard this, she uttered her former spells. She repeated her plan. Tiamat also cried vehemently with a loud voice. From its roots, she strengthened her seat completely. She recites an incantation. She casts a spell, and the gods of battle demand for themselves their arms. Then there stood up Tiamat (and) Merodach the seer of the gods. They hurried to the combat. They met in battle. Then Bel spread out his net. He enclosed her. He sent before him the evil wind which seizes from behind, and he opened the mouth of Tiamat that she should swallow it. He made the evil wind enter so that she could not close her lips. With the violence of the winds, he fills her stomach, and her heart was prostrated and her mouth was twisted. He swung the club. He shattered her stomach. He cut out her entrails. He dissected the heart. He took her, and ended her life. He threw down her corpse. He stood upon it. When Tiamat who marched in front was conquered, he dispersed her forces. Her host was overthrown, and the gods, her allies who marched beside her, trembled (and) feared (and) turned their backs. He allowed them to fly and spared their lives. They were surrounded by a fence, without power to escape. He shut them in, and broke their weapons. He cast his net, and they remain in the meshes. [All] the quarters of the world they filled with mourning. They bear their sin. They are kept in bondage, and the eleven monsters are filled with fear. As for the rest of the spirits who marched in her rear (?), he laid cords on their hands....At the same time, he [treads] their opposition under him. And the god, Kingu, who had marshalled their [forces], he bound, and assigned him [to prison] along with [the other] gods. And he took from him the tablets of destiny [that were] upon him. With the stylus he sealed (it), and held the...of the tablet. After he had fettered (and) laid the yoke on his foes, he led the illustrious enemy like an ox. He established fully the victory of An-Sar over the foe. Merodach the hero obtained the reward (?) of Ea. Over the gods in bondage, he strengthened his watch, and Tiamat, whom he had bound, he turned head backwards. Then Bel trampled on the underpart of Tiamat. With his blows unceasing, he smote the skull. He broke (it) and caused her blood to flow. The north wind carried (it) away to secret places. He beheld, and his countenance rejoiced (and) was glad. The presents of a peace-offering he caused them (i.e. the foe) to bring to him. So Bel rested. His body he feeds. He strengthens his mind (?). He forms a clever plan, and he broke her like a dried fish in two pieces. He took one half of her and made it the covering of the sky. He stretched out the skin and caused a watch to be kept, enjoining that her waters should not issue forth. The sky is bright (?). The lower earth rejoices (?), and he sets the dwelling of Ea (the Sea-god) opposite the deep. Then Bel measured the circumference (?) of the deep. He established a great building like unto it (called) E-Sarra (the firmament). The great building, E-Sarra, which he built in the heaven, he caused Anu, Bel and Ea to inhabit as their stronghold.

'The fifth tablet describes the creation of the heavenly bodies and their appointment for signs and seasons. But unfortunately only the beginning of it has as yet been discovered':

### Tablet V

He prepared the mansion of the great gods. He fixed the stars that corresponded with them, even the Twin-stars. He ordained the year, appointing the signs of the Zodiac over it. For each of the twelve months, he fixed three stars, from the day when the year issues forth, to (its) close. He founded the mansion of the Sun-god who passes along the ecliptic, that they might know their bounds, that they might not err, that they might not go astray in any way. He established the mansion of Bel and Ea along with himself. Moreover, he opened gates on either side. He strengthened the bolts on the left hand and on the right, and in the midst of it he made a staircase. He illumined the Moon-god that he might be watchman of the night, and ordained for him the ending of the night, that the day may be known, (saying), 'Month by month, without break, keep watch in (thy) disk. At the beginning of the month, rise brightly at evening, with glittering horns, that the heavens may know. On the seventh day, halve (thy) disk....

'The rest of the tablet is destroyed, and of the sixth, only the opening lines have been preserved':

At that time, the gods in their assembly created [the beasts]. They made perfect the mighty [monsters]. They caused the living creatures [of the field] to come forth, the cattle of the field, [the wild beasts] of the field, and the creeping things [of the field]. [They fixed their habitations] for the living creatures of the field. They distributed [in their dwelling-places] the cattle and the creeping things of the city. [They made strong] the multitude of creeping things, all the offspring [of the ground].

'The following lines are too mutilated for continuous translation, but we learn from them that "the seed of Lakhama", the brood of chaos, was destroyed, and its place taken by the living creatures of the present creation. Among these, we may expect man to be finally named...'

*[*This is printed out of* The Higher Critics and the Verdict of the Monuments, pp. 63-70. *Evidently, more fragments of the* Enuma Elish *came to light after 1894, because Professor Sayce gives a much more fulsome translation in* his Early Israel and the Surrounding Nations, pp. 132-139, *restoring much of* Tablets II & III. *Later, 1989, Dalley was able to produce a translation of seven tablets of the Enuma Elish, all of them more or less complete* (*see* Myths from Mesopotamia, pp. 228-277). *But there is nonetheless no improvement for the modernist cause in the contents of the Epic. It is still as* unlike *the Book of Genesis as anything can be. It seems that the modernists and Bible critics, who have always maintained that Genesis was born of these myths, have a lot of rewriting to do.*]

# Appendix Two: The Cuneiform Inscriptions and the Kings of Genesis 14

For some strange reason, it seems to be the norm amongst modernist authors not to publish the catalogue numbers or shelfmarks of the cuneiform tablets that they rely upon. Given that there are hundreds of thousands of such tablets (and their fragments) stored in our museums, that can present any challenger, or even friendly researcher, with a daunting problem. We are fortunate indeed, therefore, that Theophilus Pinches had no such qualms when he presented his findings on the Genesis 14 kings to the Victoria Institute back in 1897.

The inscriptions that he opens up to us concern the four Mesopotamian kings that are named in Genesis 14, and are therefore an immensely important historical corroboration of one of the most maligned chapters in Genesis, as well as constituting a most important contribution to our knowledge of early Mesopotamian history. For some other strange reason, modernists mention neither these tablets nor their contents, never mind their shelfmarks, even though no serious researcher in the field can be unaware of their existence and contents. Under any other circumstances, these tablets and their kings would be famous. Yet they are never spoken of. Indeed, the academic silence which surrounds them is deafening.

The tablets concerned are kept at the British Museum, and their catalogue or shelfmark numbers are:

**Sp. II. 987**; **Sp. III. 2**; and a third which is listed as
**Sp. 158 + Sp. II. 962**

We shall examine their texts – **Sp. III. 2** in full - noting how unequivocally they corroborate the Genesis record. The tablets reveal that whoever wrote the 14th chapter of Genesis, knew exactly what he was talking about, and was one hundred percent correct in all that he tells us. Just why this evidence, which could tell us so much, is withheld from the public, is probably better pondered upon than stated.

The first tablet that we shall consider, and which is probably the most important of the three, is **Sp. III. 2**. The obverse (or front) of the tablet contains nearly 16 lines of broken text, and the reverse contains 12 lines of broken text. But more to our purpose, it contains the names of *all four* of the Mesopotamian kings that Genesis 14 speaks of! Hammurabi (the Amraphel of Genesis) appears on line 4 of the obverse; Eri-aku (Arioch) appears on line 9; Tudhula (Tidal) on line 13. On line 3 (reverse), appears Kudurlagmal, (Chedorlaomer).*

Each line of text (transliterated from the Babylonian) is numbered, with an interlinear literal translation into English (by T G Pinches) appearing underneath each word. The names of the Genesis 14 kings are highlighted as they appear, the first (broken name) appearing on line 4 (obverse), *Hammu*[*rabi*]:

## Sp. III. 2 (Obverse)

1..........................................................................................................

2..........................................................................................*su*..........................

3.........................................................................*ip-se-tu-su la*........................

.........................................................................his work not.......................

4........................................................................*su* ***Ha-am-mu***..........................

.......................................................................him **Hammu**[**rabi**].................

5.......................................................*pan* (?) *ilani* *nab-nit*.......................

.................................................before (?) the gods, the creation of............

6..........................................*lu U-mu*...............*Samas* *mu-nam-mir*.............

............................................day...................Shamash, illuminator of...........

7...........*bel* *bele* *D.P.Marduk* (?) *ina* *kun-nu* *lib-bi-su*

....the lord of lords, Merodach, in the faithfulness of his heart

8............*ardu* (?) *–us* *kip-pat* *kali-su* *ma-al-ku* *la* *za-nin*

..his servant (?) the region, all of it, the ruler not nourishing

9..........*-pa... u-sam-kit.* *Dur-sir-ilani* *.ablu* *sa* ***Eri-aku***

...........caused to be slain. Dur-sir-ilani, son of **Arioch**

10....*-na-a-tam* *is-lul* *me* *eli* *Babili D.S.* *u* *E-sag-gil*

..goods (?) he carried off, waters over Babylon and the temple E-saggil

11.....*mari (?) –su ina kakki kata-su kima (?) as-lu u-ta-bi-ih-su*

...his son (?) with the weapons of his hands, like a lamb slaughtered him

12.....*bil ik-bu* (?) *si D>P> sebu u maru ina kakki*

.....spoke (?) to her (?) , the old man and the child with the sword

13.........*maru ik-ki-is.* ***Tu-ud-hul-a*** *mar Gaz-za*........................

.........the child he cut off. **Tidal** son of Gazz[ani ?].................

14.................- *a-a-tam is-lul me eli Babili D.S. u E-sag-gil*

.......................goods (?) he carried off, waters over Babylon and the temple E-saggil

15...............*mari-su ina kakki kata-su muh-ha-su im-kut*

.................his son with the weapon of his hands upon him fell

16.....................*be-lu-u-ti-su a-na pa-an bet An-nu-nit*...........

..................of his dominion before the temple of Annunit.....

---

## Sp. III. 2 (reverse)

1..*E-lam-mat al Ah-hi* (?) *–e ana* (?) *mat Rab-ba-a-tu is-lul*

Elam the city Ahhe (?) to (?) the land Rabbatu he spoiled

2........*-ku a-bu-ba-nis is-kun ma* (?) *–ha-zu mat Akkad D.S.gab-bi Bar-si*......

............in ruins he set the fortress (?) of Akkad the whole of Borsippa (?)...

3.....*ik-lu* ***Ku-dur-lag-mal*** *mari-su ina patri parzilli sibbi-su lib-ba-su it-ta*

...ended. **Chedorlaomer** his son with the steel sword of his girdle his heart pier[ced]

4......*D.P.nakri-su il-ki-ma ab- sarrani a-nu-tu bele ar-*[*ni*]

........his enemy took and the will (?) of these (?) kings, lords of sin

5......*ru-tu ka-mu-tu sa sarri ilani D.P. Marduk i-gu-ug-su-nu*......

....rebellions (?)......who the king of the gods, Merodach was angry against them....

6....*mar-sa-a-tu i-rat-su-nu ar-rat u-sur-ta*.........

...(with) sicknesses (?) their breast was oppressed [their] place....

7....*mar* (?) *–ru ana na-me-e is-....-me-ni kul-lat-su-nu ana sari bel-i-ni* (?)

... to ruin was reduced (?) All of them to the king our lord

8......*di-e lib-bi ilani rim* (?) *–nu-u D.P.Marduk ana zi-kir sumi-su*

.[kn]owing (?) the hearts of the gods, the gracious (?) Merodach, for the renown of his name

9.....*u E-sag-gil ni-bu ana as-ri-su li – tur*

...and Esaggil proclaimed (?), to its place may he return

10.....*-bi-ka lis-kun an-na-a sarru beli-ia nis-tas*....

..........thy may he make. This, O king, my lord, we.........

11.................*limutti* (?) *–su lib-ba-su ilani ab*[*e*].....

.....................his evil (?) (from) his heart, the gods father[s ?]...

12..........................................*bel* (?) *hi-te la i-*...........

....................................lord (?) of sin shall not [exist ? ]...

------------------------------------

**The reason why the name of Chedorlaomer is transcribed here as Kudurlagmal instead of Khudur-Lagamar, as we noted earlier, is that Khudur-Lagamar is the* Elamite *spelling of his name, where the tablets we are considering are Babylonian. Given that Chedorlaomer was king of Elam, it is interesting that the writer of Genesis 14 has used the Elamite spelling in his transcription of the name into Hebrew, and not the Babylonian. Professor Sayce always believed, along with many others since his day, that Genesis 14 was but a story based on a Babylonian document.*

## Sp. II. 987 (obverse)

Chedorlaomer's name appears on line 6 of this tablet's obverse, thus:

...*ina mil-ki-su-nu ki-ni ana* ***Ku-dur-lah-ga-mal*** *sar mat E-la*[-*mat*]......
...in their faithful counsel to **Chedorlaomer**, king of the land of Ela[m]...

And Arioch's name appears on line 19 thus:

....*Dur-sir-ilani maru sa* ***Eri-e-ku*** *sa sal-lat*.....
.....Dursirilani, the son of **Arioch**, who, the spoil of....

---

## Sp. 158 + Sp. II. 962 (obverse)

This tablet is by far the longest of the three. The obverse contains 41 lines of text, more or less complete, and the reverse holds 39 lines, again more or less complete. The tablet is known as *The Legend of Chedorlaomer*, (Pinches, p. 57 – see Bibliography), though we could be forgiven for never having heard of it. Such a tablet as this should be common and famous fare, yet because it contains the exploits and adventures of a Biblical king, whom modernists, since Noldeke's day (1869), have always publicly dismissed as fictitious, it is never mentioned.

However, with his name by now stinking in the nostrils of every decent and right-thinking Babylonian, Chedorlaomer is hardly to be named throughout the tablet, being referred to mostly as 'the Elamite' (*Elam-ki-u*), and 'the enemy' (*nakru*). It is but a reflection of the turbulent political scene of the times, allies one minute (as in Genesis 14), and enemies the next, as here. But, just as we near the end of the tablet, the scribe's indignation finally boils over, and 'the Elamite' is named at last in line 21 of the tablet's reverse side:

*a-a-u* ***Ku-dur-lag-gu-***[***mal*** *e*]*-pis lim-ni-e-tu*....
Who is this **Chedorlaomer**, the maker of evils?...

Text 1.

The name of Chedorlaomer as it appears on the Babylonian tablet, Sp. II. 987 (obv.) line 6.

Text 2.

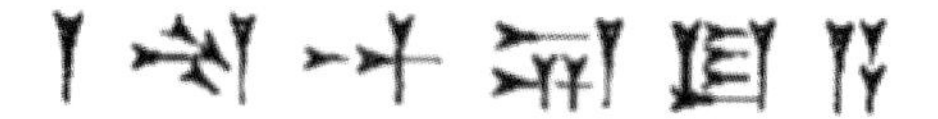

The name of Arioch (Eri-aku) as it appears on Sp. III. 2 (obv.) line 9.

Text 3.

The name of Tidal (Tud-hula) as it appears on Sp. III. 2 (obv.) line 13.

Text 4.

The name of Amraphel (Hammurabi) as it appears on line 3 of a letter concerning Chedorlaomer, full text and translation below:

## Letter from Hammurabi to Sin-iddina concerning Chedorlaomer

Free translation (by T G Pinches, *Trans. of the Victoria Inst.*, vol 29, p. 71):

> "**Hammurabi** sends thus to Sin-iddina. I shall hand over to thee the goddesses [idols] of Emutbalu (on account of) thy heroism on the day of **Chedorlaomer**. When they demand them back from thee, overthrow thou their people with the people who are with thee, and let them restore the goddesses to their shrines."

This letter (itself one of three) is yet a *fourth* source of reference for two of the Genesis 14 kings. Sin-iddina was the king of Larsa before he was displaced by Arioch (Eri-aku), who, like Chedorlaomer (perhaps a half-brother of his), was also an Elamite.

-------------------------------------

The unremitting suppression of these *four* cuneiform sources for the Genesis 14 kings is a most shameful reflection on those who dedicate their lives to convincing us that the Bible isn't true. They say - *knowingly* if they are scholars of any standing in their field - that the kings mentioned here are unknown to us from the records of the time. In the light of what we have seen here for ourselves, however, it may be instructive to contemplate the contents of the tablets and then to read once again the modernist statement that began this discussion:

> "It may be said at once that none of the names of kings mentioned in this chapter can be identified with any certainty as corresponding with the names of any kings known to us from contemporary records." *Peake's Commentary*, p. 188.

Yes. Quite so.

~ * ~

## Bibliography to Antiquity of the Book of Genesis


Albright, W F. *The Archaeology of Palestine*. 1949. Pelican Books.
Bermant, C, & Weitzman, M. *Ebla: A Revelation in Archaeology*. 1979. Times Books.
Black, M, & Rowley, H (eds). *Peake's Commentary on the Bible*. 1962. Nelson.
Bruce, F F. *The English Bible*. 1961. Lutterworth Press.
Bruce, F F. *The Books and the Parchments*. 1975. Pickering & Inglis.
Cassuto, Umberto. *The Documentary Hypothesis and the Composition of the Pentateuch*. 1961. Hebrew University. Jerusalem.
Cooper, Bill. *After the Flood*. 1995. New Wine Press.
Dalley, Stephanie. *Myths from Mesopotamia*. 1989. Oxford University Press.
Drury, J. *Critics of the Bible 1724-1873*. 1989. Cambridge University Press.
Easton, M G. *Illustrated Bible Dictionary*. 1894. Nelson.
Faber, George Stanley. *The Origin of Idolatry*. 3 vols. 1816. F & C Rivington's.
Fox Talbot, H. *The Antiquity of the Book of Genesis: Illustrated by some new Arguments*. 1839. Longman.
Gontard, Friedrich. *The Popes*. 1964. Barrie & Rockliff.
Hoffman, J M. *In the Beginning: a Short History of the Hebrew Language*. 2006. NYU.
Hogarth, D G, et al. *Authority and Archaeology*. repr. BiblioBazaar. 2009.
*Interpreters Dictionary of the Bible*. 5 vols. 1962. Abingdon Press.
Jacobsen, T. *The Sumerian King List*. 1939. University of Chicago.
Keller, Werner. *The Bible as History*. 1956. Hodder and Stoughton.
Kellogg, Alfred H. *Abraham, Joseph and Moses in Egypt*. 1887. Anson Randolph & Co.
Kramer, Samuel. *From the Tablets of Sumer*. 1956. Falcon's Wing Press.
Lopez, R E. 'The Antediluvian Patriarchs and the Sumerian King List.' *Creation Ex Nihilo Technical Journal*. December 1998. 12 (3). pp. 347-357.
Magnusson, M. BC: *The Archaeology of the Bible Lands*. 1977. Bodley Head.

McDowell, J. *New Evidence That Demands A Verdict.* 1999. Thomas Nelson Publishing.
Mitchell, T C. *The Bible in the British Museum.* 1992. British Museum Press.
Moorman, J. *Forever Settled.* 1999. Dean Burgon Society Press.
Morris, Henry. *The Genesis Record.* 1976. Baker Books.
Morris, Henry. *The Long War Against God.* 2000. Master Books.
*New Bible Dictionary.* 1980. Intervarsity Press. London. 3 vols.
Owen, J J. *Analytical Key to the Old Testament.* 4 vols. 1989. Baker Book House.
Phelan, M W J. *The Inspiration of the Pentateuch.* 2005. Two-edged Sword Publications.
Pinches, T G. *Journal of the Transactions of the Victoria Inst.*, vol. 29, (1897). pp. 56-65.
Pinches, T G. *The Old Testament in the Light of the Historical Records and Legends of Assyria and Babylonia.* 1902. SPCK.
Rogers, Robert William. *Cuneiform Parallels to the Old Testament.* 1912. Eaton & Mains.
Rohl, David. *A Test Of Time.* 1995. Random House.
Rohl, David. *Legend.* 1998. Random House.
Rohl, David. *From Eden to Exile.* 2003. Arrow Books.
Sarna, Nahum M. *Understanding Genesis.* 1970. Schocken Books.
Sayce, A H. *The Races of the Old Testament.* 1893. Religious Tract Soc. 2nd ed.
Sayce, A H. *The 'Higher Criticism' and the Verdict of the Monuments.* 1894. SPCK.
Sayce, A H. *Monument Facts and Higher Critical Fancies.* 1904. Religious Tract Society.
Sayce, A H. *Early Israel and the Surrounding Nations.* 2006. Echo Library.
Smith, George. *The History of Babylonia.* 1880? ed. A H Sayce. SPCK. London. The book can be read in its entirety at www.archive.org/stream/historyofbabylon00smitiala
Smith, George. 'The Chaldean Account of the Deluge.' *Transactions of the Society of Biblical Archaeology.* 2 [1873]. pp. 213-34.
Smith, George. *Assyrian Discoveries during 1873 and 1874.* 1875. Scribner & Armstrong.
Smith, George. *The Chaldean Account of Genesis.* 1876. Samson Low.

Tomkins, H G. *The Life and Times of Joseph in the Light of Egyptian Lore*. 1891. Religious Tract Society. repr. BiblioLife.
Unger, Merrill. *Archaeology and the Old Testament*. 1954. Zondervan.
Van Deursen, A. *Illustrated Dictionary of Bible Manners and Customs*. 1968. Oliphants.
Vos, Howard. *Genesis and Archaeology*. 1963. Moody Press.
Wallace Budge, E A. *The Babylonian Legends of the Creation*. 1921. London.
Whitcomb, J & Morris, H. *The Genesis Flood*. 1961. P & R Publishing.
Wight, Fred. *Manners and Customs of Bible Lands*. 1983. Moody Press.
Wigram, George. *Englishman's Hebrew Concordance of the Old Testament* (1874). 2003. Hendrickson Publishers.
Wiseman, D J. *Illustrations from Biblical Archaeology*. 1958. Tyndale Press.
Wiseman, P J. *New Discoveries in Babylonia about Genesis*. 1949. Marshall, Morgan.

~ * ~

## Special Appendix: The Early Writing of the Gospel

### Introduction

This concluding piece is born of great weariness – a weariness brought on by reading for the umpteenth time that the Gospels, like the Book of Genesis, are also a late compilation, and are therefore nothing more than a collection of imperfect memories and distortions of the Truth. I sigh. The scholars who make this claim must do so in utter ignorance of their subject. Either that, or they do so in full knowledge of the evidence against the idea, and deliberately mislead and deceive their readers. For be assured, evidence there certainly is which points unquestioningly to the fact that the Gospel was already written down and in circulation here in Britain - yes, *here*, as in the rest of the Roman Empire! - within only a year or two of our Lord's resurrection. What follows is an all too brief survey of that evidence. We shall hear the voices of two witnesses, namely the Lady Pomponia, (a Roman matron and one of the earliest Gentile Christians), and Gildas, an early British writer. But Gildas first.

### The Arrival of the Gospel in Britain

Gildas, who lived during the 6th century, states that the arrival of the Gospel here in Britain was indeed an early event: "This happened first, as we know [*ut scimus*], in the last years of Tiberius Caesar...."[1] Now, Tiberius reigned from AD14-37, thus placing the arrival here of the Christian Gospel within just four years of the Resurrection - a by no means impossible event, for news and documents travelled surprisingly fast throughout the Roman Empire, and four years is a very long time, even in their terms.[2] We can only lament the brevity of Gildas' statement which seems, if we are to believe the "*ut scimus*", not to have been news to his readers. Much indeed has been lost. His statement, however, paints a rather different picture to that which certain influential scholars present us with, of the Gospels coming together from various oral traditions at the end of the 1st century or even later. But was Gildas right? We shall see.

## The Lady Pomponia

Of our two witnesses, the Lady Pomponia is certainly the most interesting, for her story is surprisingly detailed. She was the wife of the Roman commander, Aulus Plautius, who was sent to Britain in AD 43 by the Emperor Claudius with orders to subdue the island during the second Roman invasion.[3] But it seems that the conquest of Britain was not the only problem that her husband had to face. We are indebted to Tacitus who tells us what happened:

> "*Pomponia Graecina, a notable lady, the wife of that Plautius who had returned from Britain [to Rome] to the honour of an ovation, was charged with being tainted with that 'foreign superstition', and was committed to her husband for his judicial verdict. According to ancient usage, he looked into this matter which affected his wife's life and reputation in the presence of her own family, and duly pronounced her guiltless. This Pomponia lived to a great age, but in continual mourning. For after the murder of Julia, the daughter of Drusus, at the connivance of Messalina, she lived for forty years without ever changing her mourning dress or her grief of heart. She was never punished for this while Claudius reigned, and it was thereafter judged to her credit.*"[4]

All of which is most intriguing. Firstly, there is her nickname (her *nomen per ludibrium datum*) of *Graecina*. It was rare, for only three other persons amongst the Roman nobility until her day were given it, and they are Julius, the father of Agricola, who was in turn Tacitus' own father-in-law;[5] an otherwise unnamed associate of one Sertorius; and lastly, to Pomponius Graecinus, who was the first to bear it and who flourished during the reign of Augustus. He was grandfather to the Lady Pomponia, who bore her first name in his honour.[6] The reason for the nickname was a fondness for and an unusual competence in Greek studies.

Secondly, there is the accusation that was laid against Pomponia that she was tainted with "that foreign superstition" [*superstitionis externae*]. This was an expression amongst the Romans that was given to the Christian faith, and to no other. The trial of Pomponia took place in AD 57, and by that date there had already been serious disturbances in Rome over certain holders of this 'foreign superstition'.[7] Suetonius tells us that in about AD 49 there had been a particularly serious riot at the instigation of the Jews in Rome concerning one "Chrestus",[8] which was when the Christians of Rome were first tainted with the suspicion of subversion and treason. As a result, the Christians were expelled from the city on Claudius' instructions, which event is referred to in Acts 18:2. Particularly serious for Pomponia, however, was the fact that the accusation was made against her whilst Nero was emperor, and it is readily seen why Aulus Plautius should avail himself of his ancient right of trying his wife himself rather than letting the State try her.

We are not told just how thorough the trial was. Pomponia's closest relations were present, as required by law, and it may reasonably be suspected that some of them were themselves tainted with this foreign superstition - perhaps even the noble Plautius himself. Certainly, his sister, Plautilla, who was hence Pomponia's sister-in-law, was at some time charged with the same offence and was banished for it.[9] Such things were not entirely unknown in the topsy-turvy world of Roman nobility, where Paul can salute those Christians that are even of Caesar's own household (Philippians 4:22), notwithstanding Caesar's [Nero's] own abhorrence of the faith.

But Pomponia's state of melancholy after the trial is equally interesting. It was stated officially by the family that her subsequent dejection was caused by the death of one Julia, the daughter of Drusus, evidently a friend or relation of Pomponia's, and Tacitus tells us that this mourning endured for the remaining years of her life. Yet, when we turn to Suetonius' account, we learn that this Julia had been put to death in Rome by the emperor Claudius some years *before* Pomponia's trial in AD 57 - in AD 43, in fact, the very year in which Pomponia had come to Britain from Pannonia with her husband Aulus Plautius, and there is no suggestion that she was in perpetual mourning then or for any of the following fourteen years up to her trial.[10] Moreover, Pomponia was a Christian, and deep mourning for the dead, while commonplace enough in pagan societies like Rome, is not found amongst those who believe in Christ.[11] So perhaps her dejection is better accounted for by her trial, and her denial under compulsion that she was a Christian at all. That, and the added burden of never thereafter being able to declare her faith.

She would have been solemnly warned by her husband, Plautius, who thereafter retired from public life, that if she did afterwards declare it, then the outcome would be certain death for herself and perpetual disgrace and disinheritance for her husband and family. Plautius, after all, was high in government, and would be aware of Nero's feelings towards Christians even before the horrors of that reign began.

Is it any wonder then that the Apostle Paul, whilst mentioning in his letters many others in Rome, should omit to mention Pomponia by name? Paul wrote his letter to the Romans the year *after* Pomponia's trial, and he would undoubtedly have been made aware - as he was made aware of much else that was happening in Rome (even the comparatively trivial absences from home of Aristobulus and Narcissus - Rom. 16:10) - of the danger in which the Lady Pomponia would now have to live out her life. If she ever chose subsequently to declare her faith as a Christian and die for it, then she would certainly enjoy Paul's every prayer and blessing. But that would not be a decision that Paul would make for her by *publicly* naming her after her trial as a continuing follower of The Way.

However, Paul *does* apparently refer to Pomponia, albeit with deliberate vagueness for her safety's sake, when he writes, "Salute Rufus [i.e. Pudens] chosen in the Lord, and his mother and mine." (Rom. 16:13). For the Lady Pomponia was indeed Pudens' natural mother (sharing with him the family surname, or *cognomen*, of Rufus). We know that Aulus Plautius, Pomponia's present husband, was not Pudens' natural father, having probably married Pomponia as a widow, for we learn from the Chichester Stone that Pudens was the son of Pudentinus.[12] Pudens had also reached manhood by the time of his mother's marriage to Plautius in ca AD 40. However, that Pomponia and Pudens were in Britain together with Aulus Plautius is known. That they all three returned to Rome is also known.[13] And what more comforting for Pomponia herself to hear in her present dejection that the Apostle Paul was not only not ashamed of her for what she had been compelled to do at her trial, but was not ashamed even now to own her as if she was his own natural mother - the highest compliment perhaps that any Christian man could have paid her?

Paul certainly would have been aware of Pomponia, for he was a very close friend of her erstwhile charge, Claudia and her family. But how can we know that Claudia was once in Pomponia's care? For the answer, we turn to one Pitiscus, who writes concerning the surname Rufus, "Rufus was also the *cognomen* of the Pomponii. Among them was L. Pomponius Rufus...."[14] We know from the poet Martial that Claudia was also known as Rufina, having taken the *cognomen* of her adoptive family. Moreover, we have further noted that Pudens, whom Claudia was to marry, was also a Rufus. All the evidence, therefore, points to this, that after their capture in AD 49, Aulus Plautius placed the family of Caradoc (Caractacus, the British king) into the care of his wife Pomponia for them to be raised and educated as Romans, a very common and expected practice of the time concerning captive royal families and the Roman nobility (Claudia was born in AD 36 according to the British records, and so was around 13 years of age when captured).[15] And so, what was once a dark and unknown episode in the history of the early Church, becomes crystal clear once the records are dusted off and examined.

## The Date of the Gospel

There is one question, however, that is raised by this evidence, and it has an important bearing upon the date by which the first Gospel was written and published. Pomponia, we have seen, was adept in Greek studies, sufficiently enough for her to be named for it, and we need hardly state the obvious conclusion that as the Gospel was written in Greek she may well have encountered it during the normal course of her scholarly pursuits. Now, we know that Pomponia was a believing and practising Christian some years prior to AD 57 when her trial took place, and certainly before AD 49 when Claudia came into her care. Could Pomponia therefore possibly have encountered a Greek copy of one of the Gospels at such an early date - as early as the mid-40s, or further still, as early as *before* the year AD 43 when she came to Britain? The answer, contrary to all the claims made by some scholars, is yes, she certainly could.

Our attention is drawn to the work of Dr Carsten Thiede who found it necessary to depart from the conventional path of biblical criticism. Why he was compelled to depart from that path is explained in his book, *The Jesus Papyrus* (see Bibliography). Suffice it here to say that a thorough and scientific analysis undertaken by Dr Thiede of the Gospel fragments known to scholars as the *Magdalen Papyrus* (named after Magdalen College Oxford where it is kept), dates this particular copy of Matthew's Gospel to times so close to the Resurrection, that it could easily have been written down by an eyewitness of our Lord's entire ministry.

To be brief, there is every indication that the *Magdalen Papyrus* was copied out in the AD 40s (and no later than the AD 50s). But we must also bear in mind that this particular papyrus was itself but a copy of an earlier original, though by how many removes we cannot know. The fragments were discovered in Egypt, which tells us further that the Gospel of Matthew at least had gone overseas from Palestine at a very early date. And if an Egyptian could obtain a copy of it in such early years, then why not a Roman whose empire at that time embraced both Egypt and Palestine, the land where the Gospels were written - particularly a high-ranking Roman in the military whose duties required himself and his enquiring scholarly wife to travel and have contacts throughout the length and breadth of the empire?

On this question, it is important to trace something of the career of Aulus Plautius to see where his duties would have carried him. We know that he was Consul of Rome in AD 29,[16] and that before he came to Britain in AD 43 bringing the IX Hispania Legion with him, he served as Governor of Pannonia on the middle Danube.[17] Pannonia formed part of what is today Yugoslavia, and it bordered upon Dalmatia, an area on the southern part of Yugoslavia's coastline. Which is interesting, for later in the 1st century we hear again from Pitiscus that one Pomponius Rufus held high military command in Dalmatia under the emperor Domitian.[18] In other words, the Pomponii Rufi were a long established dynasty in Dalmatia from at least the time of Augustus to that of Domitian, and it was whilst Plautius was serving in neighbouring Pannonia that he made contact with that family, amongst whom, of course, was the Lady Pomponia whom he married.

Throughout his career he was held in the highest esteem, which is shown in the ovation that was granted him on his return from Britain to Rome, for ovations were normally reserved only for members of the Imperial Family.[19] After the trial of Pomponia, however, he retired so effectively from public life that, apart from one deeply tragic episode, all trace of him is lost.[20]

## Conclusion

There is therefore sufficient evidence for us to conclude that Pomponia, who would have married Plautius in about the year AD 40, was herself in Dalmatia from before AD 40 and until AD 43, when she accompanied her husband and her son Pudens to Britain. She might well therefore have come into contact with the written Gospel of Christ (perhaps Matthew's) *before* AD 43, within just ten years or so of the Resurrection whilst still in Dalmatia - or she may, with equal ease, have first encountered it here in Britain where it had been circulating for the past seven or eight years already by AD 43, the year she came here. So, when we draw back the pall of ignorance that modernism has lain upon the subject, it would seem that Gildas was right. The Gospel - and hence the Christian faith - had indeed arrived in this country within just a few years of our Lord's resurrection, and even whilst Tiberius, under whom our Lord was crucified, still reigned. What a pity this isn't mentioned more often.

## Footnotes to Special Appendix

1) "*Ut scimus summo Tiberii Caesaris quo....*" Gildas. *De Excidio Britonum*. trans. John Morris. 1978. (*The Ruin of Britain*). Phillimore. Chichester. p.91.

2) Thiede and D'Ancona [p.99 - see Bibliography] give us some delivery times for the post in those days: Corinth (Greece) to Puteoli (Italy) took five days; Rome to Alexandria (Egypt) took only three days, and so on. And, as they also point out, "These delivery-times surpass even today's postal services." So when we say documents travelled surprisingly fast throughout the Roman Empire, it is no exaggeration. They did, and a copy of

the Gospel could have made its way to Britain from Palestine in little more than a week!

3) It was Aulus Plautius who, in AD 49, captured the British king, Caractacus (Caradoc) and his family, and took them into his own household to educate as Romans. Amongst them were Claudia (*Gwladys*) who later married Pudens (see footnote 13), the son of Pomponia from her first marriage, and Linus (*Llyn*), who was later to become 'overseer' of the Roman Christians. The Apostle Paul mentions all three of them in his second letter to Timothy (2 Tim. 4:21).

4) "*Pomponia Graecina, insignis femina, Plautio qui ovans se de Britanniis rettulit nupta ac superstitionis externae rea.....*" Tacitus. *Annals*. 13:32 (see Bibliography).

5) Tacitus. *Agricola*. 4. (see Penguin edition, p.53).

6) Williams, p.36. Pomponia later had a nephew who also was called Pomponius Graecinus. His tombstone was unearthed in 1867 (see Edmundson. p.86).

7) ibid.

8) Suetonius, p.202.

9) Edmundson, pp.230-5.

10) Suetonius, p.204. Could it be that Julia was herself a Christian, and had rebuked the infamous Messalina for her sinful life? The record does not say, but Messalina had others put to death for lesser offences.

11) To understand more fully the profound differences that lay between the pagan and the Christian views of death, see Scott's *The Catacombs of Rome* ( - see Bibliography).

12) *Itinerum Curiosum*. INTER VII. 1776. 2nd edition. pp.196-206.

13) Pudens is also called Aulus Pudens in various sources (*eg* Martial's Epigram 4:13), thus showing his adoption of his stepfather's name. Morgan (p.101 - see Bibliography) calls him, "*Aulus Rufus Pudens Pudentinus, a young senator with large possessions in Samnium*," without, annoyingly, giving his source for that information.

14) Williams, p.36.

15) Stated by Jowett (p.115), relying on the early Welsh *Achau Saint Prydein* (Genealogies of the Saints of Britain).

16) Salway, p.72.

17) ibid.

18) cit. Williams, p.37.

19) Both Suetonius and Tacitus mention Plautius' ovation.

20) The tragedy in question writes a sorry footnote to the story of Aulus Plautius. Shortly after the trial of Pomponia in AD 57, his son, also named Aulus Plautius, fell foul of the murderous Nero. As Suetonius tells us, "He [Nero] committed an indecent assault on young Aulus Plautius and then put him to death, remarking, 'Now Mother may come and kiss my successor'; he explained that Agrippina [Nero's mother] had been in love with Aulus and had induced him to make a bid for the throne." (Suetonius, p.234). The allegation was nonsense, of course, being nothing other than an act of spite against the elder Aulus Plautius who had so recently deprived Nero of his Christian prey by asserting his ancient right to try his wife himself. To Nero's evil mind, if he would not give up his wife, then his son would have to do.

~ * ~

## Bibliography to Special Appendix

Edmundson, G. *The Church in Rome*. 1913.

Gildas. *De Excidio Britonum*. 1978. trans. John Morris. Phillimore. Chichester.

*Itinerum Curiosum*. 1776. INTER VII. 2nd ed.

Jowett, G. *Drama of the Lost Disciples*. 1980.

Lanciani, R. *Pagan and Christian Rome*. 1895.

Morgan, R W. *The British Kymry*. 1857. Clarke. London.

Morgan, R W. *St Paul in Britain*. 1925. Covenant Publishing. London.

Peddie, John. *Invasion: The Roman Conquest of Britain*. Alan Sutton. Gloucester.

Salway, Peter. *Roman Britain*. 1981. Clarendon Press. Oxford.

Scott, Benjamin. *The Catacombs at Rome*. ca 1890. Morgan & Scott. London.

Seaman, W de M. *The Dawn of Christianity in the West*. 1993. Chrest Foundation.

Suetonius. *The Twelve Caesars*. 1989. trans. Robert Graves. Penguin Classics.

Tacitus. *Agricola*. 1970. trans. H Mattingley. Penguin Classics. Harmondsworth.

Tacitus. *Annals*. 1937. trans. John Jackson. Loeb Classical Library. Harvard.

Thiede, Carsten. *The Jesus Papyrus*. 1996. Weidenfeld & Nicolson. London.

*Trioedd ynys Prydein*. (The Welsh Triads). 1978. trans. Rachel Bromwich. Univ. of Wales.

Williams, John. *Claudia and Pudens*. 1848. Rees. London. (Glasgow University Library).

~ * ~

## Part Two

# FLOOD TRADITIONS

## from around

## THE WORLD

## Contents



~ * ~

## Introduction

The purpose and scope of this section is to gather from around the world traditions and memories of the Great Flood - the Flood of Noah that is recorded so famously in the Book of Genesis.[1] If what Genesis tells us about the Tower of Babel and how mankind was dispersed around the world is true, then it stands to reason that each group of migrant families would have carried with them memories of the Flood and other events of Genesis, and would have preserved those memories amongst themselves wherever they settled, passing them on to each succeeding generation. And that is exactly what we do find. Even the remotest peoples, separated from the rest of the world by immense distances and time, have preserved among themselves recognisable memories of the Flood of Noah, sometimes in the most startling detail, lending a remarkable corroboration to what we read in the Book of Genesis.

It is a strange phenomenon, but one which should never occur if Bible critics were right in what they have always claimed. Yet that is not the only surprise. What came as a shock to me was the discovery that our very earliest societies were *not*, as is nowadays taught, polytheistic. Nearly all of them started out with a firm belief in the One God, the Creator, and moreover, recall even the fact that He is a Trinity. Only later did they descend into paganism. This fact runs entirely counter to the modernist creed that belief in the God of the Bible 'evolved' out of pagan mythology. It did no such thing. It was there from the very beginning, its gradual loss marking a downward tumble into paganism, and not an upward 'evolution' at all.

Other incidents and persons from the Book of Genesis are encountered along with these Flood traditions – the Temptation and Fall of Man, for example - which again lend their testimony to the truth of the Genesis record. Not surprisingly, modernism has an answer for them all, or pretends to have, and we shall be examining the falsity of these 'explanations' as we proceed. We shall be looking particularly at the opinions and assurances of Sir James Frazer, the archetypal modernist who fails himself and his discipline at every turn, and yet was knighted and feted in the Victorian/Edwardian world in which he flourished, in spite of the fact that many of his dismissive assumptions were known at the time to be woefully inaccurate and misleading.[2] Amusingly, and for all his prodigious output, Frazer succeeds only in vindicating the very Word of God which he sets out to ridicule and disprove. So consistent and so pronounced was he in this, along with the persistent failure of modernism in general to disprove the Word of God, that it has taken on the force of law, and has allowed us to formulate The First and Second Laws of Frazer's Dilemma, a fascinating matter that we shall be looking into as we proceed.

In short, and for all the world's undisguised contempt for our 'naivety', if we accept the Genesis record of The Flood as accurate history, then we do so with the agreement of all the evidence that exists – a great body of evidence of global and historic proportions - which tells us that the Genesis record is indeed a fully accurate and even testable account. We can do no better than that. But what we have been careful to do is examine only those accounts of the Flood that pre-date the coming of Christianity, or the arrival of Christian missionaries and traders to the peoples concerned. That procedure forestalls any objection that these accounts are merely echoes of the Bible stories that missionaries have left behind.

## Notes to Introduction

1) Genesis, chapters 6 – 8.

2) In particular, we shall be considering his statements found in the 1923 edition of his book, *Folklore in the Old Testament.*

~ * ~

## Chapter One: Modernism – Its Rise and Methods

It would be tempting to say that Modernism – a system which ultimately denies the truth of everything – began its present mischief in the latter half of the 19th century. That was the time of not just the rise of organised evolutionary teachings (Darwin, Huxley, and so on), but also the so-called 'scholarship' of those in Germany who delighted to call themselves the 'Higher Critics' of the Bible, their leader in their heyday being Julius Wellhausen. The teachings of these critics soon spread throughout Europe and America and haunt us to this day. But we can actually see the present phase of modernism raising its deceitful and destructive head some 300 years earlier than that, in the latter half of the 16th century, and (somewhat surprisingly) in the company of no less a person than Sir Walter Ralegh.

Ralegh headed an intellectual circle in London called the Durham House Set. He, with Henry Percy (the 'wizard' Earl of Northumberland), Robert Hues (a mathematician), Thomas Hariot (an astronomer whom we shall meet again in this book), Walter Warner (who seemingly discovered the circulation of blood in the human body before William Harvey did) and others, would meet in Ralegh's home at Durham House in London and plan not just the colonisation of Virginia, but discuss matters of science, philosophy and history. Some of the company were a little too bold for the times, however, and they pronounced on matters in such a way that soon they were being spoken of in London as a circle of atheists and heretics.

Sir Walter himself, it must be said, did not always share his companions' more radical views, and there is little or no evidence that he ever abandoned his Protestant orthodoxy, in spite of many accusations of atheism being levelled against him (particularly at his trial). But one idea was raised amongst his associates at Durham House in which we see clearly the first stamp of today's modernistic notions. It was an idea concerning the Native Americans whom Ralegh's men had encountered in Virginia, and the fact that they allegedly had no recollection of the Great Flood. It was a large and, as we shall see, a wrong assumption which led to the speculation at Durham House that the 'Red Indians' of Virginia must therefore pre-date the Flood, their ancestors having survived it. Indeed, it was even mooted among them that these 'Red Indians' might even pre-date Adam himself.[1]

This, of course, runs entirely counter to what we read in the Book of Genesis concerning Adam as the first man, and the effects of the Flood of Noah being the global destruction of *all* mankind save only those eight in the Ark. In post-Reformation England, such ideas were explosive, but they soon took root amongst the more restless of London's intelligentsia, and pre-Adamites and no Flood soon became points of discussion.

The history of the development of modernistic thought is a weighty subject in its own right, and it must suffice us here merely to note that its development from its beginnings at Durham House can be traced to the birth of the Royal Society in the 17th century, from thence to the so-called Age of Enlightment in the 18th century, and so on into the 19th. It still hasn't reached its maturity in the 21st century, but in one respect it has changed not at all. It is still a force that is entirely destructive of all that it treats.

In nigh fifty years of studying it, I have not met with a single case in which modernism has added something useful to humanity's fund of knowledge. On the contrary, wherever it is applied, it darkens knowledge, making even the surest facts uncertain and everything else of doubtful value.[2] Its overriding agenda is always to pull down and not to build, and it does its work very subtly. To see how, let us pluck just one example amongst thousands out of the air.

A certain author, having written an in-depth study and translation of the Babylonian Creation and Flood accounts, finishes off her introduction to the subject with this curious statement concerning the historical evidence for the Great Flood that is found around the world, and which bears directly upon the subject of our own present enquiry:

> "Where Flood stories are found in other parts of the world, missionaries and early Christian travellers may have disseminated them; there is no reason to suppose that they are indigenous."[3]

...and with this authoritative pronouncement, the matter is closed. True, flood accounts beyond those of Mesopotamia lay outside our author's remit, so she could hardly have carried on her discussion without departing from the task in hand. But then, why make this passing shot at all? Well, it all has to do with the way in which modernism has pervaded the education systems and thought processes of the modern world. Our author has absolutely no intention of ever deceiving or misleading her readers. On the contrary, she has devoted her life to teaching and informing, and would be mortified to learn that she had passed on false information, even unwittingly. The same goes for the vast majority of today's teachers and writers. But her statement, which was made to settle a question which had clearly arisen in her own mind, raises a whole host of questions which the founders of modernism would have preferred not to see raised, let alone answered.

Considering the alleged role of missionaries in this matter, from day one missionaries have gone out into the world to preach the Gospel, and this has always meant them facing immense hardships, dangers, and sometimes even a horrible and lonely death. Are we then to believe that – on a worldwide scale – thousands of missionaries all forgot their commission and told their converts only stories of the Flood, and largely inaccurate stories at that? Whatever happened to the Gospel that they were sent to preach? Some memory of that surely should have been left behind? For be assured, unlike the Flood, the Gospel of Jesus Christ is entirely unknown and unremembered in the unevangelised nations of the world. How could it be otherwise? And how comes it that the many peoples around the globe who know about the Flood of Noah, have never heard of Jonah and the Whale, David and Goliath, and the whole host of other 'popular' Bible stories which missionaries were bound to have taught them? It is a great mystery – unless, of course, modernism is wrong in what it supposes.

It might come as a surprise to know this, but in fact it was commonly found by missionaries all over the world that the people they encountered knew about the Flood already. Their knowledge of it was faulty, to be sure, but it was knowledge nonetheless, and as we proceed we shall see that often it was startlingly in agreement with the Book of Genesis in many close details. Their folk-memory often recalled other things that Genesis mentions, although again they may be vague about the details, or had to invent names and details to fill in the gaps. But every account is recognisably of the same Great Flood of which the Book of Genesis speaks, and moreover, is entirely indigenous. After all, this was the foundation upon which the missionaries were able to build, and which explains, under God, their many successes in converting their hearers.

Our author, of course, is not alone. Let us consider the words of another scholar, one who typifies more fully the modernist mind, especially with the matter in hand – the global knowledge of the Great Flood. His objections are an education in themselves, and if we are to understand our own subject better, then we need to consider his statements carefully. As an apology for writing his book, in the opening line of the preface our author, Sollberger, says this:

> "This booklet is not concerned with the question whether there actually was a universal deluge destroying all but a few living creatures; nor does it seek to answer the much-too-often asked question, Is the Bible true?"[4]

More's the pity. The booklet in question is a British Museum publication which is again about the Babylonian account of the Great Flood, and the very fact that there is such an account seems, at the outset, to have caused our author some disquiet. The fact is, the Babylonian account, by its very existence and content (which we will examine in due course), makes it very likely that the Genesis account *is* true – not a comforting thought for a modernist scholar - hence his deep irritation at the 'much-too-often' asked question concerning the Bible's historicity.

If modernism were indeed a valid approach to history, then such issues should be of no concern to him. But he does go on to acknowledge that extra-Biblical Flood accounts are to found in:

> "...Asia – in India, Burma, China and Malaya, in Palestine and Mesopotamia; as well as in Australia and most of the Pacific Islands, and among the Indians of North America..." [listing also Greece, Lithuania, Iceland, and, for good measure, Wales. But, lest we be misled by such a weight of

> testimony, he dismisses all this with the following assurance]: "But the very fact that Flood stories are found among peoples so diverse and so far apart, both in time and space, shows that their common features cannot be but coincidences...."[5]

An impressive argument, but one that doesn't even begin to address the issue. Surely, it is a common procedure in any human enquiry to ask how many witnesses can testify to the truth of this or that, it being generally considered that the greater the number of independent witnesses that there are, then the better it is for everybody. Truth can at last be approached. Yet modernism is able to dismiss out of hand even such a global weight of evidence as this, by calling it all a great coincidence.

If so many independent accounts are indeed a coincidence, then the case is entirely unique. It occurs in no other subject around the world, so why should it occur in this? We are not told. But what we are witnessing here is something of a nervous twitch on the part of the modernist school whenever it looks as though Babylonian mythology might lend anything like a crumb of corroboration to the Book of Genesis. And so it is that modernism is driven toward the madness of inverted evidence – evidence which proves the one case is turned on its head to prove the other instead, and the uninformed reader remains just that, an uninformed reader, convinced that archaeology and all the other sciences have shown that the Book of Genesis is false.

There is method in such madness, of course. Modernism has just one agenda, and that is to give the world a very low view of Scripture. If modernism can convince the world that the Bible is just an ordinary book, a collection of primitive fables on a par with the rest of classical literature, then it has succeeded in one fell swoop in downgrading Scripture from being the very Word of God to merely a work of man's imagination. It is a grand ambition indeed, but one that is far more easily wished for than achieved, as we shall see.

## Notes to Chapter One

1) Lacey, pp. 194-201 (see Bibliography). Strangely, the very same specious argument raised at Durham House more than 400 years ago, is still current today, albeit it is couched in more 'scientific' terms than back then and given a slightly different slant (*The Genesis Flood*, p. 37 – see Bibliography).

2) I was first introduced to the strange reasoning of modernism at the age of 14 during a Latin lesson at school, when I read that Romulus (the founder of Rome) 'certainly did not exist, though some of his descendants may have'! Wonderful.

3) Dalley, p. 8 (see Bibliography).

4) Sollberger, p. 7 see Bibliography).

5) Ibid, pp. 9-10.

~ * ~

## Chapter Two: George Smith and The Flood

The history of the Bible has been one of constant crises and persecution. Around the world and down the centuries it has been sought out and burned – even along with its readers sometimes. It has been miscopied by the Alexandrian Gnostics; hacked to pieces by Marcion and his followers;[1] allegorised to the point of meaninglessness by Origen and other 'church fathers'; locked up for 1000 years or more in Latin, with a deadly ban on any attempt to translate it; and slandered and ridiculed by secular scholarship with a vehemence and determination which is unheard of for any other written work. And yet, after 2000 years and more of such treatment, it has survived it all and is with us still – unruffled, unscorched, vindicated and translated into our own and many hundreds of other languages around the world.[2] Its enemies must be exasperated beyond measure. Try as they might, they can neither destroy it, nor discredit it. But one day, shortly after the Reformation, they saw their chance and adopted a new approach.

What has always guaranteed the Bible's survival is the fact that it rightly claims itself to be the very Word of God. Indeed, the 16th-century Reformation showed that it was just that, and the Bible, instead of being destroyed as was wished and hoped for, multiplied in just a few decades to the tune of millions of copies across England and Europe, all or most of these copies certainly, ending up in the hands of the people. All outward attacks had proved utterly useless. So, enter Spinoza, stage left.

Baruch Spinoza (1632-1677) was born in Amsterdam of Sephardic Jewish descent, his ancestors having been driven out of Spain by the Inquisition in 1536. He developed a philosophy which was little more than pantheism (*Deus sive Natura* – God or Nature), but he was careful enough to give voice to his ideas anonymously in his *Tractatus,* which he published in 1670.[3] The purpose of his life's work was, strangely, to challenge the claim dear to every Jewish heart that Moses was the author of the Bible's first five books, the Pentateuch, and with him was born something that we know today as the Documentary Hypothesis that is so favoured and espoused by the 'higher critics' of the Bible.[4]

Spinoza's baton was then passed to Jean Astruc, an 18th-century French *philosophe* whose one delight as a lad was to study human corpses decomposing (*sic*!),[5] and from him it passed to Julius Wellhausen and his many colleagues in the universities of 19th-century Germany.[6] So industrious were the German critics that by the late 19th century it was nigh impossible to pursue an education in England, Europe or America that had not been weakened and poisoned by modernism. It had pervaded everything. For Bible-believers it seemed the darkest of times. As modernism was shredding the Scriptures into fables, so Darwinism was gripping the world. The Bible was defeated at last, and people's faith in it was being systematically destroyed once and for all. Or at least, that's what the critics told themselves and their public. But then, under the Providence of God, from around the corner and seemingly out of nowhere, came George Smith.

George Smith, distinguished from his many namesakes by the epithet, 'the Assyriologist', was a most unassuming man, and among the last whom one would think of as a champion. He was born on March 26th 1840 into a poor working-class London family. In the first half of the 19th century, that was a serious impediment. Children from that background could indeed be taught the rudiments of reading, writing and arithmetic, though they were warned at every turn not to expect to rise higher than the station into which they'd been born. Smith, however, was exceptionally bright, and at the age of only 14 he won an apprenticeship to become a banknote engraver at Bradbury & Evans, a famous London print shop. Socially, this was an important and very responsible career for a young man, and it seems that he excelled at the task. But his training and his fast-developing skills were merely preparing him, under God, for what was to prove his real calling.[7]

George Smith's workplace was providentially close to the British Museum, and he got to hear of some very exciting discoveries. He was already a man who loved his Bible. He read it avidly, and when he heard tell of Babylon and Nineveh, and the fact that ancient writings from these places were being unearthed and put on display at the British Museum, then the pull was irresistible. Soon he was spending every lunch hour gazing at the clay tablets and wondering what they said.

So regular and constant were his visits, and so obviously keen was his interest in the inscriptions, that soon he came to the notice of the museum staff, and they in turn spoke of him to Henry Rawlinson, the world's leading Assyriologist. Rawlinson was so taken with Smith's eagerness to learn that soon he was loaning him casts and 'squeezes' (*papier-mache* impressions) of the inscriptions to take home and study. Doubtless he also lent him lexicons and word-lists to memorise, though Smith had been reading up on the subject since he was just 14. But Rawlinson was stunned one day when George Smith mentioned in passing that he had just deciphered, on one of the displayed inscriptions (the Black Obelisk), the date of King Jehu of Israel's payment of tribute to Shalmaneser, king of Assyria.[8]

It landed like a bombshell on Rawlinson's ears. The date's decipherment was something that he and his colleagues had been grappling with for some time, but without success. Evidently, Smith's skills and eagerness to learn were bearing real fruit, and he had progressed much faster than Rawlinson had dared to hope. As a banknote engraver, George Smith possessed not just the ability to draw with great accuracy, but he had a highly-trained eye for even the tiniest detail. Moreover, being largely self-taught, he had not been blinded or seduced by the whispers of modernism in his ear. His head was clear, his eye was keen, and he had a believing heart, so that – knowing more than his teachers – he could see things that all the other experts had missed.

He was recruited immediately by Rawlinson and appointed Assistant in the museum's Assyriology department. The year was 1867, and together Smith and Rawlinson worked on volumes 3 and 4 of *The Cuneiform Inscriptions of Western Asia*.[9] Smith had meanwhile managed to date a certain eclipse mentioned in the tablets to May 763 BC, as well as the Elamite invasion of Babylonia to 2280 BC. But even that was not all. At the same time, he also contributed to a scholarly journal, *Zeitschrift fut Aegyptische Sprache*, a series of articles on the political relations between the later empires of Assyria and Egypt.

In 1871, Smith published *The Annals of Ashurbanipal* (the 'Asnapper' of Ezra 4:10), an immense labour with a transliterated as well as translated text complete with variant readings. Then followed a chronology of the reign of Sennacherib, as well as a syllabary of the Assyrian language. Whilst working on all this, he read an immensely valuable paper before the Society of Biblical Archaeology on *The Early History of Babylonia.*[10] And on top of it all – and we're still in the year 1871 – he deciphered the Cypriote Inscriptions which had hitherto baffled scholars around the world. He even helped them with their labours by supplying a Cypriote syllabary. It was an astonishing output from a truly gifted scholar, a scholar moreover who loved and believed his Bible. These were exciting and fruitful times for him, but they were about to get even more so, not only for himself but for Bible-believing Christians everywhere.

It is now 1872, and on December 3rd of that year Smith read his paper before the Society of Biblical Archaeology entitled, *The Chaldean Account of the Deluge.*[11] It stunned the world. Here was indisputable extra-Biblical evidence for the most laughed-at event in the Bible. Consider. From the late 18th century, the world had been hearing that the science of geology had disproved the silly notion that there had ever been a Great Flood. Members of the public along with scholars, writers, historians, teachers, students, preachers and clergy had abandoned the Book of Genesis in droves on the strength of these 'scientific' utterances. It was unthinkable that there was anything left to be said on the subject. Yet here it was, discovered and translated by a man who was probably the greatest scholar of his age, an account from outside the Bible of the Genesis Flood.[12]

The full text of Smith's paper is given in Appendix One of this book, and the reader will notice that, mixed though it is with blatant paganism and the names of strange gods, the account contains some startling references to the Genesis account of the Flood. It very soon becomes clear that the same event, the global Flood of Noah, is presented in both, with Genesis – and this hardly needs saying – possessing qualities and attributes both literary and historical that are way above those of the Babylonian. Nevertheless, the Babylonian is well worth the study for the many nuggets of corroboration that it lends to the Book of Genesis.

The Babylonian account makes for difficult reading in translation, being stilted and 'wooden', and is perhaps better appreciated when paraphrased into prose. Let us see how this works, beginning at line 82 of the inscription. Here, Sisit, the Babylonian Noah, gives the narrative in the first person. After the god Hea instructs Sisit to build an ark, (see line 19 onwards in the Appendix), he, Sisit, relates the coming of the Flood:

> "Shamash [the sun-god] made a flood, and he spoke [to me], saying in the night, 'I will cause it to rain mightily from heaven. Enter into the bowels of the ship and shut thy door.'.... In that day, when I [usually] celebrate his feast-day, I was afraid. I entered into the midst of the ship, and I shut my door.... In the morning, a raging storm arose. As far as heaven it thundered...." [line 101]: "The flood reached up to heaven and the earth was made a desolation. It swept the face of the earth. It destroyed all life from the face of the earth. The storm that broke over the people swept up to heaven. Brother saw not his brother. None of the people was spared" [line 121]: "Six days and nights passed, and the wind and the tempest and the storm overwhelmed all. On the seventh day, the storm was calmed in its course, and the tempest that had destroyed like an earthquake, was quieted. He caused the waters to dry, and the storm and tempest ended. I was carried through the waters. The evildoer and the whole of mankind that had turned to sin, their corpses floated like driftwood. I opened the window and light poured in." [line 135]: "– and so on.

In all, George Smith had uncovered in the British Museum's collection a document of astonishing worth. But it was incomplete. Moreover, it was a fragment of a tablet that belonged to a series of twelve, most of which were missing. It was actually eleventh in the series. Its colophon said as much. So, where were the other tablets in the series? It seemed that they were not at the British Museum, and there were people in England – some of them in *very* high places – who wanted to know.[13]

At this point, Edwin Arnold, the editor of the British newspaper, *The Daily Telegraph*, approached the British Museum and put up the then enormous sum of 1000 guineas (£1050) to send Smith to Nineveh where the Flood tablet had been found, to see if he could discover where the others lay and bring them back. In particular, Arnold hoped that a piece which Smith had complained was missing from the Museum's tablet could be found. It was, of course, a forlorn and ridiculous hope with virtually no chance at all of success. But the Museum agreed, no doubt in the more realistic hope that the talented Smith would expand its collection in any case, and at the *Daily Telegraph's* expense. And that is how, barely a month after he had read his paper to the Society, George Smith found himself saying a hurried goodbye to his wife and several small children, and being packed off in the middle of an English winter to the oppressive heat of Iraq. What he would find when he got there, he dared not think.

## Notes to Chapter Two

1) The Gnostics began to mutilate and twist the Scriptures as early as the 1st century, followed by Marcion in the 2nd. The Gnostics' perversion of the Bible has survived most notably in *Codices Alexandrinus*, *Sinaiticus* and *Vaticanus*. Marcion's, it appears, has not survived.

2) "So shall My Word be that goeth forth out of My Mouth; it shall not return unto Me void, but it shall accomplish that which I please, and it shall prosper in that thing whereto I send it." Isaiah 55:11.

3) The full title of this work is *Tractatus Theologico-Politicus*. Apart from casting doubt on the Mosaic authorship of the Pentateuch (or Torah), Spinoza also claimed that as the Torah was merely the 'political constitution of the ancient state of Israel', then because that state no longer existed, the constitution no longer applied. In other words, the first five books of the Bible were no longer valid.

4) The Documentary Hypothesis seeks to dismantle the Book of Genesis in particular by claiming to demonstrate its composition from earlier pagan myths and legends. The fact that, after centuries of enormous and untiring effort, modernism has failed dismally to prove any such thing, says

something at least for its redundancy as an intellectual pursuit. But still it flourishes. See Emil Reich's 1905 book, *The Failure of the Higher Criticism of the Bible*. Reich began his academic life as a 'higher critic', but was compelled through common sense to abandon it.

5) Jean Astruc, following Spinoza's example, published his own work anonymously in 1753. Its title (in English) was, *Conjectures on the original documents which Moses appears to have used in composing the Book of Genesis – with remarks that support or throw light upon these conjectures*.

6) Julius Wellhausen (1844-1918) was able to add many German words and phrases to the art of Biblical criticism, thus lending it a truly intellectual air. The true level of his scientific objectivity, however, is seen in his knee-jerk reaction to hearing of Karl Graf's ingenious 'hypothesis of the Mosaical law as a late addition to the original spiritual religion of the prophets'. As he himself tells us, he embraced it even before he had heard a word of Graf's reasoning on the matter! *Encyclopaedia Judaica* (2007) says a little more in its article, 'The Pentateuch'.

7) The best biographical treatment of Smith is given in Damrosch, pp. 1-80 (see Bibliography), to which, however, we may add that George Smith's interest in Assyriology began when he was 14. Perhaps as a treat for winning the apprenticeship, he was taken to the Crystal Palace Exhibition in 1854 where he picked up a copy of *The Nineveh Court* by Austen Layard. Thereafter, young Smith spent most of his money on books about Assyria and the cuneiform inscriptions. We can only imagine his joy when he discovered just how providentially close to the British Museum his employer's premises were.

8) The Bible makes no mention of this tribute of Jehu to the king of Assyria. But it is recorded on the Black Obelisk of Shalmaneser III, on which Jehu is depicted bowing in obeisance to the Assyrian king. It is the only likeness we have of an Israelite king. The date on the obelisk is (in our terms) 841 BC.

9) *The Cuneiform Inscriptions of Western Asia*, vols 3 & 4. 1861-1870. London.

10) *The History of Babylonia.* 1880. Ed A H Sayce. SPCK. London.

11) 'The Chaldean Account of the Deluge.' *Transactions of the Society of Biblical Archaeology*, vol 2 [1873], pp. 213-234 (see Appendix One of this book).

12) The Babylonian was not, of course, the very first extra-Biblical account of the Flood to come to the world's attention. Scholars had long been aware of the fact that the Greeks and Romans – and the North American Indians too by this date – had left accounts that spoke of this global cataclysm, though none of these had anything about them on this scale. Hence the impact of Smith's discovery. We shall see that the modernist camp went into, and has ever since remained in hyper-drive in its efforts to reclaim the field.

13) Amongst the audience at the Society of Biblical Archaeology when Smith read his paper, was none other than William Gladstone, the British Prime Minister. He was very likely there on instructions from Queen Victoria who had been informed about the subject of Smith's paper. However, Gladstone was himself a conservative Christian who was concerned about the recent attacks on the Bible. He had only recently held a heated exchange in the letters column of *The Times* with none other than T H Huxley, Darwin's self-appointed bulldog.

~ * ~

## Chapter Three: 'Go to Nineveh, that great city...'

Nineveh. It was once a name that struck terror into the hearts of men everywhere. It was, without a word of exaggeration, the heart of a state-sponsored terror regime that possessed a vast and dedicated army – an army, moreover, that was fully equipped and devoted to the mass destruction of cities, lands, and the wholesale slaughter of nations. But by the early 19th century, it had become a name for modernists to conjure with, laughing at it and claiming it had never existed.[1]

Unknown to the scoffers, however, was the fact that its ruins had lain under the earth for some 2500 years, ever since a 'minor' prophet of Israel had pronounced against Nineveh the words of God Himself, "I will make thy grave, for thou art vile!" (Nahum 1:14)

That grave was dug in 612 BC when Nineveh finally collapsed, and by 401 BC the city was entirely beneath the sand, not even its name or location being remembered.[2] The great mound that covered it has been known to this day as *Kouyunjik*, an interesting name meaning the 'Mound of Many Sheep.' It is a name which recalls the words of the prophet Zephaniah (2:13-14) concerning Nineveh, "He will stretch out His hand against the north and destroy Assyria, and will make Nineveh a desolation and dry like a wilderness – and flocks shall lie down in the midst of her...!"

Of further interest is the great mound that lies directly beside *Kouyunjik*, a mound that is known to this day as *Tell Neby Yunus* – the Hill of the Prophet Jonah. It is where Jonah preached to the people of Nineveh and then settled down to see whether God would destroy them. It was there that Jonah wished in himself to die, and it seems that God, after reasoning with him, granted him that prayer. Today a mosque covers his tomb.

Significantly, and this tells us more about the Book of Jonah than a thousand 'higher critics' ever could, that mound has been known as *Tell Neby Yunus* since before 612 BC, the year of Nineveh's destruction. How otherwise could the local Arabs possibly have known that Jonah was ever associated with it, the very name and location of Nineveh being so soon lost to them? Moreover, although the prophet Jonah (Arab. *Yunus*) is mentioned in the Koran (Sura 37:139-149 – a section known to Moslems as *Sura Yunus*), the name of Nineveh does not appear at all, nor anywhere else in the Koran, either in isolation or in any association with Jonah. His commission and fleeing, even his being swallowed by a great fish are all mentioned. But not Nineveh. They would not have learned from the Koran even the name of the city that he was sent to preach against. Moreover, for 1300 years after the fall of Nineveh (612 BC-AD 700), the Arabs had no Koran. They certainly had no Old Testament to tell them about Nineveh, and they were entirely strangers to the New Testament. Yet they knew that this particular mound amongst the hundreds of others in the area was Jonah's, even though Nineveh's name and location were unknown to them. But we digress.

## The Tablets

In the 1840s, when George Smith was still just a small child, the grave of Nineveh was opened, and the world, in one of its darkest hours of scoffing and ridicule and doubt, came to see once more that the Bible speaks true. The archaeologists, Rich and Botta (Rich in the 1820s, and Botta from 1840), were the first to tentatively probe the mound, but it is Austen Layard, the explorer and archaeologist, who really brought things to light, and he has left us an account of his work.[3] Given today's standards of careful and painstaking archaeology, it does not always make impressive reading. Looting and plunder were more often the rule, though it has to be said that even this brought to light some amazing treasures and information, especially in the form of clay tablets and other inscriptions. But it is the very carelessness and haphazardness of the excavations of Botta, Layard, and especially of a man named Hormuzd Rassam some twenty years earlier, that makes George Smith's discovery when he went to Nineveh all the more remarkable. Let me explain.

In 1853, Rassam had uncovered at Nineveh the palace and library of Ashurbanipal, king of Assyria (668-627 BC) – "...thanks to a combination of shrewd intuition, sheer obstinacy, and random good luck..."[4] We may like to think that Providence also had a share in the discovery, given what was found there and the timing of the whole thing. But basically, the story, as it is popularly given and understood, is this. George Smith found, amidst tons of haphazard rubble that had been shovelled and dumped to one side – and then buried again by Rassam's men – the missing piece of the British Museum's Flood tablet! It has to be said that, contrary to his sponsors' instructions and expectations, he was not actually looking for the thing. It was, as we observed earlier, a forlorn and ridiculous hope that he ever would or even could find it, or even that it still existed. But there it was, right in front of him.

> With typical modesty, George Smith recorded the find thus:
>
> "On cleaning one of them [the fragments of tablets unearthed that day], I found to my surprise and gratification that it contained the greater portion of seventeen lines of inscription belonging to the first column of the Chaldean account of the Deluge, and fitting into the only place where there was a serious break in the story"[5]

The whole episode is utterly remarkable. As more of the related tablets and their fragments came to light, the series took on a name which is now famous around the world. It was called the *Epic of Gilgamesh*. But if all this is remarkable enough, the story doesn't end here. George Smith also unearthed another series of tablets which today are known as the Babylonian *Epic of Creation*, or to use the first two words of the epic, *Enuma Elish*.

*Enuma Elish*, it has to be said, is not so much a later 'version' of the Genesis Creation account, as a distinctly hellish parody of it. It opens with the words: *e-nu-ma e-lish la na-bu-u sha-ma-mu...* – "When in the heights heaven was not [yet] named...". We discuss it in greater depth elsewhere,[6] though here we need to consider those features of the epic which correspond with some of the details that the Book of Genesis gives us. George Smith lays out for his readers a table to illustrate the points of correspondence between the two accounts, the gist of which table is as follows:[7]

Tablet 1 of *Enuma Elish* roughly corresponds with Genesis 1:1-2 (the Prologue of the Creation); Tablet 2 roughly corresponds with

Genesis 1:3-5 (the 1st day of Creation); Tablet 3 roughly corresponds with Genesis 1:6-8 (the 2nd day of Creation); Tablet 4 roughly corresponds with Genesis 1:9-13 (the 3rd day of Creation); Tablet 5 roughly corresponds with Genesis 1:14-19 (the 4th day of Creation); Tablet 6 roughly corresponds with Genesis 1:20-23 (the 5th day of Creation); and Tablet 7 roughly corresponds with Genesis 1:24-25.

Smith then goes on to mention an eighth tablet on which the creation and fall of man are recorded, and several others which describe the war between good and evil, "...but all these are very mutilated, and no number can be positively proved beyond the fifth tablet."[8]

However, Smith does go on to relate that:

> "The fifth tablet commences with the statement that the previous creations were 'delightful', or satisfactory, agreeing with the oft-repeated statement of Genesis, after each act of creative power, that 'God saw that it was good.' The only difference here is one of detail. It appears that the Chaldean record contains the review and expression of satisfaction at the head of each tablet, while the Hebrew has it at the close of each act."[9]

Smith then relates to us the Babylonian account of the fourth day of Creation, in which the stars were set out in twelve constellations. Curiously, the moon ('Uru') is described as being created before the sun ('Shamash'), reflecting (no pun intended) the Babylonian worship of the moon as the more important 'god' of the two. In a masterly understatement, Smith observes, "Here it is evident that Genesis is truer to nature than the Chaldean text."[10]

In the following pages of his book, Smith goes on to give us more of the many corresponding features between the Babylonian tablets and the Book of Genesis, among them being the fact that men are called *adami*, the very name given to the first man in Genesis. There is another race alluded to called the *sarku*, and these correspond with the enigmatic 'sons of God' mentioned in the 6th chapter of Genesis, the intermarriage of these with the daughters of men spreading and amplifying the evils begun by Adam's fall.[11]

Smith then goes on to tell us in summary, after mentioning how the tablets include the dragon in the curse for man's fall, how man fared at the Fall, and how he continues to fare thereafter in the Babylonian scheme of things. Citing one of the tablets, he says:

> "Wisdom and knowledge shall injure him (line 22); he shall have family quarrels (line 23); shall submit to tyranny (line 24); he will anger the gods (line 25); he shall not eat the fruit of his labour (line 26); he shall be disappointed in his desires (line 27); he shall pour out useless prayer (lines 28 and 30); he shall have trouble of mind and body (lines 29 and 31); [and] he shall commit future sin (line 32)."[12]

Remarkable. But perhaps we should take pause here and ponder the fact that it's just as well that George Smith came across these tablets before the modernist school got hold of them. I doubt we would ever have heard of the many close and corroborative correspondences between the clay tablets and the Book of Genesis had George Smith not been there to search them out and to tell us of them.[13] Dealing with the same material, Dalley, for example, is quick to tell us:

> "...we cannot speak of 'the Mesopotamian view of creation' as a single, specific tradition, and this in turn shows the futility of claiming a direct connection between genesis (*sic*) as described in the Old Testament and any one Mesopotamian account of creation."[14]

How very strange. George Smith found no such difficulty. But then, George Smith is not mentioned once in Dalley's book, not even in the Bibliography, even though it was he who identified and first translated virtually all the material that Dalley treats of in her book. And what are we to make of her remark concerning the futility of claiming a direct connection between the Book of Genesis and any given Mesopotamian account? Has the modernist *putsch* all these years not been firmly based upon the assumption that Genesis is *descended* from Babylonian myths?

Thousands, if not millions, have abandoned the Book of Genesis on the strength of it! Or are we being asked not to believe that now? And if so, why?

The answer to that question is clear. Reading both Genesis and the Babylonian account reveals the immeasurable superiority of Genesis over the Babylonian. Not by any stretch of the imagination could it ever be proposed that Genesis owes its origin to the often senseless, occasionally obscene, and always pagan babble of Mesopotamia, no matter how subtle or clever was the person who tried. Therefore it is better, from the modernist point of view, to disclaim any connection whatever – yes, even the traditionally held connection of the Babylonian myth descending to the Book of Genesis. Extraordinary.

Not that that will stop any future claim being made of the Book of Genesis being descended from the Babylonian legends. After all, what option remains to them? Allow Genesis just once an independence of composition, and you have the Word of God back again. Closer inspection, of course, reveals that there certainly are correspondences between the two accounts, but they all lie in the direction of the Babylonian myths trying to obscure, twist and corrupt the integrity of Genesis. The entire agenda of paganism is, and always has been, to hide God from the people, just as it is modernism's underlying agenda to hide His Word from them. That the two should walk hand in hand, in this matter especially, should therefore not surprise us.

## The Mandaeans

But before we leave the Babylonians and their tablets, we would do very well indeed to begin our exploration of the world's Flood traditions by considering a people who have lived since time immemorial in the marshland delta of the Tigris and Euphrates rivers. They are called the Mandaeans, and they are the marsh-dwellers of southern Iraq whom Saddam Hussein so recently tried to exterminate. They have a Flood tradition that, even on its own, sets a formidable challenge to modernist assumptions. They have lived in the marshlands since at least the year 553 BC when we read of them in the inscriptions of Nabonidus, king of Babylon. But we can be sure that they had settled in the delta long before that year, which is the earliest datable reference that we have for them.[15]

The first westerner to have any real contact with them was Lady Ethel Drowser in the 1920s and 1930s (she was the wife of the then British Judicial Advisor to Iraq), and such was the level of trust that she won from the Mandaeans, that she was allowed the privilege of copying and translating their ancient legends – the first outsider ever to be afforded that privilege, and amongst those legends, was their account of the Flood.

According to that account, the Creator, Hiwel Ziwa, warned Noh (*sic*) to build an ark (cube-shaped as in the old Sumerian account), because he was going to destroy the world with a Great Flood. Noh asked Him to give ample warning about when the Flood would begin, and Hiwel Ziwa said that he should look for the green shoot of a reed to appear in his oven. Shortly after, the Flood would begin. The shoot appeared 300 years later. Packing the ark with animals, Noh and his daughter-in-law entered the ark, but his son Sam (Shem?) was away tending the flocks. Almost perishing in the Flood, Sam managed to swim to the ark and sit on its roof. All the mountains of the earth were submerged, and when the waters abated (which Noh determined by sending out a crow and a dove), Noh opened the ark and saw Sam sitting on top. They all left the ark, built a clay house, and, the 'goddess' Rua assuming the shape of Noh's wife, Anhuraita, she and Noh had three sons, Sam, Tam, and Yafet.[16]

That this account long pre-dates Christianity and any of its missionaries, is shown plainly in the Sumerian model for the shape of the ark, a cube. This shape is encountered only in the Sumerian version of the Flood, and has clearly been carried over by the Mandaeans since those very early times. The fact that 'gods' and 'goddesses' are featured in their Creation and Flood accounts also places the whole thing in a pre-Christian setting. Even the pre-Abrahamic origin of their Flood account is suggested by their rejection of Abraham as a 'false prophet'. In short, the Mandaean account challenges at every level every modernist assumption that there is concerning the Flood accounts which are found around the world – which is doubtless why it is mentioned so rarely.[17]

## Notes to Chapter Three

1) No longer able to claim that Nineveh did not exist, modernists still hold up the Bible to ridicule over the statement in the Book of Jonah that Nineveh was so large a city that its circuit was a three-day journey. No city in the ancient world was ever that large, they say. Well, the walls of the city proper, standing 100 feet high and 50 feet thick, were an impressive 8 miles or so in circumference, which is large enough. But Nineveh, like London and many other cities around the world, possessed an administrative area that ranged far beyond the city walls. In this case, that area extended from Nineveh to Nimrud, to Karamles and Khorsabad, forming an urban rectangle which was indeed a three-day journey to walk around. In fact, you'd have to go some to cover it in three days.

2) The surprising speed with which this vast city was buried beneath the sand, speaks indeed of a grave in which a dead and rotting thing is quickly covered over. Many of its ziggurats, temples and palaces were higher than the 100 feet walls that surrounded them, as in the three other cities that belonged to Nineveh. But whatever forces God brought into play to make such a rapid burial even possible, He did it, and He did it thoroughly - in exact accordance with His Word. Today, only sheep graze there, just as He promised they would.

3) Layard, Austen. *Nineveh and its Remains*. 1849. 2 vols. John Murray. London.

4) Damrosch, p. 81 (see Bibliography).

5) *Assyrian Discoveries*, p. 97.

6) *The Antiquity of the Book of Genesis*, p. 33.

7) *The Chaldean Account of Genesis*, p. 75.

8) Ibid, pp. 72-73.

9) Ibid.

10) Ibid, p. 75.

11) Ibid, pp. 75-76.

12) Ibid, pp. 86-91.

13) One of the first to rush into print so that his readers could sleep safe in the knowledge that all was well, and that George Smith's discoveries carried no implication at all that the Bible might possibly be true, was the anonymous journalist who wrote the following review of Smith's book, *Assyrian Discoveries*: "As for the account of the deluge, no small share of the popular interest in it has, it must be confessed, been due to a misapprehension of its bearing on the Biblical narrative of that event. It is looked upon by many as affording weighty and independent testimony not only to the historic fact of the deluge, but also by the striking agreement in many points of detail to the literal accuracy of the Biblical account.... But all this is aside from the true meaning of these correspondences...." *New York Times*. Wednesday February 27th 1875, p. 10. In keeping with the finest traditions of the modernist school, exactly what the true meaning of these correspondences is, he forgot to say.

14) Dalley, p. 278. We may assume that the spelling of Genesis with a lower case 'g' is unintentional.

15) Kearsley, p. 985 (see Bibliography). On Sunday 4th March 2007, it was reported by the BBC that the Mandaeans faced extinction from Islamic extremists because they are 'followers of Adam, Noah and John the Baptist.'

16) Kearsley, pp. 999-1000.

17) The Mandaeans having lived in the Tigris and Euphrates delta since earliest times, it is interesting to note that this is the very part of the country to which Izdubar (Gilgamesh) travelled to meet Sisit, the Babylonian Noah (see Appendix One).

~ * ~

## Chapter Four: Further Correspondences

The fact that George Smith got to these tablets first was indeed Providential. He was himself a Bible-believer, and he had absolutely no problem with highlighting not just the discrepancies, but also the surprising correspondences between the Babylonian and Assyrian writings – which he always called Chaldean – and the Book of Genesis. And not just the Book of Genesis either, but other Old Testament books like Kings and Chronicles.[1] Indeed, it was the continuing discovery of these correspondences that drove him on in his studies and work. If he learned new words and grammars, it was only to help him to this end. If he learned ancient languages which were entirely unknown to his peers, then that again was only to help him toward confounding the Bible's critics and corroborating the Word of God that he loved so dearly. He was too modest a man to ever trumpet this abroad. He just did his work quietly and well, and then went into print.

As he points out to us, the Book of Genesis contains many details that are found to have been borrowed by those who first composed the mythologies of Babylonia.[2] They are of great importance for our present study, because they tell us that when the Flood tablets and other sources speak of a great flood, then it is the same Flood that Genesis also speaks of. Were these other details not present in these accounts, then it could easily be claimed that, seeing no other details from Genesis are evident, then another flood must be meant. As, indeed, it is often claimed anyway, as we shall see. George Smith tells us of these details which are peripheral to the subject in hand, the Flood of Noah, yet essential to its understanding. But there are others, and because we shall encounter them in the Flood accounts of other places around the world, they are worth considering here.

### Adam

The early Sumerians knew about Adam, except that they changed his name slightly by altering the last written character of his name, which they spelt *Adapu* (assuming the final character has been read correctly this time). Adapu was the first man, and he refused to eat the bread of eternal life when it was offered to him.[3] The Sumerians gave him the epithet 'atra-hasis', meaning 'most wise', which epithet was later passed down to a man called Atrahasis, the Sumerian Noah. Adapu is also said to have had 'clean' or 'holy' hands. No sin is imputed to him save that of breaking one of the wings of the south wind, but even that was morally justified.

It is interesting that in the Sumerian account of the Flood, it is not so much mankind's wickedness that destroys him, as the fact that he gets on Enlil's nerves (Enlil being the supreme deity in the Sumerian pantheon) with the constant din of his blathering and bleating. No doubt we can all sympathise, but it is worthy of note that in the Sumerian system of theology, sin is not imputed to man, and holiness is not imputed to the gods. Compare *that* with the Bible.

## Eve

One of the names or titles given to Eve by the Sumerians, is *Nin-ti*, an ingenious pun which means both 'Lady of the Living' (a harkback to Genesis 3:20 which names Eve as the mother of all living), and 'Lady of the Rib' (which name must surely speak for itself). Interestingly, Sollberger renders the name, 'Lady who gives birth', which not only disguises both meanings, but robs Eve of her unique place in human history. One wonders why such a loose translation was chosen.[4] Could it have been in the hope that those who are unacquainted with early Sumerian mythology would be unlikely to make the connection between such a rendering of *Nin-ti* and the historical Eve? We must not think so.

Modernism, though, is no stranger to loose translation. Modernist anthropologists, for example, tell us how the 'primitives' they study all around the world worship the 'sky-god'. It is a universal phenomenon. But they forget to tell their readers that the term 'sky-god' can be translated equally well out of any language on earth as 'God of Heaven'. But how would that fit in with the evolutionary and atheistic scheme of things if it were once admitted that virtually all mankind had an innate awareness of, and indeed worshipped the God of Heaven? We will meet with this awareness in the most unlikely corners of the world as we proceed. It makes very interesting reading.

## Eden

Much ink has been spilled of late in what are often silly attempts to identify the location of Eden. That land or garden was utterly destroyed by the Flood, its geology and geography altered, as all else in the pre-Flood world, beyond any recognition.[5] We will meet with concepts and dimmed memories of Eden as we proceed, but the early Mesopotamians tried to recreate Eden by naming the two main rivers of their country Tigris and Euphrates, which, Genesis tells us, were two of the four rivers which flowed through and around the original Eden.[6] Amusingly, because this recreated Eden has only two rivers and not the four of which Genesis speaks, some modern commentators have proffered the lame suggestion that the other rivers must have been canals, which needs no further comment from us. Others have proffered the Nile and Indus rivers. Given that the Nile flows through Egypt and the Indus through Pakistan, this requires even less comment.

But to be brief, the early Sumerians retained in their folk-memory much of what Genesis tells us about the pre-Flood world, certainly more than the other nations of ancient Iraq, and retained Eden's name as *edin*. The Akkadians remembered it as *edinu*, and the Assyrians as *bit-idinu*, the House of Eden.

## The Tree of Life

It is surprising how many countries and cultures around the world remember the Tree of Life. The peoples of Mesopotamia certainly remembered it, the Tree of Life figuring large in both their art and literature. They were very aware indeed that the Tree of Life was guarded by angelic creatures, these invariably being depicted in Assyrian monumental art, and on 'gems' (cylinder seals mainly), not just guarding but also tending and nurturing the Tree of Life.

George Smith, on page 88 of his *Chaldean Account of Genesis*, tells us of a mention concerning the Tree of Life on a clay tablet that he had just examined. He says:

> "There is a second tree, the Tree of Life, in the Genesis account (ch. iii. 22), which certainly appears to correspond

to the sacred grove of Anu, which a later fragment states was guarded by a sword turning to all the four points of the compass."

Unusually, Smith gives us no catalogue or shelf number for the fragment in question, and he died shortly after writing this, so the tablet cannot now be identified.

## Darkness

There is one thing that many nations do remember about the Flood, and that is the great and awful darkness that covered the earth before the rains fell. The Book of Genesis doesn't mention it, unless the Hebrew implies it in subtle and unsuspected ways, yet it forms a major component of many Flood accounts, as we shall see. Meanwhile, it was certainly remembered in the Mesopotamian versions. Tablet 11 of the *Epic of Gilgamesh* (George Smith's famous Flood tablet), for example, tells us that, "Every gleam of light was turned into darkness... Brother saw not his brother... Men could not be recognised under heaven."[7]

The Book of Exodus mentions a similar darkness (10:21-23), one that was so thick it could be felt. But the fact that the darkness which accompanied the Flood is not specifically mentioned in Genesis itself, is no great marvel. The gathering of the clouds certainly would have blotted out all sunlight, but it does mean that its being remembered so universally and so emphatically is due to another source of information, one that is little considered by the Bible's critics. I mean those who accompanied Noah aboard the Ark and who later recalled their experiences endlessly to their children, their grandchildren, and even to their great-grandchildren. How else could the information contained in Genesis have been woven so clearly into the later pagan web of mythology? The occupants of the Ark, even Noah himself, would have faced an interminable series of questions about the pre-Flood world, its people, their names, where they lived, and more morbidly, what actually happened when the Flood finally came and took them all away. Among all these details would surely have been the great darkness that presaged the Flood.

Like the *Epic of Gilgamesh*, the *Epic of Atrahasis* also carried the memories of those who were aboard the Ark and remembered the darkness:

> "None could see his neighbour. They could not be discerned in the darkness. The Flood bellowed like a bull. The winds howled, shrieking like a wild donkey. The darkness was total. No sun was there."[8]

These and many other details burned themselves into the memories of the eight who lived through the Flood, and formed the more memorable details concerning the Flood that their children and their children's children carried with them as they dispersed after Babel over the face of the earth. It is no wonder they were remembered. It would have been astonishing had they not been.

## The Tower of Babel

The Tower of Babel is also remembered around the world, and in sometimes the most startling detail too. But starting with the Akkadians, they recalled Babel as *bab-ilim*, the Gate of (or to) the Gods. Later, the Babylonian King Nebuchadnezzar had the following to say about the Tower:

> "A former king" [Nimrod no doubt] "built the Temple of the Seven Lights of the Earth" [the then seven known planets] "but he did not complete its head." [due to the sudden confusion of tongues. Genesis 11:8 specifically states that the builders stopped work at this point] "Since a remote time, people had abandoned it... Since that time, earthquakes and lightning had dispersed its sun-dried clay; the bricks of the casing had split, and the earth of the interior had been scattered in heaps."[9]

From an obscure passage out of Berosus' *Babylonaica* (ca 280 BC), translated by a 2nd-century BC diplomat named Eupolemus, we further read:

> "The city of Babylon owes its foundation to those who were saved from the catastrophe of the Flood. These were the giants, and they built the tower which is noticed in history. But the tower being overthrown by the interposition of God, the giants were scattered over all the earth."[10]

The authenticity of the piece comes through when we consider that no mention is made here of the Confusion of Tongues at Babel. A mere rehash of Genesis 11 would surely have mentioned that. Eupolemus (fl. ca 160 BC) was the Jewish ambassador to Rome under the Maccabees,[11] and he has come down to us via a circuitous route through Eusebius and Polyhistor who both quote him. We are assured by the modernist school, though, that we must never confuse him with that dastardly pseudo-Eupolemus who gave us all this nonsense about the Tower of Babel. Quite so. It never ceases to amaze me how those ancient historians who tell us of secular matters are considered genuine, while those who tell us things which corroborate the Bible are called 'pseudo' - even though it is often the same historian!

In his book, *The Chaldean Account of Genesis*, George Smith complains that there is nothing on the subject of the Tower of Babel in Berosus (he was seemingly unaware of Eupolemus' translation);[12] no representation of Babel in Babylonian art, particularly on cylinder seals; and no written reference to it in the clay tablets. But then he says:

> "Early this year [1875] I was astonished to find, on having one of the Assyrian fragments cleaned, that it contained a mutilated account of part of the story of the tower. It is evident from the wording of the fragment that it was preceded by at least one tablet, describing the sin of the people in building the tower. The fragment preserved belongs to a tablet containing four to six columns of writing, of which fragments of four [columns] remain."[13]

Smith then translates for us Column 1 of the fragment, but because he follows the Babylonian word-order, it makes for difficult and awkward reading. In modern English syntax, it says this:

> "[Line 1]... them? The father... [2]...of him, his heart was evil... [3]...was wicked against the father of all the gods, [4]... of him, his heart was evil, [5]... brought Babylon to subjection, [8]... small and great, he confounded their speech. [9] all the day their strong tower they founded. [10 & 11] in the night, he entirely made an end to their strong place. [12] thus he poured out word also in his anger. [13] he set his face to scatter abroad. [14] he gave this command. Their counsel was confused."[14]

This is a remarkably close account to that which we read in the Book of Genesis, but it appears to be all that there is from Babylon. The hope is that from amongst the hundreds of thousands of clay tablets or their fragments that still await classification and translation, a more complete account of Babel will be published. Meanwhile, we shall see that the Akkadians and Babylonians were not the only ones to remember the Tower of Babel.

## The Confusion of Tongues

Interestingly, the early Sumerians afford us a glimpse of the immediate post-Babel world and the Confusion of Tongues in their history of *Enmerkar and the Lord of Aratta*.[15] In this account, Enmerkar, king of Uruk, pleads with the 'god' Enki to restore the unity of mankind's speech – "May they all pray to Enlil in unison, in a single tongue!" Mankind in Enmerkar's day, he tell us, consisted of just the populations of "Shubur [or Subartu to the north of Babylon], Hamazi [somewhere between Elam and Assyria], Sumer, Uri-ki [Akkad], and of the land of Martu [the Amorites]"[16] – from which it is evident that mankind was still confined to Mesopotamia, showing the very early date of the account.

Of great moment to those who lived through the Confusion of Tongues was the terrifying realisation that if they could not understand one another, then maybe the 'gods' couldn't understand them either. For the emerging pagan priesthood of the day, the people's fear made them ripe for the plucking.

## The Modernist Dilemma

Such further correspondences then are the simple ingredients in the pudding of world mythology. We will meet with them all, and more, as we consider the Flood accounts of peoples around the world. They are all of them recognisably borrowed from the Book of Genesis, and there is hardly a nation on earth whose dim and distant memories of the Flood do not contain at least one of them. Usually, of course, there are several found together, and their presence leaves the modernist school with some very awkward questions to answer. It is a great dilemma in which they find themselves, and so consistent that we may formulate it into law – a law which we shall briefly examine in the next chapter.

## Notes to Chapter Four

1) When Smith unearthed and deciphered the *Annals of Tiglath-pileser II*, the inscriptions of Sargon and Sennacherib, Esarhaddon, and the *Annals of Ashurbanipal*, he found the names of numerous kings and cities that are mentioned throughout the Old Testament, not just in the Book of Genesis. The existence and historicity of every one of these, and more, have at some time been challenged by the modernist school, and would be challenged still but for George Smith's work and expertise: Kings Rezin of Syria; Hiram of Tyre; Azariah of Judah; Pekah; Hoshea; Azaiah; Jehoahaz (or Ahaz); Menahem; Merodach Baladan; Hezekiah of Judah; the city of Ashdod besieged by Sargon (an event which is covered in Isaiah 20); the city of Hamath; and so on. More importantly, and unlike most other scholars who are still encountering these things today, Smith took the trouble to tell the Bible-believing public that he had found them.

2) Mesopotamia saw four great nations and cultures in its early days: Sumer, Akkad, Assyria and Babylonia, and they each told variations on the Genesis theme.

3) Dalley, pp. 181-188. Dalley spells the name Adapa. In fairness, the pronunciation of certain Sumerian characters is constantly being revised. Who knows? When the philological

head has stopped spinning, maybe we'll be back with Adamu. *The Epic of Atrahasis* names Adam as Lullu, the word meaning 'primeval' or 'savage' man whose creation was brought about by the goddess Nin-ti mixing the blood of a sacrificed god with clay.

4) Sollberger. *The Babylonian Legend of the Flood*, p. 23.

5) Morris and Whitcomb's *The Genesis Flood* gives by far the best treatment of the question of just how destructive the Flood was.

6) See Morris' *The Genesis Record*, p. 89.

7) E A Wallace Budge, *The Babylonian Story of the Deluge and the Epic of Gilgamesh*. For online transcript see: www.sacred-texts.com/ane/gilgdelu.htm

8) My paraphrase. *Epic of Atrahasis*, Tab. 3, col 2. See Dalley, p. 31 & Sollberger, p. 21.

9) www.answers.com/topic/tower-of-babel#Sumerian_parallel

10) Charles Horne. *Sacred Books and Early Literature of the East*, p. 26.

11) 1 Maccabees 8:17 & 2 Maccabees 4:11. The Books of Maccabees are perfectly historical books belonging to a body of literature known as the Old Testament Apocrypha. It is included between the Testaments in some Bibles.

12) George Smith. *Chaldean Account of Genesis*, p. 160.

13) Ibid.

14) Ibid, pp. 160-161.

15) www.answers.com/topic/enmerkar-and-the-lord-of-aratta

~ * ~

## Chapter Five: Interlude – The First and Second Laws of Frazer's Dilemma

There is a strange phenomenon abroad in the world of scholarship. It concerns what men have been saying about the Bible for the last few hundred years, and it is so consistent, invariable, and is seen working under so many different circumstances and conditions, that it has taken on the force of law. I know of not one circumstance in which it is encountered and observed not to work, so I have taken the liberty therefore of naming and formulating that law. I have called it (or rather them), The First and Second Laws of Frazer's Dilemma. The First Law says this:

> "Whenever attempts are made to disparage, dismiss, disallow and generally to denigrate and cast doubt upon the Word of God, no matter how ingeniously or determinedly those attempts are made, the more clearly and persistently they are seen to fail."

The Second Law of Frazer's Dilemma says this:

> "Rash claims that archaeology does not support the Bible in any particular matter, are always followed by archaeological discoveries which do support it."

We will see both these laws in operation as we proceed, but first a word of explanation concerning their title. They are named after Sir James Frazer (1854-1941) for the one good reason that he is the archetypal modernist. He made the disparagement and denigration of the Bible his life's work, and published at least twenty books on its disparagement, some of them multi-volume. For his efforts, the world of academe heaped honours and titles upon him. The title page of his *Folklore in the Old Testament* (1923 ed.), for example, lists him as Fellow of Trinity College Cambridge; Fellow of the Royal Society; FBA; Hon. DCL, Oxford; Hon. Litt. D, Cambridge and Durham; Hon. LL. D. Glasgow; and finally *Doctor Honoris Causa* of the Universities of Paris and Strasbourg.[1]

That the world of academe should bestow such garlands upon him is not surprising. By his great industry over a very long life, he bolstered up, on the popular level, everything that the modernist establishment stands for, namely the denigration of the Bible. Indeed, he provided them with much ammunition which is still in uncritical use today. The truly puzzling thing is, though, that the British Government should then seek to add to the accolades by bestowing upon him, in 1914, the highest honour at its disposal, namely a knighthood. What interest the state could possibly have had in making such an endorsement of Frazer's work is as mystifying today as it was back then. The publication of his *Golden Bough* in 1890 had caused nationwide offence. Then it was only a two-volume edition, but by 1915 he had expanded it (and the offence) to twelve volumes, with a thirteenth to follow later. With this and his other works, he was conducting an all-out campaign to destroy any credibility that the Bible might enjoy among the people. And for this he was knighted.[2]

One would think, therefore, that his works must have been of a great and lasting quality, of some intrinsic worth and merit at least. But alas for the plaudits, they weren't. Many of his arguments were known to be false (by himself in many cases) at the time of publication, and today one of his biographers has to confess that:

> "His theories of totemism" [he had at least three] "were superseded... and his vision of the annual sacrifice of the Year King has not been borne out by field studies. His generation's choice of Darwinian evolution as a social paradigm, interpreted by Frazer as three rising stages of human progress – magic giving rise to religion, then culminating in science – has not proved valid."[3]

"...not borne out by field studies.... has not proved valid." – in other words, *every* assumption that Frazer built his life's work upon, was just plain wrong. That is a large statement, but we do not make it lightly. 'Magic giving rise to religion, then culminating in science' was an assumption of a three-stage evolution of human thought beloved by Frazer, and was everything that he had set out to prove. It underlay every word that he ever wrote and every thought of his working day. In a word, he set out to show that the Old Testament, and hence the

New, was nothing but bunkum, and he built all that upon a Darwinian foundation that is the greatest bunkum of all. Extraordinary. Countless souls have been turned away from the Bible on the strength of what he told them, and told them with a monumental arrogance which he pretended, with the backing of both academe and state government, was great wisdom and learning. That was an immense and tragic mistake on their part.

In the course of our present enquiry, as we refer to his book, *Folklore in the Old Testament*, we shall see just some of the many false statements that he put out about the world's Flood traditions. Particularly, we shall see the almost habitual inconsistencies that he uses to throw dust in the eyes of his readers. What he says on one page is often contradicted on a following page. We will see this as we go along, but here we may simply note that the defining word for our First Law is 'Inconsistency.'

For the Second Law, it is surely 'Irony.' Since modernism and Biblical criticism first got underway, there has been noticed a regularity of occurrence which is breathtaking, and so regular that it is now safely predictable. To remind ourselves, the Second Law states: "Rash claims that archaeology does not support the Bible in any particular matter, are always followed by archaeological discoveries which do support it." – and this has been true from day one. Consider the following example.

Balaam, the evil prophet of the Book of Numbers (chaps. 22-24), has long been dismissed as a non-historical literary device invented to adorn the Biblical fiction, as modernists are pleased to call it. But what happens then? In exact accordance with our Second Law, somebody unearths a lengthy inscription concerning Balaam, the son of Beor, and one of his prophecies. The discovery was made at Deir-Alla in Jordan, and now lies in the Archaeological Museum in Amman.[4] Is it the same Balaam? Certainly it is. Both the Bible and the inscription refer to him as Balaam, son of Beor (the inscription carrying the identification no less than three times in just its first four lines). So there can be no doubt that the Balaam of the Bible and the Balaam of the inscription are one and the same person.

One could multiply examples of archaeology and the historical record making a nonsense of modernists' claims.[5] But let us illustrate the matter this way. Before us on the table is a painted object. We can't see what it's made of, but its maker has left us a note to say that it is made of pure gold. Not willing to take the maker's word on that, we publicly denounce him to be a liar. Moreover, we also announce that we will prove him a liar by removing the paint and showing the world that underneath the paint is nothing but base metal. It would have been better science had we removed the paint first and then decided if he were a liar or no. But this is inductive modernism, and so we will call him a liar first, and then begin by removing the paint. However, on removing the paint we find that in fact the article really is made of gold, just like its maker said. So where do we go from here? Well, we prolong the proceedings by now scraping away at the gold, hoping to show the world that it is only a veneer to make us think that the object is made of solid gold. But the deeper we scrape, the more gold we find, and there's not a trace of base metal to be seen, leaving us to lamely excuse ourselves with the rejoinder, Well, it depends what you mean by gold. Now, that is Frazer's Dilemma, only it doesn't concern painted objects. It concerns the Word of God – the Old and New Testaments of the Bible.

In his *Folklore in the Old Testament*, Frazer sets out to show that because the same ingredients – the Flood, the Tree of Life, Eden and so on – are found in pagan mythologies and folklore around the world, then that proves that the Old Testament itself is nothing but folklore. But that is to confuse the fruit with the tree that it grows upon. By setting out to prove that the Old Testament is nothing more than folklore on the mistaken assumption that anything that gives rise to folklore must itself be folklore, he ends up proving the opposite. He had an inkling of his own dilemma when he first began his work, which is why his output became so immense. Writing some twenty books upon what is essentially the same subject has the air of panic about it. But like all laws, the Law of Frazer's Dilemma is implacable. The more a man tries to show that what is True is false, the more he has to explain why the evidence eludes him, from which all future Bible critics may draw a moral. In short, if you wish your scholarship to be sound, then never base it on anything that Charles Darwin ever said or did. You will only come to grief if you do.

James Frazer, of course, should have known a thing or two about the operation of law. He studied it after graduating at Trinity College and was called to the bar in 1879, though he never practiced. In his legal studies, he would have learned all about the importance of witness statements and cross examination, particularly of disinterested or even hostile witnesses. Yet he chose in his academic career to ignore it all. He amassed witness statements by their thousands, certainly. He had to, to give his work an objective and forensic air. But he used those statements and testimonies in an attempt to prove a case which he certainly knew, by every forensic rule, to be false. Today these things are a matter of record, though his works, false or no, are still eagerly pillaged by modernist authors. It says a great deal about the discipline.

It is disturbing to think how much ink has been spilt by tens of thousands of scholars over the centuries who have made it their life's work to disparage the Bible. Worse than spilling ink, they have spilled their own immortals souls to that end, deceiving millions on the way, yet still the Bible shows itself to be made of the purest gold. It is still the life-giving Word and the absolute and unassailable Truth that it has always been, and it has withstood every test and has worn out every hammer that has ever beaten against it over thousands of years past, the Frazers of this world notwithstanding.

## Notes to Chapter Five

1) *Folklore in the Old Testament*. Title page.

2) If it puzzles you as to why any state government should wish to honour, with one of the highest awards at its disposal, one who has set himself against the Word of God as thoroughly and as notoriously as Frazer did, then read Bowden (see Bibliography) and Morris' *The Long War against God.*

3) http://en.wikipedia.org/wiki/James_George_Frazer

4) Dijkdstra, Meindert. 'Is Balaam among the Prophets?' *Journal of Biblical Literature*. Vol. 114, Issue 1 (1995). pp. 43-64. & Weippert, Manfred. 'The Balaam Text from Deir 'Alla and the Study of the Old Testament.' *The Balaam Text from Deir 'Alla Re-Evaluated.* (Leiden: E J Brill. 1991). pp. 151-184.

5) Challenged by the claims of modernism, I personally once subjected the 10th and 11th chapters of Genesis to an exceedingly severe test, a test that went on for more than 25 years. What I demanded of the chapters was unreasonable, yet the more I tested them, the more these chapters showed themselves to be 100% reliable and factual history. Modernism would have had me believe that they were nothing more than folklore. That work can be seen in my book, *After the Flood* (see Bibliography).

## Chapter Six: Why not a Local Flood?

George Smith, having contributed so much to the field of Bible apologetics, died of dysentery in 1876, the year in which his *Chaldean Account of Genesis* was published. His death at such a young age (36) was a tragedy for Bible believers and for Bible scholarship. He died at Aleppo in Syria whilst on his third journey to Iraq, leaving his wife alone in London to bring up their six small children in poverty.[1]

The man who came to fill his shoes at the British Museum fared somewhat better, being blessed with long life, a knighthood, fame and much fortune. His name was E A Wallace Budge who was a rising star in modernist circles and a practicing spiritualist to boot. His appointment meant that the eagerly received supply of Bible corroborations which George Smith had constantly published, dried up almost instantly. What had been found and could not be hidden – what was already published in other words – was denigrated by Wallace Budge and others in the usual way.[2] But mostly, the information released to the public about the ongoing work of classification and translation of the tablets, was confined to talking about royal household accounts, diplomatic correspondence, wars, rumours of wars, more wars, and other such stuff, the kind of things that laundry lists are made of. And that is how it has continued to this day.

The most telling part of the tale, though, and one that is exceedingly relevant to our enquiry, is that after Smith's death – and this alone is a tribute to his many achievements – modernism had to go into hyper-drive in order to reverse what he had begun, and disprove any silly notion that the Bible had been in any way vindicated by the Babylonian finds.[3]

The appointment of Wallace Budge at the British Museum was a major part of this effort, only to falter when his spiritualism drove him to switch to Egyptology. But of special concern for the modernists was to disprove the notion that the Flood spoken of by Genesis was in any way global in its effects. This was vital for the critics, simply because Genesis speaks unequivocally of a global deluge which destroyed all mankind and every air-breathing creature from off the face of the earth – save those in the Ark. If it could once be shown that the Flood was not a global deluge, and if that could be proved by pointing to a layer of silt in Babylonia left there by a local inundation, and if someone of sufficient renown in archaeology could proclaim in a sober 'scientific' voice that that was the flood referred to in the Book of Genesis, then perhaps, just perhaps, centuries of hard toil might at last bear fruit, and the Bible might be discredited once and for all. That was the hope. The problem though was not what the Book of Genesis said about the Flood – which everyone laughed at anyway. It was what the Babylonian account said of it. It was all very awkward.

We came across the Babylonian version of the Flood in Chapter Two, where, using George Smith's more literal translation, we paraphrased a certain portion of the Flood tablet (Gilgamesh XI). We will consider it again here, whilst emphasising certain relevant lines:

> [line 101]: "*The flood reached up to heaven and the earth was made a desolation. It swept the face of the earth. It destroyed all life from the face of the earth. The storm that broke over the people swept up to heaven. Brother saw not his brother. None of the people was spared*" [line 121]: "*Six days and nights passed, and the wind and the tempest and the storm overwhelmed all.* On the seventh day, the storm was calmed in its course, and the tempest that had destroyed like an earthquake, was quieted. He caused the waters to dry, and the storm and tempest ended. I was carried through the waters. *The evildoer and the whole of mankind that had turned to sin, their corpses floated like driftwood.* I opened the window and light poured in."[4]

From this it would appear that the Babylonian version is just as emphatic in saying that the Flood was global as is the Book of Genesis, so it is odd that the critics should look to Babylonia for evidence to the contrary. As far as their writings were concerned, the Babylonians agreed with Genesis completely that the Flood was global. Every living thing that breathed air was wiped off the face of the earth. But all that was about to be challenged.

There was at this time – we are now in the 1920s and Wallace Budge is at the height of his career – another rising star in the modernist heavens, an archaeologist named Leonard Woolley. He had won his spurs (Indiana Jones-style) back in 1907 during an expedition into Nubia, and in 1914 had excavated the ancient Hittite city of Carchemish.[5] He could easily have offended his modernist colleagues by doing this, as it had long been held by them that the Hittites were but a figment of Jewish imagination. Far from being that, however, it transpired that the Hittite Empire had been the largest of all the others in the ancient world. It is hard not to laugh.

The work of localising the Genesis Flood, however, began in 1922 when Woolley was sent to dig up what was probably the most famous city in the Bible (save Jerusalem). That city was the city of Ur – or Ur of the Chaldees – once home to the patriarch Abraham. In the 1929 season, his excavations took him down to a layer of sterile silt, sterile meaning that it was devoid of any archaeology. About 12 feet (or 3.75 metres) further down, traces of archaeology were again encountered, making it plain that the sterile layer was due merely to local flooding.

How he conducted himself when he discovered the layer is best told in Woolley's own words, though as he tells us, we would do well to bear in mind that he knew perfectly well that all he was looking at was a layer of silt from a local flood. As an archaeologist of renown, he must have come across similar layers many times:

> "I got into the pit once more, examined the sides, and by the time I had written up my notes was quite convinced of what it all meant; but I wanted to see whether others would come to the same conclusion. So I brought up two of my staff and, after pointing out the facts, asked for their explanation. They did not know what to say. My wife came along and looked and was asked the same question, and she turned away remarking casually, 'Well, of course, it's the flood."[6]

Woolley, first and foremost, was at Ur to wave the modernist flag, and seemingly on the strength of his wife's remark, announced to the world that he had found Noah's Flood. But can he really have been that uncritical of the evidence before him? In his account, he gives but a weak impression of exercising any scientific rigour. Making a feeble show of objectivity, he wants us to believe that, given the immensity of the conclusion, he dared not trust to his own opinion, and so sought the opinion of others. But all he can muster at what was a well-attended dig, are two members of his staff. Whether they were, like himself, qualified archaeologists he doesn't say. They might have been secretaries. In fact, their baffled and embarrassed silence at Woolley's questioning – even after he had led them by the hand by 'pointing out the facts' – suggests most strongly that they were not qualified to give an informed archaeological opinion. And then there is his wife's clinching observation, given over her shoulder as she walked away, affecting an air of complete nonchalance. Was it really possible for her to have 'come along' and then to 'walk away' speaking over her shoulder, when she was supposed to have been standing at the bottom of a 52-feet deep pit? It just doesn't ring true, any of it.

But however it was, and notwithstanding the fact that modernists had always denied that Noah's Flood had ever occurred, the news was received with great glee around the world, for the simple reason that it showed that what Genesis described as the Flood of Noah was nothing more than a folk-memory of some local inundation in Mesopotamia. Doubtless, the fact that Abraham had come from Ur (if he had ever existed that is), meant that he must have carried into Canaan some recollections about this flood, and these stories were in turn blown out of all proportion and later incorporated into the jottings of those priestly editors who busied themselves by forging the Scriptures. More importantly, uniformitarian geologists were proved right; the Darwinists could now sleep comfy in their beds; and the Bible critics could now boast that they had – at long last! – got something right. Good for Woolley, and good for the world. That's all settled then. But alas for the critics, nothing is ever that simple when the Book of Genesis is challenged.

Not a million miles from where Woolley was digging (just 130 miles in fact) two fellow archaeologists were excavating the ancient city of Kish. They were Captain E MacKay and Stephen Langdon, and they too came across a layer of flood silt as they dug down. There were flurries of excitement all round, until somebody asked the question, Could it be dated to the time of Woolley's layer? Alas, no, it couldn't. It was every bit as impressive as Woolley's it has to be said, but it was at best merely a rival for our affections. It was – and still is – a deeply embarrassing episode for the modernist school. Rohl laments the fact that:

> "The matter is rarely discussed these days and little further research has been devoted to either dating the flood or, for that matter, demonstrating that a major flood took place at all.... Small wonder, then, that whenever the flood *is* discussed in popular works on Sumerian archaeology... [it] is then argued that the events surrounding the deposition of the silt layer at Shuruppak acted as the stimulus for the Genesis flood narrative."[7]

The mention of Shuruppak here, and not of Ur, refers to the later ill-judged attempt to pin the origins of the Genesis Flood onto the silt layers of Shuruppak and Kish, these pre-dating Woolley's layer at Ur as well as being contemporaneous with one another. Ill-judged indeed, but with nothing else to fight with, modernists continue to this day to persuade the unwary that a puddle of sludge in Mesopotamia is what gave rise to the Genesis 'legend' of the Great Flood. They even try to spoil the Genesis narrative further by pointing out that the Babylonian account has the Ark more probably coming to rest on Mount Nizir, and not upon Ararat at all.[8]

They little consider the fact – or at least, they forget to mention it to their readers – that such a flood as they propose would actually have washed the Ark out into the Persian Gulf, and in quite the opposite direction of *any* mountain, Nizir included. And there lies their problem. Since the day when men first wandered into Shinar, the largest river-induced flood that Mesopotamia has ever suffered (whichever one that was), was never deep enough to deposit a vessel the size of the Ark even halfway up a molehill, never mind a mountain. To possess such power, the flood would in any case have to come in from the sea, and have a sufficiently strong impetus to not just resist, but to overcome the waters of the Tigris and Euphrates rivers as they flowed down to the sea and away from the mountains. And, of course, it would have to have been many thousands of feet deep, even for Mount Nizir.

But, getting back to Woolley, his embarrassment, which is evident throughout his account, was deepened by his own awareness that the flooding at Ur had not even covered the entire city, which is not very large in any case. It's how he knew that it was worth extending his flood pit down another 12 feet or so to find the archaeology underneath. In any normal dig, excavations cease once sterile soil or bedrock is reached. But the waters had encroached over just part of the city, and it seems that he was entirely aware of the sheer dishonesty of the claim that he'd been asked to make. It is what made what should have been a world-shattering announcement so utterly wimpish.

No wonder there was a sudden shift away from Woolley and Ur, and on to Shuruppak and Kish for some kind of evidence for the modernist claim. At least that flooding had covered a slightly larger area than the tiny one at Ur, though even that one was itself so puny that it is no longer even discussed. If the Flood was really that tiny, then why build an Ark for animals and humans to survive in? It would have been easier to have run away to higher ground. And then, how would you get sufficient warning about the Flood to give you time to build the Ark in the first place? And, of course, if God is a fiction as they would have us believe, then who could possibly warn you of its coming? I think we should be told.

The Shuruppak-Kish idea was not, however, the last attempt to persuade us away from the universality of the Genesis Flood. It has, in fact, been superseded by the latest newcomer to the field of local flooding, and that is Ryan and Pitman's notion that the filling of the Black Sea basin represents the origin of the Flood narratives, both Genesis and pagan.[9]

Now it has to be said that Ryan and Pitman (geologists both at Columbia University) have done some stunning research, bringing to light an historical cataclysm that was hardly suspected until they began their work. But they have proffered their suggestion of this being the Genesis Flood, and they have proffered it on the wrong surmise, namely that the Flood was a local thing, albeit it put a new sea on the map. It might appear a more plausible candidate than Ur or even Shuruppak, but it is a local flood nonetheless, and not a global one. We say nothing here about the date they suggest for this event, 7200 BC. The earth, according to Biblical chronology, was not even here that long ago.

So yet another candidate fails the test and joins all the other failed candidates, including those theories of Atlantis being the source of the Flood narrative, the destruction of the Minoan civilisation being the source, and so on. Their proposers refuse to accept the fact that when Genesis speaks of a Global Flood, it isn't joking. Nor, when it speaks of a Global Flood, is it trying to deceive us. Genesis is the Word of God, and God is not a man that He should lie. He flooded the earth in its entirety, pure and simple, just as He said He would, and any 'theory' which tries to ignore or disprove that fact, has lost before it has even begun.[10]

But we have learned much in these chapters about how the peoples of Mesopotamia – the Sumerians, the Akkadians, the Babylonians, the Assyrians – preserved in their folklore and mythologies definite and recognisable memories of persons, places, things and events that are mentioned in the Book of Genesis. I don't suppose for one moment that we have exhausted the subject. The Flood of Noah has been predominant, of course. Mesopotamia *should* remember the Flood. It is where the 'heroes' of the Flood – Noah, Shem, Ham and Japheth – lived to pass on to their children and their children's children after them the things that had happened and what they had seen, some of them incidental and not mentioned in Genesis, but all of them vindicating what the Book of Genesis says.

Moreover, Mesopotamia was the land of Babel, the Confusion of Tongues, and the dispersal of the nations to all quarters of the earth. The people, as they dispersed, each carried some, though none carried all, of the memories of those events and persons, so that each isle, each nation and each continent could be global witnesses to the Truth of God's Word. Some have been unwitting witnesses, and some indeed have been unwilling witnesses, hostile as they are toward their Maker. But all are witnesses nonetheless, and we shall hear them speak as we now leave Mesopotamia and go around the world.

We have also learned something of how modernism has dealt with the subject, and when we encounter its objections and arguments against the statements of these witnesses, we shall duly weigh them. Modernism, after all, has an agenda. It has a case to prove, and its self-appointed role is to contest the Word of God and prove it false.

But as it does its work, we shall see the Laws of Frazer's Dilemma coming into play, the laws that turn modernism in upon itself to the vindication and corroboration of God's Word, the Bible. More important than any academic law, we shall also see how the Word of God, when it is tried and tested, always shows itself to be true – true to history and true to God.

## Notes to Chapter Six

1) Having been told of George Smith's death, Queen Victoria 'was pleased' to bestow a pension on Mary Smith, his widow. But it was a miserly one of only £150 a year (Damrosch, p. 77). The royal spaniels fared better. What became of Mary Smith and the children, we do not know.

2) In his *Rise and Progress of Assyriology* (1925), Wallace Budge attempted to portray George Smith nearly fifty years after his death as an emotionally-charged buffoon who was unfitted for the tasks appointed him (Damrosch, pp. 64-80), forgetting that from 1872 onwards Smith had taken him under his wing and had taught him the Assyrian language, in spite of his own horrendous workload. Wallace Budge, in other words, owed the launch of his career to George Smith's Christian kindness and patience. But Wallace Budge was no stranger to slandering his friends and colleagues, and in 1893 was even sued for it. But then, paying no more than faint lip service to 'liberal Christianity' whilst he pursued his spiritualism, there was little to restrain or improve him. His interests turned from Assyriology to Egyptology because, like himself, the Egyptians had little to say about the Bible, and they worshipped the dead. Admired by Blavatsky, the founder of the Theosophical (Luciferian) Society; involved in the Ghost Club, the spiritualist 'church' founded in 1862 by the apostate Bible critics Westcott and Hort; and a member of the occultic Hermetic Order of the Golden Dawn, Wallace Budge was steeped in devilry – and this was the man that the British Museum selected to replace George Smith. It hardly bears thinking about.

3) It seems that after nearly 140 years, little has changed. Between 13th-28th November 2008, the British Museum commissioned and staged a play about him, entitled *Smith*, as part of their Babylonian Exhibition. Astonishingly, he was portrayed as an 'overwrought' religious fool in a script that was not entirely devoid of expletives. Reversing the truth of the matter, and taking their cue from the Museum no doubt, one of its reviewers informs us that the discovery by Smith of the Babylonian Flood narrative, "constituted a weighty blow to the *Bible* both as a historical record and as revered scripture." (www.whatsonstage.com/blogs/offwestend/?p=744). Nothing could be further from the truth, and the British Museum surely knows that. It was a shameful and odious way in which to treat the memory of a man who had served the Museum so well. But the wounds he inflicted on modernism all those years ago, obviously still hurt – and hurt a lot if this 'play' is anything to go by.

4) It has to be said that the Babylonian account of the Flood is far closer to Genesis than is that of Sumer. The Flood was caused by man's sinfulness and not just by the noise and hubbub he'd been making. Moreover, it was a global Flood as opposed to Sumer's destruction of just one city. It is why George Smith's paper which he read to the Society of Biblical Archaeology caused such a storm.

5) Woolley did not discover Carchemish. George Smith did. He had discovered and identified the city almost 40 years before whilst delayed at Aleppo. A H Sayce, who wrote George Smith's obituary, tells us, "...and at Yerabolus [Smith] discovered the ancient Hittite capital Carchemish – a discovery which bids fair to rival in importance that of Nineveh itself." 'George Smith'. *Littell's Living Age*. vol 31. Issue 1687. The Bible-believing Smith is never formally credited with its discovery though.

6) Woolley. *Ur of the Chaldees*. 1982 (revised ed). London, p. 25.

7) Rohl, p. 170.

8) But see George Smith's interesting discussion of this very point towards the end of his paper in Appendix One of this book.

9) Ryan & Pitman. *Noah's Flood.* 1999. Scribner.

10) The late Dr Henry Morris lists no less than 100 scientific and literary reasons why we should take Genesis very seriously indeed when it talks of a global Flood (*The Genesis Record*, pp. 683-686). For a more in-depth treatment of the subject, see his book which he authored with Dr John Whitcomb, *The Genesis Flood.* See also his paper, 'Why Christians should believe in a Global Flood.' www.icr.org/article/842/

# Chapter Seven: Ancient Egypt and Africa

Egypt. Of all the places on this earth, Egypt has to be the least likely to yield any knowledge of the events and personages recorded in the Book of Genesis. For centuries out of mind, the entire society of Ancient Egypt was steeped in idolatry, saturated with pagan ignorance and darkness, and it seems impossible to imagine that anything resembling even a faint knowledge of the One True God, the God of Genesis, could possibly exist there. And yet, as we are about to discover, God never leaves Himself without a witness, even in such a land as this.

The land has only borne the name of Egypt since 332 BC, when Alexander the Great conquered it.[1] But before his day, the land did bear witness to the Book of Genesis in its original name, *Kamit* – or the Land of Ham, this being the name of one of Noah's sons and a favoured Biblical name for Egypt.[2] But though much, that is not all. Consider the following remarkable statement concerning the knowledge of God in Egypt during that country's very earliest days. To say the least, the information contained in the statement is unexpected, and it comes as a further surprise that it should issue not from some Bible-believer, but from a scholar of the modernist school. The scholar's name is Rudolph Anthes, and he says this:

> "It may appear striking to find both the concepts of the universal, eternal god [*sic*] and the trinity of this god as early as 3000 BC.... As for the trinity, the earliest evidence is the carving on the ivory comb of King Zet, 'the Serpent', of about 2900 BC."[3]

'Striking' is not the word for it. Modernism has done its work thoroughly in concealing this startling fact all these years. But there we have it. Before paganism took over the land – and early Egyptian paganism bears an uncanny resemblance to that of Mesopotamia – the people of Egypt were, during their most ancient times, celebrating their knowledge of the One True God. And not only that, but they were also deeply aware that God is a Trinity, three Persons in one Godhead.

"Thus," [says our author] "the idea that the eternal and universal god exists is attested at the very beginning of Egyptian history."[4]

Egyptologists have been privy to this information since the 19th century, though you'd never guess that from their books. Even Anthes, our author, tries hard to play it down, using it merely as a springboard from which to dive immediately into the tortuous twists and turns of pagan Egyptian mythology. But the cat, as they say, is now out of the proverbial bag. Instead of the favoured and much vaunted modernist teaching that the Old Testament concept of God 'evolved' out of pagan mythology, we see that precisely the opposite is the case. Even the early Egyptians *began* with the knowledge of God, but later lost it through their tumble into paganism.

But, apart from King Zet's comb, what evidence have the early Egyptians themselves left us of their knowledge of God? And just how deep did that knowledge go? Well, therein lies another surprise. The name (or one of the names) by which they knew God, was Aton, and those with a little Hebrew will know that word. It is Adonai, or Lord, which is one of God's names in the Old Testament. But their deepest awareness of God seems to have been of God as the Creator of all things. They even wrote hymns to Him, some of which have survived from those most ancient of times, and outside the Bible itself, they are among the most profoundly beautiful expressions of faith, thanks and praise that are to be found anywhere on earth. Consider this verse which an unnamed Egyptian penned to God when he considered the creation and procreation of birds. It is astonishing:

"O God alone, beside Whom there is no other,[5] when the fledgling in the egg chirps in the shell, Thou givest him breath therein to preserve him alive. When Thou hast brought him together, to the point of bursting it in the egg, he cometh forth from the egg to chirp with all his might. He goeth about on his two feet when he hath come forth therefrom."[6]

You can hear the writer's joy and wonder at the Creation and the God Who brought it all into being. When he considered all the things that had to happen just to enable a chick to hatch, he looked to the Creator of all things and praised Him. But a slightly longer hymn to the Lord and Creator, is this:

> "O God alone, besides Whom there is no other, how manifold are Thy works! They are hidden from before us, O God alone, Whose powers no other possesseth. Thou didst create the earth according to Thy pleasure whilst Thou wast alone. Men, all cattle large and small, all that are upon the earth that goeth about on their feet; all that are on high that fly with their wings.... Thou settest every man into his place. Thou suppliest his necessities. Everyone has his possessions and his days are reckoned. The tongues are diverse in speech, their forms likewise and their skins are distinguished, for Thou makest different the strangers."[7]

And in another such hymn, the writer strikes a note that would surely not be out of place in the Bible's Book of Psalms: "How excellent are Thy designs, O Lord of Eternity!"[8]

Here we have then, at the very outset of our enquiry, a profound and lively awareness amongst the early Egyptians of the One True God, the Creator of all – the God of Genesis. Who would have thought it? It was not to last though:

> "In consequence of the historical situation, this highly spiritual concept of God was not permitted to affect Egyptian popular religion..."[9]

Such was the onslaught of paganism that, once it was established, all trace of the knowledge of God amongst the Egyptians is lost to us. Doubtless, those who continued to hold dear the knowledge of God, did so out of sight and hearing of the heathen who would undoubtedly have destroyed them. But the records, such as we have, are silent.

Concerning any distinct memories of the Great Flood amongst the Egyptians, we have to say that almost all trace of them is lost - or dimmed almost to the point of obliteration. Records discovered so far make no mention of it – assuming there are no more surprises in store like the ones we have just considered. There is one faint trace though of a Flood tradition that may be discerned in a much later Egyptian work called *The Book of Going Forth by Day*, in which Atum (a later perverted memory of Adonai) says that he will submerge the world with all its gods and men in Nun (the primeval waters), and that only he and another 'god' will survive in the form of serpents.[10] It is, of course, but a satanic parody of the Genesis account, but it does indicate at least that a surer and purer knowledge of the Great Flood was known amongst the earlier Egyptians and was later perverted to this.

## 'Darkest' Africa

As we leave Egypt and go further into the African continent, we shall see not only how Africans remembered the Flood, but how both the First *and* the Second Laws of Frazer's Dilemma come into play, for we are told by Frazer and by every modernist authority that came after him that there are no recollections of the Flood there. There are as many religions amongst the indigenous and native populations of Africa as there are tribes, and between them they worship a veritable sea of 'gods' under a veritable sea of names – and in a veritable sea of languages too. Yet, according to one authority, they all hold certain beliefs in common. They all believe in a supreme God, but He is remote from them, the gulf in between being filled with intermediaries ranging from witch-doctors to tribal saints. They lack any concept of either hell or purgatory, and therefore, by extrapolation, any notion of sin. None of them have any written 'scriptures'. They have no prophets as such, and they are commonly devoted to their dead ancestors.[11] And then we come to this curious assurance:

> "In Africa, including Egypt, native legends of a great flood are conspicuously absent; indeed, no single clear case of one has yet to be reported."[12]

This somewhat emphatic statement was written by Sir James Frazer, and it appears on page 132 of his book, *Folklore in the Old Testament*. When he wrote it, however, he must have forgotten that only two pages previously he had written a rather lengthy piece on the Flood tradition that is preserved amongst the Masai, a distinctly African people if ever there was one. Quoting 'German writers' – missionaries and so on – and in particular a German officer who lived amongst the Masai, Frazer tells us how the Masai remembered the Flood of Noah, whom they called Tumbainot:

> "Tumbainot was a righteous man whom God loved. He married a wife, Naipande, who bore him three sons, Oshomo, Bartimaro, and Marmao. When his brother Lengerni died, Tumbainot, in accordance with Masai custom, married the widow Nahaba-logunja.... She bore her second husband three sons.... In those days the world was thickly peopled, but men were not good. On the contrary, they were sinful and did not obey God's commands. However, bad as they were, they refrained from murder. But at last, one unlucky day, a certain man named Nambija knocked another man named Suage on the head. This was more than God could bear, and he resolved to destroy the whole race of mankind. Only the pious Tumbainot found grace in the eyes of God, who commanded him to build an ark of wood, and go into it, with his two wives, his six sons, and their wives, taking with him some animals of every sort."[13]

Frazer goes on to relate to us how once everybody was aboard the ark, God caused it to rain so heavily that all men and beasts were drowned save those aboard the ark. Eventually the rains stopped, and Tumbainot sent out a dove to see if the waters had subsided. The dove returned, and several days later Tumbainot sent out a vulture. Finally the waters abated, and as Tumbainot left the ark, he saw four rainbows, one in each quarter of the sky, which he took as a sign that God's anger was satisfied.

Frazer is careful to suggest that this story originated from tales told by Christian missionaries, but if that were true then they must have been strange kinds of missionary. Would not the tradition of the Masai have been closer to the Genesis account if they had obtained the story so recently? There were missionaries working with the Masai to be sure, but they were not the kind of missionary that carried a Bible about with them. To put it bluntly, the German missionaries who worked among the Masai were not known for their Biblical conservatism, having been trained for the most part in the new liberal German colleges of the 'higher critics'. Vindicating and spreading the Book of Genesis was not a priority with them. Albert Schweitzer, who avowedly despised the Bible yet called himself a missionary, is perhaps the most famous of his kind, the new breed of 'missionary' which was trained and sent out to expand the west's knowledge of anthropology and exploration, paving the way for the empire of the Fatherland rather than spreading the Gospel of Jesus Christ.

For many reasons Frazer must have sensed that the Masai tradition was indigenous. He certainly sensed it in the next 'conspicuously absent' account from Africa that he gives, for he plainly states:

> "Another version of the flood story is reported by a German missionary from the same region. He obtained it at the mission-station at Mkulwe, on the Sasai or Momba River, about twenty miles from where the river flows into Lake Rukwa. His informant professed to have had it from his grandfather, and stoutly asserted that it was a genuine old tradition of the country and not borrowed from foreigners. His statement was corroborated by another truth-loving native who only differed from his fellow in opining that the African Noah sent out two doves instead of one."[14]

Frazer maintains that these accounts cannot be original because they are 'mere variations of the Biblical narrative'. But of course they are. What else could they be but variations? Would Frazer have accepted them had they been verbatim accounts? Of course he wouldn't have, and neither would we. They are variations to a greater or lesser degree because they rely on memories passed down through many generations. Naturally they will suffer distortion, but that is the very hallmark of their integrity. Frazer studied law, and in his training he was made fully aware of the phenomenon of eye-witnesses who give different accounts of the same event. To dismiss statements because they follow an entirely natural path and vary from one another is unreasonable, about as unreasonable, not to say irrational, as the following opinion of Frazer's when he dismisses a Flood tradition on the curious grounds that it doesn't resemble Genesis sufficiently:

> "In Northern Guinea, we are told, there is a 'tradition of a great deluge which once overspread the face of the whole

earth'; but it is coupled with so much that is marvellous and imaginative, that it can scarcely be identified with the same event recorded in the Bible."[15]

I would dearly love to know what these 'marvellous and imaginative' details were. Clearly, they worried Frazer sufficiently for him to avoid telling us about them. He is happy enough throughout his large book to relate other 'marvellous and imaginative' – not to say ridiculous – details when they make a mockery of the Flood and the Book of Genesis, but not these details.

In all, Frazer gives no less than six African peoples who held indigenous accounts of the Flood: those in Northern Guinea; a tribe in the Lower Congo; the Bapedi, who were a Basuto tribe of South Africa; those who live around Lake Dilolo in Angola; the Masai, whose account we have considered; and those who live in Mkulwe on the Momba River in East Africa. He damns those traditions that are close to Genesis, and damns those that aren't. Yet in the same breath, he solemnly assures us that in all Africa, "Native legends of a great flood are conspicuously absent..." – an extraordinary statement, but one that passes as scholarship amongst the Bible's critics.

But even these six are not all, for Flood traditions are also to be found in the following parts of Africa, and I don't suppose for one moment that this exhausts the supply: Ababua in Northern Zaire; Bachokwe in Southern Zaire; Bakongo in Western Zaire; Basonge; Bena Lulua on the Congo River in Southeast Zaire; Cameroon; Efik Ibibio in Nigeria; Ekoi, also in Nigeria; Kikuyu in Kenya; Komililo Nandi; Kwaya on Lake Victoria; Mandingo on the Ivory Coast; Pygmy (Congo); Southwest Tanzania; and Yoruba in Southwest Nigeria.[16]

Each of these traditions is of greater or lesser quality, but they are traditions nonetheless which the natives had held and have passed on since time immemorial, and certainly before the arrival of the white man and his missionaries. Together, they paint a rather different picture to that which modernism is pleased to present us with, a picture of a sterile Africa which knows nothing of any Flood.

The Flood, however, was not the only item or event from Genesis that was remembered among the peoples of Africa. The Tower of Babel is also commemorated. The famous Victorian explorer, Dr David Livingstone, who certainly was the first white man to reach the Victoria Falls on the Zambesi, recorded amongst the natives there an account of the Tower in which the Tower collapses, killing its builders. The A-Louyi tribe on the Upper Zambesi, the Bambala of the Congo, the people of Mkulwe, whose Flood tradition we considered earlier, and likewise the Ashantee carry strikingly similar traditions. We owe this additional information again to Sir James Frazer, who would doubtless spin in his grave if he knew what a help he'd been, for that wasn't the object of his life's work at all.[17]

But the offence of modernism is this. It pretends to know all. It assumes that its readers know little. And on the basis of a form of scholarship that is immensely sloppy at best, and downright deceitful on all other levels, its proponents – Frazer especially among them – would have us believe that it is the Word of God that is false, and God Himself – the God of all Truth – Who is the liar. It is a strange agenda for men to pursue who would have us believe that they are impartial and 'scientific' searchers after truth. What drives them to it, I wouldn't like to say.

## Notes to Chapter Seven

1) For what the Bible says about Alexander, see Daniel 8:5-8 & 21-22. He also appears in the apocryphal though perfectly historical 1 Maccabees 1:1-17.

2) 1 Chronicles 4:40; Psalm 78:51; 105:23; 105:27; & 106:22.

3) Anthes, Rudolph. 'Mythology in Ancient Egypt'. p. 34 (see Bibliography). The dates 3000-2900 BC are the conventional dates of modernism, but as any Egyptologist worth his salt will readily admit, they are tentative at best. Shaving them down by seven hundred years or so would cure all.

4) Ibid, p. 35.

5) This line heads all of the short hymns to the Creator. I have placed it here even though the quoted source for the rest of the hymn places it in the footnotes.

6) Horne, Chas. *The Sacred Books and Early Literature of the East: Egypt*. vol 2. p. 293.

7) Ibid. The word ‘heart’ is best rendered ‘pleasure’ here (line 4). And Horne’s ‘sole God’ is far better rendered ‘God alone’, which is as I have given it here.

8) Ibid, p. 294.

9) Anthes, p. 47.

10) www.philae.nu/akhet/NetjeruA.html#Atum

11) For an introduction to the subject, see: www.afrikaworld.net/afrel/community.htm

12) Frazer, p. 132 (see Bibliography).

13) Ibid, p. 130.

14) Ibid, p. 131.

15) Ibid, p. 129.

16) This after Mark Isaaks www.talkorigins.org/faqs/flood-myths.html

17) Frazer, p. 147-148.

~ * ~

# Chapter Eight: Ancient Persia (Iran)

The name of Persia does not appear in the Book of Genesis. Many other nations of the ancient world do, especially in Genesis chapters 10 and 11 (the Table of Nations), but not Persia. That is because Persia did not make its appearance on the world's stage until the year 836 BC, when the earliest mention of its name (*Parsua*) is found on an inscription from the Assyrian king, Shalmaneser III.

In Biblical history, we first encounter the Persians in Ezekiel (27:10 & 38:5).[1] They derived, in part at least, from the Medes, who certainly are mentioned in the Table of Nations (*Madai* – Genesis 10:2), and with whom they are closely associated, sharing even the same law code, 'The Law of the Medes and the Persians which changes not' (Daniel 6:8). But the question which interests us in this present enquiry is whether the Ancient Persians carried with them any knowledge or memories of the events and personages mentioned in the Book of Genesis, particularly regarding Noah's Flood?

The answer to the question is yes, they did possess such knowledge and memories. This knowledge was carried by them down a long route which we can trace through the Medes and early Iranians (Aryans), through the Indian sub-continent (Indus Valley), and then all the way back to Mesopotamia, Babel and Japheth – a route which took nigh two thousand years to travel down, and which explains why the Ancient Persians' memory of the Flood is so far departed from the Genesis account. We shall see by how much it departed shortly.

But we must ask, are other 'ingredients' from the Book of Genesis evident among the Persians which provide the hallmark of authenticity regarding their Flood tradition, as spoiled as it may be by time and loss of memory? The answer to which question is again yes, and here we come to the most intriguing part of their Genesis-inspired traditions.

It is very evident that Persia's earliest ancestors carried with them from Babel a relatively pure knowledge of God. Unquestionably, this knowledge darkened as the people wandered over 15 centuries and more toward India, then north across the Russian steppes and then into the land which we know today as Iran, the Elam of old.[2] After so long a period of time, and over so many displacements and vicissitudes, nothing else could be expected. But then, in around the 6th century BC, a philosopher who adopted the name Zoroaster sought to cleanse their knowledge of God from the paganism and idolatry that had corrupted it.

That is not to say that Zoroaster's own knowledge of God was as pure as it might have been had he had the Old Testament Scriptures in front of him. It wasn't. But it was detailed enough for him to pose as the promised Messiah. In Genesis 3:15, God promises that the Seed of the woman would bruise the serpent's head, whilst the serpent (Satan) would bruise His heel. In other words, the Messiah, the Redeemer of mankind, would destroy the power of Satan, but would Himself be slain in bringing that about. Indeed, His death would be an integral and indispensable part of the destruction of sin. This is why this Persian 'reformer' chose the name of Zoroaster. It is Chaldee, and means 'seed of the woman'.[3]

Like most false messiahs, he was of course wise enough to leave out the bit about dying. But his imposture has supplied an unexpected vindication of Genesis, for it shows that the Messianic promise of Genesis 3:15 had formed an important part of his people's folk memory. It had to, otherwise the people he hoped to deceive wouldn't have had the foggiest notion of what he was talking about.

In short, he hoped to restore or revive an already ancient knowledge of God amongst his people. But how can we know that it was indeed the God of Genesis that he spoke about, and not some other 'god' of some other faith? The question is easily answered.

Zoroaster spoke to his people of the 'uncreated Creator'. This Creator was almighty, omniscient, the Lord of all, without beginning or end.[4] This is how he described Him, and the name by which he made Him known was Ahura Mazda – the Lord of Wisdom.

In his book, *Bundahishn* 1:28 (its title means *The Creation*), Zoroaster says that of the things created:

"...the first was the sky; the second, water; the third, earth; the fourth, plants; the fifth, animals; and the sixth, mankind."[5]

This is strikingly close to the order of Creation as given in Genesis 1. How could it have come about Zoroaster and his ancestors were in possession of such knowledge as this? Compare it to any other pagan account of the Creation, yes even those of Mesopotamia whose hideous 'gods' and monsters produced the earth out of blood and mayhem, and you will see how relatively pure an account this is. But there's more.

Zoroaster's view of the universe was that it is locked in a temporary struggle between good and evil, but that good will certainly prevail. In *Bundahishn* 2:11, he speaks of mankind "becoming, at last, again unpersecuted by the adversary [Satan], perfect and immortal in the future existence, for ever and everlasting."[6]

In chapter 3 of his *Bundahishn*, Zoroaster speaks of the war in heaven between the angels of God and the devil and his angels, and how the wicked angels and the devil were cast out of heaven and into hell, with Ahura Mazda finally producing out of this war, "the renovation of the universe for ever and everlasting."[7] – which again is not a million miles from what the Bible itself says of such matters.

In *Bundahishn* 9:5, the Tree of Life that we read of in Genesis is called the Gokard tree, the purpose of which was "keeping away deformed decrepitude," and again in 18:1 as the "producer of the renovation of the universe."

In 15:10, the first created man and woman, called Mashye and Mashyane, having corrupted the Word of the Creator and having slandered His works, were, "covered with clothing of herbage."[8] Chapter 30 of the book is taken up with the resurrection of the dead, the Judgment, and the future life.

It has to be said that much else of the *Bundahishn* makes for heavy reading compared to the simple narrative of the Book of Genesis. As its title implies, the *Bundahishn* is taken up wholly with the Creation, exploring mountains, rivers and plants. But most of all it is taken up with the 'angelic' level, seeing behind every creative act of the Lord an angelic agenda and stage play of the war between good and evil. All of which tells us that Zoroaster's knowledge and understanding of the Creation was less than perfect. How could it be otherwise? But still it is astonishingly close to the order of things that Genesis speaks of concerning the Creation.

As for the Flood, the Persian tradition from Zoroaster's time onwards, although it was doubtless purer in times past, is found in a writing known as *Avesta, Venidad. Fargard* 2.[9] Very briefly, it tells us that Yima, whom we must assume is Noah or his equal, is warned by Ahura Mazda that an 'evil winter' is coming when it shall snow so thickly that even the mountains will be covered to a depth of fourteen fingers (*aredvi*). The Flood will result from the melting of the snow. Yima must build, not an ark, but a city below ground, two hathras (about 2 miles) long on every side as an abode for men and beasts. There must be houses, streets and even artificial lighting. Only the best specimens of every animal are to be taken down there, and only the finest and healthiest of men:

> "There shall be no humpbacked; none bulged forward; no impotent; no lunatic; no malicious; no liar; no one spiteful; none jealous; no one with decayed tooth; no leprous to be pent up; nor any of the brands wherewith Angra Mainyu stamps the bodies of mortals."[10]

Yima, of course, obeys all the instructions given to him, and we are left to infer (because the tradition doesn't mention it), that after the Flood he was able to repopulate the world. The considerable differences between this and the Genesis account are really unimportant. It's the similarities that grab our attention. The Persian tradition as it has come down from or through Zoroaster has a favoured righteous man who is warned by his God that a cataclysm is coming, one that will cover the mountains to a specified and measurable depth. The man is commanded to build a refuge in which he and certain others, along with selected animals, can survive the cataclysm. This refuge also has specific measurements given to it, as well as rooms and other necessities for those who are to live within it. And the man does exactly as he was commanded.

There is an interesting similarity between this tradition and that of Sumer inasmuch as no reference is made to any wickedness on man's part – or even holiness on God's. The cause of the Flood is simply overpopulation. The question arises as to whether this tradition was wholly of Zoroaster's invention, or whether it is essentially what came down to him. But this, when added to the startlingly familiar details of the Creation and so on, tells us that the Persians who lived before Zoroaster must have had purer traditions which corresponded even more closely with the Book of Genesis.

Zoroaster, we must be clear, did not speak for the entire people of Persia. He never has done that. There were many of that land, as today, who would not receive him as any kind of messiah. These kept a much older faith. Suffice it here for us to note that the Persians, and hence their forebears the Medes and Elamites, possessed a surprisingly detailed knowledge of those things that Genesis speaks of, and in that, they were not alone in the ancient world.

## Notes to Chapter Eight

1) Ezekiel 27:10 speaks of "They of Persia...", and in 38:5, he lists, "Persia, Ethiopia and Libya...", all of which gave one modernist a serious problem. His name is Torrey, and in his book, *Ezra Studies*, he asks (thinking that the question alone proves *Ezekiel* to have been a late and therefore fake composition), "How could Ezekiel make this casual mention of the Persians before that people had made its appearance on the stage of history?" (cit. Unger, p. 294 - see Bibliography). Unger enlightens him with a brief lesson in archaeology. As it happens, the fledgling Persia had long been known to the surrounding nations even by Ezekiel's traditional time (ca 600-550 BC). Even though Ezekiel did write some decades before the battle of 550 BC in which Cyrus of Persia conquered Astyages the Mede, thus propelling Persia onto the world stage, the name of Persia was nothing new to his readers. But surely Torrey was aware of the 836 BC inscription of Shalmaneser III? It seems not. The whole sorry case highlights the sheer inability of philology (the Bible critic's favourite tool) to explain history.

2) Evidently, the incoming Medes (descendants of Japheth) mingled with the indigenous Elamites (descendants of Shem), to produce the Persians who were of mixed stock, in part at least fulfilling Noah's prophecy of Genesis 9:27. Most Europeans, and hence Americans, are descended from this Aryan (ancient Iranian) stock.

3) www.thejournal.org/studylibrary/babylon/sect225.html - I am immensely grateful to my friend Dr James J Scofield Johnson for pointing out to me this etymology of Zoroaster's name. His previous adopted name was Zarathustra, meaning 'seed of deliverance, or salvation.' Under that name, he once exclaimed, "Zarathustra am I, to the false believers a forthright enemy, but to the righteous a mighty help and joy." (Yasna 43:4).

4) http://persiandna.com/101names.htm - the website gives the 101 names or attributes of Ahura Mazda according to the Zoroastrian creed.

5) http://www.avesta.org/pahlavi/bund1.html

6) Ibid.

7) Ibid, chapter 6:1.

8) Ibid.

9) For an online translation, see: http://www.avesta.org/vendidad/vd2sbe.htm - this is a transcript of Darmesteter's translation of 1898 (see Bibliography).

10) Ibid. We note the unhappy fact that causing the weak to perish that the strong might prevail was an agenda revived in recent times (1930s-1940s) by a European nation whose Nazi leadership under Himmler consciously adopted much of Zoroaster's teachings. One of their chief philosophers, Friedrich Nietzsche, made a perfect book of it called, *Also Spracht Zarathustra.* Yet what a contrast we see between the false messiah and the Lord Jesus, who, laying aside His

Majesty, made it His business to *heal* the humpbacked, the lunatic and the leprous, and to convert and save the sinful – indeed, to lay down His spotless and sinless Life for them. "Beware of false prophets which come to you in sheep's clothing, but inwardly they are ravening wolves. Ye shall know them by their fruits..." (Matthew 7:15-16). Yes, just as we know Jesus, the true Messiah, by His.

~ * ~

## Chapter Nine: India and Eastern Asia

If we felt dismay as we approached Egypt for evidence of the knowledge of God and memories concerning the events of the Book of Genesis, then India must appear as a forbidding prospect indeed. India's gods, so many more than Egypt's, are counted in their thousands, and to the Christian mind the philosophy and mythology surrounding them is utterly baffling. And yet, just as we observed with Egypt, God "Who in times past suffered all nations to walk in their own ways... left not Himself without witness." (Acts 14:16-17). Nor did He, not even in India.

India's oldest and largest religion is Hinduism (it's where India gets its name from), and there are ancient seals from the Indus Valley Civilisation whose motifs would be familiar to any Hindu living today. We may safely assume, therefore, that the religion was founded in India's very earliest days, after the arrival of the first migrants from Babel in Mesopotamia. The question which we need to address here is whether these first migrants into India brought with them any memories of the events and personages recorded in the Book of Genesis? The answer to which is yes, yes they did.

Perhaps the most striking memory that they brought with them is that of Noah's son, Japheth. And they remembered not just the man, but his name, Pra-Japati,[1] – Father Japheth. They looked to him (somewhat oddly) as the creator of all things, likening him to the sun, and, confusing him with the true Creator, even as a trinity.

As time went by, the early Hindus changed their focus slightly, and rather than worshipping Japheth in person as the creator of all things, looked instead to something they called Brahma, in which they saw, with evident dimness, the creative principle. If we had to translate this into Christian terms, then we might understand this principle as the Logos, the creative Word of John's Gospel without Whom nothing was made. At least, that would be the approximate value of the term.

There is a huge difference, however, between the Logos of the Bible and the Brahma of Hinduism in that the Brahma is not considered to be eternal. It has a beginning and an end, and a lifespan (which the

Hindus call a *mahakalpa*) of 306,720,000 years - and here's where it gets interesting for our enquiry.

At the end of this vast period of time, there occurs a *mahapralaya*, or universal Deluge which brings the old age to a close and opens the new. In the next Deluge, so they believe, everything will be destroyed, including Pra-Japati the creator, the Brahma, and so on. That is hardly a perfect memory of the teachings of Genesis, but it is how the Hindus remembered the Flood of Noah. That too was a universal Deluge which brought the old world to a close and opened the new. Not remembering the solemn promise of God never to flood the whole earth again, to the Hindus the Great Flood simply repeats itself at the end of each age in a great cyclic drama.

They also remembered Adam, calling him Manu, the first created man (our English words, man, mentality and mind, are all derived from the Hindi word Manu). But from this point on, all else concerning Adam becomes unrecognisable, the entire history of Genesis dissolving into the shadows of a mythological fog.

There is, however, a little more to be gleaned concerning Manu and the Great Flood in the *Satapatha Brahmana*, where we read that Manu was the sole survivor of the Flood.[2] But the Great Flood itself is recalled in the following strange terms:

> "When he [Manu] was washing himself, a fish came into his hands. It spake to him the word, 'Rear me, and I will save thee!' 'Wherefrom wilt thou save me?' 'A flood will carry away all these creatures; from that I will save thee!... In such and such a year that flood will come. Thou shalt then attend to me by preparing a ship; and when the flood has risen thou shalt enter into the ship, and I will save thee from it!'.... And in the same year which the fish had indicated to him, he attended to the service of the fish by preparing a ship; and when the flood had risen, he entered into the ship."[3]

The story continues with the fish towing the ship to a mountain and instructing Manu to gradually descend from the mountain as the waters subside, the northern side of that mountain being called ever thereafter,

Manu's Descent. The agency of the fish in all this is something of a surprise, because it figures in no other Flood tradition of the ancient world. However, there does seem to be an intriguing explanation for it.

In Mesopotamia, whence the ancient Hindus came from, the 'god' Ea is a water-deity that was often represented at least partially in the form of a fish. In most Flood accounts around the world, it is always a 'god' who announces the coming of the Flood, so it would seem that this early Hindu account is no exception. The pagan concept of Ea had clearly followed them into their new homeland.

## Burma

We now move on to Burma where we find some remarkably accurate traditions concerning events in the Book of Genesis. One particular tribe, the Karens, remembered the creation of Adam and Eve in these terms, saying that God:

> "...created man at first from the earth, and finished the work of creation. He created woman, and of what did he form her? He took a rib from the man and created the woman."[4]

Frazer, naturally, suspects the influence of Christian missionaries here, simply because the account is so close to that of Genesis. But had they truly learned this tradition from missionaries, then it is passing strange that the said missionaries went on to make such an appalling hash of things when teaching the Karens about the Flood:

> "According to the Karens of Burma the earth was of old deluged with water, and two brothers saved themselves from the flood on a raft. The waters rose till they reached to heaven, when the younger brother saw a mango-tree hanging down from the celestial vault. With great presence of mind he clambered up it and ate the fruit, but the flood, suddenly subsiding, left him suspended in the tree. Here the narrative breaks off...."[5]

Frazer knew perfectly well that such wayward traditions do not owe their origin to any Christian missionaries. But that is not all that the Karens have to tell us. Their ancient testimony concerning the events recorded in the Book of Genesis extends to an account of the Tower of Babel also:

> "In the days of Pan-dan-man, the people determined to build a pagoda that should reach up to heaven... When the pagoda was half way up to heaven, God came down and confounded the language of the people, so that they could not understand each other. Then the people scattered, and Than-mau-rai, the father of the Gaikho tribe, came west, with eight chiefs, and settled in the valley of the Satang."[6]

In Upper Burma, the Chingpaws also have a tradition of a great Flood. According to this account, a man named Pawpaw Nan-chaung and his sister, Chang-hko, saved themselves in a large boat. To see whether the water had subsided, they threw overboard a cock and a needle (having nine of each). Hearing neither the cock crowing nor the needle hitting anything, they remained on board. At intervals, they experimented with the next seven cocks and needles to no effect. But the ninth cock crowed and the ninth needle was heard to hit against a rock, and soon after, they were able to leave the boat.[7]

There are interesting echoes here of Noah sending forth a raven and a dove to see if the waters had abated, and there the similarity ends. But before we leave Burma, there is, amongst the Tibeto-Burmese tribes of Assam, a people called the Mikir, and they give the following testimony concerning the Tower of Babel:

> "They say that in days of old the descendants of Ram [Ham?] were mighty men, and growing dissatisfied with the mastery of the earth they aspired to conquer heaven. So they began to build a tower which should reach up to the skies. Higher and higher rose the building, till at last the gods and demons feared lest these giants should become the masters of heaven, as they already were of earth. So they confounded their speech, and scattered them to the four corners of the world."[8]

## Cochin China (Vietnam)

The Bahnars, a people of Cochin China,[9] gave their account of the Flood like this. Once, long ago, a kite pecked a crab so hard that he put a hole in the crab's shell. The crab, to avenge the injury, caused the sea and rivers to rise until the waters reached up to the heavens and all living creatures perished, save two, a brother and a sister who were inside a huge chest.[10] They took into the chest a pair of every animal, shut the lid tight and floated on the waters for seven days and nights. Eventually, a 'god' let them know that the waters were abated by the crowing of a cock, and so they and the animals were saved.[11] There are several corroborative details here which are shared with the Book of Genesis, and we meet with more in the following traditions.

## The Malay Peninsula

The Benua-Jakun, a people living in the State of Johor on the Malay Peninsula, relate how the earth beneath our feet is but a thin skin covering an abyss of water:

> "In ancient times, Pirman, that is the deity, broke up this skin, so that the world was drowned and destroyed by a great flood. However, Pirman had created a man and a woman and put them in a ship of *pulai* wood, which was completely covered over and had no opening. In this ship the pair floated and tossed about for a time, till at last the vessel came to rest..."[12]

## Yunnan Province

There is a most intriguing people called the Lolos who live in the Yunnan Province, a mountainous region of south-west China. They are intriguing because they "...invented a mode of writing, pictographic in origin, in which they have recorded their legends, songs, genealogies, and religious ritual."[13] Their records have been copied and recopied over the centuries and handed down from one generation to the next. These people look back to patriarchs whose longevity is recorded as 660 years in one case, and 990 in another. The most revered of these patriarchs among them is Tse-gu-dzih. He, it seems, is how they remember Adam, he having brought death into the world and causing the Flood. But he is also confused with the Creator.

However, the story goes that Tse-gu-dzih commanded men to bring him a human sacrifice. They all refused save one, Du-mu by name. So Tse-gu-dzih flooded the earth, but saved Du-mu and his four sons, who rode out the flood inside a log with certain animals. Nearly every legend of the Lolos begins with, or in some way refers to, Du-mu and the Flood.

Of further interest to us is the fact that the Lolos observe the Sabbath every seventh day when no ploughing or sewing is permitted. Frazer and one A Henry ascribe these remarkable facts, with tedious predictability, to the teachings of Christian missionaries. But again, we must observe that these missionaries must have been hopeless at their task to teach these people such dreadful and blatant inaccuracies. Surely, there must have been some Christian missionaries somewhere on this good earth who taught their charges from the Bible, and who even left their charges copies *of* the Bible? Not according to Frazer and his colleagues. All Christian missionaries were utterly hopeless and incompetent at their task, leaving behind them nothing but gobbledegook. That the writings containing these legends and traditions long pre-date the arrival of Christian missionaries in China, does not impress the modernist school. Why allow a simple fact to get in the way of an hypothesis - or maybe even a knighthood or two?

## Kom Chad Luek (Kamchadales) of Thailand

Frazer goes on to tell us about a people whom he knew as the ‘Kamchadales’ of Thailand, a land once known to the world as Siam. The people themselves are more properly known as the Kom Chad Luek:

> “The Kamchadales have a tradition of a great flood which covered the whole land in the early days of the world. A remnant of the people saved themselves on large rafts made of tree-trunks bound together; on these they loaded their property and provisions, and on these they drifted about, dropping stones tied to straps instead of anchors in order to prevent the flood from sweeping them away out to sea. When

at last the water of the deluge sank, it left the people and their rafts stranded high and dry on the tops of the mountains."[14]

## Eastern Tartary (Mongolia)

In a Chinese encyclopaedia of Frazer's day, there was the following entry:

> "*Eastern Tartary.* – In travelling from the shore of the Eastern Sea toward Che-lu, neither brooks nor ponds are met with in the country, although it is intersected by mountains and valleys. Nevertheless there are found in the sand very far away from the sea, oyster-shells and the shields of crabs. The tradition of the Mongols who inhabit the country is, that it has been said from time immemorial that in remote antiquity the waters of the deluge flooded the district, and when they retired, the places where they had been made[, - *sic*] their appearance covered the sand."[15]

## Sumatra and the Indian Archipelago (Indonesia)

The Batak people of Sumatra have a tradition that when the earth grew corrupt, the Creator, Debata, sent a great Flood upon the earth to destroy every living thing. When the last human couple had sought refuge on the peak of the highest mountain, the Creator repented of His decision to destroy all mankind, and made an island of earth for the couple to stand on.[16]

The people of Engano, an island to the west of Sumatra, also have a tradition concerning the Flood, as do the Ibans of Sarawak in Borneo. The Toradjas of Central Sulawesi (known to Frazer under its own Portugese name of Central Celebes) point to the sea-shells that lie more than 2000 feet up on Mount Wawo mPebato as proof of the Great Flood. Those of Rotti, a small island to the south-west of Timor, also recall a time when the waters flooded the earth so that all men and animals were drowned. And finally, Frazer tells us of the Andaman Islands in the Bay of Bengal (not strictly part of Indonesia), whose inhabitants tell of the Flood that the Creator, Puluga, sent upon the earth because of mankind's wilful disobedience.[17]

The Indian subcontinent, Eastern Asia and Indonesia are truly vast areas containing hundreds if not thousands of peoples, tribes and families, and we may not suppose for one moment that we have exhausted all the Flood traditions in this part of the world. We have hardly scratched the surface. Doubtless many more have gone unrecorded than have been written down for us. But we must now turn our enquiry toward mainland China, whose written records go back thousands of years before any Christian missionaries came along, and which have a great deal to say about the events recorded in the Book of Genesis.

## Notes to Chapter Nine

1) English, and virtually all European languages going back to Latin and Greek and beyond, are classed by philologists as Indo-European languages because they originated in India. *Pra-* is the root of the Latin *pater*, whence came the Old German *vater*, which in turn gives us our English word, father. *Japati* is simply the Hebrew name of Japheth transposed into the early Hindi tongue. So, Pra-Japati is simply Father Japheth.

2) Frazer, p. 134.

3) Ibid, pp. 78-79.

4) Ibid, p. 6.

5) Ibid, p. 81.

6) Ibid, p.150.

7) Ibid, p. 81.

8) Ibid, p. 150.

9) Cochin China became the State of Vietnam on 14th June 1949.

10) Interestingly, the Hebrew word for Noah's Ark is *aron*, meaning chest.

11) Frazer, p. 82. Note here how rain is absent from the tradition, the waters rising instead from the earth. This occurs in other Flood traditions, and appears to be a clear memory of the fountains of the deep being broken up (Genesis 7:11).

12) Ibid. *Pulai* is a low-density durable wood that is resistant to termites.

13) Frazer, p. 83.

14) Ibid, p. 84.

15) Ibid.

16) Ibid.

17) Ibid, pp. 84-88.

~ * ~

## Chapter Ten: China and the Book of Genesis

The land of China, its people, its early history, yes, even its written script, bear such a rich and invaluable testimony to the historicity of the Book of Genesis, that we need to clear the decks a little in order to get a better view of the subject. By that I mean that we must shed all later spurious mythologies and philosophies that have come down to us from the 6th century BC, and concentrate our attention entirely upon the earlier, more ancient material, the monotheistic, chronicled, historical accounts of early China.

A strange phenomenon occurred during the 6th and 7th centuries BC. That period saw the birth and burgeoning in Europe and Asia of what men are pleased to call 'philosophy'. In Europe at that time, we see the birth of Greek philosophy; in Iran and India the arrival of Zoroastrianism; in India, Buddhism; and in China the simultaneous birth of Taoism and Confucianism. It was as if the entire human race had entered a worldwide dream-phase of a long sleep, philosophy being its 'rapid eye movement'.

The problem this presents the historian with is that the simultaneous arrival on the world stage of all these ideas and philosophies acts as a veil which obscures the earlier picture. This is especially so when we consider the interchange of ideas which occurred between the various nations at this point in history. For example, we have seen how Hinduism held the notion that between each successive creation of the universe, there is a period of time which they called the *kalpa*, (actually a *maha-kalpa*, or great *kalpa*), this running into millions of years. That's what we find in India. Know then that what we find in China at that time is nothing else but an identical concept of a perpetual series of creations separated by a long period of time which they also called a *kalpa*![1]

We need not be surprised at this. China and India were, indeed still are, connected to each other by the Great Silk Road along which flowed for centuries new ideas, as well as just merchandise. Greece, India, Babylonia, and even Egypt were between them also a marketplace of innovation and ideas. But the popular misapprehension, a misapprehension which modernism does nothing to discourage, is that these later ideas are the original mythology and folk-memory of the peoples concerned. Most emphatically, they are not. They are what they are, late innovations. Here, our business is to consider what went before, and turn to the earliest written material for China, and not the later.[2]

First, let us begin with one of the most ancient books outside the Bible, the Chinese book, *Shu Jing* – The Book of History. This record takes us right back to the Creation itself as the Chinese remembered it. It is worth bearing in mind that this record pre-dates by many centuries the coming of Christianity into the world, so no man, modernist or mad, can claim with any feasibility at all that its contents were in any way tampered with or influenced by Christian missionaries. That tired old claim, at least, is redundant here. What we are about to read is an entirely indigenous account of the Creation that dates back more than 4000 years:

> "Of old, in the beginning, there was great chaos, without form and dark. The five elements [planets] had not begun to revolve, nor the sun and the moon to shine. Thou, O Spiritual Sovereign, camest forth in Thy presidency, and first didst divide the grosser parts from the purer. Thou madest heaven; Thou madest earth; Thou madest man. All things with their reproducing power got their being."[3]

There is much more than a strong echo here of the opening verses of the Book of Genesis. The knowledge of God was held in splendid isolation by the Chinese for nigh the first two thousand years of their existence, and it ran deep in their culture, reaching depths that were often truly sublime. The name by which God was known in early China is *Shang Ti* (pr. *Shang Dai*), which means Supreme Heavenly Ruler.[4] It is equally well translated as Lord Most High. We know Him as the God of Genesis, the One True God and Creator of Heaven and Earth. Now, if the modernist world-view were anywhere near to reality, then the Chinese would never have heard of the Name, let alone have had any notion of His qualities and attributes. They would have followed the Egyptians, the Canaanites, the Carthaginians, and so many others down to the road to paganism. The knowledge of God would simply have been unknown among them. Yet it was known – not perfectly, perhaps, but known nonetheless., As we have observed elsewhere and as the Bible tells us, God did not leave Himself without witness.

In considering the earlier material, we are mercifully spared the pain of investigating the many gods of Taoism, the strange agnosticism of Confucius, and the even stranger religious atheism of the Buddha. We are even spared the dizzying convolutions of Hinduism. These are simpler, untrammelled concepts, and in them we see a very clear picture of the Chinese patriarchal view of God and His Creation, a view which conforms remarkably closely to all that we are taught in Genesis.

Our main remit, of course, is to look for traces of knowledge amongst the Chinese concerning the Great Flood, and the fact is that they did have that knowledge – a greater knowledge indeed than we might reasonably have hoped for, as the following makes clear:

## *Nuah*, the Flood, and the *Miaotsu*

In remote times, ca 2000 BC, as the original Chinese settlers entered the country, they were joined by another group travelling up through Indo-China. They were soon dubbed the *Miaotsu* by the Chinese population, a somewhat derogatory term, the *miao-* element meaning 'barbarian' or 'outsider'.[5] They are more properly known as the *Hmong*, and today number some 12 million. They were a brave people. For nigh 4000 years they fought off all attempts by the Chinese to destroy them, but the interesting part of their story for our purpose is that, from the earliest times, they meticulously kept their ancestral records and pedigrees, happily recording the fact that they are descended, not from Ham as the Chinese are, but from *Jah-phu*, Japheth, the son of *Nuah*, Noah – no, I'm not making this up, really!

The *Miaotsu* recollect other named patriarchs who appear also in the Book of Genesis: *Lama* (Lamech, the father of Noah); *Cusah* (the Cush of the Bible), and *Mesay* (the Biblical Mizraim), who are both descendants of *Lo Han* (Ham); *Elan* (the Elam of the Bible), and *Nga-shur* (the Biblical Asshur), these being descended from *Lo Shen* (Shem, exactly as in Genesis); and we have *Go-men* (Gomer), the son of *Jah-phu* (Japheth, again exactly as in the Book of Genesis).[6]

Six generations after Gomer, the *Miaotsu* record that eleven tribes were descended from a patriarch named *Seageweng*.[7] Five of these tribes became the ancestors of the *Miaotsu* themselves, whilst the other six intermarried with the surrounding Chinese population.

Now that is a great deal – more, in fact, than modernism has ever been pleased to tell us about – but it is not all, not by any means. In an ancestral song recited since time immemorial by the *Miaotsu* at funerals, weddings and like occasions, and in which all the above details are included, we find the following remarkable account enshrined in that song.[8]

Of great interest to us is the fact that the song is written in couplets, which not only aids the memory of those who have to recite it, but also ensures that additions and interpolations are impossible to insert.[9] It is also worth bearing in mind that this song was already of great antiquity when Christian missionaries first encountered the *Miaotsu*, a people so introverted and shut off from the outside world, that they had no idea that the earth was even round. But the writers of this ancient song knew it, and knew it of old.[10] They knew many other things too. Consider the opening lines:

> "On the day God created the heavens and earth,
> On that day He opened the gateway of light."[11]

Compare this with Genesis 1:3. The two accounts are not a million miles removed from one another, are they? Nor are the other lines of the song removed from Genesis to any great degree. The song goes on to tell of the creation of the land, the plants, the animals and birds, and then lastly of man himself:

> "On the earth He created a man from the dirt,
> Of the man thus created, a woman He formed."

It goes on to tell how the *Miaotsu*'s Adam (named as in the Bible after the clay from which he was made) measured the earth's weight and the stars of heaven, and pondered the ways of God.

The line of his children from *Se-teh* (Seth, Genesis 5:4) to *Lama* (Lamech, the father of Noah, Genesis 5:26) is also given (as is the name of Noah's wife, *Gaw Bo-lu-en*). Their three sons, *Lo-Han*, *Lo-Shen* and *Jah-phu* (Ham, Shem and Japheth) make their appearance at this point, and:

> "So the earth began filling with tribes and with families.
> Creation was shared by the clans and the peoples."[12]

The song goes on to tell in great but independent detail (no rehash of Genesis this) how things then went between mankind and God:

> "These did not God's will nor returned His affection,
> But fought with each other defying the Godhead.
> But their leaders shook fists in the face of the Mighty..."

So, the *Miaotsu* remembered things just as the Bible describes them (Genesis 6:1-12). The earth was filled with violence. Judgment must come, and judgment did come. The song recalls further that God determined to destroy all flesh from off the face of the earth, save righteous *Nuah* and his wife and family. They build a boat and come safely through the Flood, with male and female animals on board and birds mated in pairs. But it is the *Miaotsu*'s graphic depiction of the Flood that is of particular interest to us, largely because of the fact that it radically departs from the commonly found 'seven days of rain' that most other cultures speak of:

> "So it poured forty days in sheets and in torrents,
> Then fifty-five days of misting and drizzle.
> The waters surmounted the mountains and ranges.
> The deluge ascending leapt valley and hollow.
> An earth with no earth upon which to take refuge!
> A world with no foothold where one might subsist!
> The people were baffled, impotent and ruined,
> Despairing, horror-stricken, diminished and finished."[13]

Forty days of torrential rain is exactly right and agrees with Genesis 7:4 precisely. But the added detail, which Genesis doesn't give, of a following fifty-five days of drizzle and mist rings true too. After the initial forty-day downpour, the air would have been unimaginably heavy with moisture producing constant drizzle and heavy mist, a detail that the occupants of the Ark were doubtless to pass on to their many hearers. Indeed, it may well account for the notable darkness that seems to have enveloped the earth during the Flood, and which is pointedly remembered in several Flood traditions.

This fascinating song of the *Miaotsu* goes on to tell of *Nuah* releasing a dove to see if the waters had abated, and the sacrifice which he made after leaving the Ark. God blesses him and there follows the lineage of *Nuah*'s grandsons, *Cusah* and *Mesay* (Cush and Mizraim), and *Elan* and *Nga-shur* (Elam and Asshur).

Next there follows the *Miaotsu*'s account of the Tower of Babel, the story being told like this:

> "Their offspring begotten, became tribes and peoples;
> Their descendants established encampments and cities.
> Their singing was all with the same tunes and music,
> Their speaking was all with the same words and language.
> Then they said, Let us build us a very big city,
> Let us raise unto heaven a very high tower."

The building of the Tower of Babel and the confusion of tongues described in the song, is all the more interesting to us for what it leaves out rather than what it includes. Babel itself is not named, nor any of its 'heroes' like Nimrod. We are told merely that God was angered at man's presumption, and that He made it so that no man could understand what his fellows were saying. The tower is abandoned, unfinished, and the men are scattered to all parts of the earth:

> "He's speaking in words, but they can't understand him.
> So the city they builded was never completed;
> The tower they wrought has to stand thus unfinished.
> In despair then they separate all under heaven,
> They part from each other the globe to encircle.
> They arrive at six corners and speak the six languages."[14]

Historically, the mention here of the 'six corners' of the earth is most interesting. It betrays a very early knowledge of the earth's geography, referring, of course, to the six continents. But are there not *seven* continents? Yes, today there are. They are Asia, Africa, North America, South America, Antarctica, Europe and Australia. But in the days immediately following Babel, there would not yet have been an Antarctica, which in any case has always been uninhabited. It seems that the early *Miaotsu* and their Chinese neighbours were aware of this fact. Extraordinary.

Truax, the first Christian missionary to work amongst the *Miaotsu*, tells us that the song goes on for many more pages yet, though at this point it departs from our own sphere of interest. He further points out that the *Miaotsu* knew nothing of idolatry until they learned it from the Chinese. The Chinese themselves only turned to idolatry after the teachings of the philosopher *Lao-tzu* and the establishment under him of Taoism in around 500 BC. Taoism is indeed responsible for much of China's departure from her original patriarchal faith, and the obscuring and distortion of her earlier monotheistic beliefs, so that nowadays one has to dig deep to encounter any proof of it at all. But proof there surely is.

## Shang Ti, the Lord Most High

One of the most surprising and unexpected fields of research to be opened up in recent years, is the study of ancient Chinese script as it relates to the Book of Genesis. There are four books on the subject that are currently available, and which are required reading in the subject of how the knowledge of the Book of Genesis is to be found embedded the early Chinese script. Not wishing to steal their thunder, we will not here deal with the theses of these books other than to note that the ideograms and pictograms devised by the early Chinese reveal an amazingly high level of knowledge and awareness amongst them of those events and personages that the Book of Genesis contains.[15]

Amongst those events are the Creation, the Temptation in the Garden, the Fall, the Flood, the Ark, and so on. And amongst the personages are God Himself as the Creator, Adam, Eve, the serpent, and the occupants of the Ark. It is altogether an amazing discovery.

How it came about that the Chinese had this knowledge, though, we cannot say. The invention of the Chinese script pre-dates by some centuries the writing of the Penateuch by Moses, so we cannot suppose that the early Chinese had a copy of Genesis to guide them. It is altogether a deep and profound mystery which can be explained in no other terms than that the Chinese brought this knowledge with them as they migrated from Babel to China.

But as well as encapsulating a profound knowledge of the events and personages of the Book of Genesis in the construction of their written characters, the Chinese also wrote ordinarily of such things in plain open text, so that ordinary people could read about them and understand. One such example is as follows:

> "When Te [Shang Tai], the Lord, had so decreed, He called into existence heaven, earth, and man. Between heaven and earth He separately placed in order men and things, all overspread by the heavens."[16]

The knowledge of *Shang Ti*, in any pure form, was to last for nigh 2000 years. After that period of time, it came under such a concerted assault from Taoism, that today it is barely recognisable. The memory of the patriarch *Nu Wa* (Noah), for example, was subjected to such violence that he was made to change gender more than once, so that finally the figure of Noah was reduced in the popular consciousness to one of a ridiculous woman's head grafted onto the body of a serpent.[17]

Between 475-221 BC, *Nu Wa* was represented as a female creator, making men out of clay. Then the earth goes haywire as the heavens collapse and the world is flooded. *Nu Wa* is then said to have repaired the sky by cutting off the legs of a tortoise and propping up the heavens with them. By 122 BC, *Nu Wa* is back to being a male creator with a serpentine tail. Then it's back to being a female again and the wife of *Fuxi* (pr. Foo-shee), these being portrayed as the parents of mankind – Adam and Eve in other words.[18] These hideous perversions of the Creation, Noah and the indigenous Flood tradition, are all the work of the early Taoists who sought to rewrite the spiritual history of China and eradicate all knowledge of *Shang Ti*. As we noted earlier, this is the veil that paganism threw over the picture of China's earlier beliefs and knowledge. But for all their efforts, the witness remains.[19]

## Notes to Chapter Ten

1) Werner, p. 128. See Bibliography.

2) Few realise, because few scholars ever bother to tell them, that before the arrival of Buddhism, Taoism and Confucianism (that is, up until 2500 years ago), China was a monotheistic society. Instead of the multitudinous gods and goddesses that were shared and borrowed by most other nations and which arrived very late on the scene in China, she worshipped only One, the Creator. Little wonder there are few who mention the fact.

3) Kang & Nelson, *Discovery of Genesis*, p. 15 (see Bibliography). cit. Also Ford, Ava. 'Life in the Letters.' Nov 2008. *Acts & Facts*. Institute for Creation Research, p. 5. The origin of the quote is Legge, James. *The Notions of the Chinese concerning Gods and Spirits*. 1852. Hong Kong, p. 28.

4) Kang & Nelson, p. 2. See Bibliography.

5) http://www.egeli.org/miao.htm

6) Truax, E. 'Genesis according to the Miao People.' April 1991. Impact Article. ICR. http://www.icr.org/index.php?module=articlesandaction=view*ID=341

7) The line of descent is given as: *Nuah – Jah-phu – Go-men* (Genesis 10:1-2) - ??? – *Tutan – Gawndan Mew-wan – Jenku-Dawvu – Gengen Newang – Seageweng* – from whom came 11 children or tribes. See Appendix 12 of *After the Flood*, pp. 243-246. For full text: http://www.icr.org/index.php?module=articlesandaction=view*ID=341 From the *Miao* song, *Westwards Upriver*, we glean the names of five ancestral families of the *Miaotsu*, namely *Fang*, *Fu*, *Dli*, *Ne* and *Dai Ne*. The song also carried

invaluable ancient memories of the tribe's pre-2000 BC migration into China. See Bender, pp. 169-188.

8) This particular song was translated by Edgar Truax, a missionary in the 1980s amongst the *Miaotsu* in the Kiangsi Province, an area of south-west China. See Bibliography.

9) Its poetic form, a form so often despised and denigrated by modernist critics, couldn't be better suited to our purpose. You may put this statement to the test. Write out Tennyson's historical poem, *Charge of the Light Brigade*, commemorating a British military blunder that occurred on 25th October 1854. It is a perfectly historical piece written out as a poem. But then try altering the story line by composing and inserting spurious lines and verses of your own so that the story line is now changed to that of the Battle of Hastings, fought in 1066. The insertions, additions and substitutions, though, must be seamless and undetectable. You will find it impossible. The poetic form of any ancient account or tradition is the surest guarantee against later interference and interpolation - as modernists know too well but rarely mention.

10) When describing the dispersal of the nations from Babel, the song's line says in literal translation: "They parted went live encircle world ball." (see Truax). In ancient times, long before the missionaries ever got to them, they knew that the earth was a globe, but had forgotten that fact by the time they were found.

11) See Appendix 12 of *After the Flood*, pp. 243-246, for summary, and for full text, see: http://www.icr.org/index.php?module=articlesandaction=view*ID=341

12) Ibid.

13) Ibid. The *Miaotsu* have another epic song called *The Great Flood*. But although it is centred around the historical Flood, its story line is that of a quarrel between *Jang Vang*, the ancestor of mankind (Adam), and the thunder god, both of whom fall out over a piece of property, and the thunder god,

in a sulk, returns to heaven and floods the earth. The song is written for no other purpose than hilarity – even in translation it is very funny (see Bender, pp. 157-168) – and seems in fact to be a parody of a Taoist attempt to explain the Flood.

14) Ibid.

15) The inventor of the Chinese script was, according to tradition, Tsieng Chi, otherwise Ts'ang Chieh. Nelson & Broadberry. *Genesis and the Mystery Confucius Couldn't Solve*, p. 22, quoting Hsin Cheng Yu, *Ancient Chinese History*. 1963. Taipei, p. 6.

16) Ibid, p. 27.

17) See Werner, illustration between pp. 34-35.

18) Ibid. *Fuxi* was actually a historical ruler of the Chinese, the first for whom any date is given (conventionally 2852-2737 BC), but whom the Taoists deified in their eagerness to confound and muddy the record. Interestingly, he is counted a grandson of *Nu Wa* (Noah) in the 'Three Sovereigns and Five Emperors' period of early Chinese history: http://www.answers.com/topic/three-sovereigns-and-five-emperors

19) There is so much else to do with the early Chinese which is of immense interest to Bible students, but they lie outside the remit of our present study. An example, though, is their use of the domesticated animal, *long-ma*, a 'dragon-horse', five of which used to pull the chariot of the emperor Shennong.

~ * ~

## Chapter Eleven: Australia and New Zealand

Today it is called Australia. When the Dutch first sighted the land in 1606, they named it New Holland. But before that, its name is unknown to us, although it is worth recording here that the Chinese referred to a mysterious land which lay in the direction of Australia as Fire Land, or The Land of Parrots. We know this from a map compiled in 1603 by the Jesuit missionary to China, Matteo Ricci.[1] But before that, Australia is very much *Terra Incognita* – a land unknown.

The continent, however, was not uninhabited. It was peopled by tribes and families who have been known since 1789 as 'Aborigines', a misleading term which rightly describes the native Australians as having lived there 'from the beginning', which is what the Latin phrase *ab origine* means, but gives the impression that they are all of one family and tribe. Yet, when the white man first came to Australia in the late 18th century, these 'Aborigines' spoke anywhere between 350 and 750 different languages – at least 200 of which are still spoken![2] So we are really considering a very complex collection of peoples and societies that have inhabited Australia since their ancestors arrived here from Babel.[3] This is important for us to bear in mind, for it is from among this vast collection of peoples, families and tribes, that we are to gather information concerning the Great Flood which the Book of Genesis speaks of. Another important point to consider is the fact that such a diversity of languages between groups who even shared the same territory, puts a strong restraint upon any modernist notion of information-sharing or collusion.

So, did the indigenous peoples of Australia carry with them in their migration from Babel any knowledge at all of the events preserved in Genesis – the Creation, for example? The answer to which is yes, they certainly did. One particular tribe which hailed from the Melbourne area,[4] remembered the creation of man in these most interesting terms:

> "Pund-jel, the Creator, cut three large sheets of bark with his big knife. On one of these he placed some clay and worked it up with his knife into a proper consistency. He then laid a portion of the clay on one of the other pieces of bark and

> shaped it into a human form; first he made the feet, then the legs, then the trunk, the arms, and the head. Thus he made a clay man on each of the two pieces of bark; and being well pleased with his handiwork, he danced round them for joy. Next he took stringy bark from the eucalyptus tree, made hair of it, and stuck it on the heads of his clay men. Then he looked at them again, was pleased with his work, and again danced round them for joy. He then lay down on them, blew his breath hard into their mouths, their noses, and their navels, and presently they stirred, spoke, and rose up as full-grown men."[5]

Anyone even vaguely familiar with the Book of Genesis will recognise many of the component parts of this tradition. Man being formed from clay; the joy of the Creator at his making; the Creator breathing into man the breath of life, and so on. These are remarkable details to have survived when we consider the distance in time and miles from their source in Mesopotamia, and subsequently the immense geographical isolation of the people over thousands of years who preserved the memory of them.

Significantly, Frazer, our source for the information, though he disparages the people who held this tradition in the most repugnantly racist terms, makes no attempt at all to credit the telling details of the account to Christian missionaries, something which he is very happy to do elsewhere even on the flimsiest of pretences. It seems that his own informant had made it very clear to him that the tradition is entirely indigenous.

Frazer goes on to record two Flood traditions for Australia, one of which belonged to the Kurnai people of Victoria, and another from Victoria around Lake Tyers. Both accounts put together (for they are really both parts of the same tradition), tell how the earth was dried up by a frog which swallowed all the water, only to drown the whole earth when he disgorged it.[6] A man and two or three women survived by being rescued by a pelican in a canoe.[7] Now, at first encounter, it all seems something of a silly story, which is doubtless why Frazer chose it – something to make his readers giggle. But let's remember that our witness is giving his version of events at the extreme end of memory. So let's look a little closer.

The account contains one or two component elements in common with the Book of Genesis. There is a worldwide flood. All of humanity, save for a few individuals, are drowned. Those who are not, are saved by means of a boat, and I strongly suspect that the proper name of the pelican, *Bunjil Borun*, is either a corruption of an earlier forgotten name in the Kurnai dialect, or it can be translated into something else entirely. It's a phenomenon that is not unknown in the history of translating. One example will serve.

Statues and paintings of Moses (especially from the Middle Ages) often show him sporting a pair of horns on his head. How did that come about? The answer lies in the Latin Vulgate Old Testament. In Exodus 34:29-30 & 35, the Hebrew Bible tells us plainly that Moses' face *shone*, using the word *qaran*. But, depending on the context, *qaran* can also be translated as *horned*. Jerome, when he issued the Vulgate, instead of using the common-sense translation of *qaran*, opted for the ridiculous. Hence, there are thousands of images, paintings and statues of Moses all around the world which show him wearing a pair of horns instead of having a radiant face. Mind-boggling, but true. In a similar way, *Bunjil Borun* might well prove to be mistranslated as *pelican*. One very obvious point to consider is the closeness of the name *Bunjil* with that of the Creator, *Pund-jel*. Are they in fact one and the same? I would not be at all surprised.

Happily, Frazer is not our only source for Australia. There is another Flood tradition, this time from the Wunambal tribe of Western Australia.[8] It was told by a tribal elder named Mickie Bungunie, and it runs as follows.

Back in the early days of the world, a period which the Australian aborigines refer to as the Dreamtime, there lived a man named Gajara who lived with his wife, their sons and their wives. We shall see that Gajara is none other than Noah in the Wunambal memory. One day, some children were being excessively cruel to a Winking Owl named Dumbi. They tortured the bird by plucking out his feathers and spearing him, even pushing a spear into his nose; and as they flung him into the air for the third time, yelling, "Fly!", the owl continued to ascend to the heavens until he came to Ngadja, the Supreme One or Creator, to whom he complained about what they had done to him. Ngadja was furious to learn of the children's cruelty and violence, and sent certain servants to see if it were so and whether the children were still there. Then Ngadja commanded Gajara to build a double raft. "I intend to drown everyone. I am about to send rain and a sea flood!" Ngadja told him which foods to store aboard the raft, and which animals to take on board. And when that was done:

> "Ngadja then said, 'All is ready now.'.... Then Ngadja sent the rainclouds down, shutting the clouds in upon them. The sea-flood came in from the north-northeast and the people were closed in by the saltwater flood and the tidal waters of the sea. The flood began to sweep all the living creatures together and was pushing them all along to one place.... Here the waters were spinning in a whirlpool and the people were screaming as they looked for a way of escape. Ngadja whirled the flood waters and the earth opened, drowning and flattening them all."[9]

After this harrowing description, the Wunambal account relates that the Flood waters receded and Gajara sent out some birds, the cuckoo first, which did not return to him. Then the top of the hill, Ngumbindji, appeared out of the water, and later he could see the mountain of Numbuzare. The other birds then returned. The land dried out and soon the animals found food and safety. Gajara fell overboard, and after a reunion with his family – amusingly told – his wife, Galgalbiri, cooked a kangaroo, and the pleasing smell of her cooking reached Ngadja, who was so delighted with it that he placed a rainbow in the sky. Mickie Bungunie finishes the account thus:

> "The rainbow lies bent across the sky; he [Ngadja] ties up the clouds behind it and the rain does not come. The rainbow keeps the clouds back and protects us so that the rainfall does not rise too high. Our people understand the significance of it. When we see the rainbow, we say, 'There will not be any abnormally heavy rain.'"[10]

I will leave the reader to count the number of corresponding details that there are between the Wunambal tradition and the Book of Genesis. There are many of them. Australia is rich in such traditions. One belongs to the people of the Western Desert who, most intriguingly, hark back to the 'Creation country across the sea to the west' (Mesopotamia), and go on to recall how their ancestors were led to Australia by following certain birds.[11]

Again, there is no question of any of these traditions being the products of visiting missionaries. They are too distant from the Bible's teachings concerning the Creation and the Flood to be that, yet are close enough in so many details to assure us that they are long-held memories of the same events that the Bible speaks of. As witness testimonies they are invaluable, for together they speak with great and sure authority for the historicity of the Book of Genesis. Yet these are not all from this corner of the world. The Maori of New Zealand have accounts of their own to add.

## New Zealand

> "The Maoris of New Zealand say that a certain god, variously named Tu, Tiki, and Tane, took red riverside clay, kneaded it with his own blood into a likeness or image of himself, with eyes, legs, arms, and all complete, in fact, an exact copy of the deity; and having perfected the model, he animated it by breathing into its mouth and nostrils, whereupon the clay effigy at once came to life and sneezed. So like himself was the man whom the Maori Creator Tiki fashioned that he called him *Tiki-ahua*, that is, Tiki's likeness"[12]

This is truly astonishing. Whilst many Creation accounts around the world tell of man's creation by a God, there are few indeed that bring forward the fact that God created man in His own image (Genesis 1:27). And what should we make of the startling detail that God gave His own blood in the creation of that image? There is more innate knowledge of the Gospel in fallen man than meets the eye, it seems. For God to shed His own blood for the sake of man – that man might live! – is at the very heart of the Gospel. Yet the Maori who left us this tradition, would, or rather should, have known nothing of this. It is altogether extraordinary - every bit as extraordinary, in fact, as their tradition of the Flood:

> "The Maoris of New Zealand have a long legend of the deluge. They say that when men multiplied on the earth and there were many great tribes, evil prevailed everywhere, the tribes quarrelled and made war on each other. The worship of the great god Tane, who had created man and woman, was neglected and his doctrines openly denied. Two great prophets, indeed, there were who taught the true doctrine concerning the separation of heaven and earth, but men scoffed at them, saying that they were false teachers and that heaven and earth had been from the beginning just as we see them now."[13]

It is surprising to find that the Maori traditions of the Creation and the Flood should have been challenged in such early times by the notions of uniformitarianism, something foretold in 2 Peter 3:3-6, and which infected the west only 200 years ago. Surprising indeed. Clearly, much has been lost concerning the history of this people. But let's proceed with the rest of their Flood tradition. It gets even better.

The two prophets continued to preach until the tribes cursed them. Then they made a very wide raft, equipping it with living quarters and food stores. Then they prayed that it might rain 'in such abundance as would convince men of the existence and power of the god Tane...' Three others were taken on board the raft, two men named Tiu and Reti (Tiu being a priest), and a woman named Wai-puna-hau, 'but there were other women on the raft'.[14] Tiu prayed, and it rained 'in torrents' for four or five days. But even after the rain had stopped, the flood waters kept rising. For seven months the raft rode out the flood, and by the eighth month the storm calmed and the waters began to subside. All the while, the people on board worshipped Tane, and finally the raft came to rest at Hawaiki:

> "They thought that they might find some of the inhabitants of the world still alive, and that the earth would look as it had looked before the flood. But all was changed. The earth was cracked and fissured in some places, and in others it had been

turned upside down and confounded by reason of the flood. And not one soul was left alive in the world. They who came forth from the raft were the solitary survivors of all the tribes of the earth."[15]

The Maori account is unique in many respects. It contains several components familiar to us from the Bible, but not included in other extra-Biblical versions. The preaching of righteousness by a prophet (or two prophets) in the years before the flood is so reminiscent of Noah that at least one of the prophets has to be a memory of him and his preaching. We have already noted that surprising detail of mankind rejecting the prophets' preaching on the idle supposition that all things continue as they have done from the beginning of the Creation until now – a notion which we know as uniformitarianism. But then, as if in refutation of the idea, we have this graphic and harrowing description of the devastation and signs of obliteration that marked the post-Flood earth - its signs of a ravaging destruction, its sheer emptiness, and, worst of all, its utter and mournful want of humanity.[16]

We may strongly suggest that no Maori dreamt this up out of his own head. The testimony is too detailed and too graphic to be mere invention. It is certainly too pagan to be the result of any missionary teaching. After the occupants leave the raft, they sacrifice not only to Tane, but also to Rangi and Rehua, and to all the other gods. Moreover, it omits so much from the Genesis account, that there has clearly been no reliance on the Bible, oral or written. Nevertheless, the Maori tradition is perhaps the strongest and most intriguing account of the Flood that we have encountered so far, but not *the* strongest, as we shall see later.

Even with these invaluable traditions from Australia and New Zealand, we know that we haven't exhausted the subject from these lands. There are innumerable details still to be gleaned from the various aboriginal peoples of Australia. Some remembered the Creator as Pund-jel, other tribes as Baiame. Adam was remembered as Purukupali by one people, and so on. I dare say that the Maori of New Zealand even now have more to tell us than we have noted here. But we have to move on, to the islands that lie scattered over the vast Pacific Ocean, for most of them also have traditions about the Creation and the Flood.

## Notes to Chapter Eleven

1) http://www.australianexplorer.com/australian_history.htm

2) See http://www.britannica.com/EBchecked/topic/43873/Australian-Aboriginal-languages

3) It seems that the original settlers of Australia were related to or descended from the pre-Dravidians (called Australoids by modern ethnologists) of India, and the now-almost-extinct Veddahs of Sri Lanka (Ceylon), and that they journeyed from south-eastern Asia through the Indonesian and Melanesian Islands to Australia. Roberts and Mountford's, *The Dreamtime*, p. 9 (see Bibliography).

4) Though Frazer doesn't state the fact, the tribe concerned are the Koori.

5) Frazer, pp. 4-5.

6) The frog was named Tiddalik, though Frazer doesn't name him (Roberts and Mountford's, *The Dreamtime*, p. 38.

7) Frazer, pp. 88-89.

8) Coates, H. 'Aboriginal Flood Legend.' *Creation* 4(3), pp. 9-12. October 1981.

9) Ibid.

10) Ibid.

11) Coates, H and Douglas W H. 'Australian Aboriginal Flood Stories.' *Creation* 4(1). pp. 6-10. March 1981. Also: www.answersingenesis.org/creation/v4/i1/flood.asp

12) Frazer, p. 5.

13) Ibid, p. 94. The Maori tradition names the two prophets as Para-whenua-mea and Tupu-nui-a-uta.

14) Eight persons in all? It sounds very likely.

15) Frazer, pp. 95-96.

16) We are looking here at something which we've noted before, namely telling details which can only have come from those who came through the Flood aboard the Ark. Their many listeners would have held on to the most memorable details and passed them down in their turn.

~ * ~

## Chapter Twelve: The Pacific Islands

It would not be possible in a volume of this size to cover all the many islands in the Pacific Ocean. There are thousands of them. But what we can do is consider the Flood traditions of a representative number of the islands or groups of islands. There is one important consideration that we need to bear in mind as we assess these different traditions, and that is the immense isolation of many of the communities which have left them to us. These are not peoples or tribes or nations that have lived in the mainstream of world history, be that of politics, conquest or trade. Indeed, Tahiti, which lies in the southern Pacific, only came to the attention of the French in 1844. Other island communities have only been discovered since that date. In other words, there has been no time for Christian ideas to filter down into the local mythologies. These accounts are unspoiled by any such possibility. So that the reality of that can sink in a little, we shall begin our enquiry with the traditions of a people who first met a white man barely forty years ago:

### The Biami of Papua New Guinea

The Biami of Papua New Guinea, an island in the south-western Pacific, were first contacted in 1971 by a pioneer missionary named Tom Hoey.[1] They were the last of Papua New Guinea's cannibal tribes, but it was whilst learning their language that Tom Hoey discovered that their tribal memory included traditions of both the Creation and the Great Flood. Moreover, Hoey found that their knowledge of the Creation and the Flood prepared them, once they heard the Genesis accounts, to accept the Gospel. They are now a thriving Christian community of about 5000. But exactly how did they remember the events mentioned in the Book of Genesis before Tom Hoey contacted them?

Their memory of the Creation was that in the beginning there were only men. How the men got there, they did not really understand, but they believed that the first man heard a palm tree crying one day. Feeling, no doubt, that the palm tree was lonely like himself, he carved from its wood the likeness of a woman and breathed life into her. When the Biami heard the Genesis account of how God breathed life into

Adam, it struck a deep chord within them. Interestingly, the Biami were so isolated throughout their history that they firmly believed that they, and the tribes immediately adjacent to them, were the only people on earth. Hoey's arrival must have terrified them at first, but it does mean that their memories of the Creation, faulty as they were, were entirely their own and not borrowed from anyone outside their tribe.

On the Flood, they had this to say:

> "Once a great flood came which covered the whole earth and wiped out everyone on earth except for the ancestors of the Biami people. Those ancestors climbed up into the Gobia Tree.... They took up into the tree their planting materials for crops, all their animals, their dogs and their pigs and everything else necessary for life. As the flood waters rose up on the face of the earth the people climbed further up the tree."[2]

The Biami go on to tell how the tree grew taller as the waters rose, but as the waters subsided they were able to leave the tree. The ground is described as very muddy, but soon they were able to plant and the animals began breeding again. The human survivors of the Flood became the ancestors of not just the Biami, but also of the Samos, the Kubos, the Gobasis and the Etoro peoples, all of them neighbouring tribes on the island.

Tom Hoey still returns to Papua New Guinea to continue his work among the Biami, having taught them to read and write, and translating the Scriptures into their tongue. He is adamant that these traditions that they had of the Creation and the Flood pre-date his first contact with the tribe.

### Tahiti

The Tahitian account of the creation of the first man and woman is fascinating. It bears such eloquent testimony to the Book of Genesis that the first missionary to the island, William Ellis, assumed that it must have come in from outside, in spite of the islanders' insistence that it was their tradition long before the arrival of any foreigner.

Because he is the sworn enemy of anything that may appear to corroborate the Book of Genesis, we'll allow Frazer tell us all about this tradition in his own words. It is all the more telling because he argues for the tradition's indigenous authenticity. Let's see how:

> "A very generally received tradition in Tahiti was that the first human pair was made by Taaroa, the chief god. They say that after he had formed the world he created man out of red earth, which was also the food of mankind until bread-fruit was produced. Further, some say that one day Taaroa called for the man by name, and when he came he made him fall asleep. As he slept, the Creator took out one of his bones (*ivi*) and made of it a woman, whom he gave to the man to be his wife, and the pair became the progenitors of mankind. This narrative was taken down from the lips of the natives in the early years of the mission to Tahiti. The missionary, William Ellis, who records it observes: 'This has always appeared to me a mere recital of the Mosaic account of creation, which they had heard from some European, and I never placed any reliance on it, although they have repeatedly told me that it was a tradition among them before any foreigner arrived. Some have also stated that the woman's name was Ivi, which would be by them pronounced as if written *Eve*. Ivi is an aboriginal word, and not only signifies a bone, but also a widow, and a victim slain in war. Notwithstanding the assertion of the natives, I am disposed to think that *Ivi*, or Eve, is the only aboriginal part of the story, as far as it respects the mother of the human race.' However," [says Frazer] "the same tradition has been recorded in other parts of Polynesia besides Tahiti..."[3]

William Ellis knew that it wasn't he who had inspired the Tahitians to this tale, and having no knowledge of any previous contact of theirs with missionaries, he had to guess and suppose that someone must have brought it to them.[4] He even chose to disbelieve their insistence that the tradition was entirely their own, yet was constrained to admit that the 'Eve' element did indeed belong to the people from of old. And this is the point where Frazer challenges Ellis's broad assumption by pointing out that the 'same tradition has been recorded in other parts of Polynesia...' To see Frazer with his guard down is interesting. Elsewhere in his book, he would have seized upon Ellis's hesitation as proof positive that the tale was indeed one that had been learned from missionaries. But instead, he says this:

> "Thus the natives of Fakaofo or Bowditch Island say that the first man was produced out of a stone. After a time he bethought him of making a woman. So he gathered earth and moulded the figure of a woman out of it, and having done so he took a rib out of his left side and thrust it into the earthen figure, which thereupon started up a live woman. He called her Ivi (Eevee) or 'rib' and took her to wife, and the whole human race sprang from this pair. The Maoris also are reported to believe that the first woman was made out of the first man's ribs. This wide diffusion of the story in Polynesia raises a doubt whether it is merely, as Ellis thought, a repetition of the Biblical narrative learned from Europeans."[5]

If only Frazer had been honest enough to develop his statement and see where its logic might have led him - which is why we can say with certainty that he knew all along the falsity of his reasoning and conclusions when he argued against the genuineness of the Bible on the basis that such traditions exist!

However, the Tahitians knew also of the Flood, and had their own version of events concerning it. They say how the Creator, Taaroa, was angry with mankind at their disobedience to his will, and so he overturned the world into the sea. The Flood, caused by the sea rising over the land, destroyed everything on the island, man and beast, save one couple who took refuge with their animals on top of Mount O Pitohito. After ten nights, as they watched, the flood waters receded. There is one detail unique to their account which describes a great falling of stones (meteors?) as the waters receded. The couple had two children, at which time food began to grow again, and it is from these people that all people on earth are descended.[6]

But there is another interesting sidelight on the Tahitian traditions about the Flood which may be a vivid memory of the breaking up of the fountains of the deep. Once again Frazer is of great help to us:

"It is significant... that in these Tahitian legends the flood is ascribed solely to the rising of the sea, and not at all to heavy rain, which is not even mentioned. On this point the Rev. William Ellis, to whom we owe the record of these legends, makes the following observations: 'I have frequently conversed with the people on the subject, both in the northern and southern groups, but could never learn that they had any accounts of the windows of heaven having been opened, or the rain having descended. In the legend of the Ruahatu, the Toamarama of Tahiti, and the Kai of Kahinarii in Hawaii, the inundation is ascribed to the rising of the waters of the sea. In each account, the anger of the god is considered as the cause of the inundation of the world and the destruction of its inhabitants."[7]

## Fiji

"The Fijians have a tradition of a great deluge, which they call Walavu-levu"[8] So begins Frazer, telling us how the creator-god Ndengei had a pet bird which used to wake him every morning with its cooing. Its name was Turukawa. One day, though, Ndengei's grandsons killed the bird and buried it. Sending his messenger Uto to look for the bird, on the second search Uto discovered it and accused the two grandsons. To escape Ndengei's wrath, the two fled to a village of carpenters, who built a large stockade for them to hide in. Ndengei commanded the clouds to pour rain upon the earth. As the flood waters rose, the Fijians say that Rokoro, the god of the carpenters, came to the grandsons' rescue.

The pair rode the waves in two double-canoes that Rokoro had given them, picking up drowning people as they did so. The interesting detail here is that out of all the earth's population, only eight were saved alive in the vessels. The violence which, historically, provoked God to flood the earth, is commemorated in the slaying of the bird.

## Vanuatu (New Hebrides)

Though first sighted by the Spanish in 1606, it was Captain Cook who, in 1774, named the islands. He called them the New Hebrides.

This name remained until independence was gained for the islanders on 30th July 1980, since which time the islands have borne the name, Vanuatu. Missionaries didn't arrive, though, until the 1860s, and they learned from the islanders the following indigenous account of the Flood (their name for Noah is Qat):[9]

> "In the days of Qat the ground now occupied by the lake was a spacious plain clothed with forest. Qat felled one of the tallest trees in the wood and proceeded to build himself a canoe out of the fallen trunk. While he was at work on it, his brothers would come and jeer at him, as he sat or stood there sweating away at his unfinished canoe in the shadow of the dense tropical forest. 'How will you ever get that huge canoe through the thick woods to the sea?' they asked him mockingly. 'Wait and see,' was all he deigned to answer. When the canoe was finished, he gathered into it his wife and his brothers and all the living creatures of the island, down to the smallest ants, and shut himself and them into the vessel, which he provided with a covering. Then came a deluge of rain: the great hollow of the island was filled with water, which burst through the circle of hills at the spot where the great waterfall of Gaua still descends seaward, with a thunderous roar, in a veil of spray. There the canoe swept on the rushing water through the barrier of the hills, and driving away out to sea was lost to view. The natives say that the hero Qat took away the best of everything with him when he thus vanished from sight, and still they look forward to his joyful return."[10]

This tradition of the people of Vanuatu will bear repeated reading, for there is a great deal more here that agrees with the account of the Flood in the Book of Genesis than is immediately obvious. Concerning the islanders' memory of the Creation, the people of Malekula (an island in the group) tell how the creator, Bokor, formed the first man and woman out of clay.

## Palau

Palau, sometimes called the Pelew Islands, is a widespread group of islands in the area of the Pacific known as Micronesia. Its people have inhabited the islands since long before 1000 BC, and are known to have descended from the peoples of Australia and Asia.[11] Although there was, at some undefined time since the islands were first sighted in 1543, an attempt under Spain to establish the Roman Catholic church there, it failed, and the missionary history of Palau is entirely an unknown quantity.[12]

Nonetheless, the islanders of Palau tell how the first man and woman were made out of clay mixed with animal's blood (for redness?).[13] As for the Flood, they tell how a certain man stole an eye of one of the gods (actually a star), and the gods came to earth to reclaim it. Disguised as men, they went from door to door begging, but only one old woman was kind enough to offer them food and shelter. So they warned her to make a raft, lie down on it and sleep. The flood that followed covered the islands and rent the mountains, 'and people knew not how to save themselves, and they all perished in the rising flood.' After the flood, the gods came to search for the old woman, but she had died on the raft. They revived her and she bore five children, from whom all the islanders are descended.[14]

## Hawaii

We could not think of leaving the Pacific islands without hearing the testimony of the Hawaiians regarding the Flood. It is a most intriguing account, the more so for its many startling agreements of detail with that of the Book of Genesis. And for a change, our source isn't Frazer who, not surprisingly, omits this testimony. Instead, he assures his readers with a voice of authority that the Hawaiians knew *nothing* of Noah or the Flood, nor indeed of anything called an ark.[15] Quite why he so firmly denied any such traditions for Hawaii will immediately be made plain. Judge Fornander, who lived and worked amongst the Hawaiians from 1844-1889, tells us of their tradition instead:

> "In the Hawaiian group, there are several legends of the Flood. One legend relates that in the time of Nuu, or Nanna-nuu (also pronounced *lana*, that is, floating), the flood, *Kaiakahinalii*, came upon the earth, and destroyed all living beings; that Nuu, by command of his god, built a large vessel with a house on top of it, which was called and referred to in chants as '*He waa halau Alii o ka Moku*,' the royal vessel, in which he and his family, consisting of his wife, Lilinoe, his three sons and their wives, were saved. When the flood subsided, Kane, Ku, and Lono entered the *waa halau* of Nuu, and told him to go out. He did so, and found himself on top of Mauna Kea (the highest mountain on the island of Hawaii)... Nuu left the vessel in the evening of the day and took with him a pig, cocoanuts, and *awa* as an offering to the god Kane. As he looked up he saw the moon in the sky. He thought it was the god, saying to himself, 'You are Kane, no doubt, though you have transformed yourself to my sight.' So he worshipped the moon, and offered his offerings. Then Kane descended on the rainbow and spoke reprovingly to Nuu, but on account of the mistake Nuu escaped punishment, having asked pardon of Kane."[16]

This tradition alone shows an amazing awareness amongst the Hawaiians of the historical Flood. But that is not all. They also were equally well aware of the Creation, especially that of man and woman. They also knew that the Creator was a triune Godhead, three Persons in One, namely Kane, Ku and Lono. This triune God, whom they referred to as *Hikapoloa Oie*, or The Most Excellent One, existed before the chaos. Having created the heavens and the earth (which the Creator made His footstool – *he kehina honua a Kane* (compare Isaiah 66:1), the stars, the sun and the moon, He created man thus:

> "Last of all they [Kane, Ku and Lono] created man as the model, or in the likeness of Kane. The body of the first man was made of red earth – *lepo ula*, or *alaea* – and the spittle of the gods – *wai nao*. His head was made of a whitish clay – *palolo* – which was brought from the four ends of the world by Lono. When the earth-image of Kane was ready, the three gods breathed into its nose, and called on it to rise, and it

became a living being. Afterwards the first woman was created from one of the ribs – *lalo puhaka* – of the man while asleep, and these two were the progenitors of all mankind."[17]

And even that is not all. The Hawaiians remembered Eden as *Kalana i hau ola*, or Kalana with the life-giving dew, recalling the verse in the Bible which speaks of the mist that watered the whole earth (Genesis 2:6).[18] They remembered also the Tree of Life – *Ulu kapu a Kane* – and the Tree of Knowledge – *ohia hemolele*. Judge Fornander, who collected all these traditions, tried every hypothesis to explain them. But no hypothesis would answer the fact that these accounts are ancient, long pre-dating any contact with the white man. Extraordinary. No wonder Frazer would not even mentioned them, denying their very existence.[19]

## Notes to Chapter Twelve

1) Hoey, Tom. 'The Biami Legends of Creation and Noah's Flood.' *Creation* 7(2), pp. 12-13. Oct 1984. (Introduction by John MacKay). See also the online article at: www.answersingenesis.org/creation/v7/i2/noah.asp

2) Ibid. Seeking refuge in trees is a common substitute in Flood accounts around the world for the Ark where that is either forgotten, or boats are unknown.

3) Frazer, p. 5.

4) William Ellis (1794-1872) had been a missionary in the South Pacific since at least 1822. Tahiti was not discovered until 1844, so by the time Ellis reached Tahiti, he was not exactly unfamiliar with the folklore and traditions of the islanders. If any other missionary party had been active in that area, he would surely have known about it from the natives themselves and his own people, The London Missionary Society.

5) Frazer, pp. 5-6.

6) Ibid, p. 92.

7) Ibid, p. 94.

8) Ibid, p. 90.

9) http://www.historyofnations.net/oceania/vanuatu.html

10) Frazer, p. 91.

11) http://www.1911encyclopaedia.org/Pelew_Islands

12) http://www.sandafayre.com/atlas/carois.htm

13) Frazer, pp. 96-97.

14) Ibid.

15) Ibid, p. 94.

16) http://www.bulfinch.englishatheist.org/hawaii/Chapter1.htm

17) Ibid.

18) Ibid.

19) Ibid. There is no way in which Frazer could have been unaware of the Hawaiian traditions. His omission of their accounts was born of sheer dishonesty.

~ * ~

## Chapter Thirteen: Russia, Europe and Scandinavia

The next logical step in our sweep of the world's Flood traditions is to consider the mythologies of Siberia and Russia, which border on each other and at least face the Pacific Ocean. Sadly, both countries, for all their vastness and variety of culture, have little to say on the early history of the world. Siberia was peopled by the Pazyryk, who were of Scythian stock, and were nomadic horse traders who left no literary records at all. The Xiongnu, who were of Mongol descent, (the Great Wall of China was built specifically to keep them at bay), were literate and seem to have been the ancestral stock of the Huns, but they also left nothing concerning either the history of the world or the Flood. Another Siberian tribe, however, the Bedel Tartars, left this account of the creation of woman. It is a rather bizarre corruption of that event when compared to the Book of Genesis, but it is interesting for the several telling details that agree with Genesis:

> "...the Bedel Tartars of Siberia have a tradition that God at first made a man, who lived quite alone on the earth. But once, while this solitary [man] slept, the devil touched his breast; then a bone grew out from his ribs, and falling to the ground it grew long and became the first woman."[1]

This tiny scrap speaks of a much larger body of tradition which has become lost over the centuries, and it helps us to appreciate the fullness of tradition which other cultures have passed down to us. As for Russia, this land also seems almost totally bereft of anything pre-Christian which relates to the Book of Genesis, but for this snippet concerning the creation of the first man:

> "The Cheremiss of Russia, a Finnish people, tell a story of the creation of man.... They say that God moulded man's body of clay and then went up to heaven to fetch the soul with which to animate it. In his absence he set the dog to guard the body. But while he was away the Devil drew near, and blowing a cold wind on the dog he seduced the animal by the bribe of a fur coat to relax his guard. Thereupon the fiend spat on the clay body and beslavered it so foully, that when God came back he despaired of ever cleaning up the mess and saw

himself reduced to the painful necessity of turning the body outside in. That is why man's inside is now so dirty."[2]

Again, this snippet speaks of a larger earlier tradition which has been lost, and yet even this contains some recognisable components of a tradition which once stood much closer to the history of events as described in the Book of Genesis. The scene is much more rewarding though as we enter Europe. To the south, we have Greece and Rome, both highly literate cultures which have left us traditions of immense interest concerning the Great Flood; and to the north and west we have the Baltic and Germanic peoples who likewise have left us accounts of these things. All of these versions are far superior to those of Russia and Siberia, and indeed much more plentiful. Scandinavia, as we shall see, has its own rich testimonies on the Creation and the Flood.

## Greece

Ancient Greece is fascinating for the depths of insight that its philosophers had concerning especially the Creation. Consider just this snippet from Hesiod who lived way back in the 8th century BC. It is an excerpt from his *Theogony*:

> "First of all the Void came into being... next Earth... Out of the Void came darkness... and out of the Night came Light and Day...."[3]

The rest of Hesiod's account, unfortunately, is typical of many others in its pagan deconstruction of the Creator into a multiplicity of hideous 'gods' who have not a pinch of holiness or wisdom between them. But what is interesting about Hesiod is that he pre-dates by several centuries the attempted Hellenisation of the Jews, the translating of the Old Testament from Hebrew into Greek (the Septuagint), and the coming of the Gospel to that land under the apostle Paul.

Two centuries after Hesiod, but still long before any contact of the Greeks with the Jews, lived Xenophanes who held a loftier view of God altogether:

> "[T]here is one God, greatest among gods and men, similar to mortals neither in shape nor in thought... he sees as a whole, he thinks as a whole, he hears as a whole... Always he remains in the same state, changing not at all... But far from toil he governs everything with his mind."[4]

It is interesting that Xenophanes makes no attempt to name the God of whom he speaks. Every Greek 'god' had a name but this one, and He was to remain acknowledged but unnamed among the Greeks until the day Paul came across His altar inscribed 'To The Unknown God' on Mars' Hill (Acts 17:23), and whom he declared to the Greeks so magnificently. Yet three hundred years or more before Paul did that, the Stoic philosopher, Chrysippus, gave the Greek concept of the One True God perhaps its most logical voice:

> "If there is anything in nature which the human mind, which human intelligence, energy and power could not create, then the creator of such things must be a being superior to man. But the heavenly bodies in their eternal orbits could not be created by man. They must therefore be created by a being greater than man... Only an arrogant fool would imagine that there was nothing in the whole world greater than himself. Therefore there must be something greater than man. And that something must be God."[5]

In certain accounts of man's creation, lesser Greek philosophers taught that it was not God who created man from clay, but Prometheus, whose name means 'forethought.'[6] But what interests us in such traditions is the fact that Prometheus was spoken of as the son of *Iapetos*, which is the Greek version of the name Japheth, known to us from the Book of Genesis, historically the founder of the Indo-European peoples, and a son of Noah.[7] To the Greeks, Iapetos was the son of the heaven and earth and the father of many nations.[8]

Japheth, of course, was one of those who came through the Flood aboard the Ark, which leads us naturally on to the Greeks' version of that event. As we read through it, we would do well to remember that this is an entirely Greek tradition, known amongst that people from pagan times, and long before any contact was made between the Greeks, the Jews and the Book of Genesis. The tradition comes down to us through Lucian of Samosata. In Frazer's words:

> "This gives Lucian occasion to relate the Greek story of the deluge, which according to him ran as follows. The present race of men, he says, are not the first of humankind; there was another race which perished wholly. We are of the second breed, which multiplied after the time of Deucalion [the Greek Noah]. As for the folk before the flood, it is said that they were exceedingly wicked and lawless; for they neither kept their oaths, nor gave hospitality to strangers, nor respected suppliants, wherefore the great calamity befell them. So the fountains of the deep were opened, and the rain descended in torrents, the rivers swelled, and the sea spread far over the land, till there was nothing left but water, water everywhere, and all men perished. But Deucalion was the only man who, by reason of his prudence and piety, survived and formed the link between the first and the second race of men; and the way in which he was saved was this. He had a great ark, and into it he entered with his wives and children; and as he was entering there came to him pigs, and horses, and lions, and serpents, and all other land animals, all of them in pairs. He received them all, and they did him no harm; nay, by God's help there was a great friendship between them, and they all sailed in one ark so long as the flood prevailed on the earth."[9]

With his, '...water, water everywhere...' and his, 'nay, by God's help...' Frazer is clearly trying to inject some humour into an account that has made him decidedly nervous. Such a tradition should not have been found among the Greeks (a race whom Frazer admired) if what Frazer and his colleagues had always maintained was true. However, and more intriguingly, one Greek scholar known as the 'Parian Chronicler', who compiled his chronology in 265 BC, dates the Flood to 1265 years before he wrote his work, according to which reckoning the Flood occurred in 1530 BC.[10] About a thousand years adrift, it is interesting nonetheless in that the Greeks didn't push the event far back into the mists of time, into some ethereal age of the 'gods', as certain other cultures did.[11]

## Rome

Whatever indigenous traditions the Romans may have had before their wholesale adoption of Greek ideas and culture, it seems that the Greek superseded the Roman traditions among them, especially those concerning the Creation and the Flood. There is therefore little trace of their older traditions. The names of Roman gods were substituted for those of the Greeks, of course, Iapetos (Japheth) being Latinised to Jupiter and so on, but basically the Roman accounts of the Flood are of Greek inspiration.[12] The same seems to go for the Roman ideas on the Creation. However, the Romans did have a very clear idea of what Creationism is, and their Stoic philosophers argued for it vociferously. Cicero, for example, who was perhaps the greatest advocate in law that Rome ever produced, and who knew a thing or two about the evaluation and weighing of evidence, has this to say:

> "When you see a sundial or a water-clock, you see that it tells the time by design and not by chance. How then can you imagine that the universe as a whole is devoid of purpose and intelligence when it embraces everything, including these artifacts themselves and their artificers? Our friend Posidonius as you know has recently made a globe which in its revolution shows the movements of the sun and stars and planets, by day and night, just as they appear in the sky. Now if someone were to take this globe and show it to the people of Britain or Scythia, would a single one of those barbarians fail to see that it was the product of a conscious intelligence?"[13]

Not that Rome was without its materialist philosophers, of course. These emanated from the Epicurean school, whose most able voice was that of Lucretius, and Cicero encapsulated all of his creationist arguments in his book, *On the Nature of the Gods*, in refutation of Lucretius. Where Lucretius and his colleagues could see nothing in the universe that was not just a mindless and fortuitous concourse of atoms, Cicero could look up at the night sky and say this:

> "In the heavens there is nothing accidental, nothing arbitrary, nothing out of order, nothing erratic. Everywhere is order,

truth, reason, constancy... I cannot understand this regularity in the stars, this harmony of time and motion in their various orbits through all eternity, except as the expression of reason, mind and purpose.... Their constant and eternal motion, wonderful and mysterious in its regularity, declares the indwelling power of a divine intelligence. If any man cannot feel the power of God when he looks upon the stars, then I doubt whether he is capable of any feeling at all."[14]

Cicero, alas, died in 43 BC, never having heard the Gospel, and never, as far as we know, having read the Book of Genesis – though how he would have received either we can easily imagine. But as we take our leave of Rome, we may take a moment to ponder how true it is that '...there is no new thing under the sun' (Ecclesiastes 1:9). We shall hear Cicero once more as he puts forward an argument that is not unfamiliar to us in these days of the creation/evolution controversy regarding genetics, and our understanding of how their mind-boggling complexity could never be explained by any notion of chance. In Cicero's words:

"Is it not a wonder that anyone can bring himself to believe that a number of solid and separate particles by their chance collisions and moved only by the force of their own weight could bring into being so marvellous and beautiful a world? If anybody thinks that this is possible, I do not see why he should not think that if an infinite number of examples of the twenty-one letters of the alphabet, made of gold or what you will, were shaken together and poured out on the ground it would be possible for them to fall so as to spell out, say, the whole text of the *Annals* of Ennius. In fact I doubt whether chance would permit them to spell out a single verse!"[15]

For a pagan philosopher, this is astonishing wisdom and insight, and it would seem from this that under the Providence of God, Stoicism paved the way for many in Rome to receive the Gospel when Paul arrived in that city. The Book of Genesis, which Paul preached upon just as he had with the Greeks, would have made so much sense to his listeners, prepared as they were by the teachings of Cicero and the Stoic school. Cicero considered, and then dismissed, the possibility of an infinite number of letters accidentally falling about so as to spell out a work, famous in his day, called the *Annals* of Ennius – a massive 18 volume work by Quintus Ennius covering the 1000-year period from 1184-184 BC. Today we speak of the impossibility of an infinite number of monkeys being able to randomly type out the complete works of Shakespeare. In more than two thousand years, it seems, the arguments haven't changed a bit.

## Northern Europe

The tribes and peoples of Northern Europe were held in considerable disdain by the more 'cultured' Greeks and Romans of the south, by Rome especially because her supposedly invincible armies were constantly being thrashed in battle by the northern barbarians. One Germanic tribe known to the Romans as the Cherusci, managed in AD 9 to steal the Roman battle standards from Quinctilius Varus and his legions in the Teutoberg Forest, thus humiliating the Roman army and causing worldwide embarrassment for the empire.[16] Yet even these 'howling savages' of Germania and the north had their memories of the Creation and the Flood, with one or two surprising details besides.

The pre-Christian Saxons, for example, who meticulously kept their genealogies from the most ancient times, were perfectly happy to trace their lineage all the way back to Japheth and Noah, quite oblivious of the distress that this has brought to scholars of the modernist school.[17] But there they are, inscribed in the ancient documents for all to see, the names of Japheth (*Iafet*) and Noah (*Noe*). One or two ingenious arguments (and a great many not so ingenious) have been offered to explain this most awkward phenomenon, but every one of them fails.[18]

Yet, not only did the pre-Christian Saxons remember Japheth and Noah, they also thought of the Creator as a Trinity. The recollections are dim and distant, to be sure, as with most pagan traditions, but they are there nonetheless. Sometimes, as with the pagan *Beowulf* epic, their recounting of the Creation could be truly sublime. Here it is, rendered into prose from lines 90-98 of the poem:

> "He who knew how to tell of the creation of men in the far past related the tale of how the Almighty wrought the earth, the bright and radiant expanse encircled by the waters. Exulting in victory, he set up sun and moon, lights to give light to the earth-dwellers, and he adorned the surface of the ground with branches and foliage. Life also he created for every race of beings that move and live."[19] – a perfect summary, one might say, of Genesis 1.

The pre-Christian *Beowulf* epic – it was composed before the Saxons became Christianised – also mentions the Flood, which it never should have done if what modernists have always taught were in any way true. The occasion in the poem is the presentation by Beowulf to King Hrothgar of Denmark, of Beowulf's sword-hilt, which was all that remained of his sword after his battle with Grendel's mother. It was already an ancient heirloom when Beowulf gave it to Hrothgar:

> "On it was engraved the origins of strife in time immemorial, when the tide of rising water drowned the race of giants; their end was horrible; they were opposed to the Eternal Lord, and their reward was the downpour and the flood."[20]

Regarding the triune Creator, the *Elohim* of the Bible, the Saxons remembered Him dimly as Odin, Vilja and Vilis. Later, when it came to man's creation, they named Him as Odin, Hoenir (the 'silent god'), and Lodur. This creative trinity, the Saxons understood, found two trees on the seashore. One was an ash (*askr*), and the other an elm (*embla*). To create man from the ash and woman from the elm, Odin put spirit within them; Hoenir gave them understanding; and Lodur gave them their senses and their outward form. They then breathed into them the breath of life, and the pair were named Lif and Lifthrasir, Life and Life-eager. From them, all mankind is descended.[21]

Concerning the Flood itself, no specifically Saxon tradition has come down to us, unless they shared the Scandinavian legend, which is likely. But they do refer to the Flood as a definite historical incident: "This Japheth was Noah's son, and he was borne [or carried] in the ark."[22] Moreover, the Saxons actually dated the Flood in their chronology, stating that the number of years from Adam to the Flood was, "...twa hund wintra & twu thusenda & twa & fiowertig."[23] – that is, two thousand two hundred and forty-two winters, or years.

Where did they get this figure from? It wasn't from the Latin Vulgate Bible, because that agrees with the Hebrew in giving 1656 years for this period. The Septuagint (which they had no access to anyway) gives 2256 years. We have to say that we don't know, but the figure does agree with that given by a Celtic British scholar named Nennius who wrote in the 8th century CE, long after the Saxons wrote their account.[24] More notably, the Saxons believed the earth to be very young, its Creation (and the Flood) being recent. The Creation they dated to about 5200 BC, thus placing the Flood in their view to the year 2958 BC.[25] This is altogether not what the modernist school would have us know about the Saxons.

## Scandinavia

For the most part, Scandinavia (which here includes Iceland) shared the mythology and traditions of Northern Europe. The gods and horrors were certainly the same, but an Icelandic scholar of the 13th century, Snorri Sturluson, has added greatly to our knowledge by compiling the prose *Edda*, a truly compendious collection of Norse myths and traditions.[26] Of particular interest to us in our present enquiry are the pagan accounts he passes down to us concerning the Creation, the Flood, and how the Norse people actually got to Scandinavia and where they came from.

The Norse tradition of the Creation is recounted by Snorri through a dialogue between a king disguised as an old man and calling himself Gangleri, and a trinity of 'gods' which the Vikings knew as *Har* (High), *Jafnhar* (Just-as-High), and *Thrithi* (Third). Here the three take on the form of an oracle, and answer the old man (who is actually King Gylfi of Sweden) as he asks them, "Who is the highest and most ancient of all gods?"[27]

He is told that this god is called *Alfodr* (All-Father) in Norse, but in the tongue of Old Asgard he has twelve names (we shall consider Old Asgard shortly). Meanwhile:

> "Then Gangleri asked: 'Where is this god, what power has he, and what great works has he performed?' High said, 'He lives throughout all ages and rules all his kingdom and governs all things great and small.' Then spoke Just-as-High: 'He made heaven and earth and the skies and everything in them.' Then spoke Third: 'But his greatest work is that he made man and gave him a soul that shall live and never perish though the body decay to dust or burn to ashes. And all men who are righteous shall live and dwell with him himself in the place called Gimle...'"[28]

Here the dialogue descends into pure pagan lore, telling how the heavens and earth were made from the remains of a slain frost-giant named Ymir. The vault of heaven was made from his skull, the oceans from his blood, the rocks from his teeth and bones, and so on. But there are several points of interest also. The Creator here takes on the name Odin (who was Woden to the Saxons):

> "And it is my belief [says High to his questioner] that this Odin and his brothers must be the rulers of heaven and earth; it is our opinion that this must be what he is called... and you would do well to agree to call him that too."[29]

High's words carried within them somewhat more than a veiled threat, and the king immediately complied with them – no heretic he. But importantly, we also learn at this point something of the Norse tradition of the Great Flood, and their dimmed but recognisable memory of Noah, whom they called Bergelmir. Regarding this Bergelmir, Sturluson has this to say, taking up the story of when the frost-giant Ymir was slain by Odin and his brothers:

> "...when he fell, so much blood flowed from his wounds that with it they drowned all the race of frost-giants, except that one escaped with his household. Giants called him Bergelmir. He went up into his ark with his wife and was preserved there,

> and from them are descended the families of frost-giants, as it says here: 'Countless winters before the earth was created, then was Bergelmir born. That is the first I remember, when that wise giant was laid in a box."[30]

The 'box' referred to here is, of course, the Ark. It is a curious circumstance that in many languages, even in Hebrew, the word for ark is also the word for box or chest. In this context, therefore, Faulkes, who translated the *Edda* into English for us (see Bibliography), correctly uses the word 'ark'. But Bergelmir's name is also worth pondering. It means Mountain-yeller, or Mountain-crier. Could this be yet another of those circumstantial and incidental details that were handed down after the Flood by those who had been occupants of the Ark and had come through it all? We have seen several other such authenticating details from other traditions, details which are not mentioned in the Book of Genesis, but which nevertheless might well have occurred. Did Noah cry long and loud when he disembarked from the Ark and saw the devastation around him? Genesis doesn't say so, but it is a notion. Names had meaning in olden times, and Noah had come from a world teeming with life and great beauty, into a world of indescribable emptiness and ruin.

But talking of names which had meaning, the term 'Old Asgard' is most relevant to our enquiry, because it is the name of the ancestral homeland of the Saxons and Vikings. In their tradition, Asgard is the home of the gods (the *Aesir*). But Old Asgard is the place whence Odin (and here we meet with the historical Odin, the 5th-4th century BC patriarchal ancestor of the Norse and Saxons) migrated north with his people. Snorri tells us where that land lay. It is Asia, or more specifically, the land known to us as Turkey, part of Asia Minor, which lies not a million miles from the Plain of Shinar and the site of the Tower of Babel. Moreover, the word Aesir, it turns out, is nothing more than the Norse term for Asia, and Asgard is simply Norse for Asia-garden.[31] Odin was said by the Teutons to have lived in Asaheim (Asia-home):

> "It is interesting to note, in Icelandic saga, ancient Teutons separated Asia from Europe by the River Tanakvisl (or Vanakvisl), which flows into the Black Sea. Eastward across

the river (in Asia), so legend tells us, was a land known as Asaheim or Asaland, where dwelt Odin, chief god, in his citadel named Asgard."[32]

So, it would seem that in Old Asgard we have, not an ethereal home for the gods among the stars somewhere, but a real 'flesh-and-blood' ancestral homeland for the Nordic peoples, and a tradition which sits very comfortably with the history of the early post-Flood world as told in the Book of Genesis. Indeed, an ancestral homeland in this part of the world explains much about the Vikings later migrations from Scandinavia to Russia, the North African coast and the eastern Mediterranean. It was a part of the world that they already knew and had their ancestral roots in.

But as we leave Europe and Scandinavia, we would do well to consider that out of those peoples who have left us any pre-Christian records of their past, the Icelanders, the Danes, the Norwegians, the Saxons, and even the unrelated British and Irish Celts, have all left records which state emphatically, specifically and unambiguously that they all separately and independently traced their descent from the Biblical Japheth and Noah. There is absolutely no fudging of that fact. It is clear, it is written into the records for all to see, and it is entirely inexplicable in modernist terms. Moreover, before ever they'd heard of Genesis, they all of them knew of the Creation, and they all of them knew of the Flood.[33]

## Notes to Chapter Thirteen

1) Frazer, p. 6.

2) Ibid, p. 10. There is, however, some interesting dragon-lore from Russia which will bear investigation (see, for example, Warner, *Russian Myths* – see Bibliography).

3) Hesiod, p. 15. cit. also Cooper, *After the Flood*, p. 19.

4) Barnes, pp. 95-97. cit. also Cooper, *After the Flood*, p. 19.

5) Cicero, p. 18. cit. also Cooper, *After the Flood*, p. 25.

6) Frazer, p. 3.

7) http://www.answers.com/topic/prometheus

8) Cooper, *After the Flood*, p. 199.

9) Frazer, p. 69. An interesting sidelight on the tradition of Deucalion, the Greek Noah, is the meaning of his name. It derives from *deucos*, meaning sweet new wine, and *halieus*, meaning mariner – an echo no doubt of Genesis 9:20-21. At the very least, the person who initially invented the name Deucalion must surely have been aware of this unfortunate episode in Noah's life.

10) Ibid, p. 68. Frazer erroneously says 1539 BC.

11) Frazer, against his better judgment no doubt, given his agenda, tells us that in memory of Deucalion's Flood, the people of Hierapolis commemorated the receding of the floodwaters in a twice-yearly ceremony, when great multitudes would pour seawater down a chasm beneath the temple of Hera, the chasm being in their tradition the drain down which the Flood's waters poured away. See Frazer, p. 69.

12) For a closely-argued genealogical demonstration of the identity of Jupiter with Japheth, see Cooper, *After the Flood*, pp. 241-242 (Appendix 11).

13) Cicero, p. 159. Posidonius (135-51 BC) was an accomplished polymath of the Stoic school, as was Cicero himself. By observing the star Canopus at Rhodes and Alexandria, Posidonius calculated the circumference of the earth to 24,000 miles, very close to its real circumference of 24,901 miles.

14) Cicero, pp. 144-145.

15) Ibid, p. 161.

16) For the background to this event, see: www.livius.org/q/quinctilius/varus.html

17) For a detailed discussion of these genealogies, showing their authenticity and historicity, see Cooper, *After the Flood*, pp. 83-96 & 228-230.

18) Ibid.

19) Davidson, p. 198. The *Beowulf* epic, though a poem, is an historically verifiable account of certain events and characters which belong firmly to the 6th century CE, before the Saxons were Christianised. For an in-depth treatment of the epic's historical statements and genealogies, see Cooper, *After the Flood*, pp. 146-161 & 231-240. For the Creation account in the original Anglo-Saxon, see Klaeber's *Beowulf*, pp. 4-5.

20) Crossley-Holland, p. 56. The Flood reference in *Beowulf* is contained in lines 1687-1693 of the poem. For the original Anglo-Saxon text, see Klaeber, p. 63. Interestingly, line 1562 of the poem refers to Beowulf's sword as *giganta geweorc*, giants' work, or "wrought by giants" as Crossley-Holland has it, which Klaeber – surprisingly for a modernist – links to Genesis 4:22 and the smithy of Tubalcain. The *Beowulf* epic also alludes to the murderous Cain (to whom it likens the monster Grendel) and, of course, refers to the murdered Abel. It is these pagan pre-Flood allusions that prompted Klaeber's somewhat tentative ascription. Consider also Genesis 6:4: "And there were giants in the earth in those days... the same became mighty men which were of old, men of renown."

21) Davidson, pp. 27-28 & 197-202.

22) *Reliquae Antiquae* (ed. Wright). 1841-1845. London Guildhall Library.

23) MS. Cotton. Vespasian. D. IV. Fol 69v. cit. Cooper, p. 122.

24) *A principio mundi usque ad diluvium II CC XL II* – From the beginning of the world until the Flood, 2242 (years). cit. Cooper, pp. 122 & 129.

25) Cooper, pp. 122-123.

26) Snorri Sturluson was born in 1179 into the wealthy Sturlungar family. He was twice elected Law-Speaker, or President of the Icelandic Parliament (the *Althingi*) from 1215-1218 and from 1222-1231. He wrote the *Heimskringla* (a book on Scandinavian history), *Egil's Saga* (which covers the close of the Viking era), and the prose *Edda*. The standard of his scholarship was very high indeed, but he unwisely involved himself in the turbulent politics of the time and was murdered on 23rd September 1241 on instructions from King Hakon Hakonarson of Norway.

27) Sturluson, p. 8. Just to add a little mystery to the proceedings, *Har*, *Jafnhar* and *Thrithi* are represented in manuscript illustrations of the *Edda* as Har being seated (in reverse order) on the lowest throne, Jafnhar on the next highest, and Thrithi on the highest throne.

28) Ibid, pp. 8-9.

29) Ibid, p. 11.

30) Ibid.

31) Read Sturluson's Prologue to the Edda, pp. 1-5.

32) Rydberg, Viktor. *Teutonic Mythology: Gods and Goddesses of the Northland*. 1907. Norroena Society. London. pp. 33-34.

33) See Cooper, *After the Flood*.

~ * ~

# Chapter Fourteen: South and Central America

We come now across the Atlantic Ocean to the mountains, jungles and tropical rain-forests of South and Central America. Some of the peoples whose Flood traditions we are about to consider live more remotely that even their Pacific Island counterparts. The islands of the Pacific are indeed remote, but the seas which surround them are very much easier to traverse than the impenetrable jungles which surround the tribes and families who inhabit, say, the Amazon Basin. Even today we know that there are many tribes in those forests who have yet to be discovered by us. Therefore, to find Flood traditions there at all would be most surprising, but Flood traditions there surely are, and not just in the Amazon.

We have noticed in other Flood traditions how details crept into them which are not mentioned in the Book of Genesis, but which nevertheless have a loud ring of authenticity about them. They are details which those eight who came through the Flood would have remembered and passed on to their many listeners, and which tell us that we are listening to the voice of authentic memory. Well, the traditions of South and Central America also have details which authenticate the accounts as genuine memories of the Flood. The unusual behaviour of animals in the days before the Flood are a telling detail, and one which would undoubtedly have been recounted by Noah and his sons and then passed on to others, even though the Book of Genesis doesn't mention it. Before any natural disaster, animals will appear panicky, or morose, or skittish. People who live in earthquake zones are often warned by watching the animals that disaster is about to strike long before the seismologists become aware of it. But there are other phenomena too, climatic and geological mainly, which must have presaged the Flood and which also were recalled by those who had been on the Ark, as we can see in our first account:

## Brazil (Amazon Jungle)

> "...the Pamarys, Abederys, and Kataushya, on the River Purus,[1] relate that once on a time people heard a rumbling above and below the ground. The sun and moon, also, turned red, blue, and yellow, and the wild beasts mingled fearlessly

with men. A month later they heard a roar and saw darkness ascending from the earth to the sky, accompanied by thunder and heavy rain, which blotted out the day and the earth. Some people lost themselves, some died, without knowing why; for everything was in a dreadful state of confusion. The water rose very high, till the earth was sunk beneath the water..."[2]

The account goes on to tell how soon only the tallest trees' branches were visible above the water, and amongst these the people who could swim sought refuge. But even that was in vain, for soon they perished with cold and hunger, "...and all the time it was dark and the rain fell." One couple, however, did survive, the man Uassu (their Noah) and his wife. Such was the devastation that, after the Flood had abated, these two found no trace of even a single corpse, not so much as a pile of bleached bones to say that anything, man or beast, had once lived there.

This tradition holds some fascinating details, details upon which all three tribes are agreed. Firstly, there is the unusual and fearless mingling of the wild animals and men – the fearlessness, I imagine, being entirely on the side of the animals. But then there are the strange and frightening climatic phenomena, especially the reverse-to-nature *rising* of the darkness from the earth to the sky. This is accompanied by an immense roar and would seem to have marked the breaking up of the fountains of the deep, after which began the thunder and the rain. Those aboard the Ark would have felt and seen it all, and would even have seen the climatic phenomena which had presaged the Flood a month before it began. Such stark and riveting details are entirely authentic.

## Ecuador

Our next Flood tradition is found in Ecuador, over on the west (Pacific) coast of the continent. Ecuador once formed part of the Inca Empire, whose Creation and Flood traditions we shall be looking at in the following chapter. But for now, we are interested in what the Murato people of Ecuador have to tell us about the Flood:[3]

"... a Murato Indian went to fish in a lagoon of the Pastaza River; a small crocodile swallowed his bait, and the fisherman

> killed the young animal. The crocodile's mother, or rather the mother of crocodiles in general [a goddess in other words], was angry and lashed the water with her tail, till the water overflowed and flooded all the neighbourhood of the lagoon. All the people were drowned except one man, who climbed into a palm-tree and stayed there for many days. All the time it was as dark as night. From time to time he dropped a fruit of the palm, but he always heard it splash in the water. At last one day the fruit which he let fall dropped with a simple thud on the ground; there was no splash, so he knew that the flood had subsided."[4]

Crocodiles were no doubt worshipped by the pre-Christian Muratos (and may be still), so we have a very dimmed memory here of a 'god' being offended by man's violence, and flooding the earth in retribution. Again we have the added detail of a dense darkness accompanying the Flood, which for a long time pervaded and blotted out even the days. Those who first began to lose the accuracy of their original Flood tradition did remember, however, that the survivor of the Flood employed some method of finding out whether the waters had abated or not.

## Chile

The Araucanian Indians of Chile, otherwise known as the Mapuches, were not subjugated by the incoming Spanish until the 1880s after more than 300 years of concerted military effort to bring them to heel, 1553 being a particularly bad year for the Spaniards. In earlier days, the Mapuches had likewise fought off a massive attempt by the earlier Inca Empire to invade the north of their land, which gives us a very good idea of their strength and independence of thought.

The Mapuche word 'chilli' means 'where the land ends', and probably gave the land of Chile its name.[5] It was first heard by the Spanish from the very few survivors of Diego de Almagro's 1535 somewhat over-confident 'expedition' into Peru. But as for any pre-Conquest folk-memories of the Flood, the Mapuches have left us this:

> "The Araucanians of Chili [*sic*] have a tradition of a great deluge, in which only a few persons were saved. These fortunate survivors took refuge on a high mountain called Thegtheg, the thundering, or the sparkling, which had three points and possessed the property of floating on water."[6]

Frazer, our source for the account, then takes great and ill-disguised glee in quoting a Spanish historian whom he doesn't name (but who is actually Diego de Rosales),[7] who infers that this account has nothing to do with the Flood of Noah on the rather specious argument that the Mapuches commonly run into the hills whenever there's an earthquake. But let us think about this for one moment. The Mapuches were, by their own account, fearful that after an earthquake there was the danger of the world being flooded again, and that high ground should therefore be sought. And that has nothing to do with the Flood of Noah? What of the floating refuge called Thegtheg (and 'mountain' may well be not the best translation of the word)? Does that have nothing to do with the Flood either? On the contrary, we may think that it has everything to do with it.

An earthquake (the breaking up of the fountains of the deep) presaging a world-destroying deluge, the mere memory of which still strikes such terror into the Mapuches more than 4000 years after the event, that they habitually gather provisions and flee to higher ground whenever there's a tremor, speaks to me of everything to do with the Flood. But then, with Frazer being no friend of the Book of Genesis, and with Rosales being no friend of the Mapuches, I'm surprised that anything has been mentioned at all.

To the Mapuches, the breaking up of the fountains of the deep was the most memorable thing about the approach of the Flood. They remembered that survival had depended on a large floating object, and so ingrained into their memory was the sheer magnitude of the event, that the very thought of it happening again terrified them – and the Mapuches, as both the Inca and the Spanish discovered to their cost, were not afraid of much.

## Guyana (formerly British Guiana)

> "The Arawaks of British Guiana believe that since its creation the world has been twice destroyed, once by fire and once by flood. Both destructions were brought on it by Aiomun Kondi, the great 'Dweller on High', because of the wickedness of mankind. But he announced beforehand the coming catastrophe, and men who accepted the warning prepared to escape from the great fire... Afterwards, when the destruction of the world by a deluge was at hand, a pious and wise chief named Marerewana was informed of the coming flood and saved himself and his family in a large canoe."[8]

This is a simple and plain tradition, a very brief précis of the events described in the Book of Genesis. But there is another tradition from the same country, one that belonged to the Macusis:[9]

> "...in the beginning the good spirit Makunaima, whose name means, 'He who works in the night', created the heaven and the earth. When he had stocked the earth with plants and trees, he came down from his celestial mansion, climbed up a tall tree, and chipped off the bark with a big stone axe. The chips fell into the river at the foot of the tree and were changed into animals of all kinds. When he had thus provided for the creation of animals the good spirit next created man; and when the man had fallen into a sound sleep he awoke to find a woman standing at his side. Afterwards the evil spirit got the upper hand on earth; so the good spirit Makunaima sent a great flood. Only one man escaped in a canoe; he sent out a rat to see whether the water had abated, and the rat returned with a cob of maize."[10]

We have by no means exhausted the supply from South America of indigenous traditions of the Flood. Indeed, in the following chapter we shall encounter traditions from the same continent which far surpass those we have just read. But regarding those traditions that we have from the 'lesser' tribes, Frazer alone tells us that they are held by the tribes around Cape Frio; the Caingangs (or Coroados) of Rio Grande do Sul; the Carayas of the Araguaya River; the tribes of the Orinoco;

the Tamanaques; the Canaris of Ecuador; those of Huarochiri in Peru; the Guancas; those of Chiquito; the Chiriguanos of Bolivia; and even the people of Tierra del Fuego who live at the extreme southern end of the South American continent. There are, of course, many others, but they are all traditions of the earth being flooded with only one or more survivors coming through, the rest of the world's population perishing in the waters.

Some of those traditions include a dimmed memory not just of the Flood and its devastation of a wicked and fallen world, but also the promise that God made never to flood the whole earth again, a promise which He embodied in the rainbow (Genesis 9:8-17). The Wayuu people of Venezuela provide us with one such recollection:

> "Without Kasipoluin, the rainbow, it would rain without ceasing, but the rainbow came to tell Juya, the rain, to stop. He comes to disperse the rains. The rainbow comes out at the same time as Juya, to tell him to stop: 'Don't rain any more, Juya,' he tells him."[11]

## Central America

> "The Indians about Panama 'had some notion of Noah's flood, and said that when it happened one man escaped in a canoe with his wife and children, from whom all mankind afterwards proceeded and peopled the world.' The Indians of Nicaragua believed that since its creation the world has been destroyed by a deluge, and that after its destruction the gods created men and animals and all things afresh."[12]

Today there are just seven surviving indigenous peoples in Panama: the Embera; the Wounan; the Guaymi; the Bugle; the Kuna; the Naso; and the Bribri. There were many many others when the Spaniards arrived in the early-mid 16th century. Which of them held the above tradition, we do not know. As for Nicaragua, between 1524 and 1529, the Indian population was entirely wiped out by the Spanish. The above tradition must therefore have been gleaned at some time between those years from the people who held it.

Between the years 1780 and 1781, a 'New Spanish' (*Novohispano*) Jesuit scholar, Francisco Xavier Clavigero (1731-1787), published a massive 10 volume work which he called, *La Historia Antigua de Mexico* – The Ancient History of Mexico. Clavigero had an empathy and love for the native Indians of Mexico that was rare indeed for his time, and he spent years (often getting into trouble for it from his superiors) investigating the languages, customs, and strange written records of his charges. Even more unusually, he strongly criticised the brutality of the *conquistadores*, and extols the morals and qualities of the Indians.[13] Amongst the things he tells us about them is this:

> "The Mexicans...with all other civilised nations, had a clear tradition, though somewhat corrupted by fable, of the creation of the world, of the universal deluge, of the confusion of tongues, and of the dispersion of the people; and had actually all these events represented in their pictures. They said that when mankind were overwhelmed with the deluge, none were preserved but a man named Coxcox (to whom others give the name Teocipactli), and a woman called Xochiquetzal, who saved themselves in a little bark, and having afterwards got to land upon a mountain called by them Colhuacan, had there a great many children; that these children were all born dumb, until a dove from a lofty tree imparted to them languages, but differing so much that they could not understand one another."[14]

Still in Mexico, we are told by Frazer that the following tradition of the Flood was held by the indigenous people of the province of Michoacan:

> "The natives said that when the flood began to rise, a man named Tezpi, with his wife and children, entered into a great vessel, taking with them animals and seeds of diverse kinds sufficient to restock the world after the deluge. When the waters abated, the man sent forth a vulture, and the bird flew away, but finding corpses to batten on, it did not return. Then the man let fly other birds, but they also came not back. At last he sent forth a humming-bird, and it returned with a green bough in its beak."[15]

Frazer, whose long-suffering had been sorely tested by this stage of his book, having remained silent for some time, felt obliged at this point to interject the tired old modernist assertion that this version of events 'may' have been heard through missionaries – the 'may' betraying Frazer's awareness of just how weak such an hypothesis is. But what missionaries must they have been? The hero's name is completely wrong and sounds nothing like that of Noah. Moreover, these details are known to be included in numerous other traditions from around the world where no such assertion could possibly be made. Where, for example, were the missionaries during the 2nd millennium BC when the Babylonians recorded their Flood traditions on clay tablets, and which also contain these details? What the point of Frazer's objection was, we can only guess at. But I suppose he had to say something.

One must have a heart of stone, though, not to feel his pain. It must be irksome beyond measure to have dedicated so much time, wealth and energy toward disparaging and ridiculing the Book of Genesis, only to find that every word you've written only exonerates it. The frustrations of Tantalus must have been a joy compared. But Frazer is not needed for the next stage of our enquiry. We turn now to other – native - authors and other native traditions as we hear the truly remarkable testimonies of the Inca, the Toltec, the Aztec and the Maya.

## Notes to Chapter Fourteen

1) These people live deep inside the Brazilian jungle of the Amazon. The River Purus flows into the Amazon where they live, and was explored by William Chandless in the 1860s on behalf of the Royal Geographical Society. The Society published his reports in their journal of 1866.

2) Frazer, p. 100.

3) The Muratos are part of the ethnic group, the Jibaros. The word 'Jibaros' is actually a pejorative term meaning 'savage', coined by the Spanish in the 16th century. The tribe are known to themselves as the Shuar, and live along the Maranon River in northern Peru and eastern Ecuador.

4) Frazer, pp. 100-101.

5) http://members.shaw.ca/chileanwinehouse/chile.html

6) Frazer, p. 101.

7) Diego de Rosales (1601-1677) was the author of *Historia General del Reino de Chile* – General History of the Kingdom of Chile. He arrived in Chile from Spain in 1629 as a Jesuit. He served as army chaplain in the Spanish war against the Mapuches (the Arauco War of the 1640s), which is where he learned the language and customs of the people. He was fortunate to survive the Siege of Boroa during the Mapuche uprising of 1655, and went on to become the Superior of the Jesuit Province of Chile. His second book was more ominously titled, *Conquista Espiritual del Reino de Chile*. How many Mapuche were tortured and burned alive by him during this 'spiritual conquest' we may never know.

8) Frazer, p. 103. The Arawak Indians came into British Guiana (modern Guyana) from the Caribbean Islands. As early as 1596, they recruited the help of Spain to evict and displace the indigenous tribes of the country.

9) The Macusis were one of thirteen tribes of British Guiana noted by Robert Schombergk in his 1843 survey: www.guyana.org/features/guyanastory/chapter4.html

10) Frazer, p. 103.

11) http://www.venezuelanindian.blogspot.com/2008/01/wayuu-myth-3-kasipoluin-rainbow.html

12) Frazer, p. 107.

13) http://www.newadvent.org/cathen/04008c.htm

14) cit. Frazer, p. 107.

15) Ibid, pp. 107-108.

~ * ~

# Chapter Fifteen: The Inca, Toltec, Aztec and Mayan Traditions

In case it is wondered why the Inca, the Toltec, the Aztec and the Mayan peoples were not listened to in the previous chapter, the reason is this. The Flood traditions in the previous chapter were all passed on orally by the indigenous peoples who had preserved them, and were recorded by the Spanish *conquistadores*, inquisitors and other interrogators. As far as we know, writing was unknown, and perhaps even impracticable, to the native populations. The Incas, Toltecs, Aztecs and Mayans, however, preserved their traditions in writing, and even produced native authors in the 16th and 17th centuries to tell us of them.[1] So we have both kinds of accounts from these peoples: those of the Spanish interrogators, which included Inquisitors, Jesuit administrators, and so on; and those of the native peoples themselves. That adds an immense weight to what we are about to learn.

## The Inca Traditions

The Inca Empire lasted only from 1438-1527. The name by which it knew itself was *Tahuantinsuyu*, the 'Four United Regions', these covering the whole of Peru and surrounding areas. Their accounts of the Creation and the Flood have come down to us via several early post-conquest authors, both Spanish and Quechua-speaking natives.[2] The accounts do vary slightly, depending on the area in which they were gathered, but basically they tell us this:

In the beginning was nothing but darkness out of which came the Creator, Viracocha.[3] In this primeval darkness, Viracocha is said to have created the first race of human beings. Some of the writers tell us that these were 'giants' who somehow angered Viracocha, for which reason Viracocha closed that age with a flood and turned those giants to stone – an interesting reference to the fossils, perhaps? Viracocha then called the sun, moon and stars into being and created the second race of men. He moulded their bodies out of pliable clay, making figures of men, women and even children, enough of them, in fact, to populate the entire world.[4]

One author tells us that, the earth being populated, Viracocha sent a second flood which covered the highest mountains.[5] Only two, a man and a woman, came through the flood, landing at Tiahuanaco. Viracocha commanded them to stay there, calling them *mitimaes* – 'uprooted ones'. The Creator then fashioned again the birds and animals, and repopulated the earth with humans. These he commanded to go underground into caves and tunnels, so that when he called them forth, they would emerge in that part of the world to which they had been assigned, a dimmed memory of the dispersal of the nations from Babel no doubt.

It is at this stage that we learn that the Creator was a tri-une God, named Viracocha, Imaymana Viracocha, and Tocapo Viracocha, the latter two being said to be the Creator's sons, but having the same creative powers as he. The three then travelled over the earth, each one calling forth the men who had been waiting underground to populate and care for that particular place where they were called, and telling each plant and tree when they should bear fruit. They continued on their journeys until they reached the sea, walking over that until they disappeared from mortal sight.[6]

As for the native authors and informants of some of these accounts, their predicament was perilous indeed, and it strikes a pitiful note. Terrified lest he should fall under the ever-vigilant eye of the Inquisition, once Inca chronicler, Pachacuti Yamqui, 'strongly averred' to his conquerors when questioned that Viracocha was surely no devilish pagan god, but was none other than the apostle Thomas; whilst another, Guaman Poma, asserted that the Inca creator was St Bartholomew.[7] They knew only too well what happened to Inca natives who were suspected of not being good Catholics, and felt themselves compelled to add such qualifiers. Had the Inquisition thought for one moment that there was a danger of these men even hankering to go back to the old ways, they would surely have burned them alive.

But that takes nothing away from the value of what they tell us. On the contrary, they surely would not have invented anything that would have unnecessarily endangered either themselves or their families and loved ones. The accounts that they left us of their ancestors' beliefs concerning the Creation and the Flood were quite perilous enough, and, given the dangers under which they laboured, we may rely on their honesty when they tell us of them.

Those accounts and traditions involved a Creator who, instead of making the universe out of the body parts of a slain god or giant, simply called the Creation into being. It is that and other details which allow the conclusion that the memory of the Incas was that of the Creator revealed perfectly to us in the Book of Genesis, the tri-une *Elohim* of the Bible. Likewise the detail of the Flood covering the highest mountains is an added testimony to the fact that they recalled the same historical Flood that is spoken of in Genesis.

But if anything spoiled the Inca memory and understanding of the events that Genesis speaks of, it was surely their adoption of the view that time is cyclic, and that the history of the universe consists of an endless series of creations and floods. It did little but confuse them. We shall encounter this same misconception when we come to hear how the Mayans remembered the Creation and the Flood, but whose traditions are nevertheless surprisingly close to the Book of Genesis. Meanwhile, the Toltecs had no such misconception. We are about to read what is perhaps the most astonishing testimony of all.

## The Toltec Traditions

We come now to the testimony of the Toltecs, whose account of how they came to be in their part of the world is truly astonishing, both in its close detail and in the very fulsome way in which it illuminates much that occurred after Babel. They kept a chronicled account not only of their migration, but of the length of time that that migration took, allowing us to date these events with unexpected precision. The words that you are about to read are translated from those, not of some young-earth creationist or Biblical fundamentalist, but of a native author who strongly resented what the Spaniards and their Inquisitors had done, and were still doing, to his people. He was surely no friend of this 'Christian' parody. Nevertheless, he tells us this:

> "It is found in the histories of the Toltecs that this age and first world, as they call it, lasted 1716 years; that men were destroyed by tremendous rains and lightning from the sky,

and even all the land, without the exception of anything, and the highest mountains, were covered up and submerged in water fifteen cubits [caxtolmolatli – compare Genesis 7:20]; and here they added other fables of how men came to multiply from the few who escaped from this destruction in a 'totlipetlocali'; that this word nearly signifies a close chest; and how, after men had multiplied, they erected a very high 'zacuali', which is today a tower of great height, in order to take refuge in it should the second world [age] be destroyed. Presently their languages were confused, and, not being able to understand each other, they went to different parts of the earth. The Toltecs, consisting of seven friends, with their wives, who understood the same language, came to these parts, having first passed great land and seas, having lived in caves, and having endured great hardships in order to reach this land;...they wandered 104 years through different parts of the world before they reached Hue Hue Tlapalan, which was in Ce Tecpatl, 520 years after the Flood."[8]

This is indeed an astonishing account, though in describing the events laid out here as 'fables' – the Flood, the Ark, the Tower of Babel, and the migration of the early Toltecs – our native author surprisingly but clearly tells us that he for one did not believe them.

But should *we* believe them? Surely, here if anywhere we must assume what the modernists have always claimed, the activity of Christian missionaries? The account is surely far too close to the Book of Genesis to be anything but the result of missionary activity? Well, this would be all well and good, except for one irrefutable fact: the Toltecs had left this earthly scene a full four hundred years *before* the arrival of the Spaniards and their friars and monks. They did not adopt these tales to appease their Catholic masters, simply because they were not here when those masters arrived. As a nation, they had disappeared entirely by the 12th century CE.[9] Our author was working from the written records that the Toltecs had left behind, records which he did not accept as accurate history, but which he passed on anyway because he was faithful to his task. He had no axe to grind in the matter, but speaking the same language as his Toltec predecessors, Nahuatl, he was able to understand everything that they had written. The cause of his unbelief is a matter of simple history. He was an Aztec, and as we shall see, Aztecs did not see the world in quite the same light as the Toltecs.

## The Aztec Traditions

I must say that I have yet to find a culture anywhere in the world or throughout all history as bereft of the knowledge of God as were the Aztecs. Even the Canaanites – and, yes, even the Phoenicians of Carthage! – had *some* trace of that innate knowledge of God, and the sense of human decency that comes with it, that is common around the world, as hideous as the rest of their beliefs and practices might have been. But in the Aztec world, nothing. Nothing whatever. Their 'gods' were numbered by the score, not one of them reflecting even a pretence of righteousness of any degree. For their worship, they demanded an endless blood-sacrifice of humanity in which the living heart was dug out from the body of a fully conscious victim. This bloodbath went on for centuries. We need not weary ourselves with what they did believe. That can be left to others. All we may note here is that between the Aztec notion of the Creation and the record of that event contained in the Book of Genesis, there is no resemblance at all.[10]

As for the Flood, we have better news. There is an account that the Aztecs have left us. It is not the closest to Genesis that we have seen thus far, but it does contain some surprising and very interesting details, as well as an attempt at chronology which is well worth looking at. Perhaps it was its many differences from the Toltec narrative that made Ixtlilxochitl, our Aztec author cited above, describe the Toltec tradition as 'fables'. But here it is, exactly as the Aztecs recorded it:

> "When the Sun Age came, there had passed 400 years. Then came 200 years, then 76. Then all mankind was lost and drowned and turned to fishes. The water and the sky drew near each other. In a single day all was lost, and Four Flower consumed all that there was of our flesh. The very mountains were swallowed up in the flood, and the waters remained, lying tranquil through fifty and two springs. But before the flood began, Titlachahuan had warned the man Nota and his wife Nena, saying, Make no more pulque [an alcoholic drink],

> but hollow out a great cypress, into which you shall enter [in] the month Tozoztli. The waters shall near the sky.' They entered, and when Titlachahuan had shut them in he said to the man, 'Thou shalt eat but a single ear of maize, and thy wife but one also.' And when they had each eaten one ear of maize, they prepared to go forth, for the water was tranquil."[11]

How interesting. How very interesting. The Sun Age was the period between the Creation and the Flood, which Genesis measures as 1656 years.[12] The Aztecs had it as 676, which requires only the digit for 1000 – which may well have been lost in transmission – to restore the figure to one that is amazingly close to that of Genesis – the Toltec figure was close enough at 1716 years. And then we have the name of the man Nota, which is clearly identifiable with that of Noah, and the act of Titlachahuan shutting in the occupants of the cypress ark, just as God had shut them in according to Genesis 7:16.

Noah and the other occupants of the Ark clearly subsisted on more than merely an ear of maize each, but do we have here another passed-down detail from those who had come through the Flood, this one dealing with the virtual hibernation of those on board and their subsequent ability to subsist on only small amounts of food? This would answer so many questions on the problems of food storage and preservation, cooking, and the otherwise immense problem of waste disposal for every person and animal in a closed and sealed Ark.

'Four Flower' is probably the Aztec god of flowers, Xochipilli, who is always portrayed wearing human skins.[13] As for the month Tozoztli, it ran in the Aztec calendar from 15th April to 4th May, Aztec months lasting only twenty days.[14] Intriguingly, it is the same month as that in which Noah entered the Ark (Genesis 7:11).

## The Mayan Tradition

We come now to the Mayans to see what they know about the Flood. So far, from the Incas, the Toltecs and the Aztecs, we have had three differing versions of that event, and because the Mayans were a nation quite distinct from the other three, theirs should likewise be an independent testimony.

Actually, we are very fortunate indeed to have anything at all come down to us from this people. On a night in July 1562, the officers of the Inquisition decided to make a great bonfire of all the Mayan books and records that they could find, many hundreds of them, and that takes no account of the many smaller bonfires lit over a much longer period of time by the local clergy scattered around the country. It was a deplorable and unnecessary act of vandalism. Providentially, however, and I do mean Providentially, this much, a book called *Popol Vuh*, escaped the flames. It contains all that the Mayans knew of the Creation and the Flood, Babel, the Confusion of Tongues and the dispersal of the nations. But first, their tradition concerning the Creation. It is a tradition that is not without great beauty and an obviously deep and reverent appreciation of the subject. Like most worshipful things, it begins with a profound silence:

> "This is the account of how all was in suspense, all calm, in silence; all motionless, still, and the expanse of the sky was empty....The surface of the earth had not yet appeared. There was only the calm sea, and the great expanse of the sky. There was nothing brought together, nothing which could make a noise, nor anything which might move or tremble, or could make a noise in the sky. There was nothing standing, only the calm water, the placid sea, alone and tranquil. Nothing existed...In this manner the sky existed, and also the Heart of Heaven, which is the name of God, and thus he is called. Then came the word."[15]

"Then came the word." Anyone at all familiar with the Bible will know *that* concept. The Creation, according to the Mayans, was, as with the Book of Genesis, spoken into existence. Not for them the idea of slain gods and their body parts, nor any such nonsense. The memory that the Mayans had carried with them from Babel concerning the Creation was made of purer stuff altogether.

But though a great deal, that is by no means all. As we read on, we see again that, as in so many other early cultures, the Creator is perceived as a tri-une Godhead, the *Elohim* of the Bible – why are we not told these things? The Mayans knew him as Caculha Huracan, Chipi Caculha, and Raxa Caculha, and the three persons of this tri-une Creator:

> "...talked then, discussing and deliberating; they agreed, they united their words and their thoughts. Then while they meditated, it became clear to them that when dawn would break, man must appear. Then they planned the creation, and the growth of the trees and the thickets and the birth of life and the creation of man. Thus it was arranged in the darkness and in the night by the Heart of Heaven who is called Huracan."[16]

So, whenever the Mayan thought upon the Creation, it seems that it wasn't just the event that he considered. As we can see, his thoughts ranged, as far as they were able, into the secret pre-Creation counsels of God. They were not perfect thoughts, of course. How could they be? But they were born of a deep awareness of God, the *Elohim* of the Bible, and they were reverent thoughts, full of worship and thankfulness. And they weren't so foolish or inaccurate on the historical level either. Much of the opening of *Popol Vuh* could almost serve as a commentary on the first two chapters of Genesis:

> "...then they conferred about life and light...Thus let it be done! Let the emptiness be filled! Let the water recede and make a void...Thus they spoke. Let there be light, let there be dawn in the sky and on the earth!.Our work, our creation shall be finished..."[17]

And so, we are told, God proceeded with the creation of the land, its rivers, its greenery and animals, and finally man. Sadly, it is at this point that the Mayan memory fails and begins to grow dim indeed, but not so dim that all is entirely forgotten. The first men, we are told, were made of soft mud which easily melted away (Adam was made from clay and easily fell from grace). They were incapable of much movement, and worse, were incapable of communicating with and worshipping their Creator. Therefore they were broken up and destroyed.

Then it was decided to make men out of wood. But as before, they could not communicate with God or speak anything that was meaningful. They could barely move or do anything. Therefore their destruction by a Flood was decided upon. The memory was not entirely dimmed, of course. In the Mayan account there are definite echoes of what the Book of Genesis tells us about the rebellion and wickedness and violence of pre-Flood mankind. But the impression is given, after this second attempt at creation, that all of man's faults and weaknesses were due to the fact that he had not been created properly to begin with. He was, in both beginnings, a failed experiment, a spoiled work of art.

It was this misconception that led the Mayans to adopt a cyclic and evolutionary[18] view of the universe, a universe that is repeatedly destroyed and then re-created, basically because its Maker could never get things right. It is a view that lies at the very heart of paganism. It is evident from as early as the time before Babel, when men built the Tower as a place of refuge for when the earth – ignoring God's promise (Genesis 9:8-16) – would be flooded again. It became a commonly held belief in Mesopotamia and in virtually every other pagan culture. Interestingly, it found its greatest nourishment and nurture in early India, which was the very part of the world through which the early Mayans had migrated on their way from Babel to the land that we now call Mexico.[19]

However, in Part 3 Chapter 1 of the *Popol Vuh*, we are told that finally perfect men (four in number) came into being, though not by the Creator's (Huracan's) hand. They were so perfect that they knew all things and could see all things. Naturally, the Creator resented this, so it was decided to blur man's vision so that he could see only those things that are near, and understand the earth only on a local level. This very probably recalls the fall of Adam and his acquiring the knowledge of good and evil. But things at this stage of the Mayan tradition are no longer in the order in which Genesis relates them, for now wives are created for each of the four men, which the Mayan narrative describes in this manner:

> "Then their wives had being, and their women were made. God himself made them carefully. And so, during sleep, they came, truly beautiful...."[20]

This is how the Mayans recalled the sleep of Adam at Eve's creation. Interestingly, it is said of these eight people: "They conceived the men of all the tribes, and of the large tribes, and were the origins of us, the people of Quiche."[21] – recalling no doubt that after the Flood, eight persons, four couples, had re-peopled the earth.

Yet even that is not all. The Mayans were aware of the fact that the human race was made up of just three families, the forefathers of which are called Ham, Shem and Japheth in the Book of Genesis. Though for some reason they will not name them, they say this, mentioning at the same time the migration to the Plain of Shinar from the east (Genesis 11:2):

> "Three groups of families existed; but they did not forget the name of their grandfather and father, those who propagated and multiplied there in the East....These are only the principal tribes....Many others came from each group of the people, but we shall not write their names. They also multiplied there in the East....Nevertheless, they did not sustain nor maintain [their God]; they only raised their faces to the sky, and they did not know why they had come so far as they did....The speech of all was the same."[22]

At this point, the *Popol Vuh* describes how the people migrated from the east to the city of Tulan (clearly a memory of Babel) where they began to invent and worship a whole host of 'gods', saying that at last they had found that for which they had been searching. At the common adoption of one particular 'god' called Tohil (actually another name for Huracan), they learned the secret of making fire, and when people from outside came to ask for some fire, they realised that they could no longer understand one another's speech. And there the Mayan account closes.

It makes an interesting exercise to list all the many details in the Mayan account that we also find written in the Book of Genesis. It is a surprisingly long list, and it raises the question of how they came to know all these things, albeit not perfectly. It certainly wasn't from the Spanish *conquistadores*. It is besides one of the great ironies of the Spanish conquest of these peoples that the 'pagan savages' they had come to conquer seem to have preserved in their folk memories and traditions more understanding of the events in the Book of Genesis than their conquerors ever knew, whose ignorance of the Bible and the ways of God was truly monumental. One of their number, at least, Clavigero, realised that much, and doubtless there were other individuals who shared his abhorrence of the way the natives were treated. But they were very few in number, and most of them kept silence.

But having noted the remarkable Flood traditions of the Inca, the Toltec, the Aztec and the Maya, let us now consider those traditions of the North American Indians who also remembered the Flood of Noah.

## Notes to Chapter Fifteen

1) The native Inca authors wrote down their traditions in both Spanish and their own language of Quechua using their conquerors' system of writing. Hitherto the indigenous recording method of the Inca was the *quipu*, a series of knotted strings. It is generally assumed that the *quipu* was used merely for counting and recording quantities. However, out of the 751 *quipu* that survive, only a few can be deciphered because they each contain information that ranges far beyond the mathematical. The Spaniards, fearful that *quipu* users were not always to be trusted when asked what was recorded on them, banned their use, and with that ban we lost any opportunity that we might have had of learning how to read them.

2) One work, the manuscript of which has only recently come to light (in the 1980s), is that of Juan de Betanzos' *Narrative of the Incas* - see Bibliography. Betanzos was the Spanish husband of an Inca princess, and his account is hailed for its accuracy and impartiality. He was ordered to write it in 1551 by the Viceroy of Peru.

3) In the outlying regions of the Inca Empire, the Creator's name is variously given as Con Ticci Viracocha; Thunupa Viracocha; and Viracocha Pachayachachic. He was also known as Pachacamac, the Maker of Earth and Time.

4) Urton, pp. 35-36.

5) Cristobal de Molina, author of *Las Fabulas y Ritos de los Incas* – The Fables and Rites of the Incas (1575). Urton, p. 29.

6) Urton, pp. 35-36.

7) Ibid, p. 37. Guaman Poma's knowledge of the Bible was pitifully small, as is shown when he states that the men of the first creation, the *Wari Wiracocharuna*, were not only 'the people from the time of Noah's Ark,' but were descended from the Spaniards! – Urton, p. 41. The poor man couldn't have fraudulently lifted stories from the Bible if his life had depended on it. But then, not knowing the Scriptures, nor could many of his inquisitors. Guaman Poma had reached his own abysmal level of knowledge only after years of their catechizing and 'instruction'. Never great ones for the Bible, his inquisitors seem to have accepted his qualifiers without further question, not knowing if he was right or wrong, though they'd have been happy enough to burn him if he forgot to worship a saint or two or attend mass.

8) 'Ixtlilxochitl Relaciones', in Kingsborough's *Antiquities of Mexico*, 1831, vol 9, pp. 321-322. The author of this 9-volume work, Edward King (Lord Kingsborough), was born in 1795. His life's labour was to chronicle the history of ancient Mexico, and he bankrupted himself in the process, dying in debtor's prison in 1837. His source for the information quoted above was Fernando de Alva Ixtlilxochitl (1568-1648), a native Indian convert to Catholicism and author of *Historia de la Nacion Chichemeca*, a work highly praised by scholars. In other writings, he gives courageous vent to his deep and lasting resentment concerning the oppression that he and his people were suffering daily under the heel of the King of Spain. In short, he despised the counterfeit 'Christianity' that he was being subjected to, and we may therefore count him as a hostile witness, making his testimony to the historical truth of the Book of Genesis all the more valuable and telling. Not that he was ever aware of what the Book of Genesis said. The Holy Office of the Inquisition, as it liked to call itself, never did adopt the habit of handing out Bibles, and if ever you were caught with one....

9) http://www.crystalinks.com/toltecs.html

10) It is difficult to account for the extraordinary level of debasement to which the Aztecs descended. We must allow, of course, for individuals among them who may have retained some knowledge of God (God never leaves Himself entirely without witness), but these have left us no trace of themselves.

11) http://www.honestinformation.com/ancient/great-deluge.php - The Flood tradition of the Aztecs comes from Charles Brasseur's translation into French of the *Codex Chimalpopoca* (1857-1859).

12) This is easily calculated from Genesis 5, the *Book of the Generations of Adam*.

13) http://www.answers.com/topic/xochipilli

14) http://www.aztec.com/page.php?page=religion

15) See: http://www.geocities.com/athens/academy/7286/popolvuhmain.html#anchor307278 – For the most informative translation, see Tedlock's, with its more than 160 pages of notes, commentary and other information. But for what is, in my view, the most aesthetically pleasing translation, see Goetz & Morley's first published in 1950 (see Bibliography), and readable online at the above address.

16) See: http://www.geocities.com/athens/academy/7286/popolvuhmain.html#anchor307278 – Of great interest to us is the fact that we get our word 'hurricane' from the Mayan Huracan. He was said to be the spirit, breath and wind of the Creation.

17) See: http://www.geocities.com/athens/academy/7286/popolvuhmain.html#anchor307278

18) The use of the word 'evolutionary' here does not overstate the case. Our modern evolutionists speak openly of a cyclic

universe and failed experiments. Concerning the original men who were destroyed, the Mayan account goes on to say, "And it is said that their descendants are the monkeys which now live in the forests; these are all that remain of them because their flesh was made only of wood by the Creator and the Maker. And therefore the monkey looks like man...."

19) Required reading in this field is the book, *Mayan Genesis*, by Kearsley – see Bibliography. It is all the more valuable inasmuch as it hails from the modernist stable, yet shows, through a most painstaking and erudite study, the step-by-step migration from Babylonia, through Asia, to South America of the Mayan people (and others). It is indispensable for post-Flood studies.

20) See: http://www.geocities.com/athens/academy/7286/popolvuhmain.html#anchor307278

21) Ibid.

22) Ibid.

~ * ~

## Chapter Sixteen: The North American Continent

We come now to a part of the world, a very large part, that is a continent in its own right, the continent of North America. It is much larger than the United States of America, including as it does Canada and (geographically at least) Greenland. Today's national names and boundaries were entirely unknown to the indigenous Amerindian and Inuit tribes of just a few centuries ago. There are some, in fact, who, in their wanderings and hunting, still follow their daily lives as if those boundaries had never existed and all were one land mass. But of interest to us are the many Flood traditions that are to be found amongst the varied but indigenous peoples of this continent.

### Frazer

We shall begin, though, with a statement from Sir James Frazer regarding certain North American Flood traditions. We have chosen it because it is one of the most damning statements for the modernist cause that he could possibly have made, a cause which Frazer espoused and which, by dint of his many followers' continuing admiration, he still heads even since his death in 1941. He says this:

> "When the earliest missionaries came among the Spokanas, Nez Perces, and Cayuses, who, with the Yakimas, used to inhabit the eastern part of Washington State, they found that these Indians had their own traditions of a great flood, in which one man and his wife were saved on a raft. Each of these three tribes, together with the Flathead tribes, had its own separate Ararat on which the survivors found refuge."[1]

If you wish to read that again, then please, take the time to do so. In fact, it is essential reading at this stage. The entire thesis of Frazer's book thus far, and one that is still echoed by modernists the world over, is that Flood traditions around the world are due to the proselytizing activities of Christian missionaries, or occasionally the story-telling of Moslem traders. Yet with this statement, he shows his own awareness of the fact that that assertion, which he wanted every one of his readers to believe, was entirely false and misleading. It is most shameful. Untold thousands have been deceived by this lie into turning away from the Book of Genesis, and people in their thousands are still being deceived by it today. Words fail me.

## Thomas Hariot and the Powhatans

Not that Frazer was the first of his kind, and neither, I suppose, will he be the last.[2] The first of modern times was probably Thomas Hariot - we met him in Chapter One - the astronomer who belonged to the Durham House Set in London, and who in 1588 submitted a firsthand report to Sir Walter Ralegh concerning the Powhatan Indian tribe of Virginia, with whom Ralegh's colonists were enjoying cordial relations.[3] In that report, Hariot says this of the Powhatans' beliefs regarding the Creation. It is worth quoting at length. I have retained the original spelling and silently 'corrected' the punctuation (read it just like modern English):

> "Some religion they haue alreadie, which although it be farre from the truth, yet beyng as it is, there is hope it may bee the easier and sooner reformed. They beleeue that there are many Gods which they call *Mantoac*, but of different sortes and degrees; one onely chiefe and great God, which hath bene from all eternitie, who, as they affirme, when hee purposed to make the worlde, made first other goddes of a principall order...and after the Sunne, Moone, and Starres, as pettie goddes and the instruments of the other order more principall. First, they say, were made waters, out of which by the gods was made all diuersitie of creatures that are visible or inuisible. For mankind, they say a woman was made first, which by the working of one of the goddes, conceiued and brought foorth children. And in such sort, they say, they had their beginning. But how manie yeeres or ages haue passed since, they say they can make no relation....They beleeue also the immortalitie of the soule, that after this life, as soon as the soule is departed from the bodie, according to the workes it hath done, it is eyther carried to heauen, the habitacle of gods, there to enjoy perpetuall blisse and happinesse, or els to a great pitte or hole...there to burne continually, the place they call *Popogusso*."[4]

It is surprising indeed to find no relation of the Flood among a people who otherwise are so deeply aware of other Biblical matters. One often encounters Flood traditions without the Creation and other accoutrements from Genesis, but rarely indeed does one find a Creation tradition - and one so relatively 'pure' as this - without any recollection of the Flood. Hariot, moreover, tells us himself that when the Bible was read to them, the Powhatans warmed to what they heard, and wanted to hear more, even asking permission to join the white man in prayer and worship. Their already-held belief in the Eternal Creator, the Final Judgment, Heaven and Hell, Eternity and so on, are strong indicators that a Flood tradition would not have been out of place among them, the events of Genesis being so familiar to them. But Hariot mentions none, without actually saying that they had none. Now, why should that be?

That there were none at all is very unlikely. The Powhatans were a tribe of the Algonquin confederacy, and the Algonquins certainly had their own Flood traditions.[5] But Hariot, it seems, had an agenda in what he omitted. During the years in which the Durham House Set would congregate to discuss revolutionary 'scientific' ideas, one idea in particular was beginning to cause a stir in intellectual circles, and that was the idea of pre-Adamites, a race of men (perhaps without souls) who were created before Adam. It seems to have come to prominence in 1578 amongst the Familist sect in Friesland; whilst at Frankfurt in Germany, Giordano Bruno was arguing strongly for the concept in 1591, Bruno being a friend and colleague of Galileo with whom, as a fellow astronomer and Bible-skeptic, Hariot corresponded.[6]

Such notions are, of course, contradicted entirely by the Book of Genesis. Before Adam was created, we are specifically told, "...there was *no* man to till the ground." (Genesis 2:5). The existence of pre-Adamites would have rendered that statement false. And that, it seems, was Hariot's objective. It moreover allowed a push back in time for the Creation, making the earth much older than it truly is.[7] And it was all grounded, by Hariot's very clever but subtle omission, in the fact that the Powhatans of Virginia allegedly had no Flood tradition.

If they had no Flood tradition, it was reasoned, then the Powhatans must therefore have survived the Flood, and therefore could not belong to the race of Adam which the Flood was sent to destroy. Therefore they must be pre-Adamites, and therefore the earth must be older than Genesis says. The logic of it all, if such it may be called, escapes us, but it is the philosophical domino-effect of the anti-Scripturalist (and Hariot certainly was an anti-Scripturalist), the first of the dominoes being toppled over way back in Genesis 3:1: "Yea, hath God said...?" If one part of Scripture falls, then all else falls with it, and those who actively promote the modernist agenda have always known this.

Hariot might, of course, have asked the other thirty-nine tribes of Virginia, the Monocan; Mannahoacs; Nottoways; Meherrins; Tuteloes; Chickahominies, and so on, to see if they had any Flood traditions. After all, even back in the 16th century, a database of only one, followed by a research program based upon a whole series of wrong assumptions and wilful omissions, isn't likely to lead to much that is in any way 'scientific,' least of all to the Truth. But, of course, he didn't do that. With his head full of ideas of a false Genesis, a localised Flood, and a world that was peopled by pre-Adamites, he just didn't get to know how rich North America really was in Flood traditions.

## The Yakima

We can do it though, expand the search I mean. We might well begin with those whom Frazer mentions, the Yakima people, who used to live in the eastern part of the State of Washington. Their tradition - which Frazer passes over - is as follows:

> "In early times, many people had gone to war with other tribes; even medicine men had killed people. But there were still some good people. One of the good men heard from the Land Above that a big water was coming. He told the other good people, and they decided they would make a dugout boat from the largest cedar they could find. Soon after the canoe was finished, the flood came, filling the valleys and covering the mountains. The bad people were drowned; the good people were saved in the boat. We don't know how long the flood stayed. The canoe came down where it was built and can still be seen on the east side of Toppenish Ridge. The

> earth will be destroyed by another flood if people do wrong a second time."[8]

If we list the components contained in this account, and compare them with those of Genesis, then we can see just how close to Genesis this tradition is. The violence that filled the earth; the few righteous; the warning from God (or in this case, Heaven); the building of the boat; the Flood, the water covering the mountains; the destruction of all the wicked; the receding of the waters; and the stranding of the boat. Apart from some obvious omissions, the only real departure in detail from the Genesis narrative is the warning that the earth would be flooded again if man returned to his evil ways. That is rather impressive for a tribe who held their awareness of these historical events for untold centuries before any Christian missionaries got to them. I'm not surprised that Frazer mentions the account only in passing. But one that he does include is this:

## The Papagos

> "The Papagos of South-western Arizona say that the Great Spirit made the earth and all living creatures before he made man. Then he came down to earth, and digging in the ground found some potter's clay. This he took back with him to the sky, and from there let it fall into the hole which he had dug. Immediately there came out the hero Montezuma, and with his help there also issued forth all the Indian tribes in order. Last of all appeared the wild Apaches, who ran away as fast as they were created. Those first days of the world were happy and peaceful. The sun was then nearer the earth than he is now: his rays made all the seasons equable and clothing was superfluous. Men and animals talked together: a common language united them in the bonds of brotherhood. But a terrible catastrophe put an end to those golden days. A great flood destroyed all flesh wherein was the breath of life...."[9]

The account goes on to say how the Flood had been prophesied to Montezuma by a coyote. The pair of them built a boat each, the coyote caulking his with gum, and so the Flood came and Montezuma and the coyote alone escape drowning. On the waters receding, Montezuma sent out the coyote to see what dry land was left, the coyote reporting that only to the north was dry land. Meanwhile, the Great Spirit had repopulated the earth with men and animals. I suspect that the tribal in-joke at the expense of the Apaches raised a laugh or two whenever this tradition was recited, but that detail is a strong marker (amongst many others) of the cultural origin of the tradition - through the folk memory of the Papago Indians - rather than any other proposed external source.

But to this account is added the following snippet which contains reference also to Montezuma's rebellion against the Great Spirit (recalling Nimrod's no doubt) which had led to the building of a great tower into the heavens (the Tower of Babel), the destruction of that tower by the Great Spirit sending an earthquake, and the subsequent confusion of tongues:

> "The Great Spirit, with the help of Montezuma, restocked the earth with men and animals. Montezuma, with Coyote's help, taught them and led them. Montezuma later became prideful and rebelled against the Great Mystery, thus bringing evil into the world. The Great Mystery raised the sun to its present height, and, with an earthquake, destroyed the tower that Montezuma was building into the heavens, in the process changing languages so that people could no longer understand animals or other tribes."[10]

## The Acjachemem

As for the Acjachemem Indians of California (sometimes called today the *Juanenos*), we have this interesting account. Frazer does not name his quoted source, but it may have been Geronimo Boscana, a Franciscan scholar stationed at San Juan Capistrano for more than a decade from 1812 onwards, and who compiled what is probably the closest study of ancient religious beliefs in the San Juan Capistrano valley.[11]

> "The Acagchemem [*sic*] Indians, near St. Juan Capistrano in California, 'were not entirely destitute of a knowledge of the universal deluge, but how, or from whence, they received the

> same, I could never understand. Some of their songs refer to it; and they have a tradition that, at a time very remote, the sea began to swell and roll in upon the plains, and fill the valleys, until it had covered the mountains; and thus nearly all the human race and animals were destroyed, excepting a few, who had resorted to a very high mountain which the waters did not reach.'"[12]

At some undefined time, the Acjachemem tribe split into two parts, the *Playanos,* who settled along the coast, and the *Serranos*, who, as the name implies, settled in the mountainous area. Of the *Playanos* it is said that they entertained the following tradition regarding the Creation:

> "The *Playanos* held that an all-powerful and unseen being called '*Nocuma*' brought about the earth and the sea, together with all the trees, plants, and animals of sky, land and water contained therein."[13]

## The Mandan Indians

> "The Mandan Indians had a tradition of a great deluge in which the human race perished except one man, who escaped in a large canoe to a mountain in the west. Hence the Mandans celebrated every year certain rites in memory of the subsistence of the flood, which they called *Mee-nee-ro-ka-ha-sha*, 'the sinking down or settling of the waters.' The time for the ceremony was determined by the full expansion of the willow leaves on the banks of the river, for according to their tradition, 'the twig that the bird brought home was a willow bough and had full-grown leaves on it.'"[14]

This is interesting, very interesting. The original source for the information is the painter George Catlin (1796-1872), who had a deep and abiding love for Indian peoples and culture. His visit to the Mandan tribe (who lived to the north of Fort Union on the Missouri, virtually untouched by Europeans and their ways), occurred in 1838 during one particular trip that took in eighteen tribes in all, including the Cheyenne,

Crow and Blackfoot tribes.[15] In his travels, he visited around 200 other tribes, leaving behind hundreds of paintings of them. But their customs and traditions interested him as much as their physical appearance and costumes. In the context of the tribe's Flood traditions, of the Mandan village, he tells us this:

> "In the centre of the Mandan village...is an open, circular area of a hundred and fifty feet diameter, kept always clear, as a public ground, for the display of all their feasts, parades, etc., and around it are their wigwams placed as near to each other as they can well stand, their doors facing the centre of this public area. In the middle of this ground, which is trodden like a hard pavement, is a curb (somewhat like a large hogshead standing on its end) made of planks and bound with hoops, some eight or nine feet high, which they religiously preserve and protect from year to year, free from mark or scratch, and which they call the 'big canoe': it is undoubtedly a symbolic representation of a part of their traditional history of the Flood; which it is very evident, from this and numerous other features of this grand ceremony, they have in some way or other received, and are here endeavouring to perpetuate by vividly impressing it on the minds of the whole nation."[16]

Catlin continues to tell us of this ceremony, named *O-kee-pa*, in which the part of the man who survived the Flood, whom they called *Nu-mohk-muck-a-nah*, (the first element of the name perpetuating that of Noah, it seems), was played by a 'mummer' (a mime) dressed in a white robe of wolf-skins, a hat of two ravens' skins, and a pipe of peace in his left hand. On entering the village, the mummer would stand at the door of each wigwam crying until the head of each family came out to see what was the matter. The mummer relates the history of the Flood, and asks for an edged tool from the owner of every wigwam, so that he might sacrifice it to the water, warning that if this is not done, there will be another flood.

This is all surprising enough, that a tribe of Indians in the middle of nowhere should have such a vivid recollection of the Flood burned into their collective memory, that they are compelled to celebrate it with a long and elaborate ceremony every year. But the Mandan Indians were not alone in this. Catlin goes on to tell us:

> "This tradition, however, was not peculiar to the Mandan tribe, for amongst one hundred and twenty different tribes that I visited in North and South and Central America, not a tribe exists that has not related to me distinct or vague traditions of such a calamity, in which one, or three, or eight persons were saved above the waters, on the top of a high mountain. Some of these, at the base of the Rocky Mountains and in the plains of Venezuela, and the Pampa del Sacramento in South America, make annual pilgrimages to the fancied summits where the antediluvian species were saved in canoes or otherwise, and, under the mysterious regulations of their *medicine* (mystery) men, tender their prayers and sacrifices to the Great Spirit, to ensure their exemption from a similar catastrophe."[17]

This passage again bears repeated reading. 120 tribes out of 120, all of them distant from one another both geographically and historically, some of them isolated for many centuries, yet every single one of them bearing testimony to the Flood of Noah. It's not as if Catlin was on a mission here to even hunt down such stories. His only interests were painting his native subjects (and his paintings are stunning), and capturing something for posterity of their culture and ways. That has to tell us something. But there is yet more.

### The Choctaw and the Tower of Babel

The Choctaw Indians had a tradition, none of the Creation or the Flood that I could find, but one of the Tower of Babel. They tell how, many generations ago, the Creator, Aba, created many men, all of them Choctaw, who spoke only the Choctaw language.

> "These came from the bosom of the earth, being formed of yellow clay, and no man had ever lived before them. One day, all came together and, looking upward, wondered what the clouds and the blue expanse above might be. They continued to wonder and talk among themselves and at last determined

to endeavor to reach the sky. So they brought many rocks and began building a mound that was to have touched the heavens."[18]

The men made three attempts to build the Tower, but each night the wind would blow and demolish what they had built in the day. The third night, however, the men slept close to the Tower, and when the wind blew, the rocks fell down upon the sleeping men. However:

> "The men were not killed, but when daylight came and they made their way from beneath the rocks and began to speak to one another, all were astounded as well as alarmed - they spoke various languages and could not understand one another. Some continued thenceforward to speak the original tongue, the language of the Choctaw, and from these sprung the Choctaw tribe. The others, who could not understand this language, began to fight among themselves. Finally, they separated. The Choctaw remained the original people; the others scattered, some going north, some east, and others west, and formed various tribes."[19]

## The Pawnee of Nebraska

Concerning the Flood, the Pawnee remembered it like this:

> "The first people upon the earth were giants, very big and strong. They did not believe in the creator Ti-ra-wa. They thought nothing could overcome them. They grew increasingly worse. At last Ti-ra-wa grew angry and raised the water to the level of the land so that the ground became soft. The giants sank into the mud and drowned. Their bones can still be found today. Ti-ra-wa then created a man and woman, like people of today, and gave them corn. The Pawnees are descended from them."[20]

There is more to this brief account than is immediately obvious. Again, we are surprised by the fact that, even in their pre-Christian days, the Pawnee seem to have been monotheistic, holding to a belief in a single Creator, Ti-ra-wa. They remember the increasing degradation of pre-Flood humanity, and their provocation of God by their violence and their faithlessness in Him. And then there is the post-Flood change that came over mankind. Physically, they ceased to be 'giants, very big and strong,' and became 'like people of today'. Most intriguing.

## The Cherokee

> "The Cherokee Indians are reported to have a tradition that the water once prevailed over the land until all mankind were drowned except a single family. The coming of the calamity was revealed by a dog to his master. For the sagacious animal went day after day to the banks of a river, where he stood gazing at the water and howling piteously."[21]

We noted back in Chapter Fourteen, in which we looked at the tribes of South and Central America, that some of their Flood traditions contained references to the change in animal behaviour that is noticeable before certain natural catastrophes, examples of which were very probably the transmission of accounts that those who survived the Flood aboard the Ark passed on to their many listeners. It seems that we have another reference to that phenomenon here, as with the Papago Indians with their tradition of Montezuma and the coyote mentioned above. The Cherokee go on to tell us in their narrative:

> "Being rebuked by his master and ordered home, the dog opened his mouth and warned the man of the danger in which he stood. 'You must build a boat,' said he, 'and put in it all that you would save; for a great rain is coming that will flood the land'....So the man believed, and following the directions of the faithful animal he and his family were saved, and from them the whole of the present population of the globe is lineally descended."[22]

## The Chitimacha Indians of Southern Louisiana

We have noted all through our present enquiry that although some Flood accounts are more or less fulsome than others, yet all contain some details that are recognisably memories of those events that are recorded in the Book of Genesis. The Chitimacha have left us one account that, at first appearance, has very few such details, and yet they are unmistakably present:

> "Long ago, a great storm came. The people baked a great earthen pot, in which two people saved themselves. Since rattlesnakes were then the friends of man, two rattlesnakes were saved in the pot, too. The red-headed woodpecker clung to the sky, but the waters rose so high they wet and marked his tail. When the waters sank, the woodpecker was sent to find land, but he could find none. The dove was sent next and came back with a grain of sand. When this grain was placed on the water, it spread out and became dry land."[23]

We have here the Flood; an ark of sorts; the taking on board of animals which after the Flood were to become hostile to man; the receding of the waters; the sending of the woodpecker first to seek dry land; finally the sending of the dove (presumably by those in the earthenware 'ark'); and the return of the dove with an object that led to the discovery of dry land. That comes to seven hallmark details in this one diminutive account that tell us that the Flood of Genesis is being recalled here, albeit through a very dim and faulty memory.

## The Jicarilla Apaches of New Mexico

The Jicarilla Apaches tell of the Flood in a tradition that departs from Genesis in many places, and yet has preserved some surprising corroborative details. They say that before the Apaches 'emerged from the underworld,' recalling no doubt an earlier shared belief in the Inca model of an underground population, there were yet other people on the earth. Out of these, an old man and woman were warned by God that it was about to rain for forty days and nights. They and the people were warned to seek refuge at the tops of four mountains, and not to look at either the flood waters or the sky. Those who did so would turn either into fishes or birds. After 80 days the waters receded, and the people (only a few of whom had obeyed the warning) were told to come down. Intriguingly, the tradition tells of eight people in particular who had survived the Flood, and who had the ability to travel to distant places merely by looking in their direction. These eight people, and here it gets really interesting, told the Apaches all about the Flood before entering beneath two mountains themselves (dying, in other words), being told to remain there until the earth is finally destroyed. The Apaches end their tradition with a prophecy though, saying that when they, the Apaches, dwindle sufficiently in number, the world will end by fire. The year given for this was around our year of 2000 CE - which happily has now passed.[24]

## The Montagnais and Cree of Canada

In Canada, we see the same traditions, with only slight variations, that we have seen amongst the tribes of what is today the United States of America. The Montagnais, for example, yet another tribe of the ubiquitous Algonquin family, told an early Jesuit missionary who visited them of their own tradition concerning, "a certain mighty being, whom they named Messou, [who] repaired the world after it had been ruined by the great flood."[25]

Two centuries later, another Catholic missionary was to learn from the same tribe which inhabited the Hudson Bay Territory, that they:

> "...have a tradition of a great flood which covered the world, and from which four persons, along with animals and birds, escaped alive on a floating island. Yet another Catholic missionary reports the Montagnais legend more fully as follows. God, being angry with the giants, commanded a man to build a large canoe. The man did so, and when he had embarked in it, the water rose on all sides, and the canoe with it, till no land anywhere was to be seen."[26]

The same missionary worked amongst the Cree tribe, (who also were of the Algonquin), and reported their Flood tradition; which Frazer, however, dismisses as clearly of Christian origin on the somewhat specious grounds that it features a raven and a wood-pigeon, both birds being sent out to look for dry land. Yet, again we have to ask, where were the Christians who influenced the Babylonian narrative of the Flood, which features a raven, and a dove, and even a swallow, and which is conventionally dated to around 2000 BC? If the Cree tradition were truly of Christian origin, why does it not mention Noah and all the other Genesis-derived details that a Christian would surely have passed on?[27] But, of course, it doesn't. Nor could it, pre-dating as it does the arrival of any Christian influence in that land. Interestingly, and like the Babylonian, the Cree tradition tells of mud on the pigeon's feet (see Appendix One, note 41).

## The Tinneh Tribes of Canada

We glean from Frazer that other Indian tribes of the Algonquin family left behind Flood traditions of their own; the Salteaux (or Chippeway) Indians around Bear Lake; the Tinnehs (or Denes) of North-western Canada, who belong to the great Athapascan family; and the Hareskin Indians who have left us this:

> "The Hareskin Indians, another Tinneh tribe, say that a certain Kunyan, which means Wise Man, once upon a time resolved to build a great raft. When his sister, who was also his wife, asked him why he would build it, he said, 'If there comes a flood, as I foresee, we shall take refuge on the raft.' He told his plan to other men on the earth, but they laughed at him, saying, 'If there is a flood, we shall take refuge in the trees.' Nevertheless the Wise Man made a great raft, joining the logs together by ropes made of roots. All of a sudden there came a flood such that the like of it had never been seen before. The water seemed to gush forth on every side. Men climbed up in the trees, but the water rose after them, and all were drowned. But the Wise Man floated safely on his strong and well-corded raft. As he floated he thought of the future, and he gathered by twos all the herbivorous animals, and all the birds, and even all the beasts of prey he met with on his passage."[28]

Other members of the Tinneh tribes tell that the Flood began with a great snowfall, about which the men of the time were warned by an old man. They told him that they would escape to the mountains, but all perished when the snows melted and the Flood waters rose. The same people also tell that the old man (the only survivor of the Flood) sent forth a raven which, finding corpses to feed upon, did not return. And then he sent out a turtle-dove which twice flew around the world and returned. The third time, however, she returned at dusk, exhausted, and with a sprig of fir in her beak.[29]

Our author blames it all onto Christianity, of course, though what version of the Bible these Christians must have been reading is a puzzle. But then he proceeds to tell us of the Flood traditions belonging to the Eskimo (prop. Inuit) tribes of Canada and Greenland, seemingly oblivious to the contradiction of what he has just claimed concerning the alleged activities of Christian missionaries - we shall look at those Flood traditions now.

## The Eskimo tribes of Canada and Greenland

We come now to a people who spend most of their lives in one of the most hostile environments on this earth. The expectation of finding Flood traditions that hark back to the events of the Book of Genesis must always have been low, and it would hardly have surprised us to learn that, apart from what they might have learned from the missionaries among them, they had nothing to pass on to us. But that is not the case at all. It would seem that, *per capita*, there are as many pre-Christian Flood traditions amongst the Eskimo tribes of Canada and Greenland as anywhere else.[30] We shall hear Frazer on this, his testimony as a hostile and reluctant witness being all the more valuable to our enquiry:

> "In North America legends of a great flood are not confined to the Indian tribes; they are found also among the Eskimo and their kinsfolk the Greenlanders. At Orowignarak, in Alaska, Captain Jacobsen was told that the Eskimo have a tradition of a mighty inundation which, simultaneously to an earthquake, swept over the land so rapidly that only a few persons were able to escape in their skin canoes to the tops of the highest mountains."[31]

It is the detail concerning the 'tops of the highest mountains,' to reach which a flood would have to be thousands of feet deep, that tells us that we are here listening to an account of Noah's Flood; that, and the earthquake, signifying the breaking up of the fountains of the deep (Genesis 7:11). Captain Jacobsen seems to be Johan Adrian Jacobsen, a traveller and collector who dwelt amongst the Yup'ik Eskimos in the 1880s.[32] But Frazer goes on to tell us:

> "Again, the Eskimo of Norton Sound, in Alaska, say that in the first days the earth was flooded, all but a very high mountain in the middle. Only a few animals escaped to the mountain and were saved; and a few people made a shift to survive by floating about in a boat and subsisting on the fish they caught till the water subsided. As the flood sank and the mountains emerged from the water, the people landed from the canoe on these heights, and gradually followed the retreating flood to the coast. The animals which had escaped to the mountains also descended and replenished the earth after their kinds."[33]

The detail here concerning the earth being flooded except for a "very high mountain in the middle," is interesting, for Mount Ararat, where Noah's Ark came to rest, is situated roughly in the centre of the earth's land mass.[34] It was from Ararat (elsewhere called Armenia - Isaiah 37:38) that Noah and his family, and their subsequent families, migrated east toward the Plain of Shinar (Genesis 11:2). From there, of course, which is still roughly in the centre of the earth's land mass, mankind dispersed all over the earth, each family, tribe and nation carrying with them memories of what Noah and his family had told them concerning the Flood:

> "Again, the Tchiglit Eskimo, who inhabit the coast of the Arctic Ocean from Point Barrow on the west to Cape Bathurst on the east, tell of a great flood which broke over the face of the earth and, driven by the wind, submerged the dwellings of men."[35]

Interestingly, the Tchiglit people knew not just of the Flood, but of the Creation also, even to the point of knowing that the first man, Adam, had been created from clay whilst his Maker breathed into him the breath of life (Genesis 2:7):

> “The story of the creation of mankind out of clay occurs also.... Thus the Eskimo of Point Barrow, in Alaska, tell of a time when there was no man in the land, till a certain spirit named *a se lu*, who resided at Point Barrow, made a clay man, set him up on the shore to dry, breathed into him, and gave him life.”[36]

In the following account, we have an observation that is common to the Eskimo Flood traditions, namely the evidence for the Flood covering the mountain tops. They cite, perfectly correctly, the presence on those mountain tops of fossil sea creatures, clams, seals, fishes and even whales, that were left stranded by the geological upheaval when the mountains were raised, and the waters receded:

> “The Central Eskimo say that long ago the ocean suddenly began to rise until it had inundated the whole land. The water even covered the tops of the mountains, and the ice drifted over them. When the flood had subsided, the ice stranded and ever since forms an ice-cap on the top of the mountains. Many shellfish, seals, and whales were left high and dry, and their shells and bones may be seen there to this day.”[37]

## Greenland

With the next tradition, that of the Greenland Eskimos, we note the all-important point which not even Frazer can conceal, of the Flood traditions being found already in place and up and running by the incoming missionaries. It is of further interest to note that nowhere, amongst all the peoples and nations which we have studied, have missionaries ever laid claim to having taught the people their Flood traditions. These are, in every case, indigenous to the population:

> “With regard to the Greenlanders their historian Crantz tells us that ‘almost all heathen nations know something of Noah’s Flood, and the first missionaries found also some pretty plain traditions among the Greenlanders; namely, that the world once overset, and all mankind, except one, were drowned; but some were turned into fiery spirits. The only man that escaped alive, afterwards smote the ground with his stick, and

> out sprang a woman, and these two re-peopled the world. As a proof that the deluge once overflowed the whole earth, they say that many shells and relics of fishes, have been found far within the land where men could never have lived, yea that bones of whales have been found upon a high mountain.'"[38]

If nothing else, Eskimo peoples are, and have always been, intensely practical. Living as they do in one of the earth's most inhospitable and dangerous environments, they have to be able to trust their own eyes and come to very mundane conclusions as to what it is they're looking at. Not for them some airy-fairy philosophy of uniformitarianism or geological ages. They themselves know what it is to live in an environment that is always potentially catastrophic, and they know the remains of a catastrophe when they see them. Their lives would be short indeed if they couldn't do that much:

> "Similar evidence in support of the legend was adduced to the traveller C. F. Hall by the Innuits [*sic*] or Eskimo with whom he lived. He tells us that 'they have a tradition of a deluge which they attribute to an unusually high tide. On one occasion when I was speaking with Tookoolito concerning her people, she said, 'Innuits all think this earth once covered with water.' I asked her why she thought so. She answered, 'Did you never see little stones, like clams and such things as live in the sea, away up on mountains?'"[39]

## Notes to Chapter Sixteen

1) Frazer, p. 126.

2) Dr Henry Morris's book, *The Long War Against God*, is most instructive on this point - see Bibliography.

3) It is Thomas Hariot who introduced the potato to England and Ireland; the "equals" sign = into mathematics; and he it was who first made a map of the moon by studying it through a telescope several months before his friend Galileo did. As for his opinion regarding the Book of Genesis: "But notwithstanding his great skill in mathematics, he had strange

thoughts of the scripture, and always undervalued the old story of the creation of the world, and could never believe that trite [pro]position, *Ex Nihilo nihil fit.* He made a *Philosophical Theology*, wherein he cast off the OLD TESTAMENT, so that consequently the New would have no foundation. He was a Deist, and his doctrine he did impart to the said Count [the Earl] and to Sir Walt. Raleigh when he was compiling the *History of the World*, and would controvert the matter with eminent divines of those times; who therefore having no good opinion of him, did look on the manner of his death as a judgment upon him for those matters, and for nullifying the scripture." Stevens, p. 49 (see Bibliography) quoting Wood's *Athenae* 1691. Loosely translated, '*Ex Nihilo nihil fit'* means 'Nothing comes from nothing.' It was first coined by the Greek Parmenides, and was the first point of discussion that was given to students of philosophy. Hariot, because of his 'strange thoughts of the scripture' (in which God made *everything* from nothing), could never master it. The manner of Hariot's death was cancerous ulcers of the lip.

4) Hariot, Thomas. *A Briefe and True Report of the New Found Land of Virginia.* printed 1590. John Wechell. Frankfurt. cit also http://docsouth.unc.edu/nc/hariot/hariot.html

5) An example being: "Long ago, when men had become evil, the Strong Serpent *Maskanako* came. He was the foe of people, and they became embroiled, hating and fighting each other. The small men, (*Mattapewi*) fought with *Nihanlowit*, keeper of the dead. The Strong Serpent resolved to destroy all men, and the Black Serpent brought the snake-water rushing, spreading everywhere, destroying everything. Then the waters ran off, and the great evil went away by the path of the cave." Mark Isaaks. See: http://www.talkorigins.org/faqs/flood-myths.html - citing Kelsen, Hans. 'The Principle of Retribution in the Flood and Catastrophe Myths.' 1943. *The Flood Myth.* ed. Alan Dundes. Univ Calif Press. London - but see also Frazer, pp. 115 and 127, for yet other Algonquin Flood traditions.

6) http://creationontheweb.com/content/view/453 - It is a matter of record that Galileo himself had a very low view of Scripture, stating that it should not be taken literally, and openly denying the historicity of Joshua 10:12-14. Bruno, whose own 'theology' was bizarre in the extreme (he was later burned for it), was actually in England from April 1583 until October 1585, but whether he and Hariot ever met in person is unknown. They did share mutual acquaintances though, probably through whom Hariot learned of Galileo and his unorthodox views, and thus was able to correspond with him. But in 1585, Hariot was with Ralegh's colonists in Virginia.

7) This push back in time began with the thin end of the proverbial wedge, as is witnessed by the deposition of one Richard Baines, who implicated Thomas Hariot in propagating certain heresies in the School of Night (the Durham House Set meeting at Syon House) during his depositions against the playwright, Christopher Marlowe, an erstwhile friend of Hariot's: "That the Indians and many Authors of antiquity haue assuredly written aboue 16 thousand yeares agone, wher as Adam is proued to haue lived w'hin 6 thousand yeares." Rukeyser, p. 127. The 'Authors of antiquity' included the Babylonian Berosus and the Egyptian Manetho, who had greater authority in some men's eyes than the Word of God. Today, we live at the thick end of the wedge, where the age of the universe is wrongly conjectured at many billions of years.

8) Mark Isaaks http://www.talkorigins.org/faqs/flood-myths.html - citing Clarke, E. *Indian Legends of the Pacific Northwest.* 1953. Univ Calif Press. p. 45.

9) Frazer, p. 110.

10) Mark Isaaks http://www.talkorigins.org/faqs/flood-myths.html - citing Erdoes, Richard & Ortiz, Alfonso. *American Indian Myths and Legends.* 1984. Pantheon Books. New York. pp. 487-9. Also: Gaster, Theodor H. *Myth, Legend and Custom in the Old Testament.* 1969. Harper & Row. New York. pp. 114-115. It seems that Gaster hoped to inherit Frazer's mantle.

11) http://www.newadvent.org/cathen/10532a.htm

12) Frazer, p. 111.

13) http://www.sacred-texts.com/nam/ca/bosc/bosc05.htm

14) Frazer, pp. 112-13.

15) http://www.answers.com/topic/george-catlin - In 1841, Catlin published his monumental work, *Manners, Customs, and Condition of the North American Indians*, in two volumes including some 300 engravings.

16) cited by Frazer, p. 113.

17) ibid, pp. 113-14. Catlin's testimony here makes it even more unlikely that the Powhatans of Virginia would have had no tradition of the Flood. The tribe was, as we have seen, a member of the great Algonquin confederacy, as were a great many tribes whose Flood traditions formed such an important part of their lives; the Delaware Indians, for example, an Algonquin tribe who told of a great flood from which only a few escaped alive.

18) See http://www.firstpeople.us/FP-Html-Legends/TheTowerof Babel-Choctaw.html

19) ibid.

20) Mark Isaaks http://www.talkorigins.org/faqs/flood-myths.html - citing Grinnell, G B. *Pawnee Hero Stories and Folk Tales*. 1961. Univ of Nebraska. Lincoln. pp. 355-356; repr. from 1889.

21) Frazer, pp. 114-115.

22) ibid.

23) Mark Isaaks http://www.talkorigins.org/faqs/flood-myths.html - citing Judson, Katharine B. *Myths and Legends of the Mississippi Valley and the Great Lakes*. 1914. Chicago. p. 19.

24) Opler, Morris E. *Myths and Tales of the Jicarilla Apache Indians*. Dover. 1938. pp. 111-113. Cited also: http://www.talkorigins.org/faqs/flood-myths.html

25) Frazer, p. 115.

26) ibid, p. 116.

27) ibid. For the birds mentioned in the Babylonian version, see the Appendix One of this book. The birds are found from lines 140-144 of the Gilgamesh XI Flood Tablet.

28) Frazer, pp. 121-122.

29) ibid, p. 123.

30) By pre-Christian, we do not mean before the 1st century CE. We mean a tradition that was held by a given people prior to their first contact with Christianity. In the case of the Biami tribe of Papua New Guinea, that was barely forty years ago at time of writing. In the case of Tahiti, that was any time up to 1844; with Australia, it was until the late 1700s, and so on.

31) Frazer, p. 128.

32) http://www.washington.edu/uwpress/search/books/FIETHI.html

33) Frazer, p. 128.

34) As an exercise, make a photocopy of a map of the world, and draw lines from corner to corner. Then see where the lines intersect. It is not a million miles from Ararat. Extraordinary that the Eskimos should carry such knowledge in their folk

memory, especially as they probably never realised that they did so.

35) Frazer, p. 128.

36) ibid, p. 11.

37) ibid, p. 128.

38) ibid, pp. 128-129. David Crantz published his *History of Greenland* in 1767 in 2 volumes. This was the first English edition.

39) ibid, p. 129.

~ * ~

## Chapter Seventeen: Conclusion

Well, we have reached the end of our enquiry. We have noted dozens of Flood traditions that are preserved by nations around the world, making sure that we have noted only those which date to times before any Christian influence could have placed them there. We have listened to witnesses that have often been hostile, or indeed ignorant of the issues involved. Some of the evidence heard, dates from the end of the third millenium BC; some of it to the 20th century CE, a span of 4000 years or more. It has come to us in languages as diverse as the many cultures of the world. But however old the testimony, and no matter where in the world it has come from, it has always proved remarkably consistent and faithful to the known facts as contained in the Book of Genesis. No other subject on earth has ever produced the like.

What, then, are we to say to these things? Are we to hold with Sollberger that all of these strange, independent and unexpected testimonies, found from the deserts of the Middle East to the frozen wastes of the Arctic and all stops in between, north, south, east and west, are nothing but a wonderful and happy coincidence? Or do we hold with Frazer that all this astonishingly consistent, corroborative, testimony merely exposes the Book of Genesis, and hence the entire Word of God, for what it is - at best a figment of someone's imagination, at middling the very source of all folklore and fables, or at worst a downright and deliberate lie? Or does all this evidence point to real historical events and personages? How, we might ask, would a court of law decide?

A court of law, when it hears any evidence at all, always pronounces its verdict upon the grounds of probability. Even when the accused confesses, there is no other course open to it. It has to weigh that confession against the evidence, and again pronounce on the probability or otherwise of guilt before it accepts the plea and passes sentence. After all, it is not unknown for accused persons to confess to crimes which they have not committed. Hence the need to weigh the confession against the evidence.

When witnesses are few and their testimonies inconsistent and contradictory, then the court will invariably decide that the case is not proven. But if, in any given case, witnesses, hundreds of them (some of them hostile) from all parts of the world, turn up and give independent and consistent testimony to the fact that such and such took place at such a time, then the laws of probability alone would compel the court to pronounce that the case is indeed proven. Men have been hanged on much less testimony than that of hundreds of witnesses. Would it therefore be reasonable, or just, to declare that the entire world's testimony to a Great Flood is worth nothing, and that it proves nothing? Hardly.

To evaluate the quality of the evidence that we have heard, we would do well to consider the work of Dr John Morris in this field. Dr Morris had collected (by 2001) more than 200 Flood traditions from around the world, and dismantling them down to their component parts, he found that 88% of the traditions feature a 'favored' family; 66% tell of the warning that that family received of the coming Flood; 66% tell how the coming Flood was due to man's wickedness; 95% mention that the Flood alone was responsible for the world's destruction; 95% likewise testify to the universality (global extent) of the Flood; 70% testify to a boat being the means of survival; 67% state that animals were also saved; 73% testify to the participation of animals (birds being sent out, and so on); 57% state that the survivors landed on a mountain; 82% name local places and peoples; 35% testify to the use of birds; 7% hark back to the rainbow; 13% state that the survivors offered a sacrifice; and 9% specifically state that eight persons were saved. It was a brilliant piece of research, and we may assume that the traditions we have looked at would yield a similar indication of evidential quality. Dr Morris remarks, concerning this data:

> "Putting them all back together, the story would read something like this: Once there was a worldwide flood, sent by God to judge the wickedness of man. But there was one righteous family which was forewarned of the coming flood. They built a boat on which they survived the flood along with the animals. As the flood ended, their boat landed on a high mountain from which they descended and repopulated the whole earth."[1]

Which is exactly what the Book of Genesis tells us. Courts of law the world over would love to have evidence of this abundance and quality brought before them. Gone would be the agonising doubts as they struggle to reach a verdict, fearful that the guilty might go free, and equally fearful that the innocent might be convicted. Evidence of this quality would remove all such difficulty.

I know of no other subject on this good earth that enjoys such proof as this. The Flood is, indeed, unique in this matter. In English jurisprudence, there is a legal fiction called 'the reasonable man.' It is used to help magistrates and jurors ask whether the 'reasonable man' would be persuaded by whatever evidence they are considering. Would it be reasonable, on the basis of the evidence, to suppose that this or that happened, or would the 'reasonable man' conclude that rather the opposite took place? We, in this the $21^{st}$ century, like to think of ourselves as reasonable men and women, and if we reach an unreasonable verdict in this matter, a verdict that is plainly *against* the tremendous and compelling weight of evidence that has come before us, then we shall be held responsible for that, because it would be nothing less than a *wilful* act of folly on our part. Which brings us to the following and very sobering consideration:

## The Word of God

Since the Creation, the Word of God has been manifested (or made sensible to man) in three different ways. There are His spoken words, those that He uttered on the very first day of Creation: "Let there be light!"; and those that He spoke audibly to men and women of the Old Testament, Adam, Abraham, the prophets like Jonah, and those words that He spoke to the angels (1 Kings 22:19-23); and He even spoke audibly once or twice in the New Testament (Matthew 3:17; 17:5; Mark 1:11, and so on). These words, though later written down in the Bible, were audible, spoken and uttered by the very voice of God. Sometimes they thundered and terrified those who heard them, as at Sinai; and sometimes they were barely audible, as Elijah once found. But they were, indeed, spoken.

Then there are His written words, words which the Holy Spirit inspired men to write - quite literally, 'God-breathed' words.[2] These words we find written in the Bible, those Scriptures known as the Old and New Testaments. They are words that we can put to the test should we have a mind to look into them, or the need to contend for them in a faithless world. Indeed, God Himself invites us to do just that, read the Scriptures, test them, and prove them. How otherwise could we ever learn how faithful and true those words of His are?

And then there is the third way in which His Word is made known to us - the Word that was made flesh and dwelt among us, full of Grace and Truth. I mean, of course, the Lord Jesus, the anointed Christ, the Son of God. There is indeed a strange, almost indefinable, identity between the Lord Jesus and the written Word of God. They are, in fact and in essence, the same. There simply cannot be a true Bible and a false Jesus. Neither can there be a false Bible and a true Jesus. The two are inextricably bound together, inseparable, inviolable, unbreakable, and wholly true.

It is therefore no light matter to call either of them into doubt. When a man, even though he should think himself a Christian, pronounces the Book of Genesis to be false, then he is saying in the very same breath that the Lord Jesus, whom he professes to follow, is a false witness, and he is in very real danger of crucifying the Lord afresh.[3]

Let me explain. It is often rightly pointed out that we should believe the Book of Genesis because our Redeemer also believed it. But it goes deeper than that. Much, much deeper. Our Redeemer was the Word through Whom God called all things into being. As such, He doesn't just believe the Book of Genesis. He bears an everlasting testimony to it, just as He bears testimony to the Law and the Prophets whom He came, not to destroy, but to fulfil. They, in turn, bear testimony to Him. In short, He, and the written Word of God, are the same, each testifying of the other. To say then that the Book of Genesis is not true, is to say that the Lord Jesus bears a false testimony to it (contravening Exodus 20:16), and is Himself a false witness and a liar.

That is surely reason enough for any man to believe the Book of Genesis. But God Himself, whose Word Genesis is, has gone the extra mile with us. He has given us a whole world of witnesses - a veritable *cloud* of witnesses - to persuade us of the Eternal Truth of His Word.

Consider. That part of His Word that the world has learned to laugh at the most, the Flood, is the very part that has the most witnesses to its Truth. And He has provided all those witnesses and all that testimony for this reason:

In the Book of Psalms, King David praises God. Why? - "...for Thou hast magnified Thy Word above all Thy Name." (Psalm 138:2b)

Now, we would do well to let that sink in a little. God Himself has exalted, or magnified, His Word even above His Name. That should tell us something of how seriously He takes His own Word. He sets all His Eternal Glory, His Honour, and His Holiness as God by that Word. If there were the least falsehood in that Word, then it would be found in Him too. If there were the smallest trace of ignorance or foolishness in that Word, then that too would be found in Him. And if I may speak as a fool, His Word is the one place where He is vulnerable; for if that were once known to be false, then He would lose His Eternal Glory, His Honour, and His Holiness as God.

It is why that old serpent, the devil, tempted Eve by misrepresenting the Word of God: "Yea, hath God said....?" And it is why those who knowingly promote the modernist agenda, and who are not so 'modern' after all, seek to convince the world that the Word of God is not to be trusted. They can hardly convince the world - though they try often enough - that He does not exist, for the very existence of the world testifies to the fact that He does. His Existence is self-evident through His Creation. So they try to convince the world that He is a liar, a deceiver, whose word is false. No words of mine can adequately express the danger that they are in.

In the Ten Commandments, God very solemnly warns us to avoid the sin of taking His Name in vain. Why? Because He will not hold him guiltless who takes His Name in vain (Exodus 20:7). Now if that is true for His Name, then what peril are they in who declare His Word, which He has exalted and magnified *above* His Name, to be a false thing and a lie? It hardly bears thinking about.

I remember, many years ago now, being asked by one of my Sunday School children if there was anything that God could not do, and I remember foolishly telling him that there was nothing that God could not do. If only I'd gone to the Scriptures. There I would have seen that there are several things that He is quite incapable of. He *cannot* lie. He *cannot* speak frowardly. He *cannot* forswear Himself. He *cannot* make a false promise, and He *cannot* look upon sin. But more precious to me is the knowledge that when we come to Him through Jesus, in repentance, and He puts our sins out of mind, as He promises to do, then He can no longer remember them (Isaiah 43:25).[4] Things that we have done or said or thought in the past, which come back through our conscience to haunt us, and which we constantly beat ourselves up over, He has no memory of. He has put them out of mind. He *cannot* - and will not - remember them. Now that is Mercy, and it is free to all who seek it! That Word who was made flesh and dwelt among us, and who bore our sins in His own Body upon the cross, the Lord Jesus Christ, has made it so.

## Notes to Chapter Seventeen

1) http://www.icr.org/article/570/

2) For a detailed and in-depth study of the inspiration of the Scriptures, see Louis Gaussen's, *God-Breathed: The Divine Inspiration of the Bible* - see Bibliography. It is essential reading.

3) For the latest casualty (at time of writing) in the modern falling away from sound Biblical doctrine in favour of man's foolish conjectures, go to: http://www.icr.org/article/4453/ - it is a tragic and needless loss.

4) "I, even I, am He that blotteth out thy transgressions for Mine own sake, and will not remember thy sins."

~ * ~

# Appendix: The Chaldean Account of the Deluge

*What follows is one of the most important documents in the history of Bible Apologetics. The reading of this paper before the Society of Biblical Archaeology on 3rd December 1872, marked, under God, the turning point in the battle for the Bible that was raging in the late 19th century, and which has continued to rage ever since. Its importance, now as then, can hardly be overstated, and it should never have been hidden away. All footnotes are my own and I have silently corrected any archaic punctuation and spelling. All* [ ] *mark my own insertions.*

---

## The Chaldean Account of the Deluge[1]

## by George Smith

A short time back I discovered among the Assyrian tablets in the British Museum, an account of the Flood, which, under the advice of our President, I now bring before the Society.

For convenience of working, I had divided the collection of Assyrian tablets in the British Museum into sections according to the subject matter of the inscriptions.

I have recently been examining the division comprising the Mythological and Mythical tablets, and from this section I obtained a number of tablets giving a curious series of legends, and including a copy of the story of the Flood. On discovering these documents, which were much mutilated, I searched over all the collections of fragments of inscriptions consisting of several thousands of smaller pieces, and ultimately recovered 80 fragments of these legends, by the aid of which I was enabled to restore nearly all the text of the description of the Flood, and considerable portions of the other legends. These tablets were originally at least twelve in number, forming one story or set of legends, the account of the Flood being on the eleventh tablet.

Of the inscription describing the Flood, there are fragments of three copies containing the same texts. These copies belong to the time of Assurbanipal, or about 660 years before the Christian era, and they were found in the library of that monarch in the palace at Nineveh. The original text, according to the statements on the tablets, must have belonged to the city of Erech, and it appears to have been either written in, or translated into, the Semitic Babylonian at a very early period. The date when this document was first written or translated is at present very difficult to decide, but the following are some of the evidences of its antiquity:

1st. The three Assyrian copies present a number of variant readings which had crept into the text since the original documents were written.

2nd. The forms of the characters in the original documents were of an ancient type, and the Assyrian copyist did not always know their modern representatives. So he has left some of them in their original hieratic form.

3rd. There are a number of sentences which were originally glosses explanatory of the subjects. Before the Assyrian copies were made, these glosses had been already incorporated in the text and their original use lost.

It must here be noted that the Assyrian scribe has recorded for us the divisions of the lines on the original documents.

On examining the composition of the text, some marked peculiarities are apparent which likewise show its high antiquity. One of these is the constant use of the personal pronoun nominative. In later times, this was usually indicated by the verbal form, but not expressed.

On comparing the Deluge text with dated texts from the time of Sargon I,[2] it appears to be older than these, and its original composition cannot be placed later than the seventeenth century before the Christian era - while it may be much older.

The text itself professes to belong to the time of a monarch whose name, written in monograms, I am unable to read phonetically. I therefore provisionally call him by the ordinary values of the signs of his name, Izdubar.[3]

Izdubar, from the description of his reign, evidently belonged to the 'Mythical' period. The legends given in these tablets; the offer of marriage made to him by the goddess Ishtar; the monsters living at the time;[4] Izdubar's vision of the gods; his journey to the translated Sisit,[5] with a curious account of a mythical conquest of Erech when the gods and spirits inhabiting the city changed themselves into animals to escape the fury of the conqueror; all these things and many others show the unhistorical nature of the epoch.

From the heading of the tablets giving his history, I suppose that Izdubar lived in the epoch immediately following the Flood, and I think, likewise, that he may have been the founder of the Babylonian monarchy, perhaps the Nimrod of Scripture. This, however, is pure conjecture. So many fabulous stories were current in Babylonia respecting Izdubar, that his existence may even be doubted.[6]

The fragments of the history of Izdubar, so far as I have at present examined them, remind me of the exploits and labours of Hercules, and, on the supposition that our present version of Berosus is correct as to dates, Izdubar may have been placed about 30,000 years before the Christian era. No document can belong to so remote an age. The legends of Izdubar and the account of the Flood must, however, belong to a very early period, for there are references to the story in the bilingual lists which were composed in Babylonia during the early Chaldean empires.

The question here might be asked, "How is it that we find an early Chaldean document from Erech transported to Nineveh, copied, and placed in the royal library there?" On this point we can show that it was a common custom for the Assyrians to obtain and copy Babylonian works, and a considerable portion of Assyrian literature consists of these copies of older standard writings.

Assurbanipal, the Assyrian monarch in whose reign the Deluge Tablets were copied, had intimate relations with the city of Erech. Erech remained faithful to him when the rest of Babylonia revolted, and to this city Assurbanipal restored the famous image of the goddess Nana, which had been carried away by the Elamites one thousand six hundred and thirty-five years before.[7]

---

In order to properly understand the reason why the narrative of the Flood is introduced into the story, it will be necessary to give a short account of the tablets which precede it before giving the translation of the Deluge inscription itself.

It appears that Izdubar, the hero of these legends, flourished as before stated, in the Mythical period soon after the Flood, and the centre of most of his exploits was the city of Erech, now called Warka, which must have been one of the most ancient cities in the world. Four cities only are mentioned in these inscriptions: Babel, Erech, Shuruppak, and Nippur. Two of these, Babel and Erech, are the first two capitals of Nimrod, and the last one, Nippur, according to the Talmud, is the same as Calneh, the fourth city of Nimrod. Of the first five tablets of the history of Izdubar, I have not recognised any fragments. But in the mass of material which I have collected, it is possible that some portions may belong to this part of the story.

The following passage forms the opening of the sixth tablet and shows the style of the writing. Before giving the translation, I must notice that in various places the tablets are broken and the texts defective. As I cannot point out each of these defective passages, I will endeavour to indicate them by pausing in my reading.

1. ....Belesu, he despised Belesu
2. Like a bull his country he ascended after him
3. He destroyed him, and his memorial perished
4. The country was subdued and after he took the crown
5. Izdubar put on his crown, and after he took the crown
6. For the favour of Izdubar the princess Ishtar lifted her eyes
7. And she spake thus, "Izdubar, thou shalt be husband

8. Thy word me shall bind in bonds
9. Thou shalt be husband, and I will be thy wife
10. Thou shalt drive in a chariot of Ukni stone[8] and gold
11. Of which its body is gold and splendid its pole
12. Thou shalt ride in days of great glory
13. To Bitani, in which is the country where the pine trees grow
14. Bitani is thy entrance
15. To the Euphrates shall kiss thy feet
16. There shall be in subjection under thee kings, lords and princes
17. The tribute of the mountains and plains, they shall bring to thee taxes
18. ....they shall give thee. Thy herds and flocks shall bring forth twins
19. ....the mule shall be swift
20. ....in the chariot shall be strong and not weak
21. ....in the yoke a rival shall not be permitted."

Ishtar, who was the same as Venus, was queen of beauty, but somewhat inconstant, for she had already a husband, a deity called the 'Son of Life'. She however led her husband a poor life, and of this Izdubar reminds her in his answer to her offer.

One of the next exploits of Izdubar, and Heabani his servant, was the conquest of the 'winged bull', a monster supposed to have existed in those days. But I must pass over this and other matters to approach the subject of the Flood.

In course of time, Izdubar, the conqueror of kings and monsters, the ruler of peoples, fell into some illness and came to fear death, man's last great enemy. Now, the Babylonians believed in the existence of a patriarch named Sisit, the Xisuthrus[9] of the Greeks, who was supposed to have been translated [to paradise] and to have attained to immortality without [first having to suffer] death. Izdubar, according to the notions of the time, resolved to seek Sisit to ascertain how he became immortal, that he might attain to a similar honour. The passage reads as follows:

1. Izdubar to Heabani his servant
2. Bitterly lamented and lay down on the ground
3. I the account took from Heabani and
4. Weakness entered into my soul

5. Death I feared and I lay down on the ground
6. To find Sisit, son of Ubaratutu[10]
7. The road I was taking, and joyfully I went
8. To the shadows of the mountains I took at night
9. The gods I saw, and feared
10. ....to Sin[11] I prayed
11. And before the gods my supplication came
12. Peace they gave unto me
13. And they sent unto me a dream

The dream of Izdubar is unfortunately very mutilated, few fragments of it remaining, and his subsequent journey is not in much better condition. It appears that he went through a number of adventures, and three men are represented, in one place, to be telling each other the story of these adventures.

After long wanderings, Izdubar falls into company with a seaman named Urhamsi,[12] a name similar to the Orchamus of the Greeks. Izdubar and Urhamsi fit out a vessel to continue the search for Sisit, and they sail along for a month and fifteen days, and arrive at some region near the mouth of the Euphrates where Sisit was supposed to dwell. In this journey by water, there are fresh adventures and, in their course, Urhamsi tells Izdubar of the waters of death, of which he states, "The waters of death thy hands will not cleanse."

At the time when Izdubar and Urhamsi are approaching him, Sisit is sleeping. The tablet here is too mutilated to inform us how they came to see each other, but it appears probable from the context that Sisit was seen in company with his wife a long distance off, separated from Izdubar by a stream.

Unable to cross this water which divided the mortal from the immortal, Izdubar appears to have called to Sisit and asked his momentous question on life and death. The question asked by Izdubar, and the first part of the answer of Sisit, are lost by the mutilation of the tablet. The latter part of the speech of Sisit, which is preserved, relates to the danger of death, its universality &c. It winds up as follows: "The goddess Mamitu, the maker of fate, to them their fate has appointed. She has fixed death and life, but of death the day is not known." These words, which close the first speech of Sisit, bring us to the end of the tenth tablet. The next one, the eleventh, is the most important of the series as it contains the history of the Flood.

The eleventh tablet opens with a speech of Izdubar who now asks Sisit how he became immortal, and Sisit, answering, relates the story of the Flood and his own piety as the reason why he was translated. The following is the translation of this tablet.

1. Izdubar, after this manner, said to Sisit afar off
2. " ....Sisit
3. The account do thou tell to me
4. The account do thou tell to me [*sic*]
5. ....to the midst to make war
6. ....I come up after thee
7. Say how thou hast done it, and in the circle of the gods, life thou hast gained."
8. Sisit, after this manner, said to Izdubar
9. "I will reveal to thee, Izdubar, the concealed story
10. And the wisdom of the gods I will relate to thee
11. The city, Shuruppak, the city which thou hast established....placed
12. Was ancient, and the gods within it
13. Dwelt. A tempest....their god, the great gods
14. ....Anu
15. ....Bel
16. ....Ninip
17. ....Lord of Hades
18. Their will revealed in the midst of....
19. ....hearing, and he spoke to me thus
20. "Shuruppakite,[13] son of Ubaratutu
21. Make a great ship for thee....
22. I will destroy the sinners and life....
23. Cause to go in the seed of life, all of it, to preserve them
24. The ship which thou shalt make
25. ....cubits shall be the measure of its length, and
26. ....cubits the amount of its breadth and its height.[14]
27. Into the deep launch it."
28. I perceived and said to Hea[15] my lord,
29. "Hea, my lord, this that thou commandest me

30. I will perform. It shall be done."
31. ....army and host
32. Hea opened his mouth and spake, and to me, his servant
33. "....thou shalt say unto them
34. ....he has turned from me, and
35. ....fixed....."

Here there are about fifteen lines entirely lost. The absent passage probably described part of the building of the ark.

51. It....
52. Which in....
53. Strong....I brought
54. On the fifth day....it
55. In its circuit, fourteen measures....its sides
56. 14 measures it measured....over it
57. I placed its roof on it....I enclosed it
58. I rode in it, for the sixth time I....for the seventh time
59. Into the restless deep....for the....time
60. Its planks the waters within it admitted
61. I saw breaks and holes....my hand placed
62. Three measures of bitumen I poured over the outside[16]
63. Three measures of bitumen I poured over the inside
64. Three measures, the men carrying its baskets took they....fixed an altar
65. I unclosed the altar....the altar for an offering
66. Two measures the altar...Pazziru[17] the pilot
67. For....slaughtered oxen
68. Of....inthat day also
69. ....altar and grapes
70. ....like the waters of a river and
71. ....like the day I covered and
72. ....when....covering my hand, placed
73. ....and Shamash....the material of the ship completed
74. ....strong and
75. Reeds I spread above and below
76. ....went in two thirds of it
77. All I possessed, I collected it. All I possessed, I collected of silver
78. All I possessed, I collected of gold

79. All I possessed, I collected of the seed of life, the whole
80. I caused to go up into the ship all my male and female servants
81. The beasts of the field, the animals of the field, and the sons of the army of all of them I caused to go up.
82. A flood Shamash made, and
83. He spake, saying in the night, "I will cause it to rain from heaven, heavily.
84. Enter into the midst of the ship and shut thy door."
85. A flood he raised, and
86. He spake, saying in the night, "I will cause it to rain from heaven, heavily."
87. In the day that I celebrated his festival[18]
88. The day which he had appointed, fear I had
89. I entered into the midst of the ship and shut my door
90. To guide the ship, to Buzursadirabi[19] the pilot
91. The palace I gave to his hand
92. The raging of a storm in the morning[20]
93. Arose from the horizon of heaven, extending and wide
94. Vul in the midst of it, thundered, and
95. Nebo and Saru went in front
96. The throne-bearers[21] went over mountains and plains
97. The destroyer, Nergal, overturned
98. Ninip went in front and cast down
99. The spirits[22] carried destruction
100. In their glory they swept the earth
101. Of Vul, the flood reached to heaven
102. The bright earth to a waste was turned[23]
103. The surface of the earth like....it swept
104. It destroyed all life from the face of the earth
105. The strong tempest over the people reached to heaven
106. Brother saw not his brother. It did not spare the people. In heaven
107. The gods feared the tempest, and
108. Sought refuge. They ascended to the heaven of Anu.
109. The gods, like dogs with tails hidden, crouched down
110. Spake Ishtar a discourse
111. Uttered the great goddess her speech
112. "The world to sin has turned, and
113. Then I, in the presence of the gods, prophesied evil.

114. When I prophesied in the presence of the gods evil
115. To evil were devoted all my people,[24] and I prophesied
116. Thus, 'I have begotten man, and let him not
117. Like the sons of the fishes, fill the sea.'"
118. The gods, concerning the spirits, were weeping with her
119. The gods in seats, seated in lamentation
120. Covered were their lips for the coming evil
121. Six days and nights
122. Passed. The wind, tempest and storm overwhelmed
123. On the seventh day in its course, was calmed the storm, and all the tempest
124. Which had destroyed like an earthquake[25]
125. Quieted. The sea he caused to dry, and the wind and tempest ended.
126. I was carried through the sea. The doer of evil
127. And the whole of mankind who turned to sin
128. Like reeds their corpses floated
129. I opened the window and the light broke in. Over my refuge
130. It passed. I sat still and
131. Over my refuge came peace
132. I was carried over the shore at the boundary of the sea
133. For twelve measures it ascended over the land
134. To the country of Nizir went the ship
135. The mountain of Nizir[26] stopped the ship, and to pass over it, it was not able
136. The first day and the second day, the mountain of Nizir the same
137. The third day and the fourth day, the mountain of Nizir the same
138. The fifth and sixth day, the mountain of Nizir the same
139. On the seventh day, in the course of it
140. I sent forth a dove, and it left. The dove went and searched, and
141. A resting place it did not find, and it returned
142. I sent forth a swallow, and it left. The swallow went and searched, and
143. A resting place it did not find, and it returned
144. I sent forth a raven, and it left
145. The raven went and the corpses on the water it saw, and
146. It did eat. It swam and wandered away, and did not return[27]
147. I sent the animals forth to the four winds. I poured out a libation[28]
148. I built an altar on the peak of the mountain[29]

149. By seven, herbs I cut

150. At the bottom of them I placed reeds, pines and simgar[29]

151. The gods collected at its burning. The gods collected at its good burning

152. The gods, like flies, over the sacrifice gathered[30]

153. From of old also, the great God[31] in his course
154. The great brightness of Anu had created. When the glory
155. Of these gods, as of Ukni stone on my countenance, I could not endure
156. In those days, I prayed that for ever I might not endure
157. May the gods come to my altar
158. May Bel not come to my altar
159. For he did not consider, and had made a tempest

160. And my people he had consigned to the deep[32]
161. From of old also Bel, in his course
162. Saw the ship, and went Bel, with anger filled, to the gods and spirits
163. "Let not anyone come out alive. Let not a man be saved from the deep."
164. Ninip his mouth opened, and spake and said to the warrior Bel

. . . . . . . . . . . . . . . . . . . . . . . . . . . . . . . . . . . . . . . .

[*There follows from this point a further 125 lines, most of which are taken up with silly arguing and bickering amongst the 'gods'. We need not weary ourselves with the matter as the tablet has nothing more to say about the Flood or Genesis. We pick up George Smith's paper again at the point where he has finished reading his translation, and considers a comparison between the Genesis narrative and the account that Berosus translated into Greek. Berosus is interesting for the departures that he gives from the version of the Flood tablet (Gilgamesh 11), and for the many corroborative details common both to his account and the Book of Genesis.*]

. . . . . . . . . . . . . . . . . . . . . . . . . . . . . . . . . . . . . . . .

Before entering into the details of the tablet, I must first refer to the accounts of the Deluge given in the Bible, and by Berosus the Chaldean historian, as I shall have to compare these with the cuneiform record.[33]

The Biblical account of the Deluge, contained in the sixth to the ninth chapters of Genesis, is of course familiar to us all, so I will only give the outline of the narrative.

According to the Book of Genesis, as man multiplied on the earth, the whole race turned to evil except the family of Noah. On account of the wickedness of man, the Lord determined to destroy the world by a flood, and gave command to Noah to build an Ark, 300 cubits long, 50 cubits broad, and 30 cubits high. Into this Ark, Noah entered according to the command of the Lord, taking with him his family and pairs of each animal. After seven days, the Flood commenced in the 600th year of Noah, the seventeenth day of the second month, and after 150 days, the Ark rested upon the mountains of Ararat, on the seventeenth day of the seventh month. We are then told that after 40 days Noah opened the window of the Ark and sent forth a raven, which did not return. He then sent forth a dove, which, finding no rest for the sole of her foot, returned to him. Seven days after, he sent forth the dove a second time [and] she returned to him with an olive leaf in her mouth. Again after seven days, he sent forth the dove which returned to him no more. The Flood was dried up in the 601st year, on the first day of the first month, and on the twenty-seventh day of the second month, Noah removed from the Ark and afterwards built an altar and offered sacrifices.

The Chaldean account of the Flood, as given by Berosus, I have taken from Cory's *Ancient Fragments*,[34] pages 26 to 29, as follows.

"After the death of Ardates, his son Xisuthrus reigned eighteen sari.[35] In his time, happened a great Deluge, the history of which is thus described: The deity Chronos appeared to him in a vision, and warned him that upon the fifteenth day of the month Daesius,[36] there would be a flood by which mankind would be destroyed. He, therefore, enjoined him to write a history of the beginning, procedure and conclusion of all things, and to bury it in the City of the Sun at Sippara,[37] and to build a vessel and take with him into it his friends and relations, and to convey on board everything necessary to sustain life, together with all the different animals, both birds and quadrupeds, and trust himself fearlessly to the deep.[38] Having asked the deity whither he was to sail, he was answered, "To the gods." - upon which he offered up a prayer for the good of mankind. He then obeyed the divine admonition and built a vessel five stadia[39] in length and two in breadth. Into this he put everything which he had prepared, and last of all conveyed into it his wife, his children and his friends."

"After the Flood had been upon the earth and was in time abated, Xisuthrus sent out birds from the vessel, which, not finding any food, nor any place whereupon they might rest their feet,[40] returned to him again. After an interval of some days, he sent them forth a second time, and they now returned with their feet tinged with mud. He made a trial a third time with these birds, but they returned to him no more, from whence he judged that the surface of the earth had appeared above the waters. He, therefore, made an opening in the vessel, and looking out found that it was stranded upon the side of some mountain, upon which he immediately quitted it with his wife, his daughter, and the pilot. Xisuthrus then paid his adoration to the earth, and having constructed an altar, offered sacrifices to the gods, and, with those who had come out of the vessel with him, disappeared."[41]

"They who remained within, finding that their companions did not return, quitted the vessel with many lamentations, and called continually on the name of Xisuthrus. Him they saw no more, but they could distinguish his voice in the air, and could hear him admonish them to pay due regard to religion, and likewise informed them that it was upon account of his piety that he was translated to live with the gods, [and] that his wife and daughter, and the pilot, had obtained the same honour. To this he added that they should return to Babylonia, and, as it was ordained, search for the writings at Sippara, which they were to make known to all mankind. Moreover, that the place wherein they were, was the land of Armenia."[42]

"The rest, having heard these words, offered sacrifices to the gods, and, taking a circuit, journeyed towards Babylonia.. The vessel being thus stranded in Armenia, some part of it yet remains in the Corcyraean mountains."

In pages 33 and 34 of Cory's *Fragments*, there is a second version, as follows:

"And then Sisithrus. To him the deity of Chronos foretold that on the fifteenth day of the month Daesius, there would be a deluge of rain. And he commanded him to deposit all the writings, whatever were in his possession, in the City of the Sun, at Sippara. Sisithrus, when he had complied with these commands, sailed immediately to Armenia, and was presently inspired by God. Upon the third day after the cessation of the rain, Sisithrus sent out birds by way of experiments, that he might judge whether the Flood had subsided. But the birds, passing over an unbounded sea without finding any place of rest, returned again to Sisithrus. This he repeated with other birds, and when upon the third trial he succeeded, for the birds then returned with their feet stained with mud, the gods translated him from among men.[43] With respect to the vessel, which yet remains in Armenia, it is the custom of the inhabitants to form bracelets and amulets of its wood."[44]

There are several other accounts of the Flood in the traditions of different ancient nations. These, however, are neither so full, nor so precise, as the account of Berosus, and their details, so far as they are given, differ more from the Biblical narrative. So I shall not notice them now, but pass at once to the examination of the text.

In comparing the text of the Deluge tablet with the accounts in the Bible and Berosus, the first point that meets us is the consideration of the proper names. This is the least satisfactory part of the subject, for, while the Greek forms show variant readings and have evidently been corrupted, the Cuneiform names on the other hand, being written mostly in monograms, are difficult to render phonetically. The father of the hero of the Flood bears in the inscriptions the name Ubara-tutu, which ought to correspond to one of the Greek forms, Otiartes or Ardates. The resemblance, however, cannot be called a close one.

The hero of the Flood, I have provisionally called Sisit. He corresponds, of course, to the Greek Xisuthrus, but no comparison of the two names can be made until we know the phonetic reading of the Cuneiform name. Neither the Cuneiform nor the Greek names appear to have any connection with the Biblical Lamech and Noah.

In the opening of the account of the Flood, there is a noticeable difference between the Cuneiform and Biblical narratives. For while, in the Jewish account, one God only is mentioned, the Cuneiform inscription mentions all the principal gods of the early Babylonian pantheon as engaged in bringing about the Flood. The Cuneiform account agrees with the Biblical narrative in making the Deluge a divine punishment for the wickedness of the world - this point is omitted in the Greek accounts of Berosus.

The gods having resolved on the Deluge, the deity whom we have hitherto provisionally called Hea, announces the coming event to Sisit. Now, in the account of Berosus, the god who announces the Deluge is stated to be Chronos. So this passage gives us the Cuneiform name of the deity identified by the Greeks with Chronos. The Greek account states that the communication of the coming Deluge was made in a dream. From the context, it is probable that the Cuneiform account stated the same, but the text is here mutilated so that the point cannot be decided.

The dimensions of the vessel in the inscription are unfortunately lost by a fracture which has broken off both numbers. The passage, which is otherwise complete, shows that the dimensions were expressed in cubits as in the Biblical account. But while Genesis makes the Ark 50 cubits broad and 30 cubits high, the inscription states that the height and breadth were the same.

The greater part of the description of the building of the Ark is lost. In the latter part of the account, which is preserved, there is mention of the trial of the vessel by launching it into the sea, when, defects being found which admitted the water, the outside and inside were coated with bitumen. These details have no parallel either in the Bible or Berosus.[45]

The description of the filling of the Ark agrees in general with the two other accounts, but it differs from Genesis in not mentioning the sevens of clean animals, and in including others beside the family of the builder.

The month and day when the Deluge commenced, which are given in the Bible and Berosus, are not mentioned in the text, unless the fifth day, mentioned in a mutilated passage, is part of this date.

The description of the Flood in this inscription is very vivid. It is said to have been so terrible that the gods, fearing it, ascended to the heaven of Anu, that is, the highest and furthest heaven. The destruction of the human race is recorded, and the corpses of the wicked are said to have floated on the surface of the Flood.

With regard to the duration of the Deluge, there appears to be a serious difference between the Bible and the inscription. According to the account in the Book of Genesis, the Flood commenced on the seventeenth day of the second month. The Ark rested on Ararat after one hundred and fifty days on the seventeenth day of the seventh month, and the complete drying up of the Flood was not until the twenty-seventh day of the second month in the following year. The inscription, on the other hand, states that the Flood abated on the seventh day, and that the ship remained seven days on the mountain before the sending out of the birds.

On this point it must be remarked that some Biblical critics consider that there are two versions of the Flood story in Genesis itself, and that these two differ as to the duration of the Flood.[46] The Greek account of Berosus is silent as to the duration of the Deluge.

With regard to the mountain on which the Ark rested, there is a difference between the Bible and the inscription which is more apparent than real. The Book of Genesis states that the Ark rested on the mountains of Ararat. According to the popular notion, this refers to the mountain of Ararat in Armenia. But these mountains may have been anywhere within the ancient territory of Ararat, and some commentators, looking at the passage in Berosus where the Ark is stated to have rested in the Gordiaean mountains, have inclined to place the mountain referred to in the Kurdish mountains east of Assyria. In accordance with this indication, the inscription states that the ship rested on the mountain of Nizir.

Now, the position of Nizir can be determined from the inscription of Assur-nazir-pal, king of Assyria. He made an expedition to this region, and, starting from an Assyrian city near Arbela, crossed the Lower Zab, and marching eastward between latitudes 35 and 36, arrived at the mountains of Nizir. These mountains of Nizir thus lay east of Assyria, but they form part of a series of mountain chains extending to the north-west into Armenia.

The vessel being stranded on the mountain, the Bible, Berosus and the inscription all agree that trial was made by birds in order to ascertain if the Flood had subsided. But in the details of these trials there are curious differences in all three narratives. According to the Book of Genesis, a raven was sent out first which did not return. A dove was sent next, which, finding no resting place, returned to Noah. Seven days later, the dove was sent out again and returned with an olive leaf. And seven days after, on the dove being sent out again, it returned no more.

The account of Berosus mentions the sending out of the birds, but does not mention what kinds were tried. On the first trial, the birds are said to have returned, and on the second trial likewise, this time with mud on their feet. On the third occasion, they did not return.

The inscription states that, first, a dove was sent out, which, finding no resting place, returned. On the second occasion, a swallow was sent, which also returned. The third time, a raven was sent out, which, feeding on the corpses floating on the water, wandered away and did not return. Thus, the inscription agrees with the Bible as to the sending out of the raven and dove, but adds to these the trial of the swallow, which is not in Genesis. In the number of trials, it agrees with Berosus, who had three, while Genesis has four. On the other hand, there is no mention of the dove returning with an olive leaf, as in Genesis, and of the birds having their feet stained with mud as in Berosus.

In the statement of the building of the altar and offering sacrifice after leaving the Ark, all three accounts agree. But in the subsequent matter, there is an important difference between the Bible and the inscription, for while the Bible represents Noah as living for many years after the Flood, the inscription on the other hand agrees with Berosus in making Sisit to be translated like the gods. This translation is, in the Bible, recorded of Enoch, the ancestor of Noah.

On reviewing the evidence, it is apparent that the events of the Flood narrated in the Bible and the inscription are the same, and occur in the same order. But the minor differences in the details show that the inscription embodies a distinct and independent tradition.

In spite of a striking similarity in style which shows itself in several places, the two narratives belong to totally distinct peoples. The Biblical account is the version of an inland people. The name of the Ark in Genesis means a chest or box, and not a ship. There is no notice of the sea, or of launching, no pilots are spoken of, no navigation is mentioned. The inscription, of the other hand, belongs to a maritime people. The Ark is called a ship, the ship is launched into the sea, trial is made of it, and it is given in charge of a pilot.

The cuneiform inscription, after giving the history of the Flood down to the sacrifice of Sisit when he came out of the Ark, goes back to the former part of the story and mentions the god Bel in particular as the maker of the tempest or deluge. There appears to be a slight inconsistency between this and the former part of the inscription which suggests the question whether the Chaldean narrative itself may not have been compiled from two distinct and older accounts.[47]

It is remarkable that the oldest traditions of the early Babylonians seem to centre round the Persian Gulf. From this sea, Oannes the 'fish-god' is supposed to have arisen, and the composite monsters who followed him in the antediluvian period, came from the same region. Into this sea, the Ark was launched. And after the subsiding of the Deluge, when Sisit was translated, he dwelt in this neighbourhood. To this sea came also the great hero Izdubar and was cured, and here he heard the story of the Flood.

In conclusion, I would remark that this account of the Deluge opens to us a new field of inquiry in the early part of the Bible history. The question has often been asked, "What is the origin of the accounts of the antediluvians, with their long lives so many times greater than the longest span of human life? Where was Paradise, the abode of the first parents of mankind? From whence comes the story of the Flood, the Ark, of the birds?" Various conflicting answers have been given to these important questions, while evidence on these subjects before the Greek period has been entirely wanting. The cuneiform inscriptions are now shedding a new light on these questions, and supplying material which future scholars will have to work out. Following this inscription, we may expect many other discoveries throwing light on these ancient periods, until we are able to form a decisive opinion on the many great questions involved. It would be a mistake to suppose that with the translation and commentary on an inscription like this, the matter is ended. The origin, age and history of the legend have to be traced, and it has to be compared with the many similar stories current among various nations.

All these accounts, together with considerable portions of the ancient mythologies, have, I believe, a common origin in the Plains of Chaldea. This country, the cradle of civilisation, the birthplace of the arts and sciences, for 2,000 years has been in ruins. Its literature, containing the most precious records of antiquity, is scarcely known to us except from the texts the Assyrians copied. But beneath its mounds and ruined cities, now awaiting exploration, lay, together with older copies of this Deluge text, other legends and histories of the earliest civilisation in the world.

## Notes to Appendix

1) Smith, George. 'The Chaldean Account of the Deluge.' *Transactions of the Society of Biblical Archaeology*. 2 [1873]. pp. 213-34.

2) Sargon I reigned about 2100 BC (conventional dating).

3) The signs for Izdubar are nowadays phonetically read as Gilgamesh.

4) This is of some interest to us. The Creation Model predicts that there will be many evidences of monstrous creatures which

today we would call dinosaurs co-existing with man, and hence appearing in early written records. For a fuller discussion of the subject, and some examples from European written records, see *After the Flood*, pp. 130-161 & 238-240.

5) As with Izdubar, Sisit's name had to be rendered phonetically. It actually reads Ziusudra. He is how the Sumerians remembered the Biblical Noah. The reference to Sisit being 'translated' refers to the god Enlil 'translating' him to paradise after the Flood, where he became immortal. The real Noah's longevity after the Flood doubtless gave rise to the tale. After the Flood, Noah, already in his 600$^{th}$ year, lived a further 350 years. In a time when men were living to only 120 years or so, he must have seemed immortal. (Genesis 9:28-29).

6) As a conservative Bible scholar, Smith entertained no doubts concerning the historicity of Nimrod. What he is saying here is that if Izdubar lived at all (and he allows that there is room for doubt), then he might well be identified with the Biblical Nimrod. Otherwise it was simply a case of the historical Nimrod having later legends woven about him.

7) That is, in 2295 BC. If we rely on Ussher's chronology, then this would be only 53 years after the Flood. That's not entirely impossible, though I would be inclined to assume that the conventional dating used here by Smith, which before his arrival at the British Museum was first laid by guesswork upon modernist foundations after all, is a little too early, perhaps by one or two hundred years.

8) 'Ukni' stone is lapis lazuli.

9) Xisuthrus was the Greek rendering, coined by Berosus, of the Sumerian name Ziusudra, the counterpart of Noah.

10) Ubaratutu is mentioned in the Sumerian king list as the second to last king to reign before the Flood.

11) Sin was the name of the moon god.

12) Nowadays the name Urhamsi is rendered Ur-shanabi.

13) A Shuruppakite was merely an inhabitant of Shuruppak, as Sisit was.

14) In his *Chaldean Account of Genesis*, pp. 264-265, Smith, having to read a damaged text, tentatively offers the figures of 600 cubits for the length of the vessel, and 60 cubits for its height and breadth. That would make the Babylonian vessel twice the size of the real Ark. The Sumerian account describes the vessel as a cube.

15. This is Ea-Enki, the 'god' who craftily betrayed to Sisit (or Ziusudra) the secret that the other gods, Enlil especially, were about to flood the earth. Enlil wanted none spared, but Ea-Enki decided to warn Sisit (Ziusudru), as with no men alive on earth, there would be no sacrifices, and the 'gods' would starve.

16. The word translated 'measures' by Smith is *sar*, one *sar* being equal to about 8,000 gallons. So three measures would be about 24,000 gallons. These close details sound suspiciously like details that would have been passed down by the builders of the real Ark, Noah and his sons, to those who later questioned them closely not only about the Flood, but also about the design and building of the Ark in which they survived.

17) Pazziru seems not to be a proper name. Later, in his *Chaldean Account of Genesis*, p. 266, Smith translates pazziru as meaning boatmen. Perhaps more accurately it should be boat-builders.

18) The feast-day of Shamash (the sun 'god') was on New Year's Day.

19) Buzursadirabi is a proper name, which nowadays is rendered Puzur-Amurru. The character is entirely mysterious in origin (he doesn't even appear in the *Atrahasis* epic). We cannot liken him to anyone on the real Ark, as we know that that had no pilot or steersman. He makes no further appearance in Gilgamesh, nor does he appear anywhere else in mythology

except once, anonymously, in Berosus' account of the Flood (see below).

20) Later, in *Chaldean Account of Genesis*, p. 268, Smith gives the line *Ragmu-seri-ina-namari* without translation.

21) More accurately, chamberlains.

22) These were the Anunnaki, judges in the Babylonian underworld.

23) From here to line 106, we have a very vivid description of conditions outside the Ark, conditions that could well have been passed down later by those who had been in the Ark.

24) Note the strong reminiscence here of Genesis 6:5, "And God saw that the wickedness of man was great in the earth, and that every imagination of the thoughts of his heart was only evil continually."

25) This is a clear memory of the fact that during the Flood, it didn't just rain. The fountains of the deep were broken up (Genesis 7:11).

26) Mount Nizir (or Nisir) is otherwise known as Mount Nimush, and is thought to lie in present-day Kurdistan. See Rohl, p. 149.

27) This is astonishingly clear evidence that Noah had passed on to his listeners the events that happened at the abating of the Flood. Note also that this narrative is given in the first person, surely indicating that his words were written down as he spoke them. In this Babylonian version the dove and raven are sent out in the wrong order, and a swallow, which Genesis makes no mention of, has mysteriously appeared on the scene. But these are simply markers of the antiquity of the piece, later corruptions that crept in over time. Otherwise it is an astounding corroboration of the Genesis account (Genesis 8:6-12).

28) The original word here is *surqinnu*. A libation was a drink offering poured out over a bare altar or over another sacrifice. Sometimes it could be poured on the ground (2 Sam. 23:15-17).

28) Again, the Genesis narrative is recalled here (Genesis 8:20-21), with the difference that Noah offered only a burnt sacrifice. Genesis makes no mention of a drink offering. In the Babylonian narrative, Sisit offers both kinds.

29) Or myrtle.

30) There is a strong reminiscence here of Genesis 8:21, "And the Lord smelled a sweet savour...." However, unlike Genesis, no promise is given in the Babylonian version that the earth will never again be destroyed by a Flood. On the contrary, the Babylonians lived in fear at around the time of Babel that another Flood would indeed be sent. Hence the building of the Tower of Babel whose top would reach to Heaven (Genesis 11:4).

31) Disappointingly, in the *Chaldean Account of Genesis*, p. 271, Smith had to amend this to read, "...of old also Rubat in *her* course...". Dalley, p. 114, translates Rubat as, "Mistress of the Gods", evidently the mythological justification for the practice of temple prostitution.

32) Again, on p. 271 of his *Chaldean Account of Genesis*, Smith had to amend Bel to Elu. Now, Elu, or El, was recognised even in Babylon as the Creator of all things (indeed, El is the name under which God is referred to sometimes in the Bible). What we have here is clear evidence of the sheer hostility that was projected toward God by the pagans after the Flood, in that Sisit, the Babylonian version of Noah, bans God from coming near his altar (as if he could). It is an immense, even blasphemous, distortion of the truth that Genesis gives us, but is nonetheless typical of how the pagans of Babylon showed their hatred of God, which, like modernism, they accomplished by distorting His Word.

33) By ‘cuneiform record’, Smith means the Flood tablet that he has just translated.

34) ‘Cory’ is Isaac Preston Cory, whose formidably titled book, *Ancient Fragments, Containing What Remains of the Writings of Sanchoniatho, Berossus* [*sic*], *Abydenus, Megasthenes, and Manetho*: *also the Hermetic Creed, The Old Chronicle, the Laterculus of Eratosthenes, the Tyrian Annals, the Oracles of Zoroaster, and the Periplus of Hanno*, was first published in 1828. Enlarged editions followed after 1832. Today, Kessinger have re-published the 1876 edition in facsimile - see Bibliography under Hodges.

35) Ardates, but only with difficulty, must be reckoned as the Greek form of the Babylonian Ubaratutu, whilst Xisuthrus is slightly more recognisable as Ziusudra.

36) Daesius was the fifth month in the Macedonian calendar, corresponding to May/June.

37) Shuruppak, later called the City of the Ark.

38) The earlier Sumerian account has it much more humorously. Enki, the friend of mankind, wants to save some of them from the devastating wrath of Enlil who wants all destroyed. But being a ‘god’ himself, Enki is unable to reveal the counsels of the gods to mortals, and cannot therefore reveal this secret to Ziusudra (or Utnapishtim, or Atram-hasis - they are all characterisations of the historical Noah). So he stands outside Ziusudra’s reed house, and speaks to the wall instead, but so that Ziusudra, who’s lying on his bed inside, can hear: “O hut, O hut! O wall, O wall! Listen, hut! Hear me carefully, wall...!” - and so Ziusudra is surprised out of his slumber, but warned about the coming Flood.

39) A *stadium* (pl. stadia) was a Greek measurement of length equalling 177.6 metres or 581 feet. So the Babylonian version of the Ark would have been one of 888 metres, or 2,904.5 feet

- somewhat bigger than the real Ark that Noah built of just 450 feet.

40) Yet another reminiscence from Genesis, in this case Genesis 8:9, "But the dove found no rest for the sole of her foot."

41) There are many corroborative details in this narrative. Apart from the fact that Noah had no daughter, only three sons, and that the Ark had no pilot (anonymous here but named as Puzur-Amurru in the earlier Babylonian narrative), we could almost be reading the Book of Genesis - the three trials involving birds, an opening being made in the Ark, an altar being built and a sacrifice being made. And then there's that touch of authenticity which is all the more interesting in that Genesis doesn't mention it, the mud on the birds' feet. Did Noah, I wonder, mention that detail to someone to whom he was recounting the abating of the Flood? Very likely, he did, and, just like mud, it stuck.

42) Interestingly, the Hebrew for Armenia is Ararat. It is where Adrammelech and Sharezer, the sons of Sennacherib, fled to after assassinating their father (2 Kings 19:37). It seems to be one of those strange facts that have so persistently avoided the modernist eye.

43) This constant belief amongst the Babylonians that Ziusudra (or Noah) was made immortal and translated by the gods into paradise after the Flood, may well be a memory of the fact that Noah, when he saw how almost all his contemporaries were turning from God to paganism, retreated to some isolated region. This might possibly have been the area between the mouths of the Tigris and Euphrates. That was where Gilgamesh was said to have searched for Ziusudra, and it lay furthermore in the direction of Dilmun, the pagan Eden (nowadays thought to be Bahrain). Add to that the fact that 350 years later it was known that he was still living, and all is explained.

44) In Syncellus's translation of Berosus, he says, "...and the people scrape off the bitumen, with which it [the Ark] had been

outwardly coated, and make use of it by way of an alexipharmic [antidote to poison] and amulet [a charm against evil]."(Charles Horne. *Sacred Books and Early Literature of the East*, p. 23. see Bibliography).

45) George Smith must have seen his mistake whilst reading it. While a trial launch is certainly not mentioned by Genesis, for the very good reason that one did not occur, God did tell Noah specifically to seal the vessel "within and without" with pitch (or bitumen. Genesis 6:14).

46) In mentioning this opinion of the so-called 'higher critics', of which there were many on the scene in George Smith's day, he was certainly not subscribing to the view. On the contrary, he saw it as his role in life to resist their ideas and properly contend for the Bible.

47) Smith, aware that his audience contained not a few modernists, is here subtly casting the notions of the 'higher critics' of the Bible concerning the origins of the Genesis narrative, back in their teeth. The Genesis narrative, they said - and still say today - is derived from the Babylonian via several different sources. Smith is saying not so. It is the Chaldean narrative that is derived from two sources at least. The point would not have been lost on his audience.

~ * ~

## Bibliography to Part Two


Anthes, Rudolph. 'Mythology in Ancient Egypt.' *Mythologies of the Ancient World.* 1961. (ed. S Kramer). Anchor Books. London. pp. 17-92.

Barnes, Jonathan. *Early Greek Philosophy.* 1987. Penguin Classics. Harmondsworth.

Bender, Mark (tr). *Butterfly Mother.* 2006. Hackett Publishing. Indianapolis.

Betanzos, Juan de. *Narrative of the Incas.* 1996. (tr. Hamilton & Buchanan). Univ Texas Press.

Bodde, Derk. 'Myths of Ancient China.' *Mythologies of the Ancient World.* 1961. (ed. S Kramer). Anchor Books. London. pp. 369-408.

Bowden, Malcolm. *The Rise of the Evolution Fraud.* (2nd enlarged edition). 2008. Sovereign Publications. Bromley BR2 9PF.

Brackman, Arnold C. *The Luck of Nineveh.* 1980. Eyre Methuen. London.

Brown, W Norman. 'Mythology of India.' *Mythologies of the Ancient World.* 1961. (ed. S Kramer). Anchor Books. London. pp. 279-330.

Chittick, Donald. *The Puzzle of Ancient Man.* 2006. (3rd ed). Creation Compass. Oregon.

Cicero. *On the Nature of the Gods.* (tr. H McGregor). 1988. Penguin Classics. Harmondsworth.

Cooper, Bill (Wm R). *After the Flood.* 1995. New Wine Press. Chichester. England.

Crossley-Holland, Kevin. *Beowulf.* 1999. Oxford University Press. Oxford.

Dalal, Roshen. *Religion in India*. 2006. Penguin Reference. New Dehli.

Dalley, Stephanie. *Myths from Mesopotamia*. 1989. Oxford Univ. Press. Oxford.

Damrosch, David. *The Buried Book*. 2006. Henry Holt. New York.

Darmesteter, James. *Avesta Vendidad*. 2004. Kessinger Publishing.

Davidson, H R Ellis. *Gods and Myths of Northern Europe*. 1979. Penguin. Harmondsworth.

Doneger, Wendy. *Hindu Myths*. 1975. Penguin Classics. London.

Dresden, M J. 'Mythology of Ancient Iran.' *Mythologies of the Ancient World*. 1961. (ed. S Kramer). Anchor Books. London. pp. 331-366.

Eliade, Mircea. *A History of Religious Ideas: From the Stone Age to the Eleusinian Mysteries*. 1979. Collins. London.

*Encyclopaedia Judaica*. 2007.

Frazer, James George. *Folklore in the Old Testament*. 1923. Macmillan. London.

Gaussen, Louis. *God-Breathed: The Divine Inspiration of the Bible*. 2001. Trinity Foundation.

Goetz, Delia, & Morley, Sylvanus. *Popol Vuh*: *Sacred Book of the Ancient Quiche Maya*. 1991. University of Oklahoma Press.

Gordon, Cyrus H. 'Canaanite Mythology.' *Mythologies of the Ancient World*. 1961. (ed Kramer).Anchor Books. London. pp. 183-218.

Guterbock, Hans. 'Hittite Mythology.' *Mythologies of the Ancient World*. 1961. (ed. S Kramer). Anchor Books. London. pp. 141-179.

Hesiod. *Theogony*. (tr. Norman Brown). 1953. Bobbs-Merrill Co. New York.

Hislop, Alexander. *The Two Babylons*. 1959. Loiseaux Bros. New Jersey.

Hodges, E Richmond (ed). *Cory's Ancient Fragments*. 1876. Reeves & Turner. London. Reprinted by Kessinger.

Hoffner, Harry A. *Hittite Myths*. 1998. Society of Biblical Literature. Scholars Press. Atlanta.

Horne, Charles F. *Fragments of the Babylonian Historian Berosus 300 BC*. Kessinger Publishing. Extracted from *Sacred Books and Early Literature of the East*.

Horne, Charles F. *The Sacred Books and Early Literature of the East: Egypt*. (vol 2). 1917. Parke, Austin & Lipscomb. London. reprinted by Kessinger Publishing.

Jameson, Michael H. 'Mythology of Ancient Greece.' *Mythologies of the Ancient World*. 1961. (ed. S Kramer). Anchor Books. London. pp. 221-276.

Leon-Portilla, Miguel. 'Mythology of Ancient Mexico.' *Mythologies of the Ancient World*. 1961. (ed. S Kramer). Anchor Books. London. pp. 443-472.

Jones, David M. *Mythology of the Aztecs and Maya*. 2003. Southwater. London.

Kang C H, & Nelson E R. *The Discovery of Genesis*. 1979. Concordia. St Louis.

Kearsley, Graeme. *Mayan Genesis*. 2001. Yelsraek. London.

Klaeber, F. *Beowulf*. 1950. D C Heath & Co. Boston.

Kramer, Samuel Noah. *From the Tablets of Sumer*. 1956. Falcon's Wing Press. Colorado.

Kramer, Samuel Noah (ed). *Mythologies of the Ancient World.* 1961. Anchor Books. London.

Lacey, Robert. *Sir Walter Ralegh.* 1973. History Book Club. London.

Lao-tzu. *Tao-te-ching.* (tr. Derek Bryce). 1991. Llanerch Publishers. Lampeter.

Layard, Austen. *Nineveh and its Remains.* 1849 (2nd edition). 2 vols. John Murray. London.

Lucretius. *On the Nature of the Universe.* (tr. Ronald Latham). 1951. Penguin Classics.

Lund, Erik. *A History of European Ideas.* 1976. C Hurst & Co.

Morris III, Henry. *After Eden.* 2003. Master Books. Arizona.

Morris, Henry M. *The Genesis Record.* 2008. Baker Books. Grand Rapids.

Morris, Henry M. *The Long War Against God.* 2008. Master Books. Arizona.

Murray, Gilbert. *Five Stages in Greek Religion.* 1925. Oxford.

Nelson E, & Broadberry R. *Genesis and the Mystery Confucius Couldn't Solve.* 1994. Concordia.

Nelson E, Broadberry R, & Tong Chock G. *God's Promise to the Chinese.* 1997. Read Books.

Nelson E, Broadberry R, & Tong Chock G. *The Beginning of Chinese Characters.* 2001. Read Books.

Page, R I. *Norse Myths.* 1990. British Museum Publications. London.

Plato. *The Laws.* (tr. Trevor Saunders). 1970. Penguin Classics. Harmondsworth.

Plato. *Timaeus and Criteas*. (tr. Desmond Lee). 1965. Penguin Classics. Harmondsworth.

Poignant, Roslyn. *Oceanic Mythology*. 1967. Paul Hamlyn. London.

Reed, A W. *Aboriginal Myths*. 1998. Reed New Holland. Sydney.

Reich, Emil. *The Failure of the Higher Criticism of the Bible*. 1905. Cincinnati

Riplinger, G A. *New Age Bible Versions*. 2000. A V Publications. Virginia.

Roberts, A & Mountford C. *The Dreamtime*. 1965. Rigby Limited. Adelaide.

Rohl, David. *Legend: The Genesis of Civilisation*. 1998. Random House. London.

Rukeyser, Muriel. *Traces of Thomas Hariot*. 1972. Gollancz. London.

Ryan, William & Pitman, Walter. *Noah's Flood*. 1999. Scribner.

Sallustius. 'On the Gods and the World.' Murray, Gilbert. *Five Stages in Greek Religion*. 1925. Oxford. pp. 241-67.

Smith, George. *Assyrian Discoveries..during 1873 and 1874*. 1875. Scribner, Armstrong & Co.

Smith, George. 'The Chaldean Account of the Deluge.' *Transactions of the Society of Biblical Archaeology*. 2 [1873]. pp. 213-34. This paper is given in full in Appendix Two.

Smith, George. *The Chaldean Account of Genesis*. 1876. Samson Low. London.

Smith, George. *The History of Babylonia*. 1880? ed. A H Sayce. SPCK. London.

Sollberger, Edmond. *The Babylonian Legend of the Flood.* 1984. British Museum Publications.

Stevens, Henry. *Thomas Hariot*. 2006. Echo Library. London.

Stewart, R J. *The Elements of Creation Myth*. 1991. Element. Dorset. England.

Sturluson, Snorri. *Edda*. (tr. & ed. Anthony Faulkes). 1995. Everyman. London.

Tedlock, Dennis (tr.). *Popol Vuh*. 1996. Simon & Schuster. New York.

Unger, Merrill F. *Archaeology and the Old Testament*. 1954. Zondervan. Michigan.

Urton, Gary. *Inca Myths*. 1999. British Museum Press. London.

Vanderburgh, F A. *Sumerian Hymns*. 1908. Columbia University Press. New York.

Warner, Elizabeth. *Russian Myths*. 2002. British Museum Press. London.

Werner, E T C. *Myths and Legends of China*. 1922. Harrap & Co. London.

Whitcomb, John C, and Morris, Henry M. *The Genesis Flood.* 1961. P & R Publishing.

Wilson, Elizabeth. *Lights and Shadows of European Mythology*. 1881. Partridge & Co. London.

## Published Articles

Coates, Howard. 'Aboriginal Flood Legend.' *Creation* 4 (3), pp. 9-12. October 1981.
See also www.answersingenesis.org/creation/v4/i3/flood.asp

Coates, H and Douglas W H. 'Australian Aboriginal Flood Stories.' *Creation* 4 (1): 6-10. March 1981. See also www.answersingenesis.org/creation/v4/i1/flood.asp

Ford, Ava. 'Life in the Letters.' November 2008. Acts & Facts. Institute for Creation Research.

Hoey, Tom. 'The Biami Legends of Creation and Noah's Flood.' Creation 7 (2): 12-13. October 1984. (Intro. John Mackay). See also www.answersingenesis.org/creation/v7/i2/noah.asp

Johnson, James J Scofield. 'How Young is the Earth?' October 2008. Acts & Facts. Institute for Creation Research. Dallas.

Lorey, Frank. 'The Flood of Noah and the Flood of Gilgamesh.' www.icr.org/article/414/

Morris, Henry. 'Why Christians Should Believe in a Global Flood.' www.icr.org/article/842/

Morris, John D. 'Why Does Nearly Every Culture Have a Tradition of a Global Flood?' www.icr.org/article/570/

Sage, Bengt. 'Noah and Human Etymology.' www.icr.org/article/166

Truax, E. 'Genesis According to the Miao People.' April 1991. Impact Article. Institute for Creation Research. El Cajon.

# Part Three

# The Genesis Flood Tablet

**Contents**



~ * ~

## Introduction

We have all of us heard of the *Epic of Gilgamesh*, and we have all of us heard the tired old refrain from the modernist camp that the 'Flood narrative' of the Book of Genesis is derived from it; that the story of Noah is nothing more than a Hebrew recension of this Babylonian myth. Well, those who tell us such things should think again.

The standard text of the *Epic of Gilgamesh* is known to us from clay tablets once stored in the library of King Ashurbanipal at Nineveh. These tablets, dating from only the 7th century BC, are thought to be copies of much older versions of the epic which are supposed, on linguistic grounds, to have been composed no earlier than ca 1800 BC. Thus the Bible critics say that because this is earlier than the earliest possible writing of the Book of Genesis, then the Flood narrative of Genesis must have been borrowed from the earlier Babylonian myth. They bolster their contention by pointing out the details that Genesis and *Gilgamesh* share: the wickedness and violence of mankind; the decision by God (or 'gods') to flood the earth; the choosing of a righteous man to build a vessel that will withstand the Flood; the taking on board that vessel selected animals; the global destruction of mankind; the release of birds to see if the waters had abated; the vessel coming to rest upon a mountain; the making of a sacrifice by the righteous man on leaving the vessel, and so on. And it must be confessed that these shared details are indeed remarkable, but they are remarkable for reasons other than those proposed by the modernist school.

That the Bible critics should claim what they do is no surprise. What is a surprise, though, is to learn that the modern trumpeting of the *Gilgamesh*-Genesis idea has been brought about by a sleight of hand which has concealed the true state of affairs from the public eye for the past 100 years or so. That sleight of hand has to do with the covering up of a discovery which, if once made known at a such a critical time (1900-1920), would have derailed the modernist putsch. It was the discovery of a clay tablet which makes a nonsense of the *Gilgamesh*-Genesis notion. In this section, we shall consider the discovery of that tablet, known here as the 'Genesis Flood Tablet', its remarkable nature, its early date, what it says, why it has remained out of public sight and hearing for the past 100 years, and what the implications of it are for the so-called 'science' of Bible criticism.

~ * ~

## Chapter One: The Battle Begins

In these heady days of the History Channel, the internet, and a whole world of educational software, it is hard to imagine how exciting it must have been for our Victorian forebears to hear of the first archaeological finds to come out of Mesopotamia. 150 years ago, the western world was in the throes of the Industrial Revolution. Empires were being built, and explorers were reaching the farthest corners of the globe. On the popular level at least, the Christian faith was still very much taken for granted, though ominous rumours in the press spoke of men, so-called scholars and critics, who were beginning to undermine the Bible. From elsewhere came a sense of optimism and a confidence in man's ability to forge his own world out of the fires of industry and invention. A sense of materialism was in the air, one which promised to replace the old order of things with a new. The world was moving fast – too fast - and it frightened many of the public.

Then news began to filter through the press of a new breed of men. They were archaeologists whose mission was to dig up the ancient past, and they set off to dig up the lands which were mentioned in the Bible. Soon the names of cities and countries of the Bible were being heard – Nineveh, Babylon, Assyria – all of them mentioned in that book of the Bible which the new-born scholars of Germany were now denigrating, the Book of Genesis.
Strange artifacts and inscriptions were soon gracing the west's museums, but among the usual motley collections of statues, pots and pans, were clay tablets bearing strange impressions which no one as yet could read. The writing was given the name *cuneiform*, 'wedge-shaped', and soon scholars – the more gifted among them – were devoting all their energies to discovering its meaning. The scale of their accomplishment is breathtaking.

If only one language had been involved, its discovery and translation would have been remarkable enough. But these clay tablets were written in several languages, and in some of the collections which had been unearthed from palaces and ancient libraries, tablets of all languages were found jumbled together in diplomatic archives. But that was not the worst of it, not by a long chalk.

There were those who, taken with the new Darwinian fashion in thinking, were convinced that languages must have been simple and uncomplicated when first they were uttered, becoming more complex as societies and humanity 'evolved'. The cuneiform tablets soon relieved them of that notion. Speaking of just one of these early languages, Babylonian, A H Sayce tells us:

> "The cuneiform syllabary contains nearly five hundred different characters, each of which has at least two different phonetic values. In addition, each character may be used ideographically to denote an object or an idea. But this is not all. The cuneiform script was invented by the primitive population of Chaldaea [the Sumerians] who spoke, not a Semitic, but an agglutinative language, and in passing to the Semitic Babylonians not only did the pre-Semitic words denoted by the single characters become phonetic values, but words denoted by two or more characters became compound ideographs, the characters in combination representing a Semitic word the syllables of which had no relation whatever to the phonetic values of the separate characters which composed it. It thus became necessary for the learner not only to commit to memory the actual syllabary, but also the hundreds of compound ideographs which existed by the side of it."[1]

So much for simplicity and the idea that languages and writing had 'evolved'. The story of how these languages and their scripts were deciphered, and by whom, is a long and complex tale. But the important thing is that they did it, and they did it well. Chronicles, histories, fables, royal accounts, astronomical tables, mathematical treatises, even maps, were suddenly brought out into the light of day after having been buried in the sands of Mesopotamia for thousands of years, and the public were enthralled by what they read.

One of the heroes of this new learning was an unprepossessing man named George Smith, soon to become known worldwide as 'the Assyriologist'. He had begun his career as a banknote engraver, a highly specialised skill which required immense abilities in the arts of observation and technical drawing, and he worked sufficiently close to the British Museum in London to visit each day its displays of cuneiform tablets and inscriptions. Soon he was translating what he saw, and such were his knowledge and skill in this that he was employed by the British Museum in its new department of Assyriology.

His output was immense, but what was to bring him to the world's attention was his discovery and translation of a tablet which told of the Flood, the same Flood which the Book of Genesis speaks of - the Flood of Noah.

On December 3rd 1872, Smith read before the Society of Biblical Archaeology a paper titled *The Chaldean Account of the Deluge*,[2] and it took the world by storm. Here was an independent pagan account of an event which the Bible critics had been teaching the world to laugh at for the past twenty years. Moreover, it was a highly detailed account which corresponded with the Genesis Flood narrative in many places.

Unlike most of his peers, George Smith was a Bible-believer, and part of his immense output was informing the public of documents and monuments which mentioned kings, peoples, cities and lands – and sometimes customs and laws - which the Bible also mentions, but which the critics had been telling the public were 'mythological' and 'non-historical'. In short, he was undermining the modernist effort to re-educate the public away from the Bible and the Christian faith, and there was nothing they could do about it – for the present.

In the event, they didn't have to do anything. George Smith died in 1876 on his third trip to Iraq. He was just 36 years of age and on the threshold of wonderful discoveries. But with his death came a great silence on Biblical matters. A curtain was drawn over anything which smacked of support for the Bible's integrity. In short, from this time on, the public would only know what the newly-established scholars wanted them to know. In exactly the same way in which news agencies today let out only those stories which they want the public to hear, so the educational establishments and publishers of Victorian times publicised only those things which they wanted the public to learn, and those establishments had an agenda.

Quite how this was accomplished and by whom is a story which is told elsewhere.[3] We may merely note here that it is an agenda which has not gone away. Shortly after George Smith's death, the Flood epic which he had uncovered was given a new name. It was called, *The Epic of Gilgamesh*, and soon this epic was being portrayed to the public not as an independent witness to the Genesis account of the Flood, but as its very origin. In other words, the Flood chapters of Genesis were merely a much-edited version of this earlier myth. The effect was to denigrate the Bible utterly in the public mind, and no serious educator would risk his career by attempting to vindicate the Bible in any way, whatever the evidence might say.

It is a state of affairs which has continued to the present day. Material which surfaces from the field of archaeology and which supports or vindicates the Biblical record – and there's plenty of it! - is quickly and methodically suppressed. And if it happens to be brought to the public notice, then a host of 'experts' will arise to denigrate that evidence and to cast doubt upon its authenticity, its place of discovery, its date, and sometimes even the moral integrity of its discoverer. Modernism is a well-oiled and highly efficient machine, and it knows well how to protect its own interests.

We can see it at work even by the mid-1870s when the Gilgamesh epic first burst onto the scene. But so that issues do not become obscured by generalities, let us consider exactly what it was that George Smith had discovered. Let us consider the *real* nature of the beast, and its true place in the archaeological and Biblical record, for this is evidence for the Bible's integrity which has been turned on its head to prove the modernist cause, that the Book of Genesis in particular is not only unreliable, but is not even an original document; it is but a cleverly-edited copy and a rehash of older fables. So, let's test that assertion.

## Notes to Chapter One

1) Sayce, *The Higher Criticism…*, pp. 50-51. (see Bibliography).

2) 'The Chaldean Account of the Deluge.' *Transactions of the Society of Biblical Archaeology*. Vol. 2 [1873]. pp. 213-34. A

good biography of George Smith may be found in Damrosch, pp. 10-80 (see Bibliography).

3) See Bowden, Malcolm. *The Rise of the Evolution Fraud.* (2nd enlarged edition). 2008. Sovereign Publications, & Morris, Henry M. *The Long War Against God.* 2008. Master Books. Arizona.

~ * ~

## Chapter Two: What exactly *is* the Epic of Gilgamesh?

The physical remains of the *Epic of Gilgamesh* consist of a series of twelve clay tablets. This was the size of the epic by the 7th century BC when King Ashurbanipal of Assyria ordered it copied and archived in his library at Nineveh.[1] The surviving tablets from that series are in a more or less fragmentary condition, and gaps in the text of that copy have been tentatively filled in from more than 160 other fragments of the epic discovered elsewhere. The result is that we have a more or less complete text, though work is still ongoing.

As literature, the epic, as its name implies, is an epic poem celebrating the life and adventures of one Gilgamesh.[2] But he was no mythical figure. His name appears among those of the early kings of Uruk (the Biblical Erech, Gen. 10:10 – mod. Warka), and he is famed and feted throughout Mesopotamian literature, Sumerian, Akkadian, Babylonian and Assyrian. As recently as April 2003, even the tomb of Gilgamesh was unearthed in Iraq, so there can be no doubt whatever that he lived.[3]

The epic is an intriguing (if sometimes obscene) work of literature, but of more interest to the Bible student are the many remarkable parallels between the epic and some of the early chapters of the Book of Genesis. Some of these parallels are more general than specific, but they are well worth considering for the picture that they give us of the state of knowledge in early Babylonia concerning the events, places and people that are mentioned in the Book of Genesis. We shall consider some of them in due course.

When a place, person or event is mentioned in just one ancient document, then there is room for doubt as to whether that place, person or event is historical or not. It doesn't guarantee either its historicity or non-historicity. It merely allows for the possibility that it may be non-historical. But when the same place, person or event is mentioned in two or more widely separate and independent sources – sources that are written in different languages! -then we can rightly assume that that place, person or event *is* historical and real. In the case of persons, even if their proffered words and deeds cannot be verified, then at least we can be sure that they did exist, and that is the case with Gilgamesh, one-time king of Uruk.[4]

The series of twelve tablets containing the *Epic of Gilgamesh* were, according to an inscription on the tablets themselves, copies of an epic which came from the temple of Uruk, the home city of Gilgamesh.[5] That explains the several references in the epic to certain historical events concerning Uruk, the building of its wall and temple, and the war against the invading Elamites for example, events that we know from other sources. In other words, there is a level of authenticity to the epic which may be unsuspected at first. But briefly, the story that the tablets tell us is as follows:

Tablet 1 opens with praise and adulation for Gilgamesh and his deep wisdom concerning the world as it was before the Flood. Greatly expanding and fortifying the city of Uruk, he becomes as its 'shepherd' or king, its tyrant instead. So the 'gods' create a rival to him, a wild man named Enkidu who lives in the forests as an animal. When Enkidu is reported to Gilgamesh by a frightened hunter, the king urges that a harlot be used as bait to bring him from the wild into Uruk, there to be civilised.

Tablet 2 relates the civilising of Enkidu and his summons to appear before Gilgamesh. The king claims his right to Enkidu's harlot and the two engage in a great fight over her, which results in their becoming fast friends.

Tablet 3 Gilgamesh confides in Enkidu his wish to go into the forest and destroy the evil giant Khumbaba. Enkidu tries to dissuade him, but Gilgamesh says that if he is to die like a mortal (he was only two-thirds 'god'), then he would rather die in pursuit of a glorious enterprise like this than die in peace. The two have special weapons made and set off to a cheering crowd.

Tablet 4 has the two mighty warriors encouraging each other to enter Khumbaba's realm, only for Enkidu to fall sick for twelve days with fright. Eventually Gilgamesh manages to persuade him to the battle.

Tablet 5 relates their entry into Khumbaba's realm and the various dreams that Gilgamesh has, one of which fills him with terror. Then, with the help of the 'sun-god', Khumbaba is entrapped, and the fragment ends with him pleading for his life. Enkidu warns Gilgamesh against granting it.

Tablet 6 has the pair returning to Uruk (presumably having slain Khumbaba), where the 'goddess' Ishtar falls in love with Gilgamesh. He spurns her advances by relating the woes that always befall those who consort with her. Ishtar complains to the 'god' Anu that Gilgamesh has blasphemed her, and Anu creates a great bull, the Bull of Heaven, to destroy Gilgamesh. With Enkidu to help, Gilgamesh slays the bull and Ishtar curses him in her rage. At the crowd's adulation, Gilgamesh holds a great feast during which everyone falls asleep. Enkidu has a dream, and relates it to Gilgamesh.

Tablet 7 (from fragments found elsewhere) relates how in the dream the 'gods' decree that Enkidu must die. As he dies, he heaps curses on the harlot who brought him to Gilgamesh. Then, admonished by the 'sun-god' for his ingratitude, Enkidu reverses the curses and blesses her instead. Then in another dream a monster drags him off to the underworld where he witnesses the terrible state of the dead.

Tablet 8 is taken up wholly with Gilgamesh uttering lamentations over Enkidu's death.

Tablet 9 has Gilgamesh realising the finality of death and uttering his wish to escape it. After meeting the 'scorpion-men' Gilgamesh is overcome with terror. One of them recognises that Gilgamesh is himself part 'god', and Gilgamesh discloses his desire to find his ancestor Utnapishtim (the Babylonian Noah) who was granted eternal life after the Flood. He wishes to discover the secret of immortality. Not heeding the scorpion-man's warning not to proceed, Gilgamesh sets off and soon comes into a garden that is reminiscent of Eden, even coming across the 'tree of the gods'. The 'sun-god' warns him that his quest is in vain, and Gilgamesh re-states his determination to escape death.

Tablet 10 relates how Gilgamesh encounters the 'goddess' Siduri who also warns him that his quest is in vain, for death has been decreed for man since the Creation. Gilgamesh then encounters a boatman named Ur-Shanabi who repeats the goddess's warning but nonetheless takes him to see Utnapishtim.

Tablet 11 is the famous Flood tablet that relates the Flood in details that are strikingly close to those mentioned in the Book of Genesis. Utnapishtim relates everything concerning the Flood to Gilgamesh, but again warns him that none may know when he will die, nor can he ever avoid death. But he does tell Gilgamesh of a plant that grows under the sea which will perpetually renew his youth. Gilgamesh fetches the plant, but loses it on the way home when it is eaten by a serpent.

Tablet 12 has Gilgamesh resigned to dying, but calling up the spirit of Enkidu who tells him how terrible a thing death is. And on that happy note of optimism, the epic closes.

It is wonderful to think that such a tale as this can be seriously proposed by the modernist school as a major source for the Book of Genesis. The *Epic of Gilgamesh* presented the early Babylonians with their greatest opportunity ever of putting down their thoughts about the Creation, the Fall of Man, the Flood, and so on. And yet this is the best that they could come up with. Apart from some interesting if incidental parallels which we shall consider in due course, and which indicate a definite if dimmed memory among the Babylonians of events contained in Genesis, there is, apart from the 11$^{th}$ tablet of the series, virtually no resemblance between this epic tale and the opening book of the Bible. And yet the public are continually fed the notion that Genesis is dependent upon such tales as this.

Even the 11$^{th}$ tablet, the famous Flood tablet of the Gilgamesh epic, cannot be said to bear any of the qualities and characteristics necessary to have served as a foundation document for Genesis. At most, it can only be said that Genesis and *Gilgamesh* independently recall the same historical event, but more likely it is that *Gilgamesh* is a later corruption of the account of the Flood which had already been given out by the time that *Gilgamesh* was composed. How do we know this? Let's see.

## Notes to Chapter Two

1) Rarely for a king of any land, Ashurbanipal (the Asnapper of Ezra 4:10) had a deep love of writing and literature. He was himself trained in all the arts of writing, even to the making and baking of clay tablets, and being fluent in the writing of cuneiform – see Wallis Budge, p. 10.

2) George Smith originally transcribed the name of the epic's hero as Izdubar, reading the three cuneiform characters which made up the name as pictographs. He hadn't yet realised that these pictographs had a phonetic value beyond the pictographic. Once that was realised by later scholars, the name of Gilgamesh supplanted that of Izdubar. The first scholars to include the name Gilgamesh in their translation's title of the epic were Arthur Ungnad and Hugo Gressmann in their *Das Gilgamesch-Epos* of 1911. Ten years before that, Haupt titled his translation *Das Babylonische Nimrodepos* – 'The Babylonian Nimrod Epic' (published in Leipzig 1884-1901). This was due to his belief that Izdubar (or Gilgamesh) was synonymous with Nimrod..

3) The bulletin concerning the tomb's discovery was put out by the BBC on 29th April 2003. See: http://news.bbc.co.uk/1/hi/sci/tech/2982891.stm

4) The first dynasty of the kings of Uruk are listed as: Mesh-ki-ang-gasher, Enmerkar, Lugalbanda, Dumuzi, Gilgamesh and Ur-nungal. All of these kings are historical, not mythical. In the Sumerian history titled *Enmerkar and the Lord of Aratta*, Enmerkar, king of Uruk, pleads with the god Enki to restore the unity of mankind's speech, ("May they all pray to Enlil in unison, in a single tongue!"), harking back to the days before Babel. Gilgamesh himself is credited in the records with building the walls and temples of Uruk, notably the temple of Eanna (Ishtar) whose ruins have been unearthed, as well as a great storehouse, feats which we know he accomplished and which are mentioned also in Tablet 1 of the epic.

5) Peters, ii, p. 108.

## Chapter Three: One Amongst Many

It is a notable fact that the Flood account contained in the 11th tablet of the Gilgamesh epic was not originally a part of that epic. In fact, each 'chapter' of the epic began as a separate story. We know this from Sumerian clay tablets which have survived from much earlier times:

> "It has long been recognised that the Gilgamesh Epic constitutes a literary compilation of material from various originally unrelated sources, put together to form one grand, more or less harmonious, whole. The composite character of our poem is apparent from the following considerations. To begin with, there can be no doubt that Tablet XII [12] was drawn from an independent source, for we now have the Sumerian counterpart to it, showing unmistakeably that the Gilgamesh Epic used only the second half of the original story."[1]

Likewise, the Khumbaba portion of the epic, spread over Tablets 3–5, has been discovered on Sumerian clay tablets which were written out long before the epic was even born or thought of. Ishtar's descent to the underworld, her attempted seduction of Gilgamesh and the creation of the 'Bull of Heaven' to destroy him (Tablet 6), also originated in separate compositions of both Sumerian and Semitic Babylonian origin. In other words, the *Epic of Gilgamesh* as it exists in the series of twelve tablets, is a mish-mash, a hotch-potch of earlier tales tacked together to form a much longer tale.[2] As such, it can be no fit foundation for the Book of Genesis or for any part of it. It is too late a compilation for that. But, returning to the Flood account contained on Tablet 11 of the epic, we discover a most interesting fact.

It is only one among several such accounts from Mesopotamia, each of which is different in many ways to the others. Even the names of the various 'Noahs' are markedly different. The Sumerian account tells of Ziusudra, for example. The Babylonian version (the Gilgamesh Epic) speaks of Utnapishtim, whilst another calls him Atrahasis. The name Ziusudra belongs to one who gained 'distant days' - immortality in other words. Atrahasis is the name of one who is exceedingly wise. Utnapishtim's name is conventionally held to mean one who has gained everlasting life, as in the Sumerian account, although, as we shall see, the Genesis Flood Tablet sheds a more interesting light altogether on that name.

The number of other differences between just these three accounts, even disregarding Genesis for the moment, is surprising. The Sumerian Flood account, for instance, has Ziusudra keeping the coming of the Flood a close secret from his contemporaries. They have had previous scourges in the form of dire famines (one lasting six years in which parents ate their own children), but still they continue to multiply and make an unbearable din – which strangely is the cause of their divine judgment rather than any concept of sin and iniquity. The mechanical cause of the Flood is merely the *amaru* (rainstorm). There is nothing said of the breaking up of the fountains of the deep. The *amaru* lasts for seven days and nights, after which the 'sun-god' comes out.

In the Gilgamesh account, Utnapishtim is instructed to deceive mankind when asked why he is preparing the Ark, and say that he is going to the gods to pray for mankind and that mankind will prosper and be happy as a result. The Flood lasts six days and seven nights. Strangely, the Ark is an exact cube of 120 cubits and has seven storeys. (Another Flood account from Mesopotamia which Berossus passed down to us in Greek, has an Ark which is some 3000 feet in length and 1200 feet wide!)

The Atrahasis Epic (whose fragments we consider in the next chapter) has details which again vary from the other accounts, so, given the undoubted popularity and importance of Flood traditions in Mesopotamia, how do we account for these many differences between traditions, accounts and narratives concerning just one event, the Flood, which were all born at about the same time (before 2000 BC) and in the same small area? There seems to be only one plausible explanation.

For such a muddle of detail to occur in accounts that are all born at the same time and in largely the same place, there has to have occurred a sudden and great change in language – so sudden and so great as to make straightforward translation impossible. It could no longer be a matter of simply copying details from an original document, or indeed of verbally asking questions of those who know, so memory, guesswork and invention had to be resorted to, and when memory and guesswork are relied upon, then mistakes and errors and inconsistencies are wholly inevitable.

The accounts we are considering have come down to us in different languages, and the birth of those languages must have been sudden and simultaneous, otherwise each language would have been learned and mastered, and simple translation would then have been possible. The result of that translation would at least have been a consistency of detail between these Flood accounts. And yet they are all in a hopeless muddle and in marked disagreement with one another over simple details.

The Book of Genesis tells us of such a time when, in a moment, languages were confounded (11:1-9), but Genesis is by no means a lone voice in this. We have the same information come down to us from many independent and ancient sources, and these sources are surprisingly consistent. One such source we have already encountered. It is the Sumerian epic, *Enmerkar and the Lord of Aratta*.

Enmerkar was the second king of the 1st Dynasty of Uruk, and he wished fervently that men could address their gods again in one single language, like they used to.[3] Now, why on earth should that sentence ever have been written if language had always been diverse? Such a sentiment would have had no place in men's thinking, and the remark would have been nonsensical. We take diversity of language as a fact of life. We know of no time in our own history when languages were not diverse. Yet here is an early Sumerian king yearning for a return to the then recent days when language was merely one universal speech. And interestingly, Enmerkar makes no mention of Babel in his sentiment, so the Genesis account of Babel cannot have been copied from or influenced by this epic.

But neither was Enmerkar's a lone voice. Interestingly, the extent of mankind's spread upon the earth in Enmerkar's day consisted of the 'cities' of Shuber, Hamazi, Sumer, Uri and Martu, all of them situated in the one small area within Mesopotamia. Undoubtedly there were other lesser settlements in the area, these named places being administrative towns and cities, but importantly no great migration had yet taken place. But then we have a sudden burgeoning not just of kingdoms, but of languages and systems of writing. Why – and *how*? – if the dispersal of peoples and the confounding of language had not taken place?

Closer detail about these events comes to us from a clay tablet which George Smith came across and translated back in 1875. Only four fragmented columns of writing from an original six survive, but in translation they read:

> "[Line 1]....them(?) the father....[2]....of him, his heart was evil....[3]....was wicked against the Father of all the gods, [4]....of him, his heart was evil (*sic*), [5]....brought Babylon to subjection, [6] Small and great He confounded their speech. [7]....brought Babylon to subjection (*sic*), [8] Small and great He confounded their speech (*sic*). [9] All the day their strong tower they founded. [10 & 11] In the night, He entirely made an end to their strong place. [12] Thus He poured out word also in his anger. [13] He set his face to scatter abroad. [14] He gave this command, their counsel was confused."[4]

There are other ancient accounts of Babel from far and wide, so its historicity cannot sensibly be ignored. It was an event which was, in every sense, earth-shattering, and it is more than sufficient to explain the multiplicity of disagreements and inconsistencies between the various Flood accounts of Mesopotamia.

But even these three Flood traditions, Gilgamesh, Atrahasis and Ziusudra aren't all. There are others which are simply not in the standard canon (if there ever was such a canon) of the three that we have just considered. One of them especially is of great importance to us, and we shall see in the following chapters how it came to light. Equally important is how that tablet, which we will call for convenience the Genesis Flood Tablet,[5] was treated after its discovery. Meanwhile, so that we may consider the Genesis Flood Tablet in a better and clearer context, we shall briefly consider the fragments of the *Atrahasis Epic*, a Mesopotamian account of the Great Flood which even today is sometimes still known under the unexpected and most intriguing title of, *A Hebrew Deluge Story in Cuneiform*.[6]

## Notes to Chapter Three

1) Heidel, p. 13.

2) Ibid, pp. 13-14.

3) Kramer, *From the Tablets of Sumer*, p. 259.

4) Smith, *The Chaldean Account of Genesis*, p. 160. Smith provides a literal translation which, due to its awkwardness, I have modified here, bringing it more into line with good English.

5) Its catalogue number at the Philadelphia Museum is CBM 13532.

6) Clay, Albert T. *A Hebrew Deluge Story in Cuneiform; and Other Epic Fragments in the Pierpont Morgan Library*. 1922. Yale University Press.

~ * ~

## Chapter Four: A Hebrew Cuneiform Tablet about the Flood

Albert Tobias Clay (1866-1925), Professor of Semitic Philology and Archaeology at the University of Pennsylvania, was not your run-of-the-mill modernist don. On the contrary, he was passionately concerned about the denigration of the Bible that was being published by the school of the 'Higher Critics', and he wrote and spoke against it on many occasions. Indeed, his book, *Amurru; the Home of the Northern Semites*, which he had published in 1909, was written with the express purpose of countering the thrust of those who would teach that the Bible owes its existence, not to God or even the Children of Israel, but to the peoples and mythologies of Babylonia. The book was well received in the press, earning a full-page spread in a *New York Times* review. The headline ran:

"PROOF THAT THE BIBLE IS AUTHENTIC.
Prof. Clay's Book on the Origin of the Old Testament
a Revelation to Those who Doubt."[1]

This was a rare treat indeed for Bible-believers of the day, even though the review did begin with the somewhat deflating qualifier, "...if the author's arguments are accepted".[2] But even so, for five long columns the review continued in glowing terms, and readers' hearts – or *some* readers' hearts at least – were lifted. Of course, the author's arguments were not accepted, not in the realms of academe at any rate. Modernism does not lightly give ground on any point, and it never smiles kindly upon those whose work embarrasses the movement. Hence, the aptly-named Clay saw his book ignored. Not so with the chap in the very next room to where Clay was sitting at the time of his newspaper interview. Dr Hugo Radau was his name, and his book, *Bel, the Christ of Ancient Times*, a pointedly blasphemous assertion that the Lord Jesus Christ was merely a coded memory of the ancient and hideous 'god' Bel, *was* embraced by the establishment.

It certainly wasn't that Clay lacked learning and qualifications in his discipline and Radau didn't. Clay was a leading authority on cuneiform, Mesopotamian literature and archaeology, fluent in Hebrew, Greek, and the Semitic Babylonian tongue among others. Far cleverer than Radau could ever hope to be, he really did know what he was talking about. It's what he said about the *Bible* that made the difference between the establishment's ignoring of his book and its acceptance of Radau's. Nothing changes, it seems. But apart from his *Amurru*, which may still be had in modern reprints,[3] Clay published a learned and valuable paper on the fragments of a certain clay tablet which lay in the Pierpont Morgan Library of New York. The year is 1922, Clay is clearly still on the warpath, and what he tells us in his monograph on the tablet is most interesting.[4] Certainly, it paves the way for our better understanding and appreciation of the Genesis Flood Tablet.

What Clay had translated was the fragmentary remains of the first tablet of what is now known as the *Atrahasis Epic*. The epic originally consisted of three tablets, fragments of the other two in the series being found in the rubble of King Ashurbanipal's library at Nineveh. The interesting thing about Clay's is that it is older by some 1200 years than the other two, both of which were 7th-century BC copies of an older text. According to information supplied on the tablet itself, the total work consisted of 1245 lines of text,[5] which lines were written out by the scribe Ellit-Aya on the 28th day of Shabatu (the 11th month of the Babylonian calendar) in the year when King Ammizadugga of the 1st dynasty of Babylon rebuilt Dur- Ammizadugga at the mouth of the Euphrates.[6] In our more concise terms, that is around the year 1800 BC.

In spite of the title that Clay gave his monograph, the tablet isn't written in what we know as Biblical Hebrew. Clay's thrust was always that the Amorites, the people of Amurru, were the source of the tablet, and that because they were of common stock with the Hebrews, then many Hebrew words which are found in the Bible are also to be found in the tablet. He was perfectly right, of course. Semitic languages had always prevailed in the 'land of the Amorites' – a vast territory which stretched from Babylonia to the Mediterranean and down through Canaan as far as Arabia, so his thesis is in perfect accord with archaeology. It is incidentally also in accord with the Bible, where God, through Ezekiel, says to Jerusalem, "Thy father was an Amorite, and thy mother an Hittite." (Ezek. 16:3).

But though the earlier tablet of the *Atrahasis Epic* holds such a close affiliation with Hebrew, it is nonetheless polytheistic, and hence pagan. In line 4 of the tablet, God, indeed, is referred to by His Hebrew (Biblical) Name of Ilu (Heb. El), but then come the 'great gods', in particular Adad (the Amorite rain-god).

Interestingly, on line 10 of the tablet appears, "In their bellies let vegetables be wanting." This refers to an earlier punishment of mankind before the Flood, namely a famine which, elsewhere we are told, lasted for six years and was so severe that parents ate their children. But that, and a certain pestilence which was supposed to diminish the world's population, were failed experiments, and so the Flood was finally decided upon. Now Genesis makes no mention of famines or pestilences before the Flood, but it does tell us that mankind were purely vegetarian. In Genesis 1:8-16, God has specifically created and ordained the plants, fruits and vegetables to be food for man. After the Flood, however, God says to Noah, "Every moving thing that liveth shall be meat for you, even as the green herb...." (Genesis 9:3). The Atrahasis Flood tablet seems to recall the fact that mankind had previously lived solely on plants and vegetation.

The Atrahasis narrative differs from that of Gilgamesh in that it is given in the third person and not the first. But there are a sufficient number of correspondences between the two to force the conclusion that they are both independently referring to the same historical Flood, but are both dependent, more or less, on the Genesis account. In other words, Atrahasis and the later Gilgamesh epic are both corruptions and borrowings from the Genesis original. This is entirely counter to the modernist thrust, but it is true nonetheless.

We shall see why it is true in the next chapter when we consider the Genesis Flood Tablet itself. But the Atrahasis Epic is interesting in many ways. It certainly did not originate amongst the Babylonians, the source of all Flood narratives - Genesis included, according to the 'higher critics'. It is an independent Amorite (Clay would say Hebrew) version of the events surrounding the Flood, events which were very well known in the ancient world and written about in many languages.

We may wonder then why it was not more faithful in its details to the Genesis account, given that its language and terms are so close to the Hebrew of Genesis. Yet language alone is not necessarily a unifying force when it comes to religion. The image-worshipping Israelites and Jews of the Old Testament, particularly, found themselves at odds with God in spite of their fluency in the Hebrew of the Old Testament. They spoke exactly the same language as the prophets, yet were entirely divorced from them in matters of faith. It seems that it takes more than just language to make a man of God.

There is a predominantly Jewish school of thought which holds, very seriously, that Hebrew, Biblical Hebrew that is, is the original language of mankind (and of God) that was spoken before the Confusion of Tongues at Babel. The very words of God Himself are recorded in Hebrew. The Ten Commandments were written by the finger of God in Hebrew. The question is therefore raised, Could the Old Testament be the pure and unadulterated Word of God if it were merely a translation from some other language? Translations, no matter how well done, are always flawed to a greater or lesser degree – that much is unavoidable - so there is great force to the argument. It is interesting, therefore, that the language of our next tablet, the Genesis Flood Tablet, is not Biblical Hebrew, but what is known as Semitic Babylonian, an offshoot of the original Hebrew tongue.

## Notes to Chapter Four


1) *New York Times*, 9th January 1910.

2) Ibid.

3) Clay, Albert T. *Amurru, the Home of the Northern Semites*. 1909.

4) Clay, Albert T. *A Hebrew Deluge Story in Cuneiform; and Other Epic Fragments in the Pierpont Morgan Library*. 1922. Yale University Press.

5) Heidel, p. 106.

6) Ibid, p. 107.

## Chapter Five: The Genesis Flood Tablet

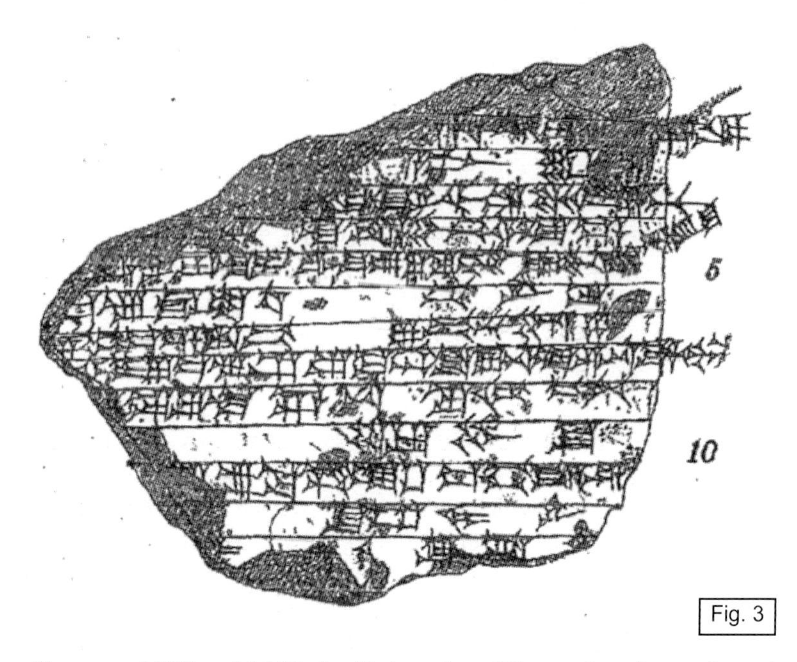


Fig. 3

Between 1889 and 1900, the University of Pennsylvania conducted four seasons of archaeological digs at the ancient Babylonian city of Nippur. Part of their yield was the excavation of a mound which the archaeologists nicknamed 'Tablet Hill,' which was all that remained of the Temple Library that had been destroyed by the Elamites in ca 2100 BC. The name speaks for itself, but among the many tablets found there during the last season's dig of 1900, was a rather sorry-looking fragment. It was encrusted, as many were, with nitre crystals and was sensibly and wisely boxed up with many others for shipment to the university workshops before any attempt could be made to read it.

As well as being a leading member of the dig, the tablet's discoverer, Hermann Vollrath Hilprecht was a professor at the university, and back in Philadelphia in October 1909 he was going through the boxes of unread tablets. One of those he looked at was the fragment just mentioned. Initially he could make nothing of it, simply because the layer of nitre crystals obscured the text beneath (providentially preserving it). But then he noticed that one word was just visible. The three cuneiform signs read *a-bu-bi*, meaning deluge or flood. He quickly searched the rest of the box to see if any other fragment of the tablet remained, and finding none he put all else to one side and turned his attention to cleaning and deciphering the fragment. (See Fig. 3)

It was extremely difficult and delicate work, requiring immense skill and patience. Removing nitre crystals from a clay tablet can very easily damage or even remove the text beneath, but by 1st December 1909, he had completed his task, and was able to read and decipher every surviving sign in the text. What he had stumbled upon is one of the most remarkable texts from the ancient world *ever* discovered, and this is its story.

The fragment, which Hilprecht catalogued as CBM 13532, had been unearthed, along with 17,500 other tablets or fragments, from the lowest of three strata which had once formed part of the Temple Library at Nippur. Due to its presence among dateable tablets from the same stratum in which it was found, and its clear palaeographical characteristics, Hilprecht was able to say that the fragment was written out at sometime between the years 2137 and 2005 BC, giving a mean date of ca 2100 BC. It was, he said, "the very latest date to which this fragment possibly can be assigned, both according to its place of discovery and the palaeographical evidence presented by the tablet itself."[1] – to which he might have added that the Elamite invasion of ca 2100 BC which had buried the tablet was another clinching factor.

The fragment was a sorry-looking thing even when cleaned, measuring just 2.75 inches wide, by 2.375 inches long (6.9cm x 6cm). Its obverse (or front) had entirely crumbled away, leaving just 14 lines of text on the reverse. It was made of dark brown unbaked clay, this alone accounting for its ruinous condition. Hilprecht was able to say, however, that, assuming that the tablet had conformed to the typical proportions of its day, the entire tablet had originally measured some 7 inches by 10 inches (18 x 25.4 cm), and had carried between 130 and 136 lines of text on its two sides.

The language in which the text was written was not the Sumerian of most of the accompanying tablets unearthed. It was Semitic

Babylonian (Hilprecht calls it Akkadian), and hence was closely related to the language that we know as Biblical Hebrew. It is indeed among the very earliest tablets discovered in that language.

Its closeness to Biblical Hebrew is revealed in the many words and phrases which it shares with the Genesis account.[2] It is such an unexpected and major characteristic of the fragment's text, even its phraseology being close to Genesis, that Hilprecht, though he was certainly no Biblical fundamentalist, was compelled to say,

> "But its significance is further enhanced by the fact that in most important details it agrees with the Biblical Version of the Deluge in a very remarkable manner, - much more so than any other cuneiform version previously known."[3]

100 years on, we might add to that, 'More than any other version since discovered'. Hilprecht translated the fragment into English, giving in square parentheses [ ] his reconstructions according to context of some of the missing or damaged sections. His transliteration of the text and his translation of it into English, are as follows:[4]

1..........................................(?)-*sha*(?)-*shi-il*(?) *i*-(?)-...-(?)-*ka*

..............................................................................................thee,

2..............................................................*a-pa-ash-* *shar*

........................[the confines of heaven and earth] I will loosen,

3.....................................................*ka-la ni-si is-ten-is i-za-bat*

...[a deluge will I make, and] it shall sweep away all men together;

4...........................................-*ti* *la-am a-bu-bi wa-si-* *e*

............[but seek thou l]ife before the deluge cometh forth;

5.....(?)-*a ni ma-la i-ba-as-su-u lu-kin ub-bu-ku lu-pu-ut-tu hu-ru-su*

...[For over all living beings], as many as there are, I will bring overthrow, destruction, annihilation.

6.....................*isu elippu ra-be-tu bi- ni- ma*

.................................Build a great ship and

7................*ga-be- e gab-bi lu bi-nu-uz- za*

.......................total height shall be its structure.

8................*si-i lu isu magurgurrum ba-bil- lu na-at- rat na-pis-tim*

..................it shall be a houseboat carrying what has been saved of life.

9...........................*-ri*(?) *zu lu-la dan-na zu- ul- lil*

.......................................with a strong deck cover (it).

10...........................................................*te-ip- pu- su*

...........................................[The ship] which thou shalt make

11..................................*-lam*(?)*u-ma-am si-rim is-sur sa-me-e*

.........[into it br]ing the beasts of the field, the birds of heaven,

12...........................................................................*ku-um mi- ni*

..[and the creeping things, two of everything] instead of a number,

13..............................................-(?) *u ki*[*n*]- *ta ru*(?)-

.....................................................................and the family.................

14...........................................................*u*]

...........................................................and

The text holds several points of interest for us. To begin with, it is entirely monotheistic. Had it been of truly pagan origin, the text would have had a fair sprinkling of the names of Babylonia's various and many gods even within the mere fourteen lines of text which have survived. Moreover, it would not have conformed so closely to the wording and presentation of the Genesis account. It is clearly an attempt to tell the story of the Flood just as Genesis tells it, yet without being a verbatim copy of Genesis.

In Line 8 of the tablet appears the word *ma-gurgurrum*, which Hilprecht translates as 'houseboat'. *Ma-gurgurrum*, however, is related to an old Semitic word, *ma-kurru*, meaning 'ark',[5] - a translation which Hilprecht shrank from giving doubtless because he already had good reason to fear that a storm might break when he published his findings. However, he does justify his choice of 'houseboat' by pointing out to us that the word signifies "a boat which can be closed by a door,"[6] – a definition which has some significance for the student of Genesis (see Gen. 6:17).

Another close feature of the tablet with the Book of Genesis is the command in line 9 of the tablet to cover the Ark with a 'strong deck' or roof. In Genesis 8:13, this covering is referred to where we are told that, when preparing to leave the Ark, Noah removed this covering or roof. The boats and ships of Babylonia commonly lacked such a covering.

As for the name of the Ark, we turn to Heidel's later translation of the fragment, particularly of line 8: *shi-i lu* *isu* *magurgurrum ba-bil-lu na-at- rat na-pish-tim*; which he renders as: The same [ship] shall be a giant boat, and its name shall be 'Preserver of Life'.[7]

The word for life here is *napishtim*, and readers of the Atrahasis Epic will recognise that element in the name under which the Sumerians knew Noah, Ut-napishtim. The Man of Napishtim, or the Man of the Ark, would seem to be the proper interpretation of the name, which, we may deduce from our fragment, is not a name at all, but a title.

The very fact that such a tablet should exist, one that is monotheistic, rational, and which doesn't depart from the Book of Genesis in even the smallest detail, is anathema to the modernist mind.

Moreover, the tablet is several centuries *older* than the earliest possible date proposed by the modernist school for the alleged sources of the Genesis account. No wonder it is studiedly ignored. Better to simply let it lie buried in some obscure scholarly paper somewhere so that it should never come to the public's attention. Let the public continue to be persuaded by endless mantras that Babylonian myth is the birthing-stool of the Book of Genesis. Do this, ignore the Flood tablet, and all shall be well.

Modernism, however, and the so-called 'Higher Critics' in particular, have a severe problem with this tiny fragment. You see, in spite of objections from some quarters in his day, the accuracy of Hilprecht's translation is beyond dispute, as is the age of the fragment. It presents immense and damning implications for the modernist cause by its mere existence. To publicly dispute any one point that is raised by the tablet, would mean the modernist school betraying to the public the deception that underlies all its reasoning. It would mean bringing into the light of day the very falsity of the entire 'science' of Bible criticism, and in this unbelieving age, that simply would not do.

We shall see in the following chapter the weak and unconvincing attempts that were made to disparage the fragment, but these very soon ceased. It is as if the school of modernism suddenly found itself with nothing to say on the matter, and little wonder.

## Notes to Chapter Five

1) All technical details concerning the tablet have been taken from Hilprecht's monograph, *The Babylonian Expedition of the University of Pennsylvania.* Series D: Researches and Treatises. Volume V, fasciculus I: *The Earliest Version of the Babylonian Deluge Story and the Temple Library of Nippur*, Philadelphia, published by the University of Pennsylvania, 1910, pp. 33-65.

2) Ibid, pp. 49-65. where Hilprecht gives an in-depth discussion of the occurrences in which the Akkadian words are identical to those of the Hebrew of Genesis.

3) Ibid, Preface, p. vii.

4) The transliteration and translation are taken from pages 48 and 49 respectively of Hilprecht's monograph.

5) Pinches, 'The Oldest Library in the World....', p. 366. *Makurru* was also used for 'chest' or 'box', and sometimes for a portable box-like household shrine. Interestingly, the Hebrew *aron* also means both 'ark' and 'chest' (as in the Ark of the Covenant, which was simply a chest). An ark or chest, of course, performs the sole function of safe containment and carrying. Otherwise, like the Ark of Noah which was not a navigable ship, it is an entirely passive object.

6) Hilprecht's monograph, p. 55.

7) Heidel, Alexander. *The Gilgamesh Epic and Old Testament Parallels*. 1946. p. 106.

~ * ~

## Chapter Six: A Cry of Fraud!

If Hilprecht showed signs of circumspection in his translation of the Genesis Flood Tablet, it's because he was expecting a storm to break over its publication. He knew all about the rivalries and jealousies of academe. He was, in fact, still riding out such a storm which had erupted a full five years earlier, and which had involved a most trivial matter compared. Some academic rivals, particularly the Rev Dr Peters of Columbia University, were incandescent over Hilprecht's failure to mention in his book, *Explorations in Bible Lands*, the provenance of two clay tablets which he had nevertheless correctly labelled and catalogued for the University of Pennsylvania's museum.

Peters' fury in particular was exceptional, but its real cause had nothing to do with clay tablets. In his *Explorations*, Hilprecht had been critical of Peters over the latter's lack of archaeological method when he was the leader of the first expedition to Nippur, and with that criticism was born a hatred that was to consume Peters for the rest of his life. Hilprecht had written of his tormentor-to-be:

> "It will always remain a source of deep regret that Dr Peters did not rely more upon the judgment and scientific advice of his Assyriologists" [meaning himself] "in deciding strictly technical questions, but that in his anxious but useless efforts to arrange all the essential details of this first expedition in person, he allowed himself frequently to be led by accidents and secondary considerations rather than by a clearly definite plan of methodical operations."[1]

Ouch. The words may have been true enough, but they were not perhaps the wisest that Hilprecht ever published. To have such words published about himself in a popular book on what was then American society's most fashionable and heroic enterprise, archaeology, caused Peters deep pain, and he was determined that Hilprecht should pay.

Not that Hilprecht's words in his *Explorations* were the first time they had crossed swords. In 1889, on the first expedition, Hilprecht had moaned all the way to Nippur. His delicate health, the insects, the natives, even the travel arrangements which he deemed were beneath the dignity of himself and the University, were all sources of friction between himself and Peters who had organised everything. Thoroughly disgruntled, Hilprecht even complained by letter to the University that the "demonic" Peters had even had the nerve to refuse to issue him with a handgun.[2] Given their geographical isolation as well as Hilprecht's very open disdain for him, Peters no doubt considered it a point of wisdom to deny such a request, but it was a wound that was to fester.

Two years after the publication of *Explorations*, and having nothing else to batter his critic with, Peters complained so bitterly to the University about Hilprecht's failure to identify the provenance of the two clay tablets that he caused an enquiry to be set up by the Board of Trustees. Thus, in March 1905, Hilprecht was hauled before an investigating committee appointed by the trustees of the University of Pennsylvania, where was born the famous Peters-Hilprecht Controversy. The newspapers loved every minute of it, and kept the pot boiling for years afterwards, but at the enquiry Hilprecht obviously gave a good account of himself. Peters and his fellow 'witnesses' left in a rage because the committee had had the gall to question Peters over his accusations against Hilprecht's 'unscholarly' omission.[3] That was a mistake on his part. To take Hilprecht to task over something that he had written in *Explorations*, meant that the Board would have to read through the whole book where they would have come across Hilprecht's words of criticism against Peters. So, not fooled for a moment, the Board exonerated Hilprecht. Five years later, and with the Controversy still ringing in his ears, Hilprecht was to find out what his rivals would now make of his discovery and publication of the Flood tablet. As it happened, he didn't have to wait long.

Hilprecht had published his monograph on the Flood tablet in March 1910. Barely two weeks later, on April 1st, the storm broke. The *New York Times* took up the story:

> "The tablet which Professor Herman V Hilprecht of the University of Pennsylvania announced two weeks ago that he had discovered on an expedition to Palestine," [*sic!*] "and which he alleged upheld the Biblical story of the deluge, was denounced to-day at a meeting of the American Oriental Society at the John Hopkins University as a fabrication and

> as an exploitation of an archaeological fraud for purely sensational purposes."[4]

The accuser was a Dr George A Barton of Bryn Mawr College, Philadelphia, and as one reads through the report it becomes clear that he was fast becoming unhinged. Nothing was too scathing to say about Hilprecht, and what should have been an academic presentation fast descended into a torrent of abuse:

> "Dr Barton said that the scholarship which Prof. Hilprecht manifested in the translation of the text of his tablet was hardly worthy of a first-year student in Hebrew...."[5]

The world is still waiting, of course, for Dr Barton's correct translation to appear, though in reality he offered none. The rest of his talk that day consisted of denigrating the tablet itself, mainly by assigning it to a date several centuries later than that which Hilprecht had claimed for it (though he'd never seen it), and by stating emphatically that Hilprecht's conclusions had rested upon, "a misunderstanding of the Hebrew text and upon the pure unbridled imagination of the translator."

This roused the audience, and two academics of note joined in the one-sided fray.[6] Doubtless the presence of a *New York Times* reporter had encouraged them to shout loud enough for him to hear and maybe publish their opinions. But it was an unseemly mess, and anyone reading the *New York Times* report would surely become inclined to side with Hilprecht who was maintaining a quiet dignity throughout it all. Someone therefore encouraged Barton to write a more scholarly appraisal of Hilprecht and his tablet in the American Oriental Society's academic journal. After all, he seemed to know more about the subject than anyone else, and right now the modernists needed a champion. Barton duly obliged, though his encouragers can hardly have foreseen the somewhat embarrassing disappointment that his 'appraisal' would turn out to be. He began it with these words:

> "In the present paper it is proposed: 1. To examine the interpretation of the text. 2. To discuss the evidence for the

age of the document, and 3. To discuss its bearings on the Bible."[7]

Briefly, the first two promises which he made merely showed up the fact that he was very much out of his depth when challenging Hilprecht. The entire paper is taken up with sophistry, a most wearisome and nit-picking pedantry designed to overwhelm any reader, and a vitriol which energizes it all to the very last shout. That much, we may suppose, is standard scholarly fare in some quarters, but the overriding disappointment in Barton's paper is his notable failure to discuss, as he had promised to do, the tablet's bearings on the Bible. The newspaper report on his talk at John Hopkins made clear that what had really rubbed the sore was Hilprecht's alleged opinion that the tablet "upheld the Biblical story of the deluge." Interestingly, Hilprecht said no such thing. All he had stated in his monograph was that the tablet bore an unprecedented closeness to the Genesis account of the Flood. He'd said not a word about it exonerating the Bible in any way. But then, he didn't have to.

What had anathematized Hilprecht in the eyes of his modernist colleagues was, firstly, his expressed belief in the historicity of Abraham,[8] this showing to the world that he had completely lost his marbles and had forever forfeited the name of scholar; and his publishing of a clay tablet's text which demolishes everything that modernism holds dear, namely the idea that the Book of Genesis was compiled in ca 500 BC by a group of editors whom the critics named, J, E, P and D. Their entire case has always rested upon that assumption.

Hilprecht points out in his monograph that his Flood tablet resembles most closely Genesis 6:13-20, and 7:11.[9] And he is perfectly correct. It does. The problem for the critics, however, is that this is precisely one of those portions of Genesis which modernism ascribes to the so-called priestly editor, 'P'. By Hilprecht's day, every modernist was of the declared opinion (in public at least) that 'P' did his work in ca 500 BC, yet here were practically his very words on a tablet which dated back to ca 2100 BC. It was all very awkward. No wonder Barton fell suddenly silent halfway through his written critique and forgot his third promise to mention the tablet's bearing on the Bible. Either that, or his effort had been blue-pencilled out by the journal's editors, Jewett and Oertel.

After Barton's foray, the critics fell silent. There were one or two mumblings in the ranks that the tablet might be later than Hilprecht believed, belonging to the Cassite dynasty of Babylon perhaps. But even if it had, it would make no difference. Even the Cassite dynasty was far too early for the comfort of the critics. And so modernism took a very deep breath and stepped back. In spite of Barton's brave effort, Hilprecht's translation could not be faulted, and the date of the tablet, 2100 BC, is still the most sensible estimate.

In the following year, 1911, Hilprecht was forced out of the university. The trustees had promoted an underling over Hilprecht's head while he was away, and had changed the locks to his office and cabinets. When he returned, Hilprecht had no choice but to resign. He returned to Germany, later to move back to America where he lived as a private citizen until his death in 1925. But his career in Assyriology was never resumed. All the doors of academe were closed to him. What his enemies could never expunge, though, were his published writings, those on the Flood tablet included. But they could ignorc them and wait for the press and the public to forget – which they did. The outbreak of World War I saw to that.

## Notes to Chapter Six

1) Hilprecht, *Explorations in Bible Lands*, p. 308.

2) http://penn.museum/documents/publications/expedition/
PDFs/52-2/ousterhout.pdf

3) *New York Times*, April 16th 1905.

4) *New York Times*, April 2nd 1910.

5) Ibid.

6) These were Professors Haupt of John Hopkins, and Albert Clay of Yale who had both previously sided with Peters in the Controversy.

7) Barton, George A. 'Hilprecht's Fragment of the Babylonian Deluge Story'. *Journal of the American Oriental Society*. vol 31. Part 1. December 1910. pp. 30-48.

8) Hilprecht's monograph, p. 62.

9) Ibid, p. 59.

~ * ~

# Epilogue

For an ancient book penned by a pack of nomads in a desert somewhere, and which the world would have us believe is loaded with nothing but fairy stories, the Book of Genesis shows a surprising resilience when it is put to the test. The greatest test for any statement which claims to be historical, is to see whether what it says actually came to pass. If evidence is there to say yes, it did happen, then we can accept that statement as historical and factual. Which brings us to the statements of the modernist school.

Since Noldeke wrote his denial in 1869, members of the modernist school have been virtually unanimous in declaring that the 14th chapter of Genesis is unhistorical, and that, "*none* of the names of kings mentioned in this chapter can be identified with *any* certainty as corresponding with the names of *any* kings known to us from contemporary records." (Italics mine).[1] And yet we have seen, in Part One Chapter Thirteen *and* in Appendix Two of Part One, that these kings are all known to us from the inscriptions that were made about them in their lifetimes. Not only are their names mentioned, but their relationships to one another and the cities over which they ruled, are all as Genesis records. Genesis even gets the spelling of their names correct and according to dialect. So the question must be addressed, which of the two has got its facts completely wrong here, modernism or the Book of Genesis?

The same consideration can be given to *every* item of evidence which we have discussed in this book. On whose side does the evidence – the hard, archaeological and documentary evidence – stand? Does it support, exonerate and vindicate the statements of the 'Higher Critics' or those of the Book of Genesis? In modern parlance, and in the light of what we have just read, this is surely what is known as a 'no-brainer'. Yet strangely, however great, convincing and indisputable the evidence might be, it will make no difference whatever to what our schools, colleges, seminars and universities teach. It will make no difference to the media who love to slam the Bible whenever some critic or other says wrongly that the Bible has been shown by his 'theory' to be false. Clearly then, evidence - good or bad - has nothing to do with it.

The vast majority of those millions upon millions of people who have taken the Bible to their hearts, accepting it and believing it to be the very Word of God, will have done so with absolutely no reference to archaeology, palaeolinguistics, or any other discipline. Most of them have never even heard of the modernists or the 'Higher Critics', which is why modernism is and always has been a waste of time. Men have forfeited their very souls in their quest to convince the world that God is a liar, that His Word is false and faith in Him vain, and they have done it all for nothing. The world was busy rejecting God long before Wellhausen and his colleagues were even born or thought of. It needed no encouragement whatever in that direction - which is why modernism has been able to get away for so long spouting its doctrines and ideas without any requirement at all for the production of evidence and facts. The world doesn't need evidence either way. It has always rejected God without it.

So why should men – very talented men in most cases – take it upon themselves to deride the Bible as they do? Those who study their subject know full well that the evidence is against them, yet still they pursue their goal with a grit and determination which defies all logic. They are not that dishonest in other areas of their lives. So why are they so dishonest with themselves - and with others - in this? It is a mystery which would take 66 volumes to explain, the first of which is the Book of Genesis.

So much for the critics; but what about the hundreds of millions of men, women and children from around the world who take the Bible as the Word of God and who love it dearly? Well, as we noted just now, they began their acceptance without archaeology, and indeed without recourse to any kind of academic discipline. It is the Spirit of God who enlivened their hearts and Who placed the light of His Word within them, not some archaeologist or don. Nevertheless, the world has seen to it that such as these shall be assailed from every quarter with statements of doubt, with the lie that that Word is false. It is for them that this book has been written. It is as if to say, You believe the Bible to be true, and that's very good. Here is why you should continue to believe it.

It is no small comfort to read that the Word of God is exonerated in the face of all that the world says against it. Each nugget of information brings with it a profound interest and pleasure, and it means that our faith is very much an informed faith and not one of ignorance and darkness. Let the world say what it likes. We know Whom we have believed, and He is no deceiver. His Word is Truth, even as He Himself is Truth, and that is how it shall remain - for evermore!

*Bill Cooper.*

*1) Peake's Commentary*, p. 188.

## Bibliography

*Not every book listed here has been quoted in this present section, but each will add something to the student's understanding of the subject in hand. Many Victorian and early 20th-century academic titles are listed, but though the originals are hard to get, most of them are now available in modern reprints. To find them, just 'Google' the title.*

Bowden, Malcolm. *The Rise of the Evolution Fraud.* (2nd enlarged edition). 2008. Sovereign Publications. Bromley BR2 9PF.

Brackman, Arnold C. *The Luck of Nineveh.* 1980. Eyre Methuen. London.

Clay, Albert T. *Amurru, the Home of the Northern Semites*. 1909.

Clay, Albert T. *A Hebrew Deluge Story in Cuneiform; and Other Epic Fragments in the Pierpont Morgan Library*. 1922. Yale University Press.

Cooper, Bill (Wm R). *After the Flood.* 1995. New Wine Press. Chichester. England.

Dalley, Stephanie. *Myths from Mesopotamia*. 1989. Oxford Univ. Press. Oxford.

Damrosch, David. *The Buried Book*. 2006. Henry Holt. New York.

Dresden, M J. 'Mythology of Ancient Iran.' *Mythologies of the Ancient World*. 1961. (ed. S Kramer). Anchor Books. London. pp. 331-366.

Frazer, James George. *Folklore in the Old Testament*. 1923. Macmillan. London.

Gaussen, Louis. *God-Breathed: The Divine Inspiration of the Bible*. 2001. Trinity Foundation.

Heidel, Alexander. *The Gilgamesh Epic and Old Testament Parallels.* 1946. U of Chicago.

Hilprecht, H V. *Old Babylonian Inscriptions.* 1896. University of Pennsylvania.

Hilprecht, H V. *Explorations in Bible Lands.* 1903 (1st Edition). T & T Clark. Edinburgh.

Hilprecht H V (ed.). *The Babylonian Expedition of the University of Pennsylvania.* Series D: Researches and Treatises. Volume V, fasciculus I: *The Earliest Version of the Babylonian Deluge Story and the Temple Library of Nippur*, by H V Hilprecht, Philadelphia, published by the University of Pennsylvania, 1910.

Hislop, Alexander. *The Two Babylons.* 1959. Loiseaux Bros. New Jersey.

Hodges, E Richmond (ed). *Cory's Ancient Fragments.* 1876. Reeves & Turner. London. Reprinted by Kessinger.

Horne, Charles F. *Fragments of the Babylonian Historian Berosus 300 BC.* Kessinger Publishing. Extracted from *Sacred Books and Early Literature of the East.*

Kraeling, Emil G. 'The Earliest Hebrew Flood Story.' *Journal of Biblical Literature.* Vol 66. No 3. September 1947. pp. 279-293.

Kramer, Samuel Noah. *From the Tablets of Sumer.* 1956. Falcon's Wing Prcss. Colorado.

Kramer, Samuel Noah (ed). *Mythologies of the Ancient World.* 1961. Anchor Books. London.

Layard, Austen. *Nineveh and its Remains.* 1849 (2nd edition). 2 vols. John Murray. London.

Morris, Henry M. *The Genesis Record.* 2008. Baker Books. Grand Rapids.

Morris, Henry M. *The Long War Against God*. 2008. Master Books. Arizona.

Peters, J P. *Nippur: Explorations and Adventures on the Euphrates*. (2 vols). 1898. Putnams. New York.

Pinches, T G. *The Old Testament in the Light of the Historical Records and Legends of Assyria and Babylonia*. 1902. SPCK. London.

Pinches & Hommell, 'The Oldest Library in the World and the New Deluge Tablets.' *Expository Times*. 1910. Vol. XXI. pp. 364-369.

Reich, Emil. *The Failure of the Higher Criticism of the Bible*. 1905. Cincinnati.

Rogers, R W. *Cuneiform Parallels to the Old Testament*. 1912. Eaton & Mains. New York.

Rohl, David. *Legend: The Genesis of Civilisation*. 1998. Random House. London.

Ryan, William & Pitman, Walter. *Noah's Flood*. 1999. Scribner.

Sayce, A H. *The 'Higher Criticism' and the Verdict of the Monuments*. 1894. SPCK.

Smith, George. *Assyrian Discoveries..during 1873 and 1874*. 1875. Scribner, Armstrong & Co.

Smith, George. 'The Chaldean Account of the Deluge.' *Transactions of the Society of Biblical Archaeology*. 2 [1873]. pp. 213-34.

Smith, George. *The Chaldean Account of Genesis*. 1876. Samson Low. London.

Smith, George. *The History of Babylonia*. 1880? ed. A H Sayce. SPCK. London.

Sollberger, Edmond. *The Babylonian Legend of the Flood*. 1984. British Museum Publications.

Unger, Merrill F. *Archaeology and the Old Testament*. 1954. Zondervan. Michigan.

Vanderburgh, F A. *Sumerian Hymns*. 1908. Columbia University Press. New York.

Wallis Budge, E A. *The Discovery of the Babylonian Story of the Deluge and the Epic of Gilgamesh*. 1929. British Museum. London.

Whitcomb, John C, and Morris, Henry M. *The Genesis Flood*. 1961. P & R Publishing.

## ICR Published Articles

Lorey, Frank. 'The Flood of Noah and the Flood of Gilgamesh.' www.icr.org/article/414/

Morris, Henry. 'Why Christians Should Believe in a Global Flood.' www.icr.org/article/842/

Morris, John D. 'Why Does Nearly Every Culture Have a Tradition of a Global Flood?' www.icr.org/article/570/

## Captions to Illustrations

Fig 1: The Adam and Eve (or Temptation) seal. This steel engraving of the seal was made by George Smith in 1875. A photo of the original (BM. ME 89326) is shown on the British Museum's website.

Fig 2: The Tepe Gawra seal. The seal is kept today at University Museum of Pennsylvania. It was discovered in 1932 at Tepe Gawra near Nineveh. Public domain.

Fig 3: The Genesis Flood Tablet, CBM 13532, University of Pennsylvania. Drawing by Hilprecht, 1910. Public domain.

~ * ~

# Index

**B**

**E**

**I**



**J**

**K**



**L**



**M**

**N**

**O**



**P**

**Q**



**R**



**S**

**T**

**U**



**V**



**W**



**X**

**Y**



**Z**



~ * ~